I0760209

Jeffersonians in Power

Jeffersonian America

Peter S. Onuf and Andrew O'Shaughnessy, Editors

Jeffersonians in Power

The Rhetoric of Opposition Meets the Realities of Governing

Edited by
Joanne B. Freeman
and Johann N. Neem

University of Virginia Press / Charlottesville and London

University of Virginia Press
© 2019 by the Rector and Visitors of the University of Virginia
All rights reserved
Printed in the United States of America on acid-free paper

First published 2019

9 8 7 6 5 4 3 2 1

Library of Congress Cataloging-in-Publication Data

Names: Freeman, Joanne B., 1962– editor. | Neem, Johann N., editor.
Title: Jeffersonians in power : the rhetoric of opposition meets the realities of governing / edited by Joanne B. Freeman and Johann N. Neem.
Description: Charlottesville : University of Virginia Press, 2019. | Series: Jeffersonian America | Includes bibliographical references and index.
Identifiers: LCCN 2019018770 | ISBN 9780813943053 (cloth : alk. paper) | ISBN 9780813943060 (ebook)
Subjects: LCSH: Jefferson, Thomas, 1743–1826. | Republican Party (U.S. : 1792–1828)—History. | Opposition (Political science)—United States—History—18th century. | Federal government—United States—History. | United States—Politics and government—1789–1815.
Classification: LCC JK2316 .J44 2019 | DDC 324.2732/6—dc23
LC record available at https://lccn.loc.gov/2019018770

Cover art: Cartoon protesting the Embargo Act of U.S. President Thomas Jefferson in 1807; hand-colored woodcut (North Wind Picture Archives/Alamy Stock Photo).

We dedicate this volume to our mentor, Peter S. Onuf

Contents

Acknowledgments ix

Introduction 1

Part I The Jeffersonian Coalition

1 Friends and Enemies in the Declaration of Independence *Robert G. Parkinson* 15

2 The Mississippi Question in Jeffersonian Political Economy *Martin Öhman* 38

3 A Religious Republican and a Republican Religion *John A. Ragosta* 59

4 Beyond Strict Construction: Jeffersonians in the 1790s *Mark Smith* 80

Part II The Challenges of Holding Power

5 Thomas Jefferson's Virginian Revolution *Kevin R. C. Gutzman* 105

6 Jefferson's Embargo: National Intent and Sectional Effects *Benjamin L. Carp* 128

7 How the Jeffersonians Learned to Love the State: Consumption, Finance, and Empire in the Madison Administration *Leonard J. Sadosky* 148

8 Lower South Jeffersonians: States and the Federal Imagination *Brian Schoen* 178

PART III JEFFERSON AND MADISON

9 Apocalypse Now: Thomas Jefferson's Radical Enlightenment *Andrew Trees* 199

10 "The Strongest Government on Earth" Proves Its Strength: The Jefferson Administration and the Burr Conspiracy *James E. Lewis Jr.* 222

11 Taking Root Deeper Than Ever: Jeffersonians and Slavery *Christa Dierksheide* 242

12 The Constitutional Statesmanship of James Madison *Richard Samuelson* 262

Afterword *Andrew Burstein* 283

Notes on Contributors 301

Index 305

Acknowledgments

The editors would like to thank the contributors to this volume for their hard work and commitment. All of the contributors, ourselves included, received our PhD training under Peter Onuf at the University of Virginia. Peter, to us, is a beloved mentor who taught us what it means to be scholars and teachers. His intellect, his compassion, his loyalty, and his support are worthy of emulation. As more than one of us has said more than once, Peter intuitively gets to the essence of his students and their work, and always improves them immeasurably. His commitment to his students was recognized by the American Historical Association, which awarded him the Nancy Lyman Roelker Mentorship Award in 2013. We dedicate this volume to him as a token of our thanks and appreciation.

As the volume was nearing completion, our dear friend and colleague Leonard Sadosky passed away. Leonard left this world much too early, but he left it better than he found it. He cared so deeply for his friends. He was not only a brilliant scholar but an honest one. He strove to offer a truthful past that challenged all of us to think more deeply, as his contribution to this volume demonstrates. He will be missed.

We met and discussed the ideas for this volume at a conference honoring Peter's work at the International Center for Jefferson Studies at Monticello. We thank Andrew O'Shaughnessy and Christa Dierksheide at the Thomas Jefferson Memorial Foundation for supporting the event and helping us organize it. The conference brought together Peter's colleagues, friends, and family to discuss his work's impact on early American history. The themes from that conference inform every page of this volume.

Dick Holway at the University of Virginia Press was an early advocate of this volume. He recognized that recent scholarship had led us to the point where new perspectives on Jeffersonians in power were possible and needed. We hope this volume provides fresh insights to some longstanding questions in American history. We thank Dick for his guidance and for shepherding this volume to completion.

Joanne Freeman and Johann Neem

Introduction

In the 1790s, the Jeffersonian Republicans were the party of "no." With the Federalists in power, the Jeffersonians' strength was in reacting. Republicans opposed Alexander Hamilton's centralizing policies and decried Federalist attempts to expand the government's role in society. They criticized the Washington administration's national bank as a state-empowering boon to moneyed men. During the nation's Quasi-War with France in 1797–99, they railed against the idea of a standing army, condemning it as a stepping-stone on the road to a monarchical nation-state; they were no more pleased with declaring war against France, America's longstanding ally in politics and revolutionary fervor. They bemoaned even the spirit of the Federalist regime, which, they claimed, favored the wealthy, flaunted aristocratic pomp, and seemed ever ready to suppress the murmurings of democracy.

Thus Thomas Jefferson's utter conviction that his election as president in 1801 was a "revolution." The "reign of witches," as he had called Federalist rule in the 1790s, had passed. With Republicans in power, the nation could be set right. The national government could be stripped down in size and strength. The rights of the common man could be celebrated rather than suppressed. And the spirit of governance could be restored to its republican roots. Jefferson's ideal, he explained, was "a wise and frugal Government, which shall restrain men from injuring one another, shall leave them otherwise free to regulate their own pursuits of industry and improvement, and shall not take from the mouth of labor the bread it has earned. This is the sum of good government, and this is necessary to close the circle of our felicities."[1] For many Americans, the appeal of this image was undeniable. It perfectly captured the essence of America's national identity as a virtuous republic in a world of monarchies, peopled by independent yeoman strivers living in peace under a limited government.

But there was a paradox at the heart of this image—a paradox that has led generations of commentators to brand Jefferson and his supporters as hypocrites.[2] Maintaining the security, stability, and prosperity of this virtuous small-state republic required aggressive statecraft, which Jeffersonians used in abundance. To open trade channels and create freer markets, they grabbed at western land, doubling the size of the nation with the Louisiana Purchase, despite Jefferson's concerns that the purchase was not authorized by the Constitution. In the same spirit, they fought against Native Americans and Barbary pirates, and engaged in a full-fledged war against Great Britain during the War of 1812. They bolstered their war efforts by reforming the military establishment and founding West Point. Jeffersonians were no less aggressive economically, deploying state power to reduce taxes and the national debt, enforcing the Embargo, and ultimately embracing the idea of a national bank during the Madison administration.[3]

In short, even as they preached the virtues of a limited federal government, Jeffersonians made strong and ample use of state power. This book explores this paradox, seeking to understand the logic and logistics of Jeffersonian statecraft. Scholars have long studied parts of this conundrum, analyzing Jeffersonian small-state ideals or tracking the outcomes of their policies. *Jeffersonians in Power* aims at a middle ground. Focusing on Jeffersonian statecraft in action, it explores the meeting place of ideology and policy as Republicans shifted from being an oppositional party to exercising power as the ruling coalition.

We are not the first to approach Jeffersonian statecraft in this manner. Noble E. Cunningham brought attention to the challenges Republicans faced as they took power from their Federalist foes, but he focused on what made the party's gears turn, rather than on Republican ideas and practices, grappling with questions of patronage, party management, and practicalities of power at a point when basic processes of government were still being worked out. Approaching the process of governing as a practical activity, Cunningham set the stage for the questions we ask, but whereas he was interested in party operations, we are interested in the ways in which those operations joined with political principles and ideals to create public policy.[4] Because we focus on the logic as well as the impact of policy decisions, we are particularly sensitive to questions of political culture—the constraints, fears, assumptions, and expectations that animate political motives and actions.[5]

Drew R. McCoy's study of Jeffersonian ideology and policies—*The Elusive Republic* (1980)—is also attuned to political culture. Noteworthy for its sensitivity to Jeffersonian ideals in relation to statecraft, McCoy explored the underlying mindset that guided Jeffersonian economic and foreign policies. In the midst of a raging debate over whether Jeffersonian Republicans were backward-looking republicans or forward-looking liberals, McCoy demonstrated how their fear of the seemingly inevitable decay of republics over time led them to engage in aggressive expansion over space, driving them to seek western lands to sustain the republic's agrarian core. Arguing that assertive Jeffersonian statecraft was intended to preserve the nation's limited republican government, *The Elusive Republic* probes the Jeffersonian paradox through close study of their worldview.[6]

Missing from McCoy's analysis, however, is the shaping impact of government institutions. Above and beyond their explicit acts of statecraft, Jeffersonians in power shaped society through their control of the institutions of government, a point that has been made recently by scholars working under the rubric of "American political development." Such scholars argue that government institutions are, in Richard R. John's words, "agents of change." This means that political institutions shape society, culture, and the economy, and are not simply responsive. Jeffersonians knew this; indeed, they believed that the character of a regime affected the character of the citizenry. Whether under Federalist or Jeffersonian leadership, the founding generation understood that political institutions had an impact on the daily lives of ordinary Americans, as this volume shows.[7]

Recognizing the shaping influence of the state, however, should not require discounting the importance of ideas. Rather, the two must come together, as they do amid the vagaries and practicalities of real-life politics. In a 1987 essay on the origins of the Constitution, Peter S. Onuf urged scholars to return to "narrative," by which he meant focusing on politicians as they solved problems in real time. He worried that scholars of political culture had abstracted politicians too far from the worlds they inhabited and the problems that confronted them. *Jeffersonians in Power* heeds Onuf's advice. The essays in this volume show the interplay of Jeffersonian principles with the challenges of ground-level statecraft and criticism from within their own coalition.[8]

These critics were not misguided, yet we do not presume, as some of Jefferson's critics did then and do now, that the deployment of state power was *prima facie* proof of Jeffersonian hypocrisy. Jeffersonians themselves were well aware that they needed to use state power to achieve their goals. Brian Balogh's *A Government Out of Sight* (2009) offers some crucial insight into how they met this challenge. Balogh argues that as the United States became increasingly democratic and commercial, Jeffersonian statesmen sought to tap into and encourage Americans' own self-interest as a tool of statecraft, thereby producing a "government out of sight." Rather than using levers of government to enforce their vision on unwilling Americans, as the Federalists had done, Jeffersonians used government to structure and make possible what ordinary Americans wanted. In other words, Jeffersonian statecraft enabled Americans to benefit from government without knowing it.[9]

This mode of governance had its challenges, as this volume shows. Different Jeffersonians had different conceptions of optimal levels of federal and state power. There were many shades of Jeffersonian Republicanism, and these differences became all the more apparent when Jeffersonians had some power to deploy. Confronted by the challenges of satisfying their varied coalition as well as by the challenges of governance, Jeffersonians struggled to accommodate ideals with realities. Wrestling with the size and shape of state power in a republic-in-the-making, they were engaged in a balancing act that continues to the present day: the desire to preserve individual rights, manage a federal system, and maintain high ideals while dealing with the demands of real-world statecraft. Exploring the nexus of political culture and ground-level politics casts this struggle in a new light, revealing how Jeffersonians did—and did not—stay true to their ideals, explaining how they reasoned and rationalized their decisions, and casting light on what they did—and did not—accomplish while in power.

The challenge of balancing ideals and realities is hardly unique to the Jeffersonians. To some degree, it represents the essential question of democratic politics. But Jeffersonians *did* face some unique challenges. An opposition party that came to power in a nascent republic still engaged in the heady project of self-definition and precedent-setting, they had to determine how their fundamental faith in the common people could mesh with political realities and the mandates of power-holding in the new nation. But they were not starting with a *tabula rasa.* At the national level, Jeffersonians inherited a government whose basic administrative organization and practices had been established by their opposition. It was up to Jeffersonians to figure out how to reorient this infrastructure to serve their own political ends.[10]

There was no single solution to this problem, in part because the Republican coalition was manifold and conflicted from its very outset. As the essays in this volume make clear, there was a spectrum of ideas and ideals encompassed by the Republican Party, some of them friendlier toward Federalist precedents than others. Exercising state power even as they distrusted it, and faced with dissension and disagreement within their ranks, Jeffersonians in power confronted key tensions at the core of democratic governance in America.

Structure of the Volume

The volume is divided into three sections. Part 1, "The Jeffersonian Coalition," examines the rise of the Jeffersonians and their years in power at the state, territorial, and national levels. Part 2, "The Challenges of Holding Power," turns to tensions within the Jeffersonian coalition, and their causes and outcomes. Part 3, "Jefferson and Madison," puts the coalition's two titular leaders in the spotlight, examining their efforts to reconcile their ideas and aspirations with the realities of governing a diverse democracy in an unstable world.

Part 1: The Jeffersonian Coalition

Our volume opens with Robert G. Parkinson's essay, "Friends and Enemies in the Declaration of Independence." Parkinson raises one of the core conundrums of Jeffersonian governance. While Federalists proclaimed themselves the party of the common good, Jeffersonians claimed to be the party of the people. But "the people" are always a fiction, far too diverse and fragmented to be effectively represented by any one party, no matter how popular. Parkinson argues that Jeffersonians confronted this challenge through a process of exclusion, reading certain people—African Americans and women, for example—out of the body of the people. By setting boundaries and constructing "the people" as they saw fit, Republicans enabled *some* Americans to see themselves as part of something larger than themselves.

Yet white Americans too were deeply divided and did not necessarily see themselves as sharing a common Jeffersonian faith. In "The Mississippi Question in Jeffersonian Political Economy," Martin Öhman reveals that during the 1790s, westerners and southerners had serious economic differences that threatened to divide the Jeffersonian coalition. During debates over the Jay Treaty, westerners favored anything that might encourage trade and foster the commercial development of the trans-Appalachian region. Southerners, on the other hand, worried about western economic competition. The Louisiana Purchase solved the problem, *not* by achieving a Jeffersonian consensus but rather by satisfying diverse interests. There was "never a natural coalition. . . . The coalition took form on the fly as Old South planters and western communities struggled to address specific challenges and conditions brought on by the protracted instability of the Atlantic World." Unlike Drew McCoy, Öhman sees the Jeffersonian ideal of a western agrarian republic developing ad hoc in response to events on the ground, rather than existing *a priori* and guiding public policy.

Such ad hoc politicking does not mean that Jeffersonians downplayed their political ideals. Although they appealed to interests, they also sought to make good on their principles. In the case of the relationship between church and state, John Ragosta argues in "A Religious Republican and a Republican Religion," northern Jeffersonians were consistent and constant in their desire to end religious establishments. Whereas recent scholars have sought to prove that Jefferson and his party did not seek an absolute separation of church and state, Ragosta argues that they sought to build a high, impermeable wall that kept church and state apart.

Mark Smith's essay, "Beyond Strict Construction: Jeffersonians in the 1790s," shows the Republican concern with ideals from another angle. Noting the diversity of the Jeffersonian coalition, Smith argues that even as some Jeffersonians focused on constitutional arguments about the federal government's legitimate powers, others were more concerned with questions of policy and the common good. For these more policy-minded Jeffersonians, being in power was a chance to use the levers of state power to achieve better outcomes. Rather than simply striving to limit the federal government's reach, such Jeffersonians wanted to guide it toward policies that, they believed, would better serve ordinary Americans.

Part 2: The Challenges of Holding Power

The Jeffersonian coalition, then, was an unstable entity. Not only did party mobilization require selective and strategic politicking among diverse constituencies, but finding common ground was a difficult business, even when relying on seemingly foundational Jeffersonian ideals. Some Republicans even questioned the Republican commitment to democratization. In

"Thomas Jefferson's Virginian Revolution," Kevin R. C. Gutzman shows that this was the case in Jefferson's own Virginia; Virginian Jeffersonians, it turns out, were not very Jeffersonian. There, the Republican Party was the establishment party, and it tended to resist Jefferson's more idealistic and radical ideas. To defend their prerogatives, Virginia Republicans opposed democratizing the franchise. They did not support Jefferson's efforts to revise the state constitution, to end slavery, or to establish public schools, raising interesting questions about how effectively Jefferson can stand in for his party as a whole—even in his home state.

Given the unpopularity of some of Jefferson's policies among Republicans in Virginia, it should come as no surprise that elsewhere they inspired active resistance—spurring Jefferson to use state power to enforce federal law. In "Jefferson's Embargo: National Intent and Sectional Effects," Benjamin L. Carp shows how resistance to Jefferson's unpopular Embargo during his second term as president drove him to adopt Federalist-style heavy-handed enforcement tactics. With Federalists fanning the flames, citizens of all political persuasions took to the streets to protest the Embargo's interruption of foreign commerce, demonstrating that Jefferson most certainly did not speak for all of "the people." Jefferson responded aggressively, deploying the military to enforce an unpopular federal law in an eerie echo of the Washington administration's response to the Whiskey Rebellion in 1794.

Political realities again challenged Jeffersonian ideals during James Madison's presidency, once again revealing divides within the party. Nowhere is this problem more obvious than in Madison's decision to support a charter for the Second Bank of the United States. In this case, as Leonard J. Sadosky argues in "How the Jeffersonians Learned to Love the State: Consumption, Finance, and Empire in the Madison Administration," experience proved the best teacher. Madison had led the fight against a national bank in the 1790s, grounding his opposition on its violation of the "necessary and proper" clause of the Constitution, but when the government was unable to secure credit during the War of 1812, some Jeffersonians—including Madison—reversed course, arguing that a national bank was both necessary and proper, once again echoing Federalist logic from Washington's administration. Some Jeffersonians went even further in their nationalism than Madison, ultimately forming what came to be known as the National Republican Party.

This was not the only split within the Republican ranks. As Brian Schoen shows in "Lower South Jeffersonians: States and the Federal Imagination," in the wake of the 1819 Adams-Onís Treaty, which removed Spanish threats from the region, some southerners turned against ambitious national policies. Demanding a small federal government with limited powers that left the states alone to conduct their own affairs, these Republicans out-Jeffersoned Jefferson. Ironically, as Schoen demonstrates, southerners could celebrate small government and states' rights precisely because Jefferson, Madison, and James Monroe had so successfully used state power to achieve America's security. Active governance and its ground-level aftermath paved the way for the South's celebration of small government.

Part 3: Jefferson and Madison

As several of the preceding essays show, Jefferson clung to his ideals, sometimes in the face of blatant contradiction. In "Apocalypse Now: Thomas Jefferson's Radical Enlightenment," Andrew Trees shows how he managed it. Jefferson was an abstract thinker who cared about ideas and tried to guide his policies accordingly, Trees argues. Jefferson's fundamental commitment was to the idea of an uncorrupted American people being their own best governors. When messy realities complicated this ideal, Jefferson blamed those messy realities for his political failures, in effect blaming politics for the failure of his policies, a strategy that shielded him from reconsidering and adapting his ideals.

We see Jefferson struggling with these issues during and after his response to Vice President Aaron Burr's alleged conspiracy to foment a western revolt, as James E. Lewis Jr. demonstrates in "'The Strongest Government on Earth' Proves Its Strength: The Jefferson Administration and the Burr Conspiracy." Although President Jefferson considered using military force, his response was ultimately much more limited, not because he did not consider Burr a threat but because his principles dictated it. He also opposed the idea of arresting Burr for something that had not been made a crime by specific legislation. Jefferson insisted, in Lewis's words, "that nothing was illegal that had not been made illegal by a specific act." But after the Burr Conspiracy fizzled on its own, Jefferson took it as vindication that the United States had "the strongest government on earth" because the people would always defend their common liberties. In short, Jefferson used the Burr Conspiracy to reinforce his idealized vision of America and Americans, even if in the midst of events he was less certain—and even if his own actions in New England to enforce the Embargo might suggest otherwise.

Jefferson's seeming denial of reality was most glaringly apparent in his views on slavery, as Christa Dierksheide argues in "Taking Root Deeper Than Ever: Jeffersonians and Slavery." Unable to imagine a biracial republic, he clung to the ideas of "amelioration" and "diffusion" as the best way to end slavery. By Jefferson's logic, slaveholders should improve the capabilities of African Americans and then allow them to "diffuse" across the North American continent, a process that—somehow—would make problems of race and slavery disappear. As flawed as it was, Jefferson's logic ultimately accomplished the exact opposite of his intentions. Slaveholders seized Jefferson's logic to promote their slave regime, celebrating the institution of slavery for improving the lives of African Americans and pushing for slavery's expansion. Even in the face of such proslavery promotion, Jefferson clung to the idea of diffusion, perhaps to avoid facing the unpleasant fact that the majority of his idealized American people did not want to end slavery.

President Madison, as Richard Samuelson describes him in "The Constitutional Statesmanship of James Madison," also sought to remain true to his principles in the face of changing contexts. Focusing on the same seeming Madisonian contradiction as Sadosky—Madison's support for the Second Bank of the United States—Samuelson wonders why Madison supported the bank yet vetoed another nationalist venture, the "bonus bill," which would have given federal funds to states for internal improvements. Unlike Sadosky, who concludes that Madison endorsed the bank because he learned from experience, Samuelson argues that Madison endorsed it because it was accepted as constitutional by the legislative and judicial branches of the federal government, as well as by the public. In the case of federally funded internal improvements, no such consensus existed, and in its absence, Madison felt that there was no authority for federal action. He always believed that the Constitution was a limited grant of power. The Bank of the United States had passed muster, but internal improvements required passing a constitutional amendment. In the end, Madison stayed true to his constitutional ideals.

As leaders of the Jeffersonian coalition, Jefferson and Madison knew that their principles and actions would have a lasting influence on the young nation. Worried about the implications of using state power and of *not* using it, they embodied the tensions at the heart of American governance.

Confronted with this challenge, the Jeffersonians articulated a new American lexicon, Andrew Burstein argues in this book's afterword, one that celebrated the possibilities inherent in "mild government." The Federalists did not have a place in this new national imaginary. In this sense—in the minds of Americans—it was Jefferson and his party that set the terms for American politics.

Jeffersonians did so, however, not just through words but equally through deeds. And it was here, where the rubber hit the road, that we see the real complexity of what Jefferson, Madison, and their party bequeathed us. They opposed big government but needed it. They spoke for some of the American people but not for all of them. Power-holders at a defining stage for the young republic, they were the first political coalition to struggle with the complexities of modern democratic governance. What appears to be hypocrisy was in fact a process of discovery and definition. The Jeffersonians' ongoing struggle to chart a true course is a reminder that many of America's longstanding political ideals were built on foundations of conflict and compromise, seeded with distrust but strengthened by the nation's fundamental faith in the democratic process.

Notes

1. Jefferson to John Taylor, June 4, 1798, in Merrill D. Peterson, ed., *Jefferson: Writings* (New York, 1984), 1048–51, 1050 (quotation); Jefferson, "First Inaugural Address," Mar. 4, 1801, in ibid., 494.

2. For the classic discussion of this paradox, see Henry Adams, *History of the United States during the Administrations of Thomas Jefferson* (New York, 1889–91). For an overview of the debate, as well as an interpretation that challenges Adams's assertions, see Robert M. S. McDonald, "The (Federalist?) Presidency of Thomas Jefferson," in *A Companion to Thomas Jefferson,* ed. Frank Cogliano (Oxford, 2011), 164–83. For scholars who have accused Jefferson of hypocrisy, see, for example, Leonard Levy, *Jefferson and Civil Liberties: The Darker Side* (Cambridge, Mass., 1963), and Robert W. Tucker and David C. Hendrickson, *Empire of Liberty: The Statecraft of Thomas Jefferson* (New York, 1990).

3. Bernard W. Sheehan, *Seeds of Extinction: Jeffersonian Philanthropy and the American Indian* (Chapel Hill, N.C., 1973); Frank Lambert, *The Barbary Wars: American Independence in the Atlantic World* (New York, 2005); J. C. A. Stagg, *Mr. Madison's War: Politics, Diplomacy, and Warfare in the Early American Republic, 1783–1830* (Princeton, N.J., 1983); Theodore J. Crackel Jr., *Mr. Jefferson's Army: Political and Social Reform of the Military Establishment, 1801–1809* (New York, 1987); Robert M. S. McDonald, ed.,

Thomas Jefferson's Military Academy: Founding West Point (Charlottesville, Va., 2004); Max M. Edling, *A Hercules in the Cradle: War, Money, and the American State, 1783–1867* (Chicago, 2014); John Lauritz Larson, *Internal Improvement: National Public Works and the Promise of Popular Government in the Early United States* (Chapel Hill, N.C., 2001); Peter S. Onuf and Leonard J. Sadosky, *Jeffersonian America* (Oxford, 2002), 139–71. For Jefferson in particular, see Johann N. Neem, "Developing Freedom: Thomas Jefferson, the State, and Human Capability," *Studies in American Political Development* 27, no. 1 (Apr. 2013): 36–50; Gary J. Schmitt, "Thomas Jefferson and the Presidency," in *Inventing the American Presidency*, ed. Thomas E. Cronin (Lawrence, Kans., 1989), 326–46; Jeremy D. Bailey, *Thomas Jefferson and Executive Power* (New York, 2007); and John Yoo, *Crisis and Command: A History of Executive Power from George Washington to George W. Bush* (New York, 2009), 99–143.

4. Noble E. Cunningham, *The Jeffersonians in Power: Party Operations, 1801–1809* (Chapel Hill, N.C., 1963); Cunningham, *The Process of Government under Jefferson* (Princeton, N.J., 1978).

5. On the idea of political culture, see Joanne B. Freeman, "Political History and the Tool of Culture," in *A Companion to American Cultural History*, ed. Karen Halttunen (Oxford, 2008), 416–24, and Ronald P. Formisano, "The Concept of Political Culture," *Journal of Interdisciplinary History* 31, no. 3 (Winter 2001): 393–426.

6. Drew R. McCoy, *The Elusive Republic: Political Economy in Jeffersonian America* (Chapel Hill, N.C., 1980).

7. Richard R. John, "American Political Development and Political History," in *The Oxford Handbook of American Political Development*, ed. Richard Valelly, Suzanne Mettler, and Robert Lieberman (New York, 2016), 186; John, "Governmental Institutions as Agents of Change: Rethinking American Political Development in the Early Republic, 1787–1835," *Studies in American Political Development* 11 (1997): 347–80.

8. Peter S. Onuf, "Reflections on the Founding: Constitutional Historiography in Bicentennial Perspective," *William and Mary Quarterly*, 3rd ser., 46, no. 2 (1989): 341–75. For a recent discussion of Jefferson and Madison as practical politicians with ideals *and* interests to uphold, see Andrew Burstein and Nancy Isenberg, *Madison and Jefferson* (New York, 2010). On that same mix of interests and ideals (however misguided) among Federalists, see Joanne B. Freeman, "Explaining the Unexplainable: The Cultural Context of the Sedition Act," in *The Democratic Experiment: New Directions in American Political History*, ed. Meg Jacobs, William J. Novak, and Julian E. Zelizer (Princeton, N.J., 2003), 20–49.

9. Brian Balogh, *A Government Out of Sight: The Mystery of National Authority in Nineteenth-Century America* (New York, 2009).

10. This point is made in Leonard D. White, *The Jeffersonians: A Study in Administrative History, 1801–1829* (New York, 1965), esp. 546–59, and Edling, *A Hercules in the Cradle*.

I The Jeffersonian Coalition

1 Friends and Enemies in the Declaration of Independence

Robert G. Parkinson

The challenges facing the members of the Continental Congress in 1776 were in many ways unprecedented. No one had attempted such a wide-scale colonial rebellion before. Keeping that scale as wide as possible, therefore, was the highest priority of Jefferson and his colleagues in Congress. Unity was the Revolution's greatest strength and potential fatal flaw. In order to solidify union, Jefferson and his fellow delegates had to mobilize as many of the American people as they could behind their definition of a just cause. They understood that the best strategy to cultivate was to find—and amplify—someone to unite against. The most effective cultural tools at hand for eighteenth-century Americans were colonial prejudices against Indians and African Americans. If the patriots could muster those stereotypes in the name of the "common cause," they stood a chance to stay united. In other words, Jefferson and other patriot leaders marshaled cultural prejudice to generate grassroots support for the Revolution, thus creating a line of exclusion among the inhabitants of North America. Some of them would belong to "the American people," and some would not. As many of the essays in this volume show, Jefferson and his colleagues celebrated "the American people" and put new redemptive faith in their voice, but also were more than willing to use exclusion to create that populist fiction.

The founders' embrace of exclusion in the service of unity is most evident in the Declaration of Independence. Although analysts often interpret it as a pure form of ideas crystallized from Enlightenment philosophers, it was much more than that. The Declaration was a document meant to achieve specific political ends, and in the process was an original statement that defined the borderlines—the cordon—around who belonged to "the American people."

There are lots of people in the Declaration. First are the declarers, the people identified in the document as the friends of liberty. A few are named specifically. The only names attached to the Declaration, as anyone saw the text in July 1776, were the president and secretary of the Congress, John Hancock and Charles Thomson. They were standing in for the rest of the delegates, who also appear throughout the document as "we." The pronoun "we," meaning the representatives to Congress and, by extension, the American people, appears eight times in the Declaration. The first invocation of "we" is, of course, the most well known, setting out who the declarers are: believers in human equality, defenders of man's desire to pursue happiness, and trustworthy guardians of the people's right to a government of their choosing. Consumers of the Declaration were expected to view the qualities of "we" as counterpoised by "he," the tyrant king, as shorthand for the heroes and villains of this political narrative.

Some of the Declaration's enemies are also named explicitly. The king, famously, leads the list. Eighteen times the Continental Congress accused George III of personally approving or encouraging terrible crimes against the American colonies. The Declaration also indicted the British people as a whole for their inattention to the continual pleadings of sincere American exhortations for mercy. They too were "deaf to the voice of justice and consanguinity," and because they did not "disavow these usurpations," they invited this divorce. In his rough draft Jefferson went further, swearing "manly spirit bids us to renounce for ever these unfeeling brethren."[1] Then there are the people who assisted the king in carrying out his plot to enslave America. This included Parliament, who is charged in the Declaration with aiding the king by passing "Acts of pretended Legislation," and the "swarms of Officers" the Crown dispatched to America to "harass our people, and eat out their substance."

But there are other enemies identified in the Declaration of Independence. In the last cluster of the twenty-seven grievances lodged against the king, three groups—"foreign mercenaries," "merciless savages," and "domestic insurrectionists"—are accused of assisting the British in destroying American freedom. These are the only people in America listed in the Declaration as willingly aiding the king.[2] German auxiliaries, Indians, and slaves: these three groups appear as the king's proxies in the Declaration's final indictments. Although Jefferson still suggested the villainy was primarily King George's for involving them, their inclusion is a significant one. Jefferson's featuring of those three groups at the climax of the Declaration of Independence was neither coincidental nor cursory. It was about unity.

A close look at the schedule of the Continental Congress during the weeks before the Declaration's approval suggests that the participation of those groups were central to the timing and contours of how the American colonies declared their independence. The delegates to Congress were thinking quite a bit about the role German auxiliaries, Indians, and slaves might play in the coming campaign at the start of the summer of 1776. One, Thomas Jefferson, was particularly interested in this issue. If we look at what else Jefferson was doing from the middle of May through early July 1776, it is clear that the final grievances that fixed the damning phrases "merciless savages" and "domestic insurrectionists" at the heart of America's founding document were more than an expression of the Virginians' felicitous writing style. The role these "proxies" would play in the Revolutionary War crowded Congress's agenda almost constantly early that summer.

On Sunday, May 19, 1776, New Hampshire delegate Josiah Bartlett wrote home to a fellow patriot leader, John Langdon, confiding his fears of a "severe trial this summer with Britons, Hessians, Hanoverians, Indians, negroes, and every other butcher the gracious King of Britain can hire against us."[3] The next evening, after a long Monday session in Congress, Bartlett was relaxing in a Philadelphia coffeehouse when a stranger wandered in. The man had been sent there (partly by Langdon himself) to find Bartlett and show him a set of fascinating papers. His name was George Merchant, a New Hampshire rifleman who had joined Benedict Arnold's invasion of Canada the previous year. Merchant had been taken prisoner while on sentry duty in Quebec the previous November and sent to England for interrogation. After several months in a London prison, British authorities ordered him to a facility in Bristol for long-term incarceration before a number of sympathetic gentlemen interceded on his behalf and secured his passage to Halifax. Someone procured for him copies of the treaties the Crown had recently signed with several German states for the hiring of several thousand mercenary soldiers.

Merchant sewed these precious documents into the lining of his clothes, and despite multiple searches by British officials in Halifax, they went undetected. Early in May, Merchant made his way to New England and found John Langdon in Portsmouth, New Hampshire. Langdon immediately sent Merchant on to Washington's headquarters in New York City.[4] The secreted papers were the first documented evidence the Americans had of the purchase of German soldiers, transactions that were several months old by that time. In fact, just a few days before Merchant arrived in New Hampshire, a ship captain named John Lee docked in Newburyport, Massachusetts, claiming to have seen those very soldiers being carried by an enormous fleet headed for New York. The captain's eyewitness account flooded newspapers throughout New England and the rest of the colonies just as Washington perused Merchant's papers and decided he needed to proceed to Philadelphia to inform the Continental Congress. When the former prisoner walked into the coffeehouse to find Langdon's friend Josiah Bartlett, he completed a journey of several thousand miles to bring Congress this vital information. The following morning, Bartlett brought Merchant and his treaties to Congress. The journals of the Continental Congress then report what they did with this crucial information: "Resolved, that the said letters, and papers, be referred to a committee of five; that the said committee be directed to extract and publish the treaties, and such parts of the intelligence as they think proper . . . and to prepare an address to the foreign mercenaries who are coming to invade America."[5] The five delegates assigned to this task were William Livingston, Richard Henry Lee, John Adams, Roger Sherman, and Thomas Jefferson. The latter three members of this committee, of course, would soon comprise the majority of another one, the so-called Committee of Five tasked to draft a declaration of independency.

The first part of this subcommittee's charge, to extract and publish the treaties, happened instantly. Bartlett's coffeehouse encounter with Merchant occurred Monday evening, Congress interviewed the New Hampshire rifleman on Tuesday morning, and, when two Philadelphia newspapers brought out their regular Wednesday editions, they featured the extracted text of the treaties. Adams, Jefferson, and the subcommittee must have worked fast, hustling the documents Merchant had secreted across the Atlantic down Market Street to the print shops of William Bradford's *Pennsylvania Journal* and Hall & Sellers' *Pennsylvania Gazette.*[6] From there the news spread quickly throughout the colonies.[7] In those newspaper columns the official text of the treaties sponsored by Congress appeared on the heels of Captain John Lee's eyewitness account of the fleet on its way across the sea, a story that often ran in the previous week's issue.[8] A third report giving the certainty of foreign soldiers being part of Britain's expected invasion force also appeared at that same moment. *Pennsylvania Packet* printer John Dunlap had just published an account from Dublin suggesting that there would be no peace commissioners in that fleet (as some American moderates had anticipated) but rather thousands of German mercenaries. This report too flew through the other colonial newspapers just days before the official text extracted by Congress's subcommittee.[9] In total, of the three dozen newspapers currently operating in the mainland colonies that May, only one—Dixon & Hunter's *Virginia Gazette*—did not print at least one of the three stories documenting the imminent entrance of foreign mercenaries into the American rebellion.[10]

The second task Congress assigned to the subcommittee, to prepare an appeal to the foreign soldiers, took shape in the days that followed, although not by any of the five delegates. A week after Merchant's interview, Congress resolved to draft and publish "an animated address . . . to impress the minds of the people with the necessity of their now stepping forward to save their country, their freedom and property," a move that sounds much like the task a declaration of independence was to accomplish just a few weeks later.[11] They assigned four men to write this address: Edward Rutledge, Samuel Adams, George Wythe, and Thomas Jefferson. Within the span of a week, Congress asked Jefferson to help write exhortations on both sides of the conflict, to encourage colonists to fight and foreign soldiers not to.

At some point, Jefferson asked his former law teacher to take one of these on. The addresses to the different colonies went out on Tuesday, June 4, four days before the debate over independence began. They sounded many of the same notes Jefferson's declaration soon would, including references to the "Tyrant of Britain and his Parliament," who was out to destroy them not the least because his use of numbers of foreign troops was "now about to be pour[ed]" in against them.[12] The address to the foreign mercenaries did not materialize as quickly. Wythe took the lead in drafting the address begging the colonies for support, for the manuscript copies of it in his hand are found among Jefferson's papers. Jefferson apparently asked Wythe to assist him with the other as well, for an undated draft in Wythe's hand is also in those papers.[13] It is unclear when Wythe finished his draft address to the foreign mercenaries, but it was surely before he left Congress to return to Virginia on June 13. The news of a British invasion fleet, thick with transports of hired mercenaries, encouraged Congress to take to their pens; Jefferson and his declaration were just one of the products of that hectic period in which they had to justify the "cause" to many different audiences.

"It is no small pleasure, when in this first address we ever made to you we must call you enemies, that we can affirm you to be unprovoked enemies," Wythe began his appeal to the mercenaries, searching for a reason why the Germans had agreed to participate in the Revolution. "We have not," he continued, "invaded your country, slaughtered, wounded, or captivated your towns and villages, wasted your farms and cottages, spoiled you of your goods, or annoyed your trade." Why, then, he asked rhetorically, do you interfere? Is it because of principles? monarchical oppression? bloodlust? or opportunity that you volunteer to come to "join in this quarrel with our foes . . . and at so great a distance from both you and us?" "We wish," he confessed, that opportunity "might be your motive; because we have the means, and want not inclination, to gratify your desires, if they be not hostile, without loss to ourselves, perhaps with less expense, certainly with more honor and with more advantage to you than victory can promise. Numberless Germans and other foreigners settled in this country will testify this truth." Wythe then left space for Congress to append a resolution, perhaps a plan approved by Congress to grant land to mercenaries who deserted the British. In the end, Wythe's draft turned out to be a dead letter. Congress never filled in the space left in the middle of Wythe's May address. Its members would, however, again take up the issue of inciting Germans to desert later in the summer.[14]

The premise behind Wythe's appeal was the same one that his former law student would develop just a few days later in the Declaration of Independence. Wythe cordoned off the actions and intentions of America's tyrannical enemies from proper defenders of liberty. He left space for the mercenaries' ultimate redemption, calling them "unprovoked enemies" and giving them plenty of chances to choose the "right" side of the conflict. Wythe, like Jefferson would soon do, blamed the king. Wythe's address, however, allowed the mercenaries to reconsider: "But if, exercising your own judgments, you have spirit enough to assert that freedom which all men are born to, associate yourselves with those who desire, and think they are able to secure it, with all the blessings of peace, to you and your posterity."[15] They had the capacity to change their minds and, like the patriots, embrace the universal rights of man. Of the three groups of "proxies" that lay at the heart of the declaration Jefferson was about to write, the foreign mercenaries had the greatest advantage.

The corroboration of rumors that the Crown had purchased foreign soldiers to aid in quelling the rebellion exploded across the mainland colonies in the middle of May 1776. Many patriots claimed this was the deciding factor for independence. According to one Philadelphian whose private letter later appeared in a few northern newspapers, the people of that capital, after learning that thousands of offshore foreign mercenaries were about to invade, quickly became of one mind about independence. "This," he related, "gives the *Coup de Grace* to the British and American connection. It has already wrought wonders in this city; conversions have been more rapid than ever happen'd under Mr. Whitfield."[16]

The importance of the news of Britain's hiring of these "unprovoked enemies" is also reflected in the business of the Continental Congress in late May and early June 1776. Although the delegates did not yet make policy decisions about how exactly they would encourage the foreign mercenaries to desert their posts, the power of the news on public opinion in favor of independence is clear. The members wrote and talked a great deal about what effect this news had on the colonial populace. They too saw this as the "coup de grace." As one Pennsylvania delegate opined early that June, "the Dogs of Warr are now fairly let loose upon us. We are not dismayed but expect to give a good Account of the Numerous hosts of Foes that are coming to Slaughter us, especially your Hessians, Hanoverians, Waldeckers, etc."[17] Merchant's "infamous treaties," Richard Henry Lee wrote, made independence "not [a] choice then, but necessity."[18] Just a few days after he wrote this, Lee formally proposed Congress take up the question of independence.

Given how central the sudden news about the king's hiring thousands of foreign mercenaries was to the timing of independence, it is not surprising that this act featured prominently in the final grievances Jefferson laid out to justify American independence. From the middle of May through the debate on independence, what role "the Hessians" would play in the conflict was a topic of conversation throughout the colonies. Newspaper printers delineated how many battalions were recruited and who their German commanders were. They described infantry and cavalry units and offered information about their equipment. They published descriptions to help Americans tell the differences between Brunswickers and Waldeckers.

The other two groups of "proxies" in the Declaration, Indians and slaves, did not suddenly burst onto the pages of colonial newspapers in the spring of 1776. Unlike the Germans, for more than a year—since Lexington and Concord—rumors about the role Indians and African Americans might play in the burgeoning conflict whipped around colonial North America. Starting in the summer of 1775, those rumors centered on royal governors in the southern colonies who stoked the fires by hinting that perhaps they would include enslaved people in their plans to quell the rebellion. Still more whispers about which side Indians might support abounded during those same months. Those stories centered on British agents in the New York and Carolina backcountry meeting with Native Americans to discuss whether they would be willing to enter the conflict. Both of those year-long stories—the participation of enslaved Americans and Indians in the Revolutionary War—were also evolving into a critical stage in May and June 1776, and the patriot political leadership had to concern itself with what effect those groups might have on the upcoming summer campaign. Here again, Thomas Jefferson was at the center of the patriot reaction to these developments.

Just weeks after the initial news of Lexington and Concord spread throughout the mainland colonies, the first rumors about British officers meeting with Indian leaders also began. Throughout 1775 colonists anxiously perused weekly reports in their newspapers about seemingly remote and insignificant events, such as a dead body found in a field in rural New York or remote conferences held 1,500 miles north of Quebec, as portents of a return of the intimate, terrible bloodshed of Indian conflict that marked the Seven Years' War and its aftermath.[19] Although both sides had implored Indians either to go to war for them or to stay neutral, the patriots screamed as loudly as they could that sinister British leaders were singular in their diabolical plots to encourage Native American raids across the backcountry. On the day after Christmas 1775, for example, *Pennsylvania Evening Post* printer Benjamin Towne extracted one key paragraph of a letter from General Philip Schuyler "to perpetuate the *humanity* of the Ministers of George the Third and their Agents." Schuyler reported that a group of Iroquois Indians "related the substance of all the conferences Col[onel Guy] Johnson had with them the last summer . . . after which they were invited to FEAST ON A BOSTONIAN AND DRINK HIS BLOOD."[20] The reports also related that Johnson had offered them "a very large black war belt with a hatchet depictured in it," but the Natives refused, "and we have now a full proof that the ministerial servants have attempted to engage the savages against us." Congress ordered

Towne and his printer colleagues to publish such salacious news in their weekly newspapers. Half of them did so.[21]

This imagery connected the British with savagery—indeed, cannibalism—in a totalizing fashion, not allowing for any nuance. The enemies of the Revolution were despicable. But, at the same time, the report also suggested that all the efforts of Indian superintendent Guy Johnson and his ally in the northern backcountry, Canadian governor Guy Carleton, were for naught. The Indians were not listening to their entreaties. One of the main stories of the Revolutionary War's first year was, interestingly, that the Indians had been quite merciful toward the colonists. Despite exhortations to get involved, nearly all—from the Canadian frontier to the Carolinas—held back from choosing sides. Patriot political leaders played up every opportunity they could find to implicate British agents, publishing documents like Schuyler's as often as possible. Newspapers friendly to the patriot cause ran rumors and hearsay over and over to incriminate and damn British officials, at the same time praising Indians (and Providence) for their smart decision to stay out of the conflict.

But, just like the sudden intrusion of the news of foreign mercenaries in May 1776, that tense period of peace ended abruptly at about the same moment. In the middle of April, the American army that had invaded Canada the previous November fell back across the St. Lawrence River. Smallpox forced the army to give up their siege of Quebec and retreat south. Benedict Arnold, commander at the temporarily American-held city of Montreal, dispatched four hundred men under New Hampshire colonel Thomas Bedel to protect the retreating force by building an outpost at a place on the St. Lawrence called the Cedars.[22] Not long after construction began at the Cedars stockade, Bedel departed to negotiate with the Caughnawaga Indians and placed Major Isaac Butterfield in command. Rumors began to swirl across the Canadian border of an approaching force of Indians, numbering anywhere from 400 to a terrifying 1,300.[23] British captain George Foster, who in reality did not have nearly that many, attacked the Cedars on May 18 with a force of 36 regulars, 1 Canadian volunteer, and 160 Indians from the neighborhood of Detroit. According to one of the defenders, the Indians came "skipping and running out of the woods" with "nothing but a sort of wildgrass to secret or hide them from us."[24] Unaware that reinforcement was on the way and fearful of what the enemy might do to his sickly men, Butterfield immediately surrendered the post. His relief, consisting of

Major Henry Sherburne and 120 Continental soldiers, was also ambushed by Indians on their way to the Cedars and surrendered after a short encounter. In all, nearly one quarter of Arnold's force in Canada were captured in the debacle.

What happened to those prisoners next clinched in many colonists' minds the accusation that the Indians were indeed "merciless savages." Since the Americans had unconditionally surrendered to the Indians and not to Foster, the prisoners were under their control. The Indians, allegedly, "fell to work" on the prisoners and "stripped them stark naked" as they took the soldiers' clothing as spoils of victory. After they "dispatched the wounded by knocking them in the head," one impassioned account detailed, "the dead [were] stripped naked, and thrown by the side of the road, the remaining troops was drove like cattle by them, it was a horrible sight . . . to see the Indians brandishing their knives and tomahawks over their heads and hollering and screaming and likewise dancing like so many mad men or devils."[25]

Knowing Arnold would come after him, Foster warned the American commander that if attacked, he would allow the Indians to kill the prisoners. Foster offered to exchange Butterfield and Sherburne's forces if they each pledged never again to take up arms against the king. Outraged, Arnold refused all offers and made plans to try to reach the captives, who were now being kept on an island in the St. Lawrence, fully exposed to the Canadian elements. Foster convinced Butterfield and Sherburne to agree to the cartel, and, against his wishes, Arnold signed it. The prisoners were set free on May 27, 1776. The American leadership was incensed. Washington condemned the "cowardly and disgraceful behavior" of Bedel and Butterfield (who were later court martialed), and John Adams lamented that the Cedars was "the first stain upon American arms." Adams thought Butterfield deserved "a most infamous death."[26]

News of this surrender and the Indians' rough treatment of American prisoners stormed through colonial newspapers. Although printers still substantiated wild rumors, the first few months of 1776 had lacked much proof of British agents plotting with Indians in the backcountry. The story of the Cedars, however, provided palpable, incriminating evidence of Native Americans acting on the king's behalf. What had been just hearsay before was now tangible proof of Indians' "feasting on Bostonians." The first reports, wildly inaccurate, appeared in New York and Philadelphia papers in early June, incidentally the same day Congress opened their debate on independence.[27] The next week John Holt's *New York Journal* provided an "authentic account" from "an officer of the detachment it principally concerns." This report was nearly a column long and packed with images of savagery. Once the Americans surrendered, "then a scene of Savage barbarity ensued, and many of our people were sacrificed to their fury," the officer from Sherburne's unit related. These instances of "barbarity" were repeated as the prisoners were "again and again stripped of the small remainder of their clothes, till many of them had not sufficient to hide their nakedness." Most papers throughout the northern colonies exchanged this account throughout June.[28]

The earliest news of disaster at the Cedars reached Philadelphia by Sunday, June 2. New Hampshire delegate William Whipple wrote that day, "here is a report" that Bedel "is cut off by a party of the 8th regiment and Indians," but he did not put much stock in it.[29] The next day, an express arrived from Albany bearing a letter from Ticonderoga confirming the worst. Whipple's colleague Josiah Bartlett also hoped it would not "prove so bad as reported," but Congress took steps to improve security on the Canadian frontier just in case.[30] Armed with intelligence from the Albany express, Congress decided to provide details to a resolution passed the previous week allowing the recruitment of Indians into the Continental Army; to do, in other words, exactly what the patriots screamed their enemies were doing to them. With the expectation that the Atlantic horizon would any day start filling with British and German troop ships, they resolved that Philip Schuyler "be empowered to employ in Canada a number of Indians, not exceeding two thousand."[31] Samuel Adams, for one, fixed his hopes that, despite "displeasing" recent affairs in Canada, this controversial step would rescue patriot fortunes on the northern frontier.[32] The situation was indeed dire.

Samuel's cousin, ever the pessimist, was in a panic. John Adams believed the loss of Canada could mean the concession of all northern Indians to Britain, a potentially fatal blow to the "common cause." Not only would the British have control of the St. Lawrence and Great Lakes, and uninterrupted communication among Niagara, Detroit, and Michilimackinac, he argued, but "they will have a free Communication with all the numerous tribes of Indians, extending along the frontiers of all the colonies, and by their trinkets and bribes will induce them to take up the hatchet, and spread blood and fire among the inhabitants by which means, all the frontier inhabitants will be driven in upon the middle settlements, at a time when the inhabitants of the seaports and coasts, will be driven back by the British Navy. Is this picture too high colored?" he asked, recovering his nerve. "Perhaps it is."[33]

Others in Congress were shaken by the news from Canada too. It was two days after receiving the news about the Cedars that Congress approved an address, written by Jefferson, Wythe, Adams, and Rutledge, imploring colonists to remain steadfast in the "cause" in spite of the bad news. In the five days since they had received this assignment, the situation, especially the "melancholy aspect" in Canada, had only gotten far worse.[34] Once the delegates sent those beseeching messages with express riders galloping off in all directions, Congress then opened an investigation to find out exactly what had gone wrong in Canada.

From the middle of May through the first days of June, in other words, foreign mercenaries or Indians dominated a significant portion of Congress's attention. This absorption matched the newspapers during those weeks: papers in many locales published accounts from the Cedars either together with or closely behind the news of Hessians on their way, or the text of the German treaties themselves. During the weeks when they were weighing the question of independence, the delegates to the Continental Congress were in fact working arduously on crafting addresses to convince the people to keep faith, quietly issuing orders to recruit northern Indians to defend New England, and concocting plans to convince German mercenaries to desert as soon as they arrived in America. Concerns about hostile Indians threatening from the St. Lawrence or German troops sailing across the Atlantic dominated those hectic days of early June.

Then, on Friday, June 7, Richard Henry Lee introduced a motion to propose American independence. After two heated days of debate, the following Tuesday, June 11, Congress appointed five men to draft a declaration of independency: Roger Sherman, Robert Livingston, Benjamin Franklin, John Adams, and Thomas Jefferson. At some point over the next day or two, the members of the "Committee of Five" placed the quill in Jefferson's hands, a moment lodged deeply at the core of American mythology ever since.[35] Although American lore would rather us linger about Jefferson's Philadelphia apartment while he wrote what would become a sacred civil text, writing the Declaration was hardly all Jefferson was doing with his time.

He had other responsibilities in Congress. On Friday, June 15, Congress took Jefferson away from his writing duties to act as secretary to investigate the Cedars prisoner debacle. The four-man Committee on the Cedars Cartel interviewed Major Henry Sherburne and presented their report two days later, a paper with language that included prisoners being delivered into the "hands of the Savages," a "horrid act," "cruel and inhuman death," and a "gross and barbarous violation of the laws of nature and nations."[36] Everything having to do with the Cedars investigation, from the reports issued by the subcommittee to the notes on their interview with Sherburne, was in Jefferson's hand, a task that took one of the three precious weekends away from his time to draft the Declaration.

At the same time, during the dwindling days Jefferson had left that June, news also began to circulate in Philadelphia and other American cities that the "common cause" might be just as vulnerable in the southern backcountry as in the North. In the spring, Southern Indian superintendent John Stuart, who had been exiled from Charleston under suspicion of "instigating" Indian attacks, sent his brother Henry into Cherokee country to explore their willingness to fight for the king. Following in his brother's footsteps, Henry's efforts to engage the Cherokee and Creek Indians were also discovered by patriot leaders. On May 18, Henry wrote a public letter warning frontier inhabitants across the South who refused to join him that they would soon be at risk from "five hundred warriors" each from the Creeks, Chickasaws, and Cherokees, who were about to "take possession of the frontiers of North Carolina and Virginia."[37] This letter was intercepted, sent to Williamsburg, instantly given to *Virginia Gazette* printer Alexander Purdie, and forwarded to Jefferson and his colleagues in Philadelphia, where it arrived by June 18, just after Jefferson filed his report on the Cedars and went back to his writing desk to work on the Declaration.[38] While Congress considered what to do about potential hostile Indians in the South, twelve more printers from Maryland north exchanged this fresh threat from one of the patriots' old nemeses in June and July.[39]

In other words, even though Indians had largely stayed out of the conflict over the first fourteen months of the Revolutionary War, just at the moment that Jefferson drafted the Declaration questions about their participation seized the attention of patriot leaders. Jefferson and his colleagues spent the same time they were thinking about, writing about, or debating independence dealing with old and new threats from the backcountry.

Jefferson paid particular attention to these threats. When he was not transcribing Sherburne's description of how American soldiers were "continually insulted, buffeted, and ill-treated by the savages" or writing the

Declaration draft, Jefferson was also penning a model constitution for an independent state of Virginia.[40] That document contained a preamble that rehearsed many of the grievances Jefferson would soon submit to Congress for its approval, including the final ones enshrined in the Declaration. He completed this draft in the first half of June, a few days before the Cedars committee completed its report and just two weeks before finalizing the Declaration draft. The Virginia constitution preamble accused the king of "endeavoring to bring on the inhabitants of our frontiers the merciless Indian savages whose known rule of warfare is an undistinguished destruction of all ages, sexes, and conditions of existence."[41] One wonders what Jefferson thought about this powerful, loaded sentence he had recently crafted for the Virginia constitution as he listened to Major Sherburne describe the prisoners' plight at the Cedars. This was no rhetorical flight of fancy but documented fact. After this corroboration, there was little doubt he would repeat it verbatim in the Declaration draft.

There was one other accusation Jefferson leveled at the king in his draft of the Virginia constitution. In addition to listing "merciless Indian savages" and "a large army of foreign mercenaries" as the king's proxies to destroy American freedom, he also indicted George III for "prompting our negroes to rise in arms among us; those very negroes whom by an inhuman use of his negative he hath refused us permission to exclude by law."[42] This grievance differed significantly from what would soon be enshrined in the text of Congress's Declaration. Unlike the rather opaque reference to "domestic insurrectionists" that would appear in the Declaration, Jefferson specifically called attention to enslaved people who responded to British calls to trade military service for emancipation.

As with Indians, rumors about British officials "tampering," "inciting," or "whispering" to slaves on southern plantations started immediately with the news of war with Britain. Patriots linked southern governors and Royal Navy officers to foiled insurrectionist plots in the summer and fall of 1775. When Virginia's governor, Lord Dunmore, issued his notorious emancipation decree to all able-bodied, male slaves of rebels who joined his forces in November, he was only the most prominent of several British agents patriots accused of inciting their slaves to murder. Patriot authorities had forced North Carolina governor Josiah Martin to seek the protection of Royal Navy captain John Collet's fleet, and they executed Thomas Jeremiah, a black pilot accused of plotting to aid South Carolina governor William Campbell land troops and emancipate slaves in Charleston.[43]

Dunmore had threatened slave emancipation when first confronted by patriot resistance in late April 1775. When he made good on these warnings in November, his scheme to end the rebellion in Virginia was part of a growing chorus of patriot exclamations—in official addresses and sponsored newspaper stories—that the king's men in America would stop at nothing to destroy them. Over the last few weeks of 1775, hundreds of slaves from Virginia and Maryland labored to reach Dunmore's forces near Norfolk. Patriot military leaders attempted to stem the tide by threatening to execute any runaways they caught, while political leaders used their pens to fight, writing essays and private letters that lambasted Dunmore and warned slaves not to be "weak" or "wicked" in placing their trust in such a treacherous man. "Be not then, ye negroes, tempted by this proclamation to ruin yourselves," one remarkable essay published in a Williamsburg paper warned. "I have considered your welfare, as well as that of the country. Whether you will profit by my advice, I cannot tell; but this I know, that whether we suffer or not, if you desert us, you most certainly will."[44]

Historians estimate about one thousand enslaved people ignored this threat, taking refuge with the governor in the months after the news of his proclamation spread throughout the colonies. In mid-December, the *Pennsylvania Evening Post* reported an encounter between a white woman and a black man on a Philadelphia street. When she reprimanded him for getting in her way, his impassioned reply laid bare the raw tension that was in the air across much of North America right then. "Stay, you damned white bitch, 'till Lord Dunmore and his black regiment come," he allegedly responded, "and then we will see who is to take the wall."[45] What that emboldened African American Philadelphian did not yet know was that such dreams would not materialize. In early December, Dunmore organized what would derisively be called his "Ethiopian Regiment" and deployed them at Great Bridge, in defense of the southern approaches to Norfolk. A force of patriot militia overwhelmed them on December 9. Not long after that encounter on a Philadelphia sidewalk, Dunmore and his loyalists were ejected from the city. By the first days of the new year, the seat of royal government in Virginia was known as the "floating town," an extensive flotilla of vessels anchored in the Chesapeake.

After spending several months gathering loyalist refugees, black and white, smallpox forced Dunmore to unload the "floating town" on Gwynn's Island, a small sandbar just a few yards off the Virginia mainland between the mouths of the York and Rappahannock Rivers. By the end of May—on the same day Benedict Arnold was being forced to sign the Cedars Cartel—the disease tearing through his fleet forced him ashore. According to one published letter, the raging epidemic cost Dunmore "9 or 10 men from his black regiment every day."[46] Nevertheless, a Royal Navy captain estimated on June 10 that the governor still gained "six or eight fresh Men every day."[47] Although many of these new recruits would tragically die as soon as they reached the purported promised land, the sustained stream of runaways even in the face of smallpox testifies to the attraction of Dunmore's proclamation. Eight of Landon Carter's slaves thought the risk worthwhile. In late June he noted in his diary that they had gone "to be sure, to Lord Dunmore," taking guns, ammunition, silver buckles, and new sets of clothes with them.[48] Dunmore quarantined most of the runaway slaves on the bay side of the island and dug fortifications nearest to the mainland to prepare for a patriot assault. *Virginia Gazette* printers John Dixon and William Hunter first published a report on June 15 that Dunmore had taken this opportunity to initiate a new stage of germ warfare. Employing the most vague, least corroborated method of introducing a story, they wrote, "We learn from Gloucester, that Lord Dunmore has erected hospitals upon Gwyn's island . . . and that they are inoculating the blacks for the smallpox." "Two of those wretches," they continued, were purposely "inoculated and sent ashore, in order to spread the infection, but it was happily prevented."[49] Nine patriot newspapers would exchange this accusation, in some cases in the same column of news with Henry Stuart's proclamation.[50]

On the weekend that Congress debated independence, both Elbridge Gerry and John Adams wrote home relating news that "we hear" Dunmore "with his Regiment of Royal Africans" had landed on Gwynn's.[51] They were not the only delegates who had Dunmore on their minds that June. Jefferson, despite being preoccupied with piles of congressional business in Philadelphia, was also thinking about the island. At some point during the seven summer weeks when the governor was camped there, Jefferson sketched an intricate map of the island. Although it is not certain when he received the information incorporated in this map or even who supplied that intelligence, the detailed sketches of the besieging American fleet and surrounding breastworks found among his papers suggest that Jefferson had more than a passing interest in the actions on Gwynn's Island as he was helping George Wythe craft an address to the German mercenaries, investigating Indian attacks in Canada, writing the preamble to Virginia's first state constitution, and drafting the Declaration of Independence.[52]

In short, when the delegates to the Continental Congress focused on resistant slaves, hostile Indians, and German auxiliaries in the final, climactic grievances against King George, they were not solely doing so for dramatic effect. True, the language of these accusations was more impassioned than many that preceded—and that was not accidental either, for in their editing sessions on July 2–4, the delegates made more changes to these last charges, more than any of the two dozen further up the page. But more importantly, the grievances about "domestic insurrectionists," "merciless savages," and "foreign mercenaries" also document the *business* that consumed Congress during the days and weeks when they considered independence. And no delegate was more at the center of those issues than Thomas Jefferson. Slaves, Indians, and German mercenaries lay at the heart of both the process of declaring independence and the Declaration of Independence. These topics were key reasons why and when Jefferson and his colleagues cast their votes for independence, and they featured at the climax of the summary statement Congress issued to explain to audiences foreign and domestic why they were taking such a fateful step. In reality and rhetoric, when the king's agents brokered deals with these three groups—all involved in crises erupting during May and June 1776—they were the ultimate deal-breakers for the American colonies.

When Jefferson featured these groups at the climax of the Declaration it was to make the case that "we"—the "one people" who "hold these truths to be self-evident"—were distinct from and superior to their "British brethren." It was a profoundly exclusionary rendering of the "common cause." At the crucial founding moment, the definition of what it meant to be an American was a negative one: not British. But the heated language of the Declaration's final grievances gave it other shapes, especially not slave and not savage. Those negative constructions reinforced the patriots' positive assessment of themselves as holding the moral, philosophical, and political high ground in this conflict. Because those tropes plugged into deeply embedded colonial prejudices about Africans and Native Americans, however, they were more than just stock scripts about not behaving in manners that were slavish or savage. These renderings had the effect of casting out real Indians and African Americans. Jefferson's words, ratified by the Continental Congress and broadcast to the world, eliminated the nuanced political realities patriot leaders had sought to manage in the weeks leading up to the Declaration. The Declaration elided the potentially friendly Indians they tried to enlist, erased the foreign mercenaries they sought to seduce, and abandoned all attempts to speak directly to runaway slaves. Jefferson's rhetoric did not match the realities of his own busy agenda throughout May and June 1776.

But it was more than that. One month after finishing the Declaration, Jefferson wrote his Virginia friend John Page, now lieutenant governor of Virginia, about the news of Cherokee attacks along the Carolina backcountry. "Nothing will reduce those wretches so soon as pushing the war into the heart of their country," Jefferson advised. "But I would not stop there. I would never cease pursuing them while one of them remained on this side [of] the Mississippi." Jefferson had already supervised the rhetorical removal of all friendly Indians in the Declaration by lumping them together as merciless enemies. Now he also called for physical removal: "So unprovoked an attack and so treacherous [a?] one should never be forgiven while one of them remains near enough to do us injury."[53] When the Declaration elided friendly Indians, German mercenaries, and African Americans and fused them all as enemy proxies of the tyrant king, Jefferson created a new political reality. This was especially powerful for African Americans and Indians, groups that carried significant cultural baggage, prejudices, and stereotypes inherited from generations of colonialism. German mercenaries, especially after patriot leaders were able to cast them as pathetic soldiers following the debacle at Trenton, lacked these deep prejudices and were able to slip the onus of being excluded at the founding. They were, after all, "unprovoked enemies" and still redeemable. For the remainder of the war, patriot political and communications leaders cast them as fellow victims of monarchical tyranny and opened pathways for them to become American citizens. But for "merciless savages" and "domestic insurrectionists," those doors remained closed. Of course, white Americans' notions of Native Americans' and blacks' inferiority—which gathered speed and force in the eighteenth century—predated Jefferson's sitting down at his writing desk for those few June days in 1776. And they helped determine just how Jefferson would categorize and cordon them off as being the antithesis of "we," the American people.

The Declaration, moreover, created a new American reality, and not just in the sense of first establishing a new nation. When the portrayal of African Americans and Native Americans as King George's proxies merged with existing prejudices, a new political reality justified taking action against these enemies. Jefferson and his colleagues fashioned policies that planted racial exclusion deep into the political heart of the new republic. In the name of presenting a clean, powerful statement of the "common cause," Jefferson cast aside all the opacity of Congress's business at the moment of independence. Some of the people listed as enemies in the Declaration became enemies of the United States. In private, Jefferson and many of his patriot colleagues might have had qualms about drawing such distinctions, but in the name of unity and making the "cause" common, they obliterated nuance. In the process of trying to turn the British into aliens, they further cemented notions that "merciless savages" and "domestic insurrectionists" had no claims to enjoy the liberties and privileges of American citizens. In the first decades of the early republic, the totalizing rhetoric of the Declaration—of heroes and villains at the founding—would gain ascendancy over the complexity and gradations of the actual experience of the summer of 1776.

Notes

1. Jefferson, "'Original Rough Draught' of the Declaration of Independence," in Julian P. Boyd, ed., *Papers of Thomas Jefferson* (Princeton, N.J., 1950), 1:423–28, 427 (quotation) (hereafter *PTJ*).

2. The Declaration does mention Americans fighting for the Crown, but they are represented as being forced to "become the executioners of their friends and Brethren or to fall themselves by their Hands" after being captured.

3. Josiah Bartlett to John Langdon, Philadelphia, May 19, 1776, in Paul H. Smith et al., eds., *Letters of Delegates to Congress* (Washington, D.C., 1979), 4:39.

4. For Merchant's story, see John Langdon to George Washington, May 10, 1776, in W. W. Abbott, ed., *Papers of George Washington: Revolutionary War Series* (Charlottesville, Va., 1985), 3:255–57, and Caesar Rodney to Thomas Rodney, May 22, 1776, in Smith et al., eds., *Letters of Delegates to Congress,* 4:61–63.

5. Worthington C. Ford et al., eds., *Journals of the Continental Congress, 1774–1789* (Washington, D.C., 1904), 4:369–70.

6. *Pennsylvania Gazette* (Philadelphia), May 22, 1776; *Pennsylvania Journal* (Philadelphia), May 22, 24, 1776.

7. *Pennsylvania Packet* (Philadelphia), May 27, 1776 (2 entries); *New York Constitutional Gazette,* May 29, June 1, 1776; *Connecticut Journal* (New Haven), May 29,

June 5, 1776; *Connecticut Gazette* (New London), May 31, 1776; *New York Gazette and Weekly Mercury,* June 3, 1776; *Norwich [Conn.] Packet,* June 3, 10, 17, 1776; *Newport [R.I.] Mercury,* June 3, 6, 1776; *Connecticut Courant* (Hartford), June 3, 10, 17, 1776; *Maryland Gazette* (Annapolis), June 6, 1776; *New England Chronicle* (Salem, Mass.), June 13, 1776; *Freeman's Journal* (Portsmouth, N.H.), June 15, 1776.

8. *Providence Gazette,* May 4, 1776; *Norwich Packet,* May 6, 1776; *New York Constitutional Gazette,* May 8, 1776; *New England Chronicle,* May 9, 1776; *New York Gazette and Weekly Mercury,* May 9, 1776; *Pennsylvania Evening Post* (Philadelphia), May 9, 1776; *Connecticut Gazette,* May 10, 1776; *Connecticut Journal,* May 15, 1776; *Pennsylvania Gazette,* May 15, 1776; *Pennsylvania Journal,* May 15, 1776; *Pennsylvania Ledger* (Philadelphia), May 18, 1776; *Maryland Gazette,* May 23, 1776; *Virginia Gazette* (Purdie), May 24, 31, 1776. Because the law stipulated that the lucrative contract of printing the colony's currency and legal proceedings would go to the printer of the *Virginia Gazette,* all three Williamsburg newspapers active in 1776 shared that same title. They are, therefore, differentiated by the printer's name.

9. *Pennsylvania Packet,* May 6, 1776; *Pennsylvania Evening Post,* May 7, 1776; *Pennsylvania Journal,* May 9, 1776; *New York Journal,* May 9, 1776; *New York Packet,* May 9, 1776; *Pennsylvania Ledger,* May 11, 1776; *Maryland Journal and Baltimore Advertiser,* May 13, 1776; *Norwich Packet,* May 13, 1776; *Connecticut Courant,* May 13, 1776; *New York Gazette and Weekly Mercury,* May 13, 1776; *Maryland Gazette,* May 16, 1776; *New England Chronicle,* May 16, 1776; *Connecticut Gazette,* May 16, 1776; *Virginia Gazette* (Purdie), May 17, 1776; *Providence Gazette,* May 18, 1776; *Boston Gazette,* May 20, 1776; *Freeman's Journal,* May 25, 1776.

10. This is not to suggest that Virginia's capital was in the dark, however. Edmund Pendleton, writing to Thomas Jefferson from Williamsburg on May 24, said, "We have heard much of the Arrival of Russians, Hessians, and Comm[issione]rs to the Eastward, but nothing we can rely on." See Pendleton to Jefferson, May 24, 1776, in *PTJ,* 1:297.

11. Ford et al., eds., *Journals of the Continental Congress,* 4:401–2.

12. John Hancock to "Certain Colonies," June 4, 1776, in Smith et al., eds., *Letters of Delegates to Congress,* 4:136–37. These addresses went out to New Hampshire, Massachusetts, Connecticut, New York, New Jersey, Delaware, and Maryland. A separate address that used similar language went to Pennsylvania, for which see ibid., 4:138.

13. For the provenance of these addresses, see Smith et al., eds., *Letter of Delegates to Congress,* 4:111–12. Lyman Butterfield suggested Jefferson probably asked Wythe to write the draft address in "Psychological Warfare in 1776: The Jefferson-Franklin Plan to Cause Hessian Desertions," *Proceedings of the American Philosophical Society* 94 (June 1950): 233–41.

14. "George Wythe's Draft Address to the Foreign Mercenaries," May 1776, in Smith et al., eds., *Letters of Delegates to Congress,* 4:110–12.

15. Ibid., 4:111.

16. *New York Journal,* May 9, 1776; *New York Gazette and Weekly Mercury,* May 13, 1776; *Connecticut Journal,* May 15, 1776; *Connecticut Gazette,* May 16, 1776.

17. Robert Morris to Silas Deane, Philadelphia, June 5, 1776, in Smith et al., eds., *Letters of Delegates to Congress,* 4:147.

18. Richard Henry Lee to Landon Carter, Philadelphia, June 2, 1776, in ibid., 4:117.

19. For the dead body meaning "the commencement of Hostilities," see *New York Journal,* July 27, 1775; *New York Gazette and Weekly Mercury,* July 31, 1775; *Connecticut Journal,* Aug. 2, 1775; *Connecticut Gazette,* Aug. 4, 1775; *Norwich Packet,* Aug. 7, 1775; *Massachusetts Spy* (Worcester, Mass.), Aug. 16, 1775; *New Hampshire Gazette* (Portsmouth), Aug. 22, 1775. For the meeting 1,500 miles north of Quebec, see *New Hampshire Gazette,* July 11, 1775; *Pennsylvania Ledger,* July 22, 1775; *Pennsylvania Packet,* July 24, 1775; *Pennsylvania Journal,* July 26, 1775; *Virginia Gazette and Norfolk Intelligencer,* Aug. 2, 1775; *Virginia Gazette* (Pinkney), Aug. 3, 1775; *Virginia Gazette* (Purdie), Aug. 4, 1775.

20. *Pennsylvania Evening Post,* Dec. 26, 1775.

21. *Pennsylvania Gazette,* Dec. 27, 1775; *Pennsylvania Journal,* Dec. 27, 1775; *Pennsylvania Ledger,* Dec. 30, 1775; *New York Constitutional Gazette,* Dec. 30, 1775; *Pennsylvania Packet,* Jan. 1, 1776; *New York Gazette and Weekly Mercury,* Jan. 1, 1776; *Maryland Journal and Baltimore Advertiser,* Jan. 3, 1776; *Maryland Gazette,* Jan. 4, 1776; *New York Journal,* Jan. 4, 1776; *Virginia Gazette* (Purdie), Jan. 5, 1776; *Norwich Packet,* Jan. 8, 1776; *New England Chronicle,* Jan. 11, 1776; *Massachusetts Spy,* Jan. 12, 1776; *Connecticut Gazette,* Jan. 12, 1776; *Providence Gazette,* Jan. 13, 1776; *Boston Gazette,* Jan. 15, 1776; *Pennsylvania Magazine,* Dec. 1775, 581.

22. For the Cedars debacle, see Elizabeth A. Fenn, *Pox Americana: The Great Smallpox Epidemic, 1775–1782* (New York, 2001), 72–74; Robert McConnell Hatch, *Thrust for Canada: The American Attempt on Quebec in 1775–1776* (Boston, 1979), 197–208; and Robert S. Allen, *His Majesty's Indian Allies: British Indian Policy and the Defence of Canada* (Toronto, 1993), 47–48.

23. John Greenwood, Journal, 33, James S. Schoff Revolutionary War Collection, Clements Library, University of Michigan, Ann Arbor.

24. Zaphaniah Shepardson, "Journal," 7, quoted in Hatch, *Thrust for Canada,* 198.

25. Greenwood, Journal, 34, 36.

26. George Washington to Philip Schuyler, New York, June 16, 1776, in W. W. Abbott, ed., *Papers of George Washington: Revolutionary War Series* (Charlottesville, Va., 1993), 5:8; John Adams to John Sullivan, Philadelphia, June 23, 1776, in Robert J. Taylor et al., eds., *Papers of John Adams* (Cambridge, Mass., 1979), 4:330. See also Hatch, *Thrust for Canada,* 206. The Cedars Cartel is in Papers of the Continental Congress, item 29, pp. 251–56, National Archives, Washington, D.C.

27. *New York Constitutional Gazette,* June 8, 1776; *New York Gazette and Weekly Mercury,* June 10, 1776; *Connecticut Journal,* June 12, 1776; *Continental Journal* (Boston), June 13, 1776; *New England Chronicle,* June 13, 1776; *Freeman's Journal,* June 13, 1776; *Essex Journal* (Newburyport, Mass.), June 14, 1776; *Pennsylvania Evening Post,* June 15, 1776; *Providence Gazette,* June 15, 1776; *American Gazette* (Salem, Mass.), June 18, 1776; *Virginia Gazette* (Purdie), June 21, 1776; *Virginia Gazette* (Dixon & Hunter), June 22, 1776. A different account started with *Connecticut Courant* printer

Ebenezer Watson and had the following publishing run: *Connecticut Courant,* June 10, 1776; *Connecticut Journal,* June 12, 1776; *New England Chronicle,* June 13, 1776; *Continental Journal,* June 13, 1776; *Essex Journal,* June 14, 1776; *Pennsylvania Evening Post,* June 15, 1776; *Boston Gazette,* June 17, 1776; *Newport Mercury,* June 20, 1776. For a different letter from Canada, see *Pennsylvania Magazine,* June 1776, 294. Another report that originated in Philadelphia telling of Arnold's rush to reinforce Bedel appeared in the *Pennsylvania Evening Post,* June 8, 1776; *Pennsylvania Ledger,* June 8, 1776; *New York Constitutional Gazette,* June 12, 1776; *Connecticut Journal,* June 12, 1776; *Providence Gazette,* June 15, 1776.

28. *New York Journal,* June 20, 1776; *Pennsylvania Evening Post,* June 22, 1776; *New York Gazette and Weekly Mercury,* June 24, 1776; *Pennsylvania Packet,* June 24, 1776; *Connecticut Courant,* June 24, 1776; *New England Chronicle,* June 27, 1776; *Essex Journal,* June 28, 1776; *Newport Mercury,* July 1, 1776; *Norwich Packet,* July 1, 1776; *American Gazette,* July 2, 1776; *Maryland Gazette,* July 4, 1776; *Connecticut Gazette,* July 5, 1776; *Freeman's Journal,* July 6, 1776; *Virginia Gazette* (Dixon & Hunter), July 6, 1776.

29. William Whipple to John Langdon, Philadelphia, June 2, 1776, in Smith et al., eds., *Letters of Delegates to Congress,* 4:120.

30. Josiah Bartlett to John Langdon, Philadelphia, June 3, 1776, in ibid., 4:126.

31. Ford et al., eds., *Journals of the Continental Congress,* 4:412.

32. Samuel Adams to James Warren, Philadelphia, June 6, 1776, in Smith et al., eds., *Letters of Delegates to Congress,* 4:150.

33. John Adams to James Warren, June 16, 1776, in ibid., 4:228–29.

34. John Hancock to "Certain Colonies," June 4, 1776, in ibid., 4:136–37.

35. Pauline Maier, *American Scripture: Making the Declaration of Independence* (New York, 1997), 99.

36. "Report of the Committee on the Cedars Cartel," June 17, 1776, in *PTJ,* 1:400–404.

37. Henry Stuart to John Stuart, Toquah, Overhill Cherokee Nation, May 7, 1776, in K. G. Davies, ed., *Documents of the American Revolution* (Dublin, 1972), 12:130–33; Henry Stuart to southern frontier inhabitants, May 18, 1776, in Peter Force, ed., *American Archives,* 4th ser. (Washington, D.C., 1839), 6:497.

38. Elbridge Gerry gave particulars of this letter, including his hopes that Henry Stuart's "vile designs would be frustrated," in his June 18, 1776, letter to Joseph Trumbull, Philadelphia, in Smith et al., eds., *Letters of Delegates to Congress,* 4:263–64.

39. *Virginia Gazette* (Purdie), June 7, 1776; *Maryland Journal and Baltimore Advertiser,* June 17, 1776; *Dunlap's Maryland Gazette* (Baltimore), June 19, 1776; *Maryland Gazette,* June 20, 1776; *New York Journal,* June 27, 1776; *New York Packet,* June 27, 1776; *Pennsylvania Ledger,* June 29, 1776; *Pennsylvania Packet,* July 1, 1776; *New York Gazette and Weekly Mercury,* July 1, 1776; *Norwich Packet,* July 8, 1776; *Connecticut Courant,* July 8, 1776; *Massachusetts Spy,* July 10, 1776; *Newport Mercury,* July 11, 1776.

40. "Major Sherburne's Testimony on the Affair at the Cedars," June 17, 1776, in *PTJ,* 1:399.

41. Jefferson, "'First Draft' of Declaration of Independence," before June 13, 1776, *PTJ,* 1:338–39.

42. Ibid., 1:338.

43. For more of these developments, see Robert G. Parkinson, *The Common Cause: Creating Race and Nation in the American Revolution* (Chapel Hill, N.C., 2016), 102–13, 141–48.

44. *Virginia Gazette* (Pinkney), Nov. 23, 1775.

45. *Pennsylvania Evening Post,* Dec. 14, 1775; *Norwich Packet,* Dec. 25, 1775; *Virginia Gazette* (Purdie), Dec. 29, 1775.

46. *New York Constitutional Gazette,* June 22, 1776; *Providence Gazette,* June 29, 1776; *South Carolina and American General Gazette* (Charleston), Aug. 2, 1776

47. Narrative of Captain Andrew Snape Hamond, HMS *Roebuck,* June 10, 1776, in William B. Clark, ed., *Naval Documents of the American Revolution* (Washington, D.C., 1964), 5:840.

48. Jack P. Greene, ed., *The Diary of Landon Carter of Sabine Hall, 1752–1778* (Richmond, Va., 1987), 2:1051–52.

49. *Virginia Gazette* (Dixon & Hunter), June 15, 1776. For more on the accusations that Dunmore purposely spread smallpox, see Fenn, *Pox Americana,* 58–61.

50. *New York Journal,* June 27, 1776; *New York Packet,* June 29, 1776; *Pennsylvania Ledger,* June 29, 1776; *New York Gazette and Weekly Mercury,* July 1, 1776; *Massachusetts Spy,* July 5, 1776; *Connecticut Courant,* July 8, 1776; *Boston Gazette,* July 8, 1776; *Freeman's Journal,* July 13, 1776; *American Gazette,* July 16, 1776. Three papers (*New York Journal, New York Gazette and Weekly Mercury,* and *Connecticut Courant*) published this alongside the Henry Stuart letter.

51. Elbridge Gerry to Joseph Trumbull, June 8, 1776; John Adams to William Cushing, June 9, 1776, in Smith et al., eds., *Letters of Delegates to Congress,* 4:170, 178.

52. Even the famously thorough Julian Parks Boyd could not deduce exactly when Jefferson drew this map. See his explanation in *PTJ,* 1:566. For more on the connections between Dunmore and the Declaration, see Sidney Kaplan, "The 'Domestic Insurrections' of the Declaration of Independence," *Journal of Negro History* 61 (1976): 243–55.

53. Thomas Jefferson to John Page, Aug. 5, 1776, in *PTJ,* 1:485–86.

2 The Mississippi Question in Jeffersonian Political Economy

Martin Öhman

In the spring of 1803, the French government unexpectedly sold the Louisiana Province to the United States. For about three cents an acre, U.S. diplomats James Monroe and Robert Livingston obtained just over 520 million acres of land, roughly doubling the republic's domain. Federal officials were taken by surprise when the news arrived in early summer. American diplomatic objectives had initially been confined to protecting trade on the Mississippi River system and, if possible, liberalizing trade relations between the two countries. The Jefferson administration never authorized the purchase of territory west of the Mississippi River. There is in fact nothing in the historical records to suggest that Jeffersonian policymakers ever considered such a transaction. "An acquisition of so great an extent was, we well Know, not contemplated by our appointment," Monroe and Livingston admitted as they reported of the affair. When the sale was first proposed to them, they "proceeded to treat for the whole," believing that it might be possible to "conclude eventually a treaty for a part." French officials, however, never showed any inclination to sell specific portions of the province, and instead of jeopardizing the negotiations, Monroe and Livingston agreed to purchase the entire province. The decision was not dictated by necessity alone. Possession of the "left bank of the river" would have secured most of U.S. objectives but not all, they stressed. Shared control over the Mississippi River—especially if new French colonies came under military command—would sooner or later have created tensions. But thanks to the treaty, there were now excellent prospects for rebuilding trust between the former allies. "We adjust by it the only remaining Known cause of variance with this very powerful nation," Monroe and Livingston explained to Secretary of State James Madison.[1]

In retrospect, the Louisiana Purchase stands out as the Jefferson administration's greatest foreign policy triumph. But in the summer of 1803, the affair appeared to involve substantial challenges. The province's economic and geopolitical benefits were not by any means self-evident. Federal officials, let alone Americans in general, knew very little about Louisiana, and besides, there was little to suggest that the United States was in need of additional territory. Politically, the affair was a risky move. Jeffersonian officials recognized that the Constitution did not contain any explicit support for incorporating foreign territory, and they feared that Federalists might use the opportunity to stir up opposition. In a letter to Monroe and Livingston, Madison raised concerns that "the *acquisition* may *produce criticism and censure.*" Yet despite some initial doubts, the administration and its allies in Congress decided to support the treaty and resolutely pushed for its ratification. Madison hoped that benefits derived from the treaty would soon "amply justify the arrangement."[2]

Possession of the western bank of the Mississippi and of New Orleans secured the main commercial transportation routes for the Mississippi and Ohio River Valleys. Leaders in the southern Atlantic states, moreover, certainly recognized that protecting western commercial interests was essential to countering secessionist tendencies in the republic's far-flung borderlands.[3] But what advantages, if any, did the treaty present to tobacco planters and grain farmers primarily interested in expanding market opportunities in Europe and the West Indies? Why did Chesapeake leaders consistently advocate policies that portended heightened competition from western staple producers? Instead of examining how economic and geopolitical realities shaped outlooks and policy positions, historians have conventionally sought to arrange Jeffersonian statecraft within intangible arguments about territorial expansion. Drew R. McCoy and others see the Louisiana Purchase as the realization of an agrarian political economy. By spreading across the continent, the argument goes, Americans would postpone the social decay already visible in parts of the Old World. Scholars less convinced by the explanatory power of yeoman ideals see the pursuit of western lands as driven by the wasteful practices that characterized southern agriculture. Others take a more expansive view, arguing that a commitment to expansion became a core component of an emerging American identity.[4]

The existing literature fails to explain how the economic and geopolitical course of the Ohio and Mississippi River Valleys—what Arthur Preston

Whitaker once labeled "the Mississippi Question"—factored into the concerns of Atlantic-focused southern planters.[5] A credible account of early American expansionism needs to explain in concrete terms how the interests of Tidewater and Piedmont planters converged with those of western elites in the decades after the American Revolution. Dictated by time-specific conditions, this convergence made possible the Jeffersonian coalition. This essay considers the evolution of Jeffersonian political economy, which came to predicate the realignment of U.S. foreign trade and the revival of struggling staple economies on an assertive policy in the West.

American revolutionaries demanded a separate and equal station in the international community of states, confident that independence would secure them a more advantageous position in the Atlantic system of trade. Liberated from the British yoke, farmers, merchants, and artisans would be in a better position to capitalize on the bountiful resources of land, produce, and raw materials. But separation from the mother country proved difficult. Large areas suffered greatly during the war. Problems were particularly acute in the southern states, where trade disruptions and wartime taxes strained an already cash-strapped and debt-ridden economy. Extensive devastation and the escape of tens of thousands of slaves exposed the region's vulnerabilities. Independence did little to improve the situation, and staple economies soon plunged into a sustained depression. Carolina rice barons never fully recovered their prerevolutionary markets, indigo producers faced increased competition from the French colonies, and new British duties and the creation of a single French purchasing agency kept down tobacco prices. The European colonies in the West Indies only admitted grain, lumber, and other U.S. articles in times of scarcity.[6]

Increasingly concerned with their region's vulnerabilities, Chesapeake leaders labored to craft a political economy that would enhance the position of struggling staple producers in the Atlantic system of exchange. Genuine independence, they argued, could only be achieved by a commercial realignment that undercut British dominance over the former colonies. In the decades to come, politicians like Jefferson and Madison consistently argued for the use of retaliatory measures against countries refusing reciprocity in trade. They recognized that the best markets for tobacco, rice, wheat, and other staple crops were located outside the British Empire—in Continental Europe, around the Mediterranean, and in the French and Spanish West Indies. Although Jefferson and Madison did not want to replace a dependence on Britain with subordination to France, they nevertheless concluded that a realignment of U.S. trade and the opening of a more profitable direct trade depended on working out new arrangements with Paris. France was an attractive commercial partner thanks to its substantive domestic market, its rich colonies, its skilled workforce, and its awesome economic potential. A better understanding between the two countries also made sense from a geopolitical perspective. Equally interested in undermining British commercial hegemony, the French court—traditionally exercising a degree of influence over the Barbary powers and Spain—might help further U.S. commercial objectives in the Mediterranean.[7]

As minister plenipotentiary to France, Jefferson did more than theorize about commercial realignment. After arriving in the late summer of 1784, he met repeatedly with Louis XVI's foreign minister, Charles Gravier, comte de Vergennes, to discuss ways to promote trade between the two countries. He devoted particular energy to tobacco, the Chesapeake's prime export. Working closely with a select committee, headed by the Marquis de Lafayette, Jefferson sought to terminate the import monopoly held by the Farmers-General, a private company that farmed certain taxes for the royal treasury. In this matter, the monarchy's severe financial difficulties impeded a more liberal arrangement. Since the Farmers-General generated revenue of close to 30 million livres, French officials were reluctant to make any radical changes.[8] Jefferson also made strenuous efforts on behalf of South Carolina rice producers, examining the kinds and quantities sold in French markets and informing his correspondents back home of French tastes. He requested samples for distribution to potential buyers and sought to convince leading South Carolinians of the benefits of shipping cargoes directly to French markets, instead of through British ports.[9] When Americans arrived to explore business opportunities, Jefferson provided them with commercial information and letters of introduction to French mercantile houses.[10]

Through no lack of effort, Jefferson largely fell short in his exertions to promote Franco-American relations and lay the foundation for commercial realignment. Growing French frustration with Congress's inability to honor the war debt, combined with concerns that U.S. commerce was drifting back into the British orbit, greatly complicated his efforts. By early 1786, the Virginian was forced to admit that only minor progress had been achieved.[11] Meanwhile, as Jefferson was struggling in Paris, widening conflicts back home over public lands, commerce, boundaries, and debts seemed to portend the collapse of the union. Instead of working toward a common policy with respect to foreign trade, individual states began pushing their own measures in response to foreign restrictions. As the systemic weaknesses under the Articles of Confederation became increasingly evident, momentum started to build for establishing a more "energetic" central government, strong enough to deal with foreign powers and counter centrifugal forces within the union.[12]

Diplomatic developments exacerbated existing tensions. In August 1786, Secretary for Foreign Affairs John Jay brought before Congress an outline for a commercial treaty with Spain. In exchange for access to ports in Spain proper and in the Canary Islands, the United States would recognize Spain's exclusive navigation rights on the Mississippi River over a period of twenty-five to thirty years. The treaty's proponents believed it would expand important export markets for New England fisheries, secure an inflow of specie (Spain agreed to pay for specified U.S. articles in hard currency), and provide a much-needed stimulus to the languishing shipping industry. Grain farmers would benefit from trading with the Iberian Peninsula and perhaps, by way of the Canary Islands, with South America. Moreover, a deal with Madrid might safeguard American vessels from Barbary depredations and open up trade in the Mediterranean basin. The potential benefits to U.S. trade were considerable, especially when weighed against the limited surplus production in the Ohio and Mississippi Valleys in the mid-1780s.[13]

Led by Virginia delegate James Monroe and South Carolina's Charles Pinckney, southerners in Congress immediately denounced the "partial" benefits of the "proposed agreement," loudly complaining that it would benefit one region at the expense of the rest of the union. Indeed, the arrangement conveyed few if any direct benefits to the Chesapeake and Lower South states. Import duties from the expected growth of trade with the Iberian Peninsula would primarily benefit the larger seaports in New England and mid-Atlantic. Markets in the West Indies would remain closed, and tobacco would still be prohibited in metropolitan Spain. While the treaty would not alter existing commercial relations—the lower Mississippi River had been closed to U.S. traders since 1784—it was reasonable to expect that a formal relinquishment of navigation rights would slow down western migration and the appreciation of land titles.[14]

Virginia delegate William Grayson warned that both "the western Inhabitants" and the people of "the S States" would be greatly disaffected, seeing their "dearest interests sacrificed & given up."[15] In light of later sectional conflicts, it is tempting to see opposition to the treaty as evidence of southern expansionist aims. But in the years after the Revolution, it was by no means self-evident that opening the Mississippi River trade would actually benefit southern states. To be sure, Tidewater and Piedmont elites had long taken a keen interest in improving waterways between the backcountry and the Atlantic coast. For the Chesapeake region, there were obvious benefits in facilitating the exchange of goods over the Potomac, the Rappahannock, the James, and adjacent rivers connecting eastern and western districts. The same was not necessarily true with respect to the commerce on the Mississippi River. Quite the contrary, in fact—an opening of this route involved substantial risks. Madison, for one, clearly recognized that increased competition with farmers in the Mississippi and Ohio River Valleys in all likelihood would depress the price of tobacco, Chesapeake's prime staple, along with other important export articles, including indigo, corn, and rice. European demand would not keep pace with the growth of U.S. exports, he warned in a letter to Jefferson. In fact, only "an impolitic and perverse attempt in Spain to shut the mouth of the Mississippi against the inhabitants above" would counter the price reduction of export articles.[16] In a draft version of this letter, Madison elaborated on the effects of western growth:

> The only sufferers by the encouragement of the Western settlements will be those [who] remain in the Atlantic states. They may it's true be relieved from taxes in proportion to the price added to the vacant land by the freedom of the Missi. but this danger will be greatly outweighed by the danger to the Confederacy from multiplying the parts of the machine, by the depopulation of the country, by the depreciation of their lands, and by the delay of that marine strength which must be their only safety in case of war. N.Y. Pa. and Va. will also lose the advantage of being Merchants for the Western States in proportion their trade has a ready passage thro' the Missi.

Virginia would "suffer a loss of her staple [tobacco]." From this perspective, then, the Jay-Gardoqui proposal seemed to accord with Chesapeake interests. The one advantage Madison could perceive in western growth was that the Atlantic South at the same time would be "disburdened of the slaves who will follow the culture of that plant."[17] In the decades to come, the revolution in Saint-Domingue and incidents like Gabriel's Rebellion would strengthen southern anxieties and perceptions that territorial expansion provided a safety valve for potentially dangerous slaves.[18] But in the 1780s, there was little to suggest that U.S. navigation rights on the Mississippi River would stabilize Chesapeake society and revive its stagnating economy. New Englanders were not alone in fearing that rapid westward migration would weaken the older states and impede economic development along the Atlantic seaboard. In the southern Atlantic states too, concerns about a loss of political power, sluggish economic growth, and depopulation informed debates over western development.

To understand Chesapeake leaders' opposition to the Jay-Gardoqui agreement, it is necessary to examine how it corresponded with efforts to realign U.S. foreign commerce. First, the proposed treaty threatened to alienate backcountry communities, and the volatility of western allegiances was well understood.[19] Second, the navigation issue was particularly sensitive in the spring and summer of 1786, since western disquiet threatened to derail the push for a stronger central government better equipped to deal with foreign powers.[20] In the development of the trans-Appalachian West, Chesapeake leaders saw opportunities to alter U.S. relations with the rest of the world. Leaders like Jefferson and Madison understood from experience that diplomacy alone would not bring about desired changes in foreign commerce. Treaties, however advantageous, would only go so far toward altering long-established trade routes. Commerce was ultimately based on a host of other factors: mutual trust and shared practices, complementary demands and tastes, and personal networks. Anglo-American commercial connections, however unprofitable in the Jeffersonian view, were a product of the empire. Having matured over a long period of time, these connections were immensely difficult to deconstruct. The commerce of the Mississippi and Ohio Valleys, on the other hand, was still in an embryonic stage, offering opportunities to build new connections for beneficial and expanding exchange. Madison envisioned that transatlantic migrations would strengthen bonds between the United States and France. "The habits & prepossessions of the emigrants & their descendants will naturally prefer the articles brought from their former Country," he noted. French settlers, moving into the unoccupied lands in the western country, would, as their numbers increased, promote Franco-American trade and help rebalance the republic's foreign trade. At this time, the mercantile establishment in New Orleans was predominantly French, and Madison was convinced that these houses were eager to trade with Americans upstream. Therefore, he wrote, "the more populous parts of the U. S. have a national interest in not discouraging emigrations to the less inhabited parts."[21]

Jeffersonian leaders clearly believed that French and American interests converged on the matter of western development. In 1784, Madison sought to enlist French support in negotiations with Spain. A rupture between the United States and Spain would only benefit British interests, he reasoned. If for no other reason, imperial rivalries gave France "a great interest in a trade with the western country thro the Mississippi."[22] In a letter to the Marquis de Lafayette—Madison no doubt intended that the message be shown to French officials—he elaborated on how the Mississippi trade might draw the two nations together. If "the Island of N. Orleans" were under French instead of Spanish control, Madison conjectured, a great "metamorphosis" would take place. Opening the Mississippi would speed up settlement, increase production of "tobacco indigo & other articles for exportation," and, as a result, reduce the price of these articles for European consumers. The outlet of the river "would become the Grand Cairo of the New World." With appreciating western lands and a more profitable foreign trade, the United States would become financially solvent and be able to pay its debtors.[23]

The Jeffersonian opposition that coalesced in the 1790s was a heterogeneous coalition of discontented groups. Throughout the 1790s, a series of incidents contributed to widening the rift between westerners and the federal administration. In Middle Tennessee, wealthy land speculators turned against the Washington and Adams administrations in large part because of the lack of federal protection against Indian raids. Owing to extensive violence, particularly between 1792 and 1795, land values stagnated and the rate of migration declined. From a purely financial perspective, the federal government had little to defend in the Southwest Territory. Federal neglect frustrated western settlers.[24] Peace with the Indians, secure land titles, and open navigation, Kentucky politician and surveyor Hubbard Taylor reminded Madison, would make Kentucky "the happiest & richest Country in the world."[25] In late 1793, the Democratic Society of Kentucky complained of congressional inaction and of being treated "with a neglect bordering on contempt." Its address reminded Congress of the previous attempt "to barter away" the right of navigation, thanking "a part of the Union"—that is, the South—for its opposition on that occasion.[26]

Discontent was also brewing in the Chesapeake throughout the 1790s, where many had supported constitutional reform in the hope that the new federal government would actually use its expanded powers to challenge British commercial policy. Uneven regional growth intensified political conflict. The wars of the French Revolution indeed promoted U.S. trade in colonial goods and grain, but tobacco markets remained depressed. Between 1790 and 1796, Virginia's exports were cut by more than half.[27] Sensing an opportunity to capitalize on a growing dissatisfaction with administration policies, Jefferson renewed the push for an overhaul of the nation's trade policies in late 1793.[28] Madison followed up by moving that the House of Representatives consider discriminatory duties against countries lacking a commercial treaty with the United States. By placing British goods and ships at a disadvantage, the Virginians hoped to expand direct trade in non-British markets.[29]

A diplomatic crisis erupted before Congress had time to act. On November 6, 1793, the British Privy Council issued orders that all neutral ships carrying goods to France or its colonies were liable to seizure. Sizeable captures in the West Indies and European waters followed. In an attempt to allay tensions, the president appointed Chief Justice John Jay to a diplomatic mission to London. During Jay's negotiations at the Court of St. James, European power relations underwent great changes. A series of French military triumphs combined with signs of British economic distress bolstered expectations that Jay would return home with a favorable deal. Chesapeake leaders were greatly disappointed when the details of the treaty became known. Instead of taking advantage of propitious geopolitical circumstances, the Jay Treaty granted Great Britain most-favored-nation status. The treaty also prohibited the use of discriminatory duties, eliminating the policy option that Jefferson and Madison believed would be most effective in enhancing staple producers' economic prospects.[30]

Diplomatic historians have generally tried to assess the merits of the treaty in relation to a set of constructed "national" interests, rather than exploring its differential regional impact. Scholars focused on domestic politics generally downplay the significance of the actual substance of the treaty, arguing instead that the struggle over ratification reflected ideological tensions about the republic's social order. But as Lawrence B. A. Hatter persuasively argues, the opposition was firmly grounded in concerns about the effects of specific provisions. The treaty provided for a transfer of the western posts yet granted the British subjects residing there the option to remain on U.S. soil. They had one year to decide whether to remain British subjects or, by default, become Americans. Article 3, moreover, stipulated that "it shall at all Times be free" for all British subjects, American citizens, and Indians, regardless of their place of residence, to "pass and repass" the boundary between the United States and British North America and to "freely carry on trade and commerce" in perpetuity. Not only would the Mississippi River be "entirely open" to British subjects; they would also be allowed to use "all the ports and places on its Eastern side." While reciprocal in theory, the provision ensured that British houses, with their longstanding ties of trade and kinship with Indian nations, would continue to exercise a great deal of influence in the western states and territories.[31]

News of the treaty immediately sparked anxiety and outrage among western settlers. In November 1795, Kentucky lawyer and politician George Nicholas reported that "western and local politicks" had "all been swallowed up by Jay's treaty." He urged Madison to oppose it in the House of Representatives and obstruct its implementation. The treaty, especially when considered in light of the recent peace settlement between France and Spain, had "destroyed all just expectation of our obtaining the navigation of the M——I by negociation." Discontent was brewing all over the trans-Appalachian West, Nicholas noted.[32] Not only did the treaty seem to impede negotiations with Spain; it also opened a backdoor to British commercial enterprise and intrigue. An anti-treaty meeting in Clarke County, Kentucky, warned that, in case the Senate moved to ratify, "western America is gone forever—lost to the union, and grasped by the voracious clutches of the insatiable and iniquitous George the third of Britain."[33] William Findley, a U.S. representative from western Pennsylvania, complained that the treaty "increases that connexion with Great Britain which was already too great."[34] Indirectly, however, news of the treaty helped the objectives of western settlers. Weakened by the European war and fearing a British-American alliance, Spanish officials opted for concessions. In October 1795, U.S. minister to Madrid Thomas Pinckney finalized the Treaty of San Lorenzo. That agreement settled boundary disputes in the Southwest, opened the Mississippi River to U.S. navigation, and granted U.S. traders the right to "deposit their merchandise and effects in the Port of New Orleans" or some equivalent place.[35] When Jay's allies in Congress sought to make the ratification of the Jay Treaty a precondition for ratifying the Treaty of San Lorenzo, western districts quickly began petitioning Congress urging the implementation of both.[36]

Although several town meetings and leaders in the West pushed for ratification of the Jay Treaty in the late winter and spring of 1796, the agreement remained widely unpopular and reaffirmed the alliance between Chesapeake planters and settlers in the trans-Appalachian West. While the Mississippi trade expanded as a result of the Treaty of San Lorenzo, the U.S. economy as a whole plunged into a serious depression in the late 1790s. Noting the stagnation of trade, massive business failures, and the severe depreciation of the land market, western critics sarcastically pointed to "the blessed effects of the Jay Treaty."[37] A correspondent for the *Kentucky Gazette* identified the "British Treaty" as "the cause of our present ruinous state of our commerce; it is the cause of the present bankruptcies and misfortunes of our merchants; it is the cause of the fall in the prices of wheat and flour." It was, moreover, the cause of "the serious misunderstanding between this country and the French Republic."[38]

Reports of growing French hostility were particularly disconcerting to Chesapeake leaders, who saw reconciliation with leaders in Paris as vital to realigning America's foreign commerce. When Franco-American relations deteriorated into quasi-war, producer groups dependent on continental markets, notably Chesapeake tobacco planters, suffered great losses.[39] French hostility also created significant concern among western communities. By 1796, rumors were already circulating of the French Directory's interest in obtaining the Louisiana Province. With Spain increasingly looking like a French client state, secure access to the Mississippi River over the long haul seemed to require a good understanding with Paris.[40]

The Treaty of San Lorenzo did not provide a final resolution of the Mississippi question. On October 16, 1802, the Spanish intendant at New Orleans, Juan Morales, revoked the right of deposit. Outraged westerners demanded that the federal government take action.[41] Morales's proclamation was particularly disquieting in light of unconfirmed rumors that Spain had ceded Louisiana to France. Reports to that effect had been circulating since mid-1801. Officials in Washington recognized that the presence of a new powerful neighbor threatened to destabilize the union. But the administration and its allies in Congress had no interest in going to war over the intendant's proclamation. Nor did they support a military strike for the purpose of preventing French troops from taking command of Louisiana. The administration's preference for negotiations was not grounded primarily in an ideological aversion to war but in economic considerations. The Quasi-War and the depression it deepened and prolonged had badly damaged the tobacco economy. Chesapeake leaders understood that renewed conflict with France or its ally Spain would be counterproductive to their long-term commercial objectives.

Jefferson acted with speed to diffuse western belligerence. Contacts with Carlos Fernandez Martínez de Yrujo, the Spanish minister at Washington, and statements from the governor of New Orleans convinced administration officials that Morales had acted without authorization from Madrid. Jefferson and Madison then turned to trusted western leaders to spread that information.[42] On January 11, 1803, Jefferson announced the appointment of James Monroe as minister plenipotentiary to the courts of France and Spain. The appointment of Monroe was a judicious move. Westerners had not forgotten his opposition to the Jay-Gardoqui agreement. An opinion piece addressed "To the People of Kentucky" declared that Monroe was "eminent for his abilities, his services, and his attachment to the object of his mission."[43] The administration also wanted guarantees that U.S. navigation and deposit rights, as stipulated by the Treaty of San Lorenzo, would be honored in case Louisiana came under French control. The prospect of French possession of territory on the North American mainland worried federal officials, but such a development also offered opportunities. In light of the increasing likelihood of renewed war with Great Britain and the problems in Saint-Domingue, the administration believed that France might be willing to support U.S. policy objectives with regards to New Orleans and the Floridas. Monroe's mission, Jefferson explained, was undertaken "for the purpose of enlarging, and more effectually securing, our rights and interests in the river Mississippi, and *the territories eastward thereof*."[44] Kentucky senator John Breckinridge assured his constituents a few weeks later that the administration was not only determined to resolve the present crisis but also to find "new arrangements," designed to prevent future obstructions of the Mississippi trade.[45]

The French government's offer to sell the Louisiana Province surprised leaders in Washington.[46] Although little was known about the acquired territory, Jeffersonian publicists and politicians quickly came out in support of the treaty, enumerating the benefits it would bring.[47] With rapid settlement of the West, trade would increase and, as a result, so would federal revenue from land sales and import duties. In the end, the purchase would pay for itself—it was, wrote one westerner, "rather to be considered as a donation than sale."[48] New Orleans would become the nexus of an expanding trading network encompassing the Ohio and Mississippi Rivers and all their tributaries, the ports around the Mexican Gulf, the West Indies, and perhaps even South America. Although few maps or surveys existed, Jeffersonian publicists confidently asserted that Louisiana abounded in iron, lead, copper, salt, live oak, and cedars. Its rich soil would yield ample volumes of flax, hemp, sugar, and cotton for export markets.[49] Men of capital would be attracted to New Orleans and commercial hubs upriver. As commerce on the western river system expanded, the specie-draining land trade to Philadelphia and Baltimore, by way of Pittsburgh, would decline. In addition, the purchase would remove the threat of foreign-instigated "Indian aggression and negro insurrections."[50] Some projections went even further, claiming that possession of Louisiana would spur "a more direct and rapid trade" with China and the East Indies.[51]

Before Monroe and Robert Livingston concluded the agreement, no leading public official or publicist was arguing for territorial expansion across the Mississippi River. A political economy in support of the acquisition had to be constructed after the details of the treaty became known. Jeffersonians quickly hailed the Louisiana Purchase as a triumph of enlightened diplomacy and a vindication of republican principles. Without firing a single shot, the United States had managed to double its domain and enhance its geostrategic position. Kentucky governor James Garrard believed that the treaty offered "fair prospects of security, peace, increased freedom from collision with foreign powers."[52] Lexington lawyer Allan Bowie Magruder agreed that the acquisition of Louisiana—by preventing French colonization in the American neighborhood—would ensure peace and prosperity for the Mississippi and Ohio Valleys. "Every war with France," he argued, "would have shut up the Mississippi and given a sudden check to the prosperity of all the fluvial states West of the Allegheny."[53]

Federal officials recognized that France was a far more formidable power than Spain and that French command of Louisiana threatened to destabilize the American union. At the same time, anxieties about French ambitions should not be exaggerated. Jeffersonian policymakers did not see the establishment of French colonies in North American as a military threat.[54]

While writers like Magruder argued that the Louisiana Purchase effectively removed the French presence from the area, leading Jeffersonian policymakers still hoped that western development would bring the two countries closer together and pave the way for a realignment of U.S. foreign trade. Many took for granted that France would have an important role to play in the emerging western trading system. In April 1803, before Monroe and Livingston announced the purchase, Kentucky representative John Fowler dismissed anxieties about French colonization. There were no reasons to consider the French "dangerous neighbours," he asserted, adding, "and as a friendly, sociable, and intelligent people, I see rather great advantages to our side of the river."[55] Others argued that French ownership of Louisiana in all likelihood would stimulate western economic growth. Rather than attempting to close the Mississippi River to American merchants, the enterprising French would encourage trade with the Mississippi and Ohio River Valleys. Stable and prosperous French settlements were premised on an open exchange with U.S. farmers and manufacturers. French capital and mercantile skill would be drawn to New Orleans. In addition, the western states would become the prime suppliers of grain, flour, hemp, staves, timber, horses, and cattle to Saint-Domingue, Guadeloupe, Martinico, and other French possessions. "Thus mutual interest, or the reciprocity of means and wants, would be the bond of amity," wrote a leading Jeffersonian editor.[56]

Such conjectures were not the product of wild speculation. Regardless of what regulations might be put in place, there was no reason to doubt that geography and historical connections in important ways would continue to shape the commerce of the Mississippi River system. French merchants had long been in a strong position at New Orleans, and before the outbreak of war in 1792 French ships had dominated the carrying trade.[57] In the years to come, French networks would retain their position. From 1804, there was a marked increase in the downriver trade of grain, flour, and other articles. Over the next decade, about 45 percent of export would go to the West Indies, primarily to the French and Spanish islands. Another 30 percent cleared for the Iberian Peninsula.[58]

In early 1803, in the midst of rumors surrounding French intentions in Louisiana, Jeffersonian representatives again proposed measures designed to expand trade outside the British orbit. A report issued by the House Committee of Commerce and Manufactures concluded that Great Britain had imposed duties in violation of the Jay Treaty to ensure British dominance over the carrying trade. France and other nations had also imposed restrictions. The committee identified two possible responses. The first was to impose countervailing duties, which might lead to "commercial warfare." The second approach, which the committee supported, would be to give up the system of discriminatory duties against foreign shipping and instead "favor such foreign nation as will agree to abolish such of their discriminating and countervailing duties, as are, in their operation, injurious to the interest of the United States."[59] Resisted by mercantile groups, the effort failed. But the administration believed that international developments had opened an opportunity for diplomatic advances and it was intent on pursuing the matter further. Madison instructed Monroe and Livingston not only to inquire with French officials about New Orleans and the Floridas but also to raise the issue of setting up a new framework for Franco-American trade, one that would be based on "just principles."[60]

In the summer and fall of 1803, there was every reason to believe that the Louisiana Treaty would be the first step in a realignment of U.S. commerce. The treaty encompassed substantial advantages to French trade and navigation. As he laid the Louisiana Treaty before Congress, Jefferson praised the "enlightened French Government" for initiating this "liberal arrangement," which, the president believed, would operate "permanently to promote the peace, interests, and friendship of both."[61] Indeed, its provisions were explicitly designed "to encourage the communication" between the contracting powers, granting French and Spanish vessels, when arriving from their respective mother countries or colonies and carrying French or Spanish productions, the same duties on merchandise and tonnage as U.S. vessels at New Orleans and other ports of entry. This arrangement would be in place for a period of twelve years in preparation for a more lasting agreement. During this period no other nation would have "a right to the Same privileges in the Ports of the ceded territory." After the twelve years, French ships would be treated "upon the footing of the most favoured nations" in the ports of entry.[62]

Once and for all, the Mississippi question appeared resolved. For Chesapeake leaders, the affair transformed a potential source of conflict with their most important trading partner to a promising new arrangement of U.S. trade. Jefferson, for one, saw the treaty as a new beginning, bringing the two countries closer together "in harmony and friendly intercourse."[63] The Louisiana Purchase also cemented Jefferson's popularity in the trans-Appalachian

West and facilitated the merger of conflicting southern and western interests into a seemingly coherent outlook on political economy. This was never a natural coalition, nor was it one that emerged because of some common commitment to Jeffersonian principles (however we choose to define them). The coalition took form on the fly as Old South planters and western communities struggled to address specific challenges and conditions brought on by the protracted instability of the Atlantic World.

Notes

1. Livingston and Monroe to Madison, May 13, 1803, in *American State Papers: Foreign Relations* (Washington, D.C., 1833–59), 2:558, 559.

2. Madison to Monroe, June 25, 1803, in Mary A. Hackett et al., eds., *Papers of James Madison, Secretary of State Series* (Charlottesville, Va., 1986–2017), 5:118 (hereafter *PJM-SS*).

3. Peter S. Onuf, *Jefferson's Empire: The Language of American Nationhood* (Charlottesville, Va., 2000); James E. Lewis Jr., "A Tornado on the Horizon: The Jefferson Administration, the Retrocession Crisis, and the Louisiana Purchase," in *Empires of the Imagination: Transatlantic Histories of the Louisiana Purchase,* ed. Peter J. Kastor and François Weil (Charlottesville, Va., 2009), 117–42.

4. On agrarianism, see Drew R. McCoy, *The Elusive Republic: Political Economy in Jeffersonian America* (Chapel Hill, N.C., 1980), and Lance Banning, *The Sacred Fire of Liberty: James Madison and the Founding of the Federal Republic* (Ithaca, N.Y., 1995). On expansion as a core element of Jeffersonian theory and policy, see John M. Murrin, "The Jeffersonian Triumph and American Exceptionalism," *Journal of the Early Republic* 20 (Spring 2000): 1–25. On wasteful agriculture, see Allan Kulikoff, *Tobacco and Slaves: The Development of Southern Cultures in the Chesapeake, 1680–1800* (Chapel Hill, N.C., 1986). On expansionism as an American ideology, see Alexander DeConde, *This Affair of Louisiana* (New York, 1976). On identity, see Eric Hinderaker, *Elusive Empires: Constructing Colonialism in the Ohio Valley, 1673–1800* (New York, 1997). On the contradictions between Jeffersonian ideals and actions, see Robert W. Tucker and David C. Hendrickson, *Empire of Liberty: The Statecraft of Thomas Jefferson* (New York, 1990).

5. Arthur Preston Whitaker, *The Mississippi Question, 1795–1803: A Study in Trade, Politics, and Diplomacy* (1934; Gloucester, Mass., 1962).

6. On problems in the Chesapeake, see Kulikoff, *Tobacco and Slaves.* On indigo, see Adam Rothman, *Slave Country: American Expansion and the Origins of the Slave South* (Cambridge, Mass., 2005), 18, 46–47. For an overview of the U.S. economy from 1775 to 1790, see John J. McCusker and Russell R. Menard, *The Economy of British America, 1607–1789* (Chapel Hill, N.C., 1985), 373–77.

7. Martin Öhman, "Ambiguous Bonds of Union: American Political Economy and the Geopolitical Origins of Interregional Cooperation and Conflict, 1783–1821" (PhD Diss., University of Virginia, 2011), 58–76.

8. Jefferson to Jay, with enclosure, May 27, 1786, in Julian P. Boyd et al., eds., *Papers of Thomas Jefferson* (Princeton, N.J., 1951–), 9:582–90 (hereafter *PTJ*).

9. Rutledge to Jefferson, Oct. 14, 1786; Jefferson to Izard, Nov. 18, 1786; Jefferson to Ramsay, Oct. 27, 1786, in *PTJ,* 10:463–65, 540–42, 490–92.

10. Jefferson to Famin, Nov. 11, 1786, in *PTJ,* 10:517.

11. Jefferson to Jay, with Report on Conversations with Vergennes, Jan. 2, 1786, in *PTJ,* 9:136–39. On French frustrations, see also Allan Potofsky, "The Political Economy of the French-American Debt Debate: The Ideological Uses of Atlantic Commerce, 1787 to 1800," *William and Mary Quarterly,* 3rd ser., 63 (July 2006): 489–516.

12. On conflicts during the 1780s, see Cathy D. Matson and Peter S. Onuf, *A Union of Interest: Political and Economic Thought in Revolutionary America* (Lawrence, Kans., 1990). On the move for constitutional reform, see also Max M. Edling, *A Revolution in Favor of Government: Origins of the U.S. Constitution and the Making of the American State* (New York, 2003).

13. King to Gerry, New York, Aug. 13, 1786, in Paul H. Smith et al., eds., *Letters of Delegates to Congress, 1774–1789* (Washington, D.C., 1976–2000), 23:469–70 (hereafter *LDC*). King used the same arguments in a speech; see Charles Thomson, "Notes of Debates," Aug. 16, 1786; Arthur St. Clair, "Notes on John Jay's Report," Aug. 16–18, 1786; Arthur St. Clair, speech, Aug. 18, 1786, in *LDC,* 23:486, 482, 492. For the speech by Sedgwick, see Charles Thomson, "Notes of Debates," Aug. 18, 1786, in *LDC,* 23:396. See also Arthur St. Clair, notes, Aug. 22[?], 1786; Livermore to Sullivan, New York, Aug. 26, 1786, in *LDC,* 23:515, 531.

14. Charles Pinckney, speech, Aug. 10, 1786, in *LDC,* 23:449–52, 452 (quotation). See also James Monroe to Patrick Henry, New York, Aug. 12, 1786, in *LDC,* 23:465. On the sectional split over the Jay-Gardoqui agreement, see H. James Henderson, *Party Politics in the Continental Congress* (New York, 1974), and Joseph L. Davis, *Sectionalism in American Politics, 1774–1784* (Madison, Wis., 1977), 109–26. On sectional commitment to territorial expansion, see McCoy, *The Elusive Republic,* 124–29. Lance Banning elaborates on this interpretation in *The Sacred Fire of Liberty,* 58–65. See also Jack N. Rakove, *The Beginnings of National Politics: An Interpretive History of the Continental Congress* (New York, 1979), 350.

15. Grayson's speech was recorded in part by Charles Thomson. See Notes of Debates, Aug. 16, 1786, in *LDC,* 23:485.

16. Madison to Jefferson, Aug. 20, 1784, in *PTJ,* 7:401–10, 403 (quotation).

17. Madison to Jefferson, Aug. 20, 1784, in William T. Hutchinson et al., eds., *Papers of James Madison, Congressional Series* (Chicago, 1962–77; Charlottesville, Va., 1978–2017), 8:108 [draft] (hereafter *PJM-CS*).

18. John Craig Hammond, *Slavery, Freedom, and Expansion in the Early American West* (Charlottesville, Va., 2007), 36.

19. Monroe to Madison, May 31, 1786, in *PJM-CS,* 9:68–73. See also Jefferson to Stuart, Jan. 25, 1786, in *PTJ,* 9:217–19.

20. Madison to Monroe, June 21, 1786, in *PJM-CS,* 9:82–85. See also Washington to Lee, Oct. 31, 1786, in W. W. Abbott et al., eds., *Papers of George Washington, Confederation Series* (Charlottesville, Va., 1992–94), 4:318–20. Even Henry Lee, who in principle supported the Jay-Gardoqui agreement, privately raised concerns that the issue would kill constitutional reform; see Lee to Washington, Aug. 7, 1786, in *LDC,* 23:438. See also Charles Pinckney, speech, Aug. 10, 1786, in *LDC,* 23:455. On William Grayson's views, see Charles Thomson, Notes of Debates, Aug. 16, 1786, in *LDC,* 23:495. On antifederalists' use of the Jay-Gardoqui agreement during the Virginia constitutional convention, see Fredrika Johanna Teute, "Land, Liberty, and Labor in the Post-Revolutionary Era: Kentucky as the Promised Land" (PhD diss., Johns Hopkins University, 1988), 30–33.

21. "Notes on Emigration, [ante 19 November] 1791," in *PJM-CS,* 14:113–16.

22. Madison to Jefferson, Sept. 7, 1784, in *PTJ,* 7:417.

23. Madison to Lafayette, Mar. 20, 1785, in *PJM-CS,* 8:250–55.

24. Andrew R. L. Cayton "'Separate Interests' and the Nation-State: The Washington Administration and the Origins of Regionalism in the Trans-Appalachian West," *Journal of American History* 79 (June 1992): 39–67; Kristofer Ray, "Progress and Popular Democracy on the Southwestern Frontier: Middle Tennessee, 1790–1824" (PhD diss., University of North Carolina, 2003), 17–18, 38–48, 59–60.

25. Hubbard Taylor to Madison, May 23, 1793, in *PJM-CS,* 15:20–21.

26. "To the Inhabitants of the United States West of the Allegheny and Apalachian Mountains," Dec. 13, 1793, Broadsides, Leaflets, and Pamphlets from America and Europe Collection, Library of Congress, Washington, D.C., https://www.loc.gov/item/rbpe.02100200/.

27. On Virginia's exports, see Kulikoff, *Tobacco and Slaves,* 157–58. On the uneven effects of the growth of the U.S. export trade, see Donald R. Adams Jr., "American Neutrality and Prosperity, 1793–1808: A Reconsideration," *Journal of Economic History* 40 (Dec. 1980): 713–37.

28. Jefferson, "Final State of the Report on Commerce," Dec. 16, 1793, in *PTJ,* 27:567–79.

29. Madison, "Commercial Discrimination," Jan 3, 1794, in *PJM-CS,* 15:167.

30. Studies of the treaty include Samuel Flagg Bemis, *Jay's Treaty: A Study in Commerce and Diplomacy* (1923; reprint, New Haven, Conn., 1962), and Jerald A. Combs, *The Jay Treaty: Political Battleground of the Founding Fathers* (Berkeley, Calif., 1970).

31. Lawrence B. A. Hatter, "The Jay Charter: Rethinking the American National State in the West, 1796–1819," *Diplomatic History* 4 (2013): 693–700. For a brief historiographical overview, see 693–94n1.

32. Nicholas to Madison, Nov. 6, 1795, *PJM-CS,* 16:118–21. Kentucky senator Humphrey Marshall voted for the treaty and was vilified at public meetings and in the press. See *Kentucky Gazette* (Lexington), Oct. 3, 1795. From November 1795 to January

1796, "A Freeman" and Humphries sparred in the *Kentucky Gazette* over the effects of the treaty, clause by clause.

33. "The Address of Sundry Inhabitants, Free Citizens of the County of Clarke and State of Kentucky, at a Meeting Held on Tuesday the 8th Day of September, 1795," *Kentucky Gazette,* Sept. 19, 1795.

34. Findley, PA, HR, Apr. 20, 1796, in *The Debates and Proceedings in the Congress of the United States* (*Annals of Congress*) (Washington, D.C., 1834–49), 4th Cong., 1st sess. (hereafter *AC* 4–1), 1112.

35. "Treaty of Friendship, Limits, and Navigation between Spain and the United States," Oct. 27, 1795, The Avalon Project: Documents in Law, History, and Diplomacy, http://avalon.law.yale.edu/18th_century/sp1795.asp.

36. The most thorough account of the negotiations remains Samuel Flagg Bemis, *Pinckney's Treaty: America's Advantage from Europe's Distress, 1783–1800,* rev. ed. (1926; New Haven, Conn., 1960). On petitions from western communities, see William Branch Giles to Jefferson, Mar. 26, 1796; Madison to Jefferson, Apr. 18, 1796, in *PTJ,* 29:48–49, 71. On pro-treaty sentiments in the western country, see also "Pittsburgh, May 14," *Pennsylvania Gazette,* May 25, 1795.

37. "Extract of a Letter from a Member of Congress, to a Gentleman in This Town, Dated Philadelphia February 12th 1797," *Kentucky Gazette,* Mar. 25, 1797. On the depression, see Richard S. Chew, "Certain Victims of an International Contagion: The Panic of 1797 and the Hard Times of the Late 1790s in Baltimore," *Journal of the Early Republic* 25 (Winter 2005): 565–613.

38. "From a Correspondent," *Kentucky Gazette,* Apr. 26, 1797.

39. On June 7, 1798, Congress passed an act to suspend commerce with France and its dependencies. See *AC* 5–2, 573, 1865–66, 3737–39. In September 1799, Jefferson estimated that Virginia planters would lose $5 million that year; see Jefferson to William Bache, Sept. 20, 1799, in *PTJ,* 31:189.

40. "Lexington, August 6," *Kentucky Gazette,* Aug. 6. 1796.

41. The order was issued on October 18; see "Frankfort, January 28," *Kentucky Gazette,* Feb. 1, 1803. In a letter to Congress, the council and house of representatives of the Mississippi Territory pledged their support of whatever measures the federal government deemed necessary. "The Memorial," *Kentucky Gazette,* Dec. 7, 1802; "Memorial," *Kentucky Gazette,* Feb. 1, 1803. The Kentucky House of Representatives unanimously resolved that the measure was an infraction of the Treaty of San Lorenzo. "Kentucky Legislature. House of Representatives," *Kentucky Gazette,* Dec. 7, 1802.

42. Jefferson's letter to Kentucky governor James Garrard appeared in "Frankfort, Feb 9," *Kentucky Gazette,* Feb. 15, 1803. See also "Washington City, Jan. 6," *Kentucky Gazette,* Feb. 1, 1803.

43. "To the People of Kentucky," *Kentucky Gazette,* Mar. 8, 1803.

44. Jefferson, Message to Congress, Jan. 11, 1803, in *AC* 7–2, 23; emphasis added. See also Madison to Livingston, Feb. 23, 1803, *PJM-SS,* 4:343–45.

45. "Letter," *Kentucky Gazette,* Feb. 15, 1803. See also John Fowler, "Circular," *Guardian of Freedom* (Frankfort, Ky.), Apr. 6, 1803.

46. Livingston and Monroe to Madison, May 13, 1803, in *American State Papers: Foreign Relations,* 2:559.

47. In late 1803, Jefferson sent "An Account of Louisiana" to members of Congress. The report was reprinted in newspapers. No reliable map of the province existed. No known survey existed, and much of the region was "imperfectly explored." Even the boundaries, the report admitted, "are at present involved in some obscurity." The first appeared in "An Account of Louisiana," *Kentucky Gazette,* Dec. 6, 1803.

48. Phocion, "Desultory Reflections on the Aspect of Politics in Relation to the Western People. No. 2," *Kentucky Gazette,* Oct. 4, 1803. Monroe and Livingston also argued that the purchase was a bargain; see Livingston to Monroe, May 13, 1803, in *American State Papers: Foreign Relations,* 2:558–60. See also Kentucky representative John Fowler's views in "Circular," *National Intelligencer* (Washington, D.C.), May 7, 1804.

49. "Louisiana," *Kentucky Gazette,* Aug. 16, 1803; A Peace-Maker, "To the Senate of the United States," *National Intelligencer,* Oct. 24, 1803; "A Letter from Dr. John Siblet," *National Intelligencer,* Jan. 13, 1804.

50. Aristides, "Reflections on Political Economy, and the Prospect before Us," *Kentucky Gazette,* Sept. 6, Nov. 22, 1803.

51. "Communication. Extension of the Empire of the United States," *Kentucky Gazette,* Aug. 16, 1803. Others, including political economist Tench Coxe, argued that the affair would promote U.S. manufacturing; see Martin Öhman, "Perfecting Independence: Tench Coxe and the Political Economy of Western Development," *Journal of the Early Republic* 31 (Fall 2011): 397–433.

52. "Governor's Speech," *Kentucky Gazette,* Nov. 15, 1803.

53. Allan Bowie Magruder, *Political, Commercial and Moral Reflections on the Late Cession of Louisiana* (Lexington, Ky., 1803), 17–18, 40, 50 (quotation).

54. Madison to Livingston, Sept. 28, 1801, in *PJM-SS,* 2:142–47; [Nicholas, VA, Sen], Feb. 25, 1803, in *AC* 7–2, 233–34. On policymakers' downplaying the military threat, see also Lewis, "A Tornado on the Horizon," 124–25.

55. John Fowler, "Circular," *Guardian of Freedom, Apr. 6, 1803.*

56. "Camillus" [William Duane], *The Mississippi Question Fairly Stated, and the Views and Arguments of Those Who Clamor for War Examined. In Seven Letters—Originally Written for Publication in the Aurora, at Philadelphia* (Philadelphia, 1803), 46. See also De Witt, "Louisiana," *Kentucky Gazette,* Sept. 24, Oct. 1, 1802.

57. On French domination of New Orleans shipping, see Arthur Preston Whitaker, "France and the American Deposit at New Orleans," *Hispanic American Historical Review* 4 (Nov. 1931): 486.

58. W. F. Galpin, "The Grain Trade of New Orleans, 1804–1814," *Mississippi Valley Historical Review* 4 (Mar. 1928): 501–2.

59. "Report from House Committee of Commerce and Manufactures," Jan. 10, 1803, in *AC* 7–2, 347–50, 350 (quotation).

60. Madison to Livingston, Feb. 23, 1803, *PJM-SS,* 4:343–45.

61. Jefferson, "To the Senate and House of Representative of the United States," Oct. 17, 1803, in *AC* 8–1, 12.

62. Hunter Miller, ed., *Treaties and Other International Acts of the United States of America* (Washington, D.C., 1931), doc. 28, 2:504.

63. James D. Richardson, ed., *A Compilation of the Messages and Papers of the Presidents, 1789–1907* (1897; reprint, New York, 1908), 1:379.

3 A Religious Republican and a Republican Religion

John A. Ragosta

Thomas Jefferson is rightly remembered as a founder of American religious freedom. His Statute for Establishing Religious Freedom and letter to the Danbury Baptists (identifying a constitutional "wall of separation between Church & State") were iconic even in the early republic. Jefferson was deeply committed to the "useful truths & principles" of the Danbury letter. Not only was religious freedom important in its own right but it was essential for a functioning republic. Historically, because of restrictions on religious freedom and the mixing of church and state, the "human mind has been held in vassalage by kings, priests and nobles." The intermingling of church and state was, to Jefferson, the foundation of tyranny. As a result, he swore "upon the altar of god eternal hostility against every form of tyranny over the mind of man" and committed himself to religious freedom. By Jefferson's logic, without that freedom, including separation of church and state, the mind could not be free and a functioning republic would be impossible.[1]

Understanding the centrality of these principles to Jefferson, and to Jeffersonians, is essential to understanding how Jeffersonians in power addressed religion and religious freedom. While Jeffersonians differed on the details and implementation of many policies, religious freedom was generally not one of them. Here there was one steadfastly Republican position, as evident in the election of 1800.

During that election Jefferson was viciously attacked for his perceived lack of religiosity (more accurately, his lack of orthodoxy). The Jeffersonian response, though, is perhaps more important: some Republican editors tried to defend his religion, but the more prominent response was to insist that under the Constitution and American ideas of freedom, Jefferson's religion was a personal matter irrelevant to the election. This became a defining issue for Republicans. In the midst of electoral attacks on Jefferson's unorthodoxy, a Philadelphia printer republished the Statute for Establishing Religious Freedom and excerpts on religious freedom from Jefferson's *Notes on the State of Virginia*—including his highly controversial insistence that "it does me no injury for my neighbour to say there are twenty gods, or no god. It neither picks my pocket nor breaks my leg." In a Jeffersonian voice, the editor declared that "upon the preservation of these sacred and inestimable rights, depends a large proportion of our felicity and prosperity at all times." This pamphlet was broadly reprinted. In 1803, while debates over religious freedom raged in Connecticut, a similar and aptly titled *Republican Notes on Religion* was printed. Later in the century, this issue was still understood to define Jeffersonian Republicans; New Hampshire editors in 1842 insisted that "to maintain their reputation as Republicans of the Jefferson school," citizens must make clear that "men's religion is a concern between themselves and their Maker; and, that, to encroach upon religious freedom, is to violate the privacy of conscience, . . . which the men of the revolution taught us to cherish and venerate." A July 4 oration in Otsego, New York, in 1832 reflected that same understanding: "Our bosoms swell with pride, as we give the name of our beloved Jefferson, who burst the polluted embrace of 'Church and State,' and unlocked the consciences of a nation. This is the proudest triumph of our Republic over Monarchal Governments." As Jefferson sought to remake the United States, creating an "empire of liberty," religious freedom, including separation of church and state, would play an essential role.[2]

Some analysts have suggested that Jefferson was inconsistent in applying these principles, particularly during his presidency. This is a serious claim as this is not an area in which Jefferson acted without thought. Yet a careful review of Jefferson and Jeffersonians in power suggests that they respected these principles. Consideration of this issue might start by distinguishing two overlapping circumstances: religious actions by government officials and government interaction with religion and religious institutions.[3]

Officials Are People Too

While Jefferson demanded a secular government, he did not demand, nor seek, a secular nation.[4] This then posed a problem: how should government officials, as opposed to the government, express their religiosity?

James Madison, Jefferson's trusted lieutenant with whom he walked in almost perfect lockstep on issues of religious freedom, explicitly addressed the problem. "In their individual capacities, as distinct from their official station," officials "might unite in recommendations of any sort whatsoever," including religious actions, prayers, and even preaching, "in the same manner as any other individuals might do. But then their recommendations ought to express the true character from which they emanate." That is, religious actions by government officials should be clearly personal, not official.[5]

Jefferson agreed. For example, unlike both of his predecessors as president, Jefferson refused to issue official prayer proclamations, insisting that to do so would violate the Constitution. His 1808 letter responding to a request for such a proclamation from Reverend Samuel Miller is worth quoting at length:

> I consider the government of the US. as interdicted by the Constitution from intermeddling with religious institutions, their doctrines, disciplines, or exercises. This results not only from the provision that no law shall be made respecting the establishment, or free exercise, of religion, but from that also which reserves to the states the powers not delegated to the U.S. . . . But it is only proposed that I should *recommend,* not prescribe a day of fasting & prayer. That is, that I should *indirectly* assume to the U.S. an authority over religious exercises which the Constitution has directly precluded them from. It must be meant too that this recommendation is to carry some authority, and to be sanctioned by some penalty on those who disregard it; not indeed of fine and imprisonment, but of some degree of proscription perhaps in public opinion. . . . I do not believe it is for the interest of religion to invite the civil magistrate to direct it's exercises, it's discipline, or it's doctrines; . . . Every religious society has a right to determine for itself the times for these exercises, & the objects proper for them,

> . . . and this right can never be safer than in their own hands, where the constitution has deposited it.

Even a proclamation calling for "voluntary" prayer would be essentially coercive, creating a "proscription perhaps in public opinion" as to who was or was not a good citizen or sufficiently patriotic. Madison, commenting on such proclamations, scoffed that "an *advisory* government is a contradiction in terms."[6]

At the same time, Jefferson, speaking for himself, prayed publicly at both of his inaugurals, as he did in several of his annual addresses to Congress. His first annual message noted that "we devoutly return thanks to the beneficent Being . . . , we are bound with peculiar gratitude to be thankful to Him that our own peace has been preserved through so perilous a season." His second annual message drew "our just attentions . . . to those pleasing circumstances which mark the goodness of that Being from whose favor they flow and the large measure of thankfulness we owe for His bounty." While later messages largely eschewed prayers, he prayed in his second inaugural, noting, "in matters of religion I have considered that its free exercise is placed by the Constitution independent of the powers of the general government. I have therefore undertaken on no occasion to prescribe the religious exercises suited to it, but have left them, as the Constitution found them, under the direction and discipline of state or church authorities." Jefferson viewed these public statements, even as made by the president, as differing fundamentally from an official proclamation because they reflected his ideas without presuming to speak for or in the name of the government or to pressure any citizen (implicitly or explicitly) to take religious action.[7]

Republican newspapers echoed the point, chiding Federalists for failing to distinguish Jefferson's role as a "*civil ruler,* clothed with *temporal power,*" from his actions "in his *private capacity,* as a *man.*" "Mr. Jefferson, in his political capacity, *lets it* [religion] *alone* . . . is not inclined to intervene with his power," but in his private capacity he supports religion and "attends public worship."[8]

Some scholars have suggested an inconsistency on Jefferson's part in this regard, arguing that his "rhetoric in official utterances . . . in terms of religious content, was virtually indistinguishable" from thanksgiving proclamations. Jefferson clearly saw things differently. By his logic, a simple statement, even in a public context, was personal. There was no "official policy" in his public prayers. (Similarly, for example, if a Jewish president attended synagogue regularly, no one would suggest that this was an official promotion of Judaism. A proclamation calling on everyone to attend synagogue would be an entirely different matter.)[9]

The same point was made in a political context by Jefferson's secretary of the treasury, Albert Gallatin. In a draft circular for customs officials, Gallatin warned appointees against any confusion of official duties and private action by officials: "Whilst freedom of opinion, & freedom of suffrage at public elections are considered by the President, as imperscriptible rights, which . . . you cannot have lost by becoming public officers; he will regard any exercise of official influence to restrain or controul the same rights in others as injurious to that part of the public administration which is confided to your care, and practically destructive of the fundamental principles of a republican Constitution." Jefferson wrote Gallatin that "I approve . . . entirely of the two paragraphs on the participation of office, & electioneering activity." The same principle applied to religious activity by officials.[10]

This fundamental distinction between an official proclamation and a president's own inaugural speech or message to Congress has been recognized by political scientists: "The form of the proclamation virtually ensures that the central rhetorical appeal of any proclamation will be the authority of the president (or of the government as a whole) rather than factors peculiar to the president's persuasive abilities. Put another way, the proclamation's persuasive power derives more from the fact that the president proclaims, or commands, than it does from a case he builds."[11]

It should be no surprise that in attempting to define the appropriate role for government and officials with respect to religion, difficult distinctions must be made. While the wall of separation may not be serpentine, as Justice Robert Jackson famously suggested in 1948, it sometimes must work its way carefully through a dense thicket. Confronted with that thicket, Jefferson seems to have hit upon an important distinction that maintained his strict commitment to keeping government out of religion and religion officially out of government, while recognizing the important role that religion would play in the lives of policymakers.[12]

Madison provides an interesting contrast to Jefferson's studied inaction in this regard. Facing the crisis of the War of 1812 and under substantial political pressure (including secessionist threats from New England), Madison accepted Congress's request that he issue prayer proclamations, but he later regretted it, concluding that they were unconstitutional as they "seem to imply and certainly nourish the erroneous idea of a *national* religion." He understood that such proclamations tended, almost inevitably, to prefer a particular religion (Christianity as a practical matter) while profaning religion by their political, rather than religious, motivations.[13]

The problem of public but nonofficial action is also presented by the fact that President Jefferson not infrequently attended religious services in the House of Representatives, a point emphasized by critics of Jeffersonian religious freedom who charge that he was a hypocrite or did not really intend the separation of church and state as understood by modern courts.[14] His private choice of where to attend church, however, even as president, in no way compromised his commitment to a strict separation of church and state, though the use of public buildings for religious purposes is more complicated, as discussed below.

Official Actions and Religion

Jeffersonians grappled with a number of issues concerning the relationship of government to religion, and here too they did so with a focus on principle. Incorporation of churches, another area in which Jeffersonians were accused of inconsistency, is a good example.

In 1811, President Madison vetoed the incorporation of an Episcopal church in Alexandria (then part of the District of Columbia). His veto message reflected his belief that the act would be a "law respecting an establishment of religion" prohibited by the First Amendment. Federalist congressman Josiah Quincy III objected that President Jefferson had signed a bill "in every material respect" the same as that vetoed by Madison. In truth, however, the two incorporation acts were very different in ways that are essential to understanding the Jeffersonians' religious freedom principle.[15]

As Madison explained, the bill that he vetoed regulated the church in some detail:

> The bill enacts into, and establishes by law, sundry rules and proceedings relative purely to the organization and polity of the Church incorporated, and comprehending even the election and removal of the Minister of the same; so that no change could be made therein, by the particular Society, or by the General Church

of which it is a member, and whose authority it recognizes. This particular Church, therefore, would so far be a religious establishment by law; a legal force and sanction being given to certain articles in its constitution and administration.

This was a far cry from the incorporation bill that Jefferson signed, which generally treated the church in a neutral manner, like any other incorporated entity. (That bill did limit the church's total annual revenue to prevent an old-world aggrandizement of church property, a not uncommon nineteenth-century concern.)[16]

Similar concerns determined how Jeffersonians approached use of the House of Representatives for religious services. In 1800, when the federal government moved to Washington, there were only two churches in the infant city—a small Catholic church and an Episcopal church. Given that, the Federalist Speaker of the House, without objection from representatives, allowed church services in the House chamber on Sundays when it was not being used for official purposes; the practice continued for a number of years.[17] Margaret Bayard Smith, one of Washington's leading socialites, reported that "preachers of every sect and denomination of christianity were there admitted—Catholics, Unitarians, Quakers. . . . Even women" were permitted to preach.[18] Significantly, in undeveloped Washington, the House was also used for other unofficial activities such as public lectures, with "the galleries serving as the 'lounging place of both sexes, where acquaintance is as easily made as at public amusements.'" For example, in 1801, a July 4 discourse "suitable to the occasion" was delivered in the House by Reverend David Austin. Congress clearly did not intend that the use of the House for various purposes, including church services on Sundays, be a precedent for more active, official support of religion. Thus, an 1802 petition, fostered by Austin himself, requesting that Congress erect a building for worship of all denominations, was referred to committee where it apparently died.[19]

The issue here is one that is described in modern terms as "neutrality." The use of public space for nonofficial purposes was not unheard of in the nineteenth century. In fact, Jefferson (admittedly somewhat reluctantly) suggested a similar strategy as he was seeking funding for the University of Virginia. When pushed to allow worship on campus, he indicated that access to a "building still to be erected" (later the university's Rotunda) under "impartial regulations" would "leave inviolate the constitutional freedom of religion, the most inalienable and sacred of human rights," and that if religious institutions were created on or adjacent to campus grounds, it should be clearly understood that such seminaries "shall be independent of the University."[20] Modern courts have understood such "impartial" or "neutral" regulations to require that if a public facility is open for nonofficial use, the government cannot prevent its use for religious purposes. The issue of neutrality continues to dominate the Supreme Court's treatment of government-church interactions.[21] This is not to say that the Speaker of the House was necessarily thinking of such neutrality when he permitted the church services, but it is significant that Jeffersonians recognized the legitimacy of such use.

The treaty with the Kaskaskia Indians, in which the federal government agreed to build a church and pay a Catholic priest one hundred dollars a year for seven years, poses a more complicated problem—as Jefferson and Madison recognized. The treaty involved the transfer of the Kaskaskia Indians' vast land holdings to the United States, and provided some detail on how the annual annuity that the United States was paying for the land was to be spent, including construction of a church and payment of a priest. While some insist that this demonstrates that Jefferson was willing to support religion financially so long as the federal government did not choose one religion in particular, in fact the treaty did choose one religion, specifying a Roman Catholic church and priest. No other treaty signed by Jefferson or Madison had similar terms.[22]

Yet the situation appears quite differently if seen in the context that the treaty was disposing of Indian money provided "as full and ample compensation for the relinquishment made to the United States," that is, Kaskaskia land in Illinois Territory; these were not government funds. It was not unusual for Indian treaties to specify how annuities—Native money—would be paid (e.g., in tools). This understanding of the funds—that they belonged to the Kaskaskia and not the U.S. government—seemed implicit when Jefferson's secretary of war, Henry Dearborn, wrote to Indiana Territory governor William Harrison about distribution of the funds in 1807: the Kaskaskia were owed "$1100—to be paid $500 in goods and $600 in cash; this last sum includes $100 to be paid annually to a Roman Catholic priest for 7 years per treaty." As the Supreme Court recognizes, private funds held in trust by the government are not subject to the same constitutional constraints as public expenditures.[23]

What is more interesting, and often overlooked, is that Jefferson and Madison obviously wanted to prevent the treaty from creating an impression that the federal government could fund religion. They had not approved the language that was inserted in the treaty text, and by the time they saw it, it was too late to change it without a major delay. Nonetheless, before sending the treaty to Congress, Madison urged that the summary provided by the president be edited to delete this fact: "May it not be as well to omit the detail of the stipulated considerations, and particularly, that of the Roman Catholic Pastor. The jealousy of some may see in it a principle, not according with the exemption of Religion from Civil power &c." Thus, in his message to Congress, Jefferson noted simply that the treaty provided for "certain annual aids in money, in implements of agriculture, and other articles of *their* choice."[24]

Certainly, no other Jefferson or Madison treaty had such a provision. Noting this, James A. Davids argues that the provision could easily have been changed and that the failure to do so in the Kaskaskia Treaty suggests a particular Jeffersonian policy on faith-based initiatives. It seems more reasonable to note the peculiarity of the treaty, the fact that such provisions were excluded from all other Jefferson and Madison treaties, and their noted reluctance to discuss these provisions in the one treaty where they appeared. After all, if Davids is correct that this provision was somehow indicative of a principled support for direct funding of religion, setting aside that it involved only a Catholic priest (and would on that basis run afoul of the establishment clause even in the most narrow interpretation), why were similar provisions not included in other treaties, and why would Madison and Jefferson correspond about ways to avoid any appearance of mixing government and church?[25]

Other examples reinforce this point. For instance, during Madison's administration, through a surveying error in the new Mississippi Territory, a Baptist church was placed on government land. Seeking to preserve the church in spite of the error, Congress passed a bill to give the church five acres on which the building sat. Madison vetoed the bill, explaining that any such grant "comprises a principle and precedent for the appropriation of funds of the United States for the use and support of religious societies, contrary" to the First Amendment. Notably, Madison was not opposed to a commercial arrangement with the church, selling it the land, but a gift was a clear violation of the principle of separation of church and state.[26]

All told, when operating in the sphere of the federal government, Jefferson and Madison consistently sought to maintain a strict separation between church and state while, at the same time, recognizing the religiosity of government officials and not discriminating against religion.

Republicanism and the States

All of this, though, begs a broader question. While Jefferson and Madison were consistent in their application of the principles of religious freedom in official actions, their actions were also circumscribed by the federal Constitution. As Jefferson noted, religion was by and large a matter to be regulated by the states: "Our citizens have wisely formed themselves into one nation as to others, and several states as among themselves. . . . To each state severally [belongs] the care of our persons, our property, our reputation, and religious freedom." Jefferson's commitment to a federal structure would allow no less.[27]

This is not to say that Jeffersonians in power ignored this vast area of potential church-state conflict or religious controversy. As Peter S. Onuf explains more broadly, for Jeffersonians, "the revolutionary challenge was to perfect republican governments that would preserve liberty . . . while enabling Americans to participate in, and contribute to, the progress of civilization." Yet that task would be impossible without progress in the states. Referring to the expected success of Republicanism in 1800, Jefferson wrote Gideon Granger, soon to be his postmaster general, that "should the whole body of New England continue in opposition to these principles of government, either knowingly or through delusion, our government will be a very uneasy one." Given how essential Jeffersonians considered religious freedom to a functioning republic, the broad role of the states, and the limited size and power of the federal government, to "perfect republican government" it was essential that Jeffersonians promote religious freedom in the states, including separation of church and state. The Revolution of 1800 required no less. While recognizing the limitations of federal authority, silence in the face of Federalist efforts to use religion to protect their waning political hegemony would have been unconscionable.[28]

Both Jefferson and Madison sought to ensure that religion in the states (particularly Calvinist, New England religion) did not interfere with republicanism or the developing Republican Party. This is the context for Jefferson's

1801 Danbury Baptist letter. Danbury Baptists complained bitterly to Jefferson about the lack of religious freedom and the mixing of church and state in Connecticut, but they recognized the limits of his federal authority: "We are sensible that . . . the national goverment cannot destroy the Laws of each State; but our hopes are strong that the sentiment of our beloved President, which have had such genial Effect already, like the radiant beams of the Sun, will shine & prevail through all these States and all the world till Hierarchy and tyranny be destroyed from the earth."[29] So what was a states'-rights president committed to religious freedom to do? While he could not change state policy directly, he could influence minds by "sowing useful truths & principles among the people." To do so, it was important for the contents of this "private" letter to the Danbury Baptists to be broadly disseminated, and Jeffersonians saw to that. The letter was quickly reprinted in a score of newspapers throughout the country, especially in New England. Jefferson used what Theodore Roosevelt would call the president's "bully pulpit" to influence states to encourage republicanism and religious freedom where federal authority was limited. "By placing new phrases into public discourse," political scientist Jeremy D. Bailey explains, "Jefferson used the presidency to direct the public's constitutional understanding and to unify public opinion."[30]

President Jefferson specifically targeted reform of the New England churches and polities that supported the unholy alliance of church and state. Henry Adams, admittedly a difficult source in many contexts, understood the challenge Jefferson perceived. "The New England church," Adams wrote, "was the chief obstacle to democratic success, and New-England society, as then constituted, was dangerous to the safety of the Union." The mixing of church and state in New England, and efforts to control the mind of nascent republicans (and Republicans), was at the heart of the problem. "If Jefferson thought he had the power to effect his object by political influence," Adams concluded, "he could hardly refuse to make the attempt." Jefferson saw in the waxing political success of Republicans in New England an opportunity to reform religious freedom.[31]

Nowhere was the problem clearer than in Connecticut, where Federalists maintained power through an intimate partnership with the established Congregational Church, and continued to do so throughout Jefferson's and Madison's administrations. Pierpont Edwards, an influential Connecticut lawyer and newly Republican politician, warned the president of the danger of the Connecticut church-state cabal in the context of federal appointments: "The federalists here are a corps most systimatically organized. The Governor and Council joined to *the corporation of Yale College,* which was originally wholly eclesiastical, (and thirteen out of twenty one are now eclesiastics,) makes all the arrangements; these are communicated to those general meetings of our established Clergy, . . .—from them it is communicated to all the true federalist[s?] of each Parish—By this means they act with perfect uniformity." Jefferson responded to Edwards:

> I consider Rho. isld. Vermont, Massachusets & N. Hampshire as coming about in the course of this year . . . but the nature of your [Connecticut] government being a subordination of the civil to the Ecclesiastical power, I consider it as desperate for long years to come. their steady habits exclude the advances of information & they seem exactly where they were when they separated from the Saints of Oliver Cromwell. and there your clergy will always keep them if they can. you will follow the bark of liberty only by the help of a tow-rope. you will greatly oblige me by continuing your information as to the effects on them produced & to be produced by our measures.[32]

Not only could Edwards provide Jefferson with information concerning developments in Connecticut and New England generally, but he was the type of opinion leader who would be needed to bring the Republican message of religious freedom and separation of church and state effectively to the state. Jefferson's efforts arguably paid off years later when Edwards became the chairman of the committee that drafted the 1818 Connecticut constitution, which effectively disestablished the Congregational Church (albeit retaining a potential preference for Christian sects) and eliminated the requirement that officeholders take the oath of fidelity (ending in "So help me god in the Lo: Jesus Christ").[33]

Seeking to protect republicanism, Republicanism, and religious freedom in the states was on Jefferson's mind as he approached the task of dismissing some Federalist political appointees. "The effects of removals will be very different in different places," Jefferson's attorney general, Levi Lincoln, suggested. "In Connecticut . . . , an attempt to get the General Government, under the influence of an arrogant official clamor, and an ecclesiastical terror, has been general." It was in this context—replacement of appointees—that Jefferson famously wrote, "From the clergy I expect no mercy. they crucified their Saviour who preached that their kingdom was not of this world, and all who practice on that precept must expect the extreme of their wrath. the laws of the present day withhold their hands from blood. but lies and slander still remain to them."[34]

Jefferson took every opportunity to use his public persona to argue against restrictions on religious freedom and support separation of church and state in the states, especially vis-à-vis New England. In his second inaugural, he used the allegory of educating Native Americans to emphasize reforms needed in New England:

> But the endeavors to enlighten them on the fate which awaits their present course of life, to induce them to exercise their reason, follow its dictates, and change their pursuits with the change of circumstances, have powerful obstacles to encounter; they are combated by the habits of their bodies, prejudice of their minds, ignorance, pride, and the influence of interested and crafty individuals among them, who feel themselves something in the present order of things, and fear to become nothing in any other. These persons inculcate a sanctimonious reverence for the customs of their ancestors; that whatsoever they did, must be done through all time; that reason is a false guide, and to advance under its counsel, in their physical, moral, or political condition, is perilous innovation; that their duty is to remain as their Creator made them, ignorance being safety, and knowledge full of danger; in short, my friends, among them is seen the action and counteraction of good sense and bigotry; they, too, have their anti-philosophers, who find an interest in keeping things in their present state, who dread reformation, and exert all their faculties to maintain the ascendency of habit over the duty of improving our reason, and obeying its mandates.

Recognizing the limits of his authority, and always preferring to seize a tool by its "smooth handle," the Native allegory allowed him to "bear[ ] witness" to the principle while not "committing himself to direct warfare upon it." Jefferson used such public addresses to transfer his "thought into public space."[35]

Political and religious reforms in the states went hand in hand. Certainly this was true in terms of amendments to state constitutions. Thus, critics of the Jeffersonian vision often point out that in 1791, when the First Amendment was ratified, twelve of thirteen states had formal religious establishments or some form of test oaths. While the First Amendment contemplated that the states would be left to devise their own systems of church-state relations, through 1879 (and the Supreme Court's unanimous embracing of Jefferson's wall of separation), each of the state constitutions moved emphatically in a Jeffersonian direction, often influenced by Jeffersonians. The first Rhode Island postindependence constitution, for example, simply adopted language from Jefferson's Statute for Establishing Religious Freedom. In North Carolina, restrictions on religious freedom were relaxed after debates in the state convention quoted, at length, Jefferson's statute. Other state constitutional reforms also followed a Jeffersonian pattern and idiom.[36]

The same pattern was evident in nonconstitutional state legal reforms. When the first Republican governor of Massachusetts supported proposals for liberalizing church-state relations by exempting dissenters from an establishment tax, Federalists and Congregationalists declared that it was a "war on . . . religion." Those reforms only succeeded after Jeffersonian Republicans came to power. When a similar religious liberty bill was adopted in Vermont, "under the lead of two Baptist and Republican members of the legislature," it was denounced in the *Dartmouth Gazette* as "another striking instance of the pernicious, the direful, the infernal consequences to which the leveling spirit of democracy must invariably tend." One hundred years ago, Professor W. A. Robinson properly concluded that it was "difficult to prove whether these public worship bills were adopted by strict party voting, but there is no question but that the Republican party held itself responsible for them and that the Federalists were strongly opposed to them."[37]

After leaving office, Madison continued to plead with states to adopt the religious freedom that was essential to a Jeffersonian republic, including separation of church and state. His so-called Detached Memorandum, written after leaving the White House, was apparently intended for eventual publication to inculcate truths much like the Danbury Baptist letter. In that essay he urged,

> Ye States of America which retain in your Constitutions or Codes, any aberration from the sacred principle of religious liberty by giving to Caesar what belongs to God, or joining together what God has put asunder, hasten to revise your systems, and make the example of your Country as pure and complete, in what relates to freedom of the mind and its allegiance to its maker, as in what belongs to the legitimate objects of political and civil institutions.[38]

Certainly, Republican newspapers and correspondents promoted the idea that the Jeffersonian influence was essential to state-level reform. While this essay does not offer a thorough review of changes in religious freedom laws and laws impacting church-state relations at the state level in the early nineteenth century, it is evident that at the time and in subsequent telling, the Jeffersonian Republicans were central players in the efforts to expand religious freedom and, in particular, the separation of church and state.[39] This will undoubtedly be a topic for further research; Steven K. Green provides an excellent example of the type of study possible.[40]

Jeffersonians not only sought to separate church from state but hoped that, in doing so, American Christianity would itself become more compatible with republican freedom. Among a deeply religious people, protecting republicanism would require, on the "other side" of the wall of separation, a thinking religion. Johann N. Neem has explained that this was part of the purpose of the Danbury letter: "Jefferson's wall was never an end in itself but the means toward a larger end: the reformation of American Christianity to make it the basis of the new nation's civil religion." While Jefferson had idiosyncratic views of true Christianity—rejecting Jesus's divinity, resurrection, and atonement, and focusing on his ethics—based on those views, Jefferson would have joined with the Republican minister Stanley Griswold in declaring Christians ideal citizens. Preaching in Milford, Connecticut, on October 12, 1800, Griswold emphatically declared, "True it is, real Christians make the best citizens in the world. And rulers actuated by the real spirit of Christ's precepts make the best rulers. . . . But this device [blending church and state], however plausible in appearance, is only opening a ready door for unprincipled hypocrites to creep through, and under the imposing garb of religion do infinite mischief."[41] Indicative of the tense nature of the election of 1800—and the fraught nature of religious concerns in Federalist Connecticut—Griswold was driven out of his church for his Republican views.

Today, Americans have so fetishized the founding that a discussion of Jefferson and religious freedom inevitably is read through a modern lens. This is particularly ironic given Jefferson's demand that laws and constitutions were for the living and should be replaced each generation. Yet in the area of religious freedom, there is arguably more reason for consideration of the founders' views than in others. As Jefferson made explicit in the concluding paragraph of his Statute for Establishing Religious Freedom, the rights implicit in religious freedom "are of the natural rights of mankind." Unlike other aspects of constitutions and laws, religious freedom was timeless; while other provisions could be and should be modified with the times and temper of a people, not so with religious freedom. This was at the center of Jefferson's Republican revolution. As Peter Onuf concludes, "justly celebrated as a landmark in the libertarian tradition," and as central to the Jeffersonian vision, Jefferson's "Inaugural Address calls for political as well as religious toleration." For Jefferson, the two were codependent and transcendent.[42]

A commitment to the separation of church and state and to religious freedom helped define the Republican Party. Jeffersonians envisioned a republican government based on freedom of the mind, for which religious freedom, including the separation of church and state, was essential. While Jeffersonians in power may have disagreed about many things, in the area of religious freedom, principle provided a consistent foundation for their politics and policies.

Notes

1. Thomas Jefferson to Danbury Baptist Association, Jan. 1, 1802; Thomas Jefferson to Levy Lincoln, Jan. 1, 1802; Thomas Jefferson to James Madison, Dec. 16, 1786; Thomas Jefferson to Benjamin Rush, Sept. 23, 1800, in Julian P. Boyd et al., eds., *The Papers of Thomas Jefferson* (Princeton, N.J., 1950–), 34:258; 36:256; 10:604; 32:168 (hereafter *PTJ*).

2. *A Test of the Religious Principles of Mr. Jefferson* (Philadelphia, 1800), ii. See also *A Test of the Religious Principles of Mr. Jefferson* (Philadelphia, 1800), i–ii; *A Test of the Religious Principles, of Mr. Jefferson* (Easton, Md., 1800); and *A Test of the Religious*

Principles of Thomas Jefferson (Pittsfield, Mass., 1800). *Republican Notes on Religion, and an Act Establishing Religious Freedom, Passed in the Assembly of Virginia, in the Year 1786, by Thomas Jefferson* (Danbury, Conn., 1803); *New-Hampshire Patriot and State Gazette* (Concord), Sept. 22, 1842; "An Address by Dr. Richard Fry in Otsego, NY on July 4, 1831," *The Watchtower* (Cooperstown, N.Y.), July 18, 1831.

3. There is a voluminous literature on Jefferson and religious freedom. See, e.g., John Ragosta, *Religious Freedom: Jefferson's Legacy, America's Creed* (Charlottesville, Va., 2013); Mark David Hall, "Madison's Memorial and Remonstrance, Jefferson's Statute for Religious Liberty, and the Creation of the First Amendment," *American Political Thought* 3, no. 1 (Spring 2014): 32–63; Johann N. Neem, "Beyond the Wall: Reinterpreting Jefferson's Danbury Address," *Journal of the Early Republic* 27 (Spring 2007): 139–54; Edwin S. Gaustad, *Faith of the Founders: Religion and the New Nation, 1776–1826* (Waco, Tex., 2004); and Paul Rasor and Richard E. Bond, eds., *From Jamestown to Jefferson: The Evolution of Religious Freedom in Virginia* (Charlottesville, Va., 2011), and works cited therein.

This chapter is not about significant developments in Jefferson's own religious views during the latter part of the 1790s and the years of his presidency, when he increasingly embraced the ethical teachings of Jesus, explaining that Jesus's philosophy was superior to others' because it emphasized loving ones' neighbors and enemies. One might interestingly explore the parallel with Jefferson's desire to create a functioning polity in a broadening democracy, but that is beyond the scope of this essay. See generally Ragosta, *Religious Freedom,* 7–39, esp. 9 and works cited therein.

4. See, for example, Jefferson to James Smith, Dec. 8, 1822, in Albert Ellery Bergh, ed., *The Writings of Thomas Jefferson* (Washington, D.C., 1905), 15:409.

5. James Madison, "Detached Memorandum," in "Aspects of Monopoly One Hundred Years Ago," *Harper's Magazine,* March 1914, 494.

6. Jefferson to Rev. Samuel Miller, Jan. 23, 1808, in Paul Leicester Ford, ed., *The Writings of Thomas Jefferson* (New York, 1892), 9:174–75; Madison, "Detached Memorandum," 494.

Jefferson's understanding stands in sharp contradistinction to arguments made by Justices Clarence Thomas and Antonin Scalia that to violate the First Amendment, government must essentially compel action through force or fines. See, e.g., *Town of Greece v. Galloway,* slip op. 12–696, 572 U.S. ___ (2014) (Thomas and Scalia concurring in part), 6–7 ("force of law and threat of penalty"), quoting *Lee v. Weisman,* 505 U.S. 577, 640 (1992) (Scalia dissenting). The narrow view of coercion seems unrealistic, certainly to those most likely to be subject to implicit coercion, and is inconsistent with Jefferson's vision.

7. James D. Richardson, ed., *A Compilation of the Messages and Papers of the Presidents* (Washington, D.C., 1897), 1:314, 330, 367–68. Richardson's text, as have others, seems to capitalize terms that Jefferson did not. See Ragosta, *Religious Freedom,* xii. Similarly, in his first inaugural, Madison prayed and articulated as a governmental principle "to avoid the slightest interference with the right of conscience or the functions of religion, so wisely exempted from civil jurisdiction." Ibid., 1:452.

8. *The Witness* (Litchfield, Conn.), Oct. 2, 1805. That paper does make perhaps too much of Jefferson's support of religion, but the fundamental distinction between official action and the action of an official, even when public, is recognized.

9. Daniel Dreisbach, *Thomas Jefferson and the Wall of Separation between Church and State* (New York, 2002), 57. The courts make essentially the same distinction in declaring unconstitutional official invocations at public school graduations but permitting a valedictorian, a private individual, albeit speaking at a public event, to include prayers (but not proselytizing). See *Lee v. Weisman,* 505 U.S. 577 (1992); *Cole v. Oroville Union High School District,* 228 F.3d 1092 (9th Cir. 2000); and *Adler v. Duval County,* 250 F.3d 1330 (11th Cir. 2001), cert. denied, 122 S. Ct. 664 (2001).

10. Albert Gallatin to Jefferson, July 25, 1801; Jefferson to Gallatin, July 26, 1801, in *PTJ,* 34:636, 644.

11. Jeremy D. Bailey, *Thomas Jefferson and Executive Power* (New York, 2010), 230n18, citing Jeffrey Tulis, *The Rhetorical Presidency* (Princeton, N.J., 1987), 52.

12. *McCollum v. Board of Education,* 333 U.S. 203, 238 (1948) (Jackson concurring).

13. Madison, "Detached Memorandum," 495.

14. See, for example, James Hutson, *Religion and the Founding of the American Republic* (Washington, D.C., 1998): 89. This pattern is interesting: Justices William Rehnquist and Clarence Thomas sought to distance religious freedom from Jefferson in an effort to distance the First Amendment from the wall of separation. See, e.g., *Wallace v. Jaffree,* 472 U.S. 38, 99 (1985) (Rehnquist dissenting), and *Elk Grove v. Newdow,* 542 U.S. 1, 45–46 (2004) (Thomas concurring). Others have tried to claim Jefferson's legacy for the same purpose. Perhaps the most notorious example is David Barton's aptly named *Jefferson Lies,* a bestselling volume that the publisher had to take off the market because of its numerous inaccuracies. David Barton, *Jefferson Lies: Exposing the Myths You've Always Believed about Thomas Jefferson* (Nashville, Tenn., 2012). See, e.g., "'The Jefferson Lies' Is Recalled by Publisher Thomas Nelson," *Christian Science Monitor,* Aug. 13, 2012.

15. *Annals of Congress,* House of Representatives, 11th Cong., 3rd sess., Feb. 21, 1811, 22:985.

16. Madison, "To the House of Representatives," Feb. 21, 1811, in Robert A. Rutland et al., eds., *The Papers of James Madison, Presidential Series* (Charlottesville, Va., 1984–), 3:176 (hereafter *PJM-PS*). See also *The Debates and Proceedings of the Congress of the United States,* 11th Cong., 3rd sess. (Washington, D.C., 1853), 982–85, http://www.constitution.org/jm/jm_estab.htm; 2 Stat. 356. Madison discusses wealth accumulation by religious organizations in his "Detached Memorandum," 492–93. See by contrast Donald L. Drakeman, *Church, State, and Original Intent* (New York, 2000), 284–85. Drakeman argues that Senator Andrew Johnson, supporting incorporation of D.C. Baptists, acted inconsistently with Madison.

17. *Annals of Congress,* House of Representatives, 6th Cong., 2nd sess., Dec. 4, 1800, 10:797. The work of the House was not interrupted by the services; as Margaret Bayard Smith noted with some indignity, a clerk would often walk to the front of the room during services to collect letters posted by House members for delivery. Margaret

Bayard Smith, *The First Forty Years of Washington Society,* ed. Gaillard Hunt (New York, 1906), 14.

18. Smith, *Forty Years,* 15. Services were also held for a period in the Treasury and War offices. See Wilhelmus Bogart Bryan, *A History of the National Capital from Its Formation through the Period of the Adoption of the Organic Act,* vol. 1, *1790–1814* (New York, 1914), 382. Some have attempted to dismiss the House services because the event was more social than religious. Chris Rodda, *Liars for Jesus: The Religious Right's Alternative Version of American History* (North Charleston, S.C., 2006), 445–46. This, though, should make little difference; the government can hardly be asked to gauge the religiosity of a church gathering before deciding whether to permit it to use public facilities.

19. James Sterling Young, *The Washington Community, 1800–1828* (New York, 1967), 72, quoting Smith, *Forty Years,* 95; Bryan, *History of the National Capital,* 1:408; *Annals of Congress,* House of Representatives, 7th Cong., 1st sess. (March 31, 1802), 11:1119; *National Intelligencer* (Washington, D.C.), June 29, 1801, 3.

20. Jefferson, Minutes of the Board of Visitors, Oct. 7, 1822, in Bergh, ed., *Writings,* 19:414–16. Jefferson's treatment of religion in the formation of the University of Virginia is discussed in Ragosta, *Religious Freedom,* 193–98.

21. See, for example, *Rosenberger v. University of Virginia,* 515 U.S. 819 (1995); *Lamb's Chapel v. Center Moriches Union Free School District,* 508 U.S. 384 (1993); and *Trinity Lutheran Church v. Comer,* slip-op. 15–577 (June 26, 2017).

22. Compare Daniel Dreisbach, *Real Threat and Mere Shadow: Religious Liberty and the First Amendment* (Westchester, Ill., 1987), 75, and Robert L. Cord, "Founding Intentions and the Establishment Clause: Harmonizing Accommodation and Separation," *Harvard Journal of Law and Public Policy* 10, no. 1 (1987): 51.

23. *Message of the President of the United States Transmitting a Treaty Lately Concluded between the United States and the Kaskaskia Tribe of Indians* (Washington, D.C., Nov. 25, 1803). See, e.g., William Henry Harrison to Henry Dearborn, July 15, 1801, in Logan Esarey, ed., *Governors Messages and Letters* (Indianapolis, 1922–24), 1:29–30, and Dearborn to Harrison, Apr. 20, 1807, in Clarence Edwin Carter, ed., *The Territorial Papers of the United States* (Washington, D.C., 1939), 7:447. See also Dearborn to Harrison, May 13, 1808, in Carter, ed., *Territorial Papers,* 7:568, and *Reuben Quick Bear v. Leupp,* 210 U.S. 50 (1908).

24. Madison, Memorandum to Jefferson, ca. Oct. 1, 1803, in Robert J. Brugger et al., eds., *The Papers of James Madison, Secretary of State Series* (Charlottesville, Va., 1986–), 5:480; Madison, Third Annual Message (Oct. 17, 1803), in Richardson, ed., *Compilation of the Messages,* 1:347, emphasis added. Jefferson's draft message on which Madison commented has not been found.

25. James A. Davids, "Putting Faith in Prison Programs, and Its Constitutionality under Thomas Jefferson's Faith-Based Initiative," *Ave Maria Law Review* 6, no. 2 (Spring 2008): 341, 377.

26. *The Debates and Proceedings of the Congress of the United States,* 11th Cong., 3rd sess., 366, http://www.constitution.org/jm/jm_estab.htm; Madison to Jesse Jones and others, June 3, 1811, in *PJM-PS,* 3:324.

27. Jefferson to the General Assembly of Rhode Island and Providence Plantations, May 26, 1801, in *PTJ*, 34:188–89.

28. Peter S. Onuf, "'We Shall All Be Americans': Thomas Jefferson and the Indians," *Indiana Magazine of History* 95, no. 2 (June 1999): 111; Jefferson to Gideon Granger, Aug. 13, 1800, in *PTJ*, 32:96.

29. Danbury Baptist Association to Jefferson, after Oct. 7, 1801, in *PTJ*, 35:408.

30. Jefferson to Levi Lincoln, Jan. 1, 1802, in *PTJ*, 36:256; Ragosta, *Religious Freedom*, 256–58n12; Bailey, *Thomas Jefferson and Executive Power*, 226.

31. Henry Adams, *History of the United States of America during the First Administration of Thomas Jefferson* (New York, 1921), 1:314–15.

32. Pierpont Edwards to Jefferson, May 12, 1801; Jefferson to Edwards, July 21, 1801, in *PTJ*, 34:92, 606–7.

33. See Charles A. Heckman, "A Jeffersonian Lawyer and Judge in Federalist Connecticut: The Career of Pierpont Edwards," *Connecticut Law Review* 28 (Spring 1996): 674; Ragosta, *Religious Freedom*, 135; Oath of Fidelity, in Donald S. Lutz, ed., *Colonial Origins of the American Constitution: A Documentary History* (Indianapolis, 1998), http://oll.libertyfund.org/titles/694.

34. Levi Lincoln to Jefferson, July 28, 1801; Jefferson to Lincoln, Aug. 26, 1801, in *PTJ*, 34:660; 35:147.

35. Merrill D. Peterson, *Thomas Jefferson and the New Nation: A Biography* (New York, 1975), 802; Adams, *History of the United States*, 1:605; Barbara Oberg, "Presidential Address: Decoding an American Icon: The Textuality of Thomas Jefferson," *Text* 15 (2003): 11.

36. See, for example, *Elk Grove v. Newdow*, 542 U.S. 1, 45–46 (2004) (Thomas concurring). See Ragosta, *Religious Freedom*, 134–40.

37. *Columbian Centinel* (Boston), Mar. 23, 1808. See the discussion in Thomas C. Amory, *Life of James Sullivan: With Selections from His Writings* (Boston, 1892), 2:209–10, and Anson Phelps Stokes and Lew Pfeiffer, *Church and State in the United States*, rev. ed. (1950; New York, 1964), 178–79. W. A. Robinson, *Jeffersonian Democracy in New England* (New Haven, Conn., 1916), 147, 78, 149, quoting *Dartmouth Gazette*, Nov. 18, 1807.

38. Madison, "Detached Memorandum," 492. For a discussion of the Detached Memorandum, see Founders Online, National Archives, Washington, D.C., http://founders.archives.gov/documents/Madison/04-01-02-0548.

39. See, e.g., Paul E. Lauer, *Church and State in New England* (Baltimore, 1892), 99–105. After the long-sought Republican political success in Connecticut, for example, Joshua Stow, a local Jeffersonian, wrote to Madison and Jefferson declaring that the success of Republicans against Federalists had defeated the religious and political "Hierarchy and Aristocracy." Stow to Madison, Sept. 20, 1817, in David B. Mattern et al., eds., *The Papers of James Madison, Retirement Series* (Charlottesville, Va., 2009–), 1:133.

40. See, e.g., generally Steven K. Green, *The Bible, the School, and the Constitution: The Clash That Shaped Modern Church-State Doctrine* (New York, 2012).

41. Johann N. Neem, "A Republican Reformation: Thomas Jefferson's Civil Religion and the Separation of Church and State," in *A Companion to Thomas Jefferson,* ed. Frank Cogliano (Malden, Mass., 2012): 92; Stanley Griswold, *Truth Its Own Test and God Its Only Judge; or, An Inquiry, How Far Men May Claim Authority over Each Other's Religious Opinions?* (Bridgeport, Conn., 1800), 18. For Jefferson's religious views, see Ragosta, *Religious Freedom,* 7–39.

42. Peter S. Onuf, *Jefferson's Empire: The Language of American Nationhood* (Charlottesville, Va., 2000), 93.

4 Beyond Strict Construction

Jeffersonians in the 1790s

Mark Smith

The scholarly depiction of Republicans in the 1790s often paints Thomas Jefferson and those of his persuasion, in Congress or in the partisan press, as objecting to Federalist policies because those policies violated Republican interpretations of the Constitution. Overly concerned with a strict interpretation of the Constitution, Jeffersonians fought Federalists as they attempted to institute policies such as the Bank of the United States, neutrality in the wars of the French Revolution, and the Alien and Sedition Acts. Historians have argued that Jeffersonians and their namesake violated those same principles when they assumed power in the subsequent decade, abandoning their previous constitutional beliefs with bold acts of statecraft such as the purchase of the Louisiana Territory and the passage and enforcement of the Embargo Act. Marked as adhering to strict construction in one decade, Jeffersonians are tarnished as hypocrites for abandoning their principles when they assumed executive and legislative power in the next.

Yet the strict constructionism label imposes too much rigidity on a diverse group and, more importantly, fails to see the full spectrum of Republican objections to Federalist policy proposals in the 1790s. Republicans in that decade surely critiqued Federalist policies for their broad interpretation of the Constitution, but Jeffersonians did more than howl for strict construction. They proposed a complex web of principles and policies in the decade before they assumed full executive and legislative power. Identifying Jeffersonians too closely with the arguments of strict construction miscasts the nature of their persuasion.

To explore that web of principles and policies, this essay focuses on three partisan debates in the 1790s—the Bank of the United States, the Neutrality

Proclamation, and the Alien and Sedition Acts. In all three cases, Jeffersonian arguments demonstrate a diverse group of ideas interacting with one another as the nascent party struggled to find cohesion and define itself. Of course, in each of those debates, there were Jeffersonians (including Jefferson himself) who argued along constitutional lines, but they also went far beyond those kinds of arguments, not just in a vain attempt to defeat Federalist proposals but because Republicans found Federalist policies objectionable for many reasons. During debates over a national bank, Jeffersonians went well beyond a constitutional critique, arguing that Federalist policies would hinder American economic development and the happiness of American citizens. Amid the foreign policy debates regarding the French Revolution, Jeffersonians were deeply concerned about projections of American power (or lack thereof), the impact that American policies would have on enemies and allies, and the moral implications of failing to aid a former ally. Finally, while debating the Alien and Sedition Acts, Jeffersonians demonstrated not only a vision for American immigration policy but also an overarching belief in the necessity of a marketplace of ideas and a fear of monarchy. The views of American society and of American politics that emerged from the Republican critique of Federalist policies reveal that Republicans had a wide array of positions in the 1790s—and that array transcends the simple portrait of Republicans as strict constructionist hypocrites who abandoned their principles when they gained power.

When Republicans and Federalists argued over matters of policy and governance, they were disagreeing about what best served the interests of the United States and its citizens. These policy concerns were not entirely separate from the Republican concept of strict construction. Rather, they were part of an overall Republican policy mindset that found fault with Federalist proposals along financial, moral, and philosophical, as well as constitutional, grounds. This essay explores that mindset and its implications, restoring those concerns to their rightful place in the Jeffersonian canon and revealing the policy dimensions of Jeffersonian politics in the 1790s alongside their strict constructionism.

Understanding Republicans in this light puts their later policies when in power in sharper focus. Their foreign policy attempts (the Louisiana Purchase, the Embargo, the Barbary Wars) as well as their domestic policies (lowering internal taxes, instituting internal improvements such as the Cumberland Road) served some of the same policies and principles that they had advocated in the 1790s. Assuming the mantle of legislative and executive authority, then, Republicans did not alter their principles and abandon their strict constructionism. They were staying true to their overall policy mindset. In short, Jeffersonians may have been strict constructionists in the 1790s, but that is not all they were.

The partisan debates over Alexander Hamilton's 1790 proposal for a national bank featured Republicans offering objections on strict construction grounds as well as on matters of policy. The constitutional objections that they offered in the halls of Congress, in the press, and in private communications to President George Washington concerned enumerated powers, abuse of the necessary and proper clause, and the importance of the reserved clause.[1] Republicans, however, also raised policy objections alongside constitutional ones. As early as the bank debates, then, Republicans were formulating specific policy complaints about the Federalist platform that highlighted their concern with individual freedoms and unfair economic advantages.

The Republican challenges to Hamilton's bank bill on strict construction grounds are well known and easily summarized.[2] Georgia congressman James Jackson noted that the bank bill "contravenes the spirit of the Constitution." Michael Stone from Maryland agreed that there was no expressed power that could support the bank bill, and Virginian William Giles warned of "sophistical deduction" in the Federalists' attempts to expand the necessary and proper clause.[3] James Madison's close reading of the Constitution found that "it was not possible to discover in it the power to incorporate a Bank." Insisting that the government was predicated on "limited and enumerated powers," Madison examined the necessary and proper clause and cited examples from state constitutions to demonstrate the importance and strength of the notion of reserved powers. Hamilton's desire for a bank, Madison reasoned, "could not even be called necessary to the Government; at most it could be but convenient."[4] Republicans in newspapers continued the assault on the constitutionality of the bank proposal.

Although the partisan press was just developing at this time, Republican polemicists and editors aggressively used it to voice their strong constitutional objections.[5] They objected to the use of the necessary and proper clause, the notion that Congress possessed powers beyond what the Constitution enumerated, and the idea that the congressional power to charter the bank stemmed from Congress's exclusive jurisdiction over the capital city. They insisted that powers not specified were retained by state governments, who could charter banks if they saw fit to.[6] Although his newspaper, the *National Gazette,* did not begin publication until after the passage of the bank bill, Philip Freneau fanned the flames of the controversy well after other printers had lost interest in the debate, arguing that the Bank of the United States was "repugnant to the genius and spirit of the federal constitution" because it was "grounded on the favorite new assumed doctrine of Discretion and the undefined Powers of Congress."[7]

While congressmen and polemicists attacked the bank on constitutional grounds, Jefferson did the same in communication with Washington. When, having voted along sectional lines, Congress passed the bank bill to the president for his signature, Washington solicited opinions from Jefferson and Hamilton on its constitutionality.[8] Jefferson's objections demonstrated his commitment to a strict interpretation of the Constitution: "The incorporation of a bank, and the powers assumed by this bill, have not, in my opinion, been delegated to the United States, by the Constitution."[9] Jefferson's view of federalism was predicated on a limited federal authority with maximum power saved for the peripheral states, a view that echoed Republican arguments in Congress and the press.[10]

Concerns about the constitutionality of the bank, however, were not the only objections Jeffersonians offered. Throughout the debates, they offered policy-based objections as well, arguing against the bank's financial necessity and its implications for American economic development. These policy arguments were not offered out of desperation to defeat the bill; they were forcefully argued and supported, and Federalists took them seriously and responded. All told, in Congress, in the press, and in Jefferson's report to Washington, Republicans harped on three main policy objections. First, they critiqued the utility of banks in general and this one in particular. Second, they warned that this bill would provide the merchant class with a particular economic advantage. Finally, even though most of his essay was concerned with his constitutional objections to the bank bill, even Jefferson himself demonstrated arguments that transcended his constitutional objections and strove at policy objections and other deeply held principles that the bank bill would contradict. The bank debates clearly demonstrate that nonconstitutional, or policy, stances concerned Republicans just as much as constitutional qualms did.

In all forums, Republicans critiqued the need for the bill, believing that the previously established Bank of North America was already doing everything that the new national bank allegedly would do.[11] Debating the "advantages and disadvantages of Banks" on February 2, 1791, in the House, Madison argued that "the most important advantages would be better obtained by several Banks properly distributed than by a single one."[12] Other congressmen noted that the existence of large national banks in Venice, Amsterdam, France, and Great Britain did not justify the need for a similar bank in the American republic with its very different needs.[13] In his final speech on the bill, just before the vote on February 8, Madison listed numerous other objections, including the way in which the bill regulated creditors and the amount of profit the public could expect to receive from it. Madison's final objection was that the bill delegated to the president the power to create subordinate banks, a power, in Madison's possibly exaggerated estimation, that "ought not be delegated to any set of men under Heaven."[14]

Republican newspapers echoed Madison's arguments about a national bank and banks in general. Writing in Benjamin Franklin Bache's *General Advertiser,* one polemicist questioned the "utility" of the bank, arguing that the English version had left that nation in an "embarrassed state," and citing both David Hume and Thomas Paine as authorities against national banks. Continuing that the nation ought not "so rudely to dismiss so old and faithful a servant," the author believed that the Bank of North America and other state banks should be allowed to grow and serve the purposes that Hamilton had proposed for the Bank of the United States.[15] "Cash or no cash, banks of deposit we shall have in abundance," argued another polemicist.[16] Federalists took such objections seriously; Elbridge Gerry, Fisher Ames, Theodore Sedgwick, John Lawrence, and Elias Boudinot of New Jersey all defended the utility of banks.[17]

The financial implications of the bill's passage also concerned the Jeffersonians. Regardless of its questionable constitutionality, Republicans strongly believed that the Bank of the United States would provide a distinct economic advantage to one part of American society at the expense of another. Representative James Jackson of Georgia felt it was "calculated to benefit a small part of the United States, the mercantile interest only; the farmers, the yeomanry, will derive no advantage from it."[18] Maryland representative Michael Stone hinted at a growing divide between the states, arguing that the law was designed "to raise the value of Continental paper," and accused eastern "manufacturers of this country" of endeavoring "to strengthen the hands of a Government by which they are so peculiarly benefited."[19] A writer in the *New York Daily Gazette* wondered if putting power in the national bank based in Philadelphia was a part of a Federalist plot to support the new capital city to the detriment of other states.[20] Madison also worried that the advantages of a bank would flow disproportionately to the merchant classes, and that "the genius of Monarchy favored the concentration of wealth and influence in the metropolis."[21]

Madison continued this line of reasoning when asked by Washington to draft a potential veto message (which would have been Washington's first). In his response, Madison perfectly blended Republican constitutional as well as policy objections.[22] In one paragraph, he listed the violation of the expressed and delegated powers clauses as the reason for the presidential veto. He immediately followed this objection with a paragraph listing economic complaints and class inequalities as further reasons for the veto.[23] Although Madison's draft did not persuade the president, it illuminates that Republicans were thinking deeply about policy concerns in addition to constitutional ones.

Republican polemicists took Madison's arguments a step further by showing their readers that the national debt and stock capitalization plans of the new bank were potentially damaging to the new nation because they favored the financial elite.[24] Starting from the general point that Hamilton had established "systems that have already produced consequences most pernicious to the interests, honor, and happiness of our country," "Caius" predicted that "seas of corruption will, if pursued, overwhelm and destroy in their poisonous current, every free and valuable principle of our government." The bank would lead to "inequality, corruption and oppression" because it would "produce the ambitious sacrifice of the *many* to the aggrandizement of the *few.*" Caius was also concerned that, in conjunction with other parts of Hamilton's financial plan, the bank would contribute to the "*consolidation* and the *annihilation* of the *state governments.*"[25] Caius cautioned readers that Hamilton and his "junto" were trying to mimic the British system to the detriment of the American people. Federalists, according to Caius, were advocating the "mistaken policy of engrafting upon the American constitution, healthful, young, and vigorous, all the weaknesses, vice, and infirmities of the decayed and expiring constitution of Britain."[26]

Caius was not alone. Numerous other newspapers criticized the bank plan as a wealth transfer. The *New Hampshire Gazette* noted that the bank "may be justly considered as a proposition made to the monied interest," and that "the terms are so advantageous that no equal object of speculation is perhaps presented in any quarter of the globe."[27] Wrapping suspicions of the "monied influence" from the public debt and speculation into the "ill-fated policy" that was the bank, one polemicist critiqued its "baseness, in fraud and in swindling." The bank was a policy designed for "throwing magnificent wealth into the hands of a favorite few."[28] A satirical advertisement in Boston's *Independent Chronicle* went further: "Wanted: A number of Stock-Jobbers, Speculators, and Negotiators for the purpose of aiding and assisting certain members of the Robin-Hood Society [that is, Congress] in accomplishing their foreign contracts."[29] Pointing at the bank's alleged favoritism of the moneyed class, Jeffersonians here voiced objections to its impact on American society at large, showing particular concern for the people at large for whom the Jeffersonians claimed to speak.

Republicans like Freneau continued to critique the bank bill's passage throughout 1792. Noting his readers' continued anger about it, Freneau published four more objections on Independence Day 1792, raising the revolutionary chant of taxation without representation and repeating the claim that the United States was following the British example.[30] Later in the year, Freneau printed a polemic that noted, "Some members of a late Congress invented a kind of machinery, called a Bank, and contrived to have the shares filled up in one day, to exclude the greater part of the community, and to raise mountains of wealth for themselves, and a few others."[31] Fearful of a creeping Hamiltonianism predicated on a national policy vision that privileged the merchant class, Freneau and Republican journalists fanned the flames of the controversy long after the Bank of the United States began operations, and they did so by continually raising policy objections.

The third way in which Republicans fought the idea of a national bank on policy grounds actually stemmed from Jefferson himself. Long credited for articulating the strict constructionist viewpoint in his opinion written for George Washington, Jefferson actually began his report opposing the bank by noting other laws, beliefs, and principles that the bill violated, citing monopoly, by giving the bank "the sole and exclusive right of banking under the national authority"; alienage, "to make alien subscribers capable of holding lands"; forfeiture, "to put the lands out of reach of forfeiture"; and mortmain, "to enable them in their corporate capacities to receive grants of land."[32] Clearly, Jefferson was arguing to Washington that the bank bill was poor policy in addition to being unconstitutional.

Interestingly, while Jefferson opposed the bank bill on strict construction as well as policy grounds, a potential veto of it challenged another of Jefferson's key principles. Although he was decidedly opposed to the bank, Jefferson told Washington that the use of the veto should not seek to overcome what the legislature had passed unless they were "misled by error, ambition, or interest." Jefferson cautioned the president to defer to "the wisdom of the legislature."[33] In addition to his strict constructionist argument, Jefferson sought to protect the supremacy of the legislature, another important principle to him.[34] When ideals that he held dear—strict construction and legislative supremacy—collided, Jefferson was able to bend his strict construction leanings. In the debates over the bank bill, then, Jeffersonians of all stripes went far beyond straight constitutional arguments. They concerned themselves with policy issues that could have a profound impact on national statecraft and American society as a whole.

The debates over the bill were not the only place that Republicans explored their policy objections. As the wars of the French Revolution engulfed Europe, American foreign and domestic policy became inexorably linked. Americans who had begun splitting into partisan groups during the bank debates found themselves in similar camps with the same opponents as foreign policy concerns drove domestic political concerns. The execution of Louis XVI, the subsequent war between France and Britain, and the arrival in Philadelphia of Citizen Edmond-Charles Genet forced Washington's cabinet to consider the proper course of action for the new nation. Following his previous script, Washington solicited opinions from Hamilton and Jefferson on whether the nation should uphold or abrogate the French treaties of 1778.[35] Those discussions culminated in Washington's decision to issue a presidential proclamation on April 22, 1793, declaring that the nation would "pursue a conduct friendly and impartial towards the belligerent powers."[36] The debates surrounding this proclamation once again show Republicans offering strict construction arguments—that the president had no constitutional authority to issue such a proclamation. But as they demonstrated in the bank debates, Republicans also offered other objections to Washington's proclamation, namely that he had rejected the will of the people, which ought to reign supreme; that the proclamation violated international law;

and that the president had not taken the opportunity to assist the nation that had helped the United States win the Revolutionary War.

In these debates, the Jeffersonians' constitutional objection to Washington's proclamation was clear: the president lacked the specific executive power to issue such a document. "A Uniform Federalist" charged that Hamilton and Washington must have had to "search the constitution" for the "Executive power" that allowed the president to issue the proclamation because "a duty imposed to execute the laws should involve the right to control or dispense with their execution."[37] While other Republican essayists argued that Washington (and Hamilton) had overstepped their constitutional limits, no objection was reprinted more than the series of essays that Madison wrote under the name "Helvidius."[38] Although Madison sketched the arguments of governmental theorists such as John Locke, Montesquieu, and Emer de Vattel, paying most attention to Locke's "federative" claim, Madison perfectly espoused the Republican strict constructionist view.[39] Arguing that the president had infringed on a legislative power, Madison examined the constitutional powers to wage war, receive ambassadors, make and keep treaties, and issue proclamations.[40]

Responding to a series of essays that Hamilton had written under the pseudonym "Pacificus," Madison challenged the constitutionality of the proclamation, but in so doing, his writings demonstrate a clear Jeffersonian policy objective: to cultivate the marketplace of ideas in which newspaper editors would serve as the vigilant guardians for the republic.[41] Although Jefferson had hired Freneau at the State Department, thereby subsidizing his newspaper, Jefferson did not like to write for the press.[42] Despite his squeamishness at entering the public fray, Jefferson was not above frantically urging Madison to confront his former polemical partner Hamilton. "For God's sake, my dear Sir," Jefferson implored Madison, "take up your pen, select the most striking of the heresies, and cut him to pieces in the face of the public."[43] Madison complied. Republicans across the country saw the press debate as a necessary alternative to a government debate that Federalists allegedly had stifled. "Philoveritas" summed up the issue for many Republicans, writing, "thus are those who question the legality and propriety of the President's Proclamation styled 'desperados' who wish to plunge the United States into war."[44]

Republican objections to the proclamation, however, went far beyond questions about its constitutionality. They questioned the policy behind the proclamation as much as they questioned Washington's constitutional authority to issue it. The president had ignored the people's wishes, they argued, and his decision was likely to harm American relations with France. Unlike the previous debate over the bank bill, in his letter to Washington about the proclamation, Jefferson rebutted the treasury secretary's arguments without leaning on a strict interpretation of the Constitution. In contrast to Hamilton's belief that the French alteration of their head of state meant that Americans could abrogate their treaty commitments, Jefferson considered "the people who constitute a society or nation as the source of all authority in that nation." Jefferson did not ascribe this authority to the Constitution, instead deferring to his understanding of the law of nations. Jefferson stressed the "moral law of our nature," "moral feelings and the reason of all honest men," and quoted Hugo Grotius, Samuel von Puffendorf, Christian Wolf, and Vattel as his authorities, not the Constitution.[45]

Along similar lines, although Jefferson understood that Washington could not aid France in its war, for the consequences would surely be disastrous for the young nation, Jefferson did not believe that the treaties could be overturned because their neglect posed no "danger" to the United States and were neither "useless or disagreeable." In fact, he feared that abrogating the treaties at this time would be "giving just cause of war to France."[46] Demonstrating his full command of the foreign and domestic policy issues in play, Jefferson also privately noted to Madison that the newly arrived French minister Genet was making defending France "immensely difficult" through his conduct.[47] At no time in his report to Washington or in his letter to Madison did Jefferson question Washington's constitutional right to issue a proclamation concerning the situation. Jefferson examined the wisdom of the policy and the way in which it adhered to international law, not the president's constitutional authority to issue it.

Like Jefferson, Republican polemicists also stressed the policy matters inherent in Washington's proclamation, in addition to noting constitutional issues. "Secretarius," "Truth," and "A Republican" avoided discussing the constitutionality of the proclamation, and instead objected to abandoning the French, who had proved so helpful to the nation during the Revolution. "Philadelphius" drove the point home: Americans should assist the French because they had aided America in the Revolution: "The money came out of the pockets of the [French] people: it was made out of the labor of their hands and the sweat of their brows."[48] "A Democrat" even admitted that the president had the constitutional authority to issue the proclamation but insisted that doing so was contrary to the national interest.[49] Taking a different approach, "Ionotus" focused on public opinion, noting that 90 percent of Americans were "friendly to the French Revolution from principle" and that Washington was "Ignorant" of their desires—suggesting that Washington's proclamation violated republican principles.[50] "A Bunker's Hill Man" also argued along republican lines, stressing that the few republics in the world needed to stay loyal to one another.[51]

In one of the most widely reprinted series of essays, "Veritas" focused on this republican argument. Noting that the proclamation was not in America's interest, Veritas argued that the American people had a historical connection to the French and that Washington had violated that link.[52] Veritas further argued that the proclamation was not in America's "interest."[53] Veritas expressed numerous times that the real problem with the proclamation was that Washington had ignored the people's wishes. Reminding readers that in America, unlike Britain, what the people thought mattered, Veritas wrote, "It ought never to be forgotten by our magistrates that popular opinion is the basis of our government."[54] In the final essay in the series, Veritas summarized the argument: "My sole object when I began this essay was to show the necessity of canvassing public measures with a manly freedom, without suffering our judgment or integrity to be warped by the slavish influence of great names." Objecting to the way in which Washington's and Hamilton's prestige (rather than reasoned argument) had been bandied about to support the proclamation, Veritas supported a vigorous and open marketplace of ideas, hoping that the names of "court-writers" would not "deter individuals . . . from a free investigation of public measures." Defending the legislative superiority that was never far from Republican minds, Veritas hoped that "the representatives of the people, who can alone express the national will" would soon speak on the matter.[55]

During the debates over Washington's Neutrality Proclamation, then, Republicans were *more* focused on policy objections than they were on constitutional objections. Republican foreign policy, as articulated in these objections, not only favored France as an ally over Great Britain but also aimed at asserting the will of the people as well as the role of the legislature in assisting the president's crafting of foreign policy. As they had in the bank debates, some Republicans offered strict construction arguments, but others moved beyond those constitutional complaints, demonstrating diversity in the group's thoughts and approaches.

In the end, Republicans forced Federalists to defend both the constitutionality of Washington's actions and the wisdom of his policy choice. In defending the proclamation, for example, Hamilton addressed the Republican complaint that it was "without authority" but spent long stretches of his argument discussing whether the proclamation was "contrary to our treaties with France," "contrary to the gratitude" the Americans owed the French, and "out of time and unnecessary."[56] The debate over this issue, like the bank bill debates before it and the Alien and Sedition debates after it, entailed both policy and strict constitutional issues.

Five years after the proclamation debates, Federalists seized on the XYZ Affair as an opportunity to smash their Republican opposition. Embarrassed and reeling from the revelations that French diplomacy was not as virtuous as they had hoped, Republicans presented themselves as targets for Federalist legislative wrath. In a bold series of laws designed to stifle Republican supporters, Federalists aimed to crush the Republican opposition in time for the election of 1800 with the Alien and Sedition Acts.[57] In the debates that followed, Republicans submitted their standard strict construction argument: that the Constitution provided no enumerated power to regulate the immigration of aliens and that the First Amendment barred Congress from limiting free speech. They also, however, set forth four main policy arguments—that the laws would limit American freedom and encourage despotism, that the laws would have a chilling impact on immigration, that the laws would ultimately harm the marketplace of ideas, and that Federalists were exaggerating the foreign threat.

As they had in previous debates, members of Congress, newspaper editors, and Jefferson himself offered strict constructionist arguments to defeat the proposed laws. In Congress, Republican Edward Livingston of New York called the Alien Friends Act a "miserable mockery of justice" for it contravened the Constitution's limitations on federal power.[58] Quoting from *The Federalist* as well as from James Wilson's notes from the Constitutional Convention, and closely reading the Constitution's reserve clause and article 1, section 8, clause 1, Albert Gallatin remarked that the general welfare clause was not separated from the power to tax because then "there would have been no need to have enumerated the powers given the Congress."[59]

Republicans in the press echoed the various arguments forwarded by their congressional counterparts. Benjamin Franklin Bache printed that the laws were "in direct violation of the Constitution."[60] Thomas Greenleaf wondered whether the sponsor of the bill, Federalist senator James Lloyd from Maryland, was "exempted from his oath" to defend the Constitution when he proposed a law that violated the First Amendment.[61] In the Kentucky Resolutions—responding to the Alien and Sedition Acts—Jefferson began by offering the strict constructionist view that he had put forth before.[62] He repeatedly submitted that the Tenth Amendment's transfer of nondelegated powers to state governments made the Sedition Act "altogether void, and of no force."[63] Jefferson also revisited arguments made earlier in the decade, noting that the necessary and proper clause "ought not be so construed as themselves to give unlimited power."[64]

In his penultimate and lengthiest resolution, however, Jefferson turned his attention toward the policy itself and to its implications for freedom. Here, his argument transcended his concern for strict construction and moved toward a consideration of the threats that the Alien and Seditions Acts posed to American democracy. These laws, he wrote, were bad policies because the "citizen" and "friendless alien" would be subjected to "the absolute dominion of one man."[65] Long concerned with despotism, Jefferson argued that the laws transferred too much power to the central government and too much power into the hands of the president. It was not necessarily strict constructionism that led Jefferson to this point but a deep and abiding passion for freedom and liberty, and a growing concern over the development of the nation.[66] Kentucky, in Jefferson's words, called on its "co-States" to consider their relationship with the federal government. In this resolution, the heart of his argument, Jefferson moved from a consideration of whether the Constitution was interpreted strictly to a consideration about whether the entire American democratic and federal experiment, a compact among states, could continue in this vein.[67] While connected in Jefferson's mind, the sovereignty of the people reigned supreme over fealty to a strict construction of the Constitution.

Republicans in Congress and in the press also offered policy objections to the new laws. In addition to objecting to the Alien and Sedition Acts on strict construction grounds, Jeffersonian representatives highlighted the flaws in the bill concerning immigration policy, the marketplace of ideas, and the accuracy of the looming foreign threat. First, many Jeffersonians argued that the bill would hinder American development by producing a chilling effect on immigration. Gallatin noted that the bill would harm immigration, especially to states like his adopted state of Pennsylvania and other middle states, "whose population is thin." Pennsylvania had, "from its establishment," encouraged "emigrants of all nations" to come.[68] Livingston likewise fretted that the "loss of wealth, of population, and of commerce" by chasing out immigrants would hurt the nation. North Carolina's Joseph McDowell concurred. He worried that the bill would ultimately drive those of "wealth . . . abilities and industry" from the nation. Maryland's Samuel Smith reminded the House of the Declaration of Independence's complaint that the king was limiting immigration and argued that immigrants had provided great service to the nation: "We ought not now . . . pass laws which will bear so hard upon them."[69]

Republicans in the press were similarly concerned about how these laws would impact new arrivals to America. A polemicist in the *Bee* wrote that the Alien Laws were "totally contrary to philanthropy, hospitality, or common justice," and that "every act of oppression towards any individual or class of men ought to be considered as an attack upon the liberties and safety of the whole and resisted accordingly," because "the spirit which can punish and banish an unfortunate stranger, without either accusation or trial, would require no great stretch to invade our own rights."[70]

In addition to being concerned with immigration policy, Republicans objected to the rationale behind the proposed law, arguing that the marketplace of ideas should be diverse enough to provide Americans with a full spectrum of opinions. Elected Republicans understood that having newspapers supporting different viewpoints was essential to intellectual and political development across the nation because "if anything was unfounded in [a] paper, it would always be contradicted in another." The people, North Carolina Republican Nathaniel Macon argued, "know that truth is not afraid of investigation."[71] Virginia congressman John Nicholas noted that Federalist attempts to silence the press were likely to prevent citizens from learning key information about elections, particularly given the preponderance of Federalist newspapers throughout the nation.[72] Gallatin admitted that the Republican press was not terribly strong, and, noting that nine out of ten newspapers in the nation were Federalist, he added, "Such is the want of confidence in the purity of their own views and motives that they even fear the unequal contest and require the help of force to suppress the limited circulation of the opinions of those who did not approve all their measures."[73] Gallatin later noted that Federalists did not seem to be hiding their intent "to prevent a free circulation of opinion," while Madison moaned to Jefferson, "It is to be regretted that these papers are so limited in their circulation."[74] Other congressmen, Federalist as well as Republican, noted that they could only locate a handful of Republican newspapers.[75] Such assessments proved prescient, given the paltry number of Sedition Act prosecutions.[76] Not surprisingly, Republican printers, the prime targets of the new laws, thought that Federalists were aiming to stifle political discourse that was beneficial to the nation.

In doing so, Republican printers argued, the Federalists were acting against the best interests of the nation.[77] A polemicist named "William Tell" asked, "What then, is it already come to this, that the American press shall only print on *one side?* That members of Congress shall not justify themselves to their constituents, by exposing the motives of their adversaries? And that nothing shall come from the mouth of an independent freeman of America, relative to the conduct of his public servants, but servile adulation and flattery?"[78] "Benedict Arnold" mockingly advised Federalists to "roar in chorus . . . Oh! SEDITION, SEDITION, SEDITION," if anyone were to "examine [laws] and point out their defects" or even suggest to "countrymen that their Government is not infallible."[79] Upset that Federalist papers in numerous cities were "pensioned and held in the pay of government," one anonymous author warned readers that "all these presses continually nauseate us with eulogiums on the British . . . and sedulously suppress every transaction that tends to give the public an idea of the infamous conduct of the English towards our commerce and our citizens."[80] To these printers, the Sedition Act and the trials that it threatened would define the future role of the press and suppress free discussion in the new republic. "The ensuing trials for libel," Bache wrote, "will determine whether the press is to be the *palladium* and *centinel of liberty,* or the mere vehicle of *madrigals, rhebus'* and *tampons* on the people."[81]

Complaints about what the nation would look like under the Sedition Act were not the only objections that Jeffersonians raised. They also questioned the necessity of the bill, accusing Federalists of either exaggerating or inventing foreign threats to national security. Congressman McDowell worried that only a "strong aversion" against the French had merited the bill. He believed Federalist stories of French spies and traitors were "trumped up for the purpose of assisting the passage of this bill." Livingston warned that passing the bill would allow "individual suspicions, our private fears, our overheated imaginations" to accuse foreigners falsely. In his final speech before the vote was held, Gallatin questioned whether Federalists, who had used uprisings in Continental Europe to show the depth of the French threat, had properly understood the histories behind those movements. For good measure, Gallatin then attacked the legality of the bill, arguing it was counter to treaties that the United States had signed with the Netherlands, Sweden, and Great Britain involving how one nation should treat citizens of another.[82]

Republican printers likewise looked to foreign policy and alliances, depicting the Alien and Sedition Acts as inimical to the nation's longstanding relationship with France and emphasizing America's popular support of that relationship, which Federalists were neglecting in violation of republican principles. Not only did Republican newspapers print the Virginia and Kentucky Resolutions, but they described the erection of liberty poles and the gatherings of citizens to express demands for change, and they printed petitions and toasts in an effort to demonstrate to their readers that the Republican movement was growing, despite Federalist efforts to clamp down on their freedoms.

Indeed, Republican newspapers went far beyond the Alien and Sedition Acts to sketch out a series of desired policies. Newark, New Jersey's *Centinel of Freedom,* for instance, printed a lengthy list of Republican desires originally printed in the Virginia *Argus.* Opposed to war with France on the basis of their assistance in the Revolution, seventeen citizens protested a standing army and taxes for a larger navy, arguing "that the foreign power of the United States is vested in the people."[83] Baltimore's *Federal Gazette* reprinted the resolutions of citizens of Clarke County, Kentucky, arguing that a federal official is "the servant of the people and is amenable and accountable to them: that being so, it becomes the people to watch over their conduct with vigilance . . . the more elevated the office . . . the more necessary is a scrutiny and examination."[84] While most such protests covered the Sedition Act and foreign policy, others included resolutions that complained about the July 1798 direct tax, enacted to fund the military buildup necessitated by the Quasi-War.[85] Because the French had no interest in attacking the United States, the nation did not need a standing army or increased taxes, Suffolk County citizens wrote to Congress, in opposition to the Federalists' "unnecessary increase of the public debt and the introduction of an oppressive system of taxation."[86] Much to the chagrin of congressional Republicans and their supporters in the press, the bills passed.

A year after the Sedition Act passed, the few Republican voices in the press that had not been silenced fought on. One Virginian, James Lyon, proposed a *National Magazine.* The magazine was necessary, its advertising copy stated, because "the American people have long enough been imposed upon by the pretended impartiality of printers—it is all delusion—every party will have its printer." Claiming impartiality in the press in the late 1790s was as ridiculous as a pastor who preached "Christianity in the morning and paganism in the evening." The magazine, Lyon promised, would "elucidate and expose the origin, progress, and alarming influence of that system of iniquity, robbery, bribery, and oppression, hypocrisy and injustice, which may be traced from the attempt of Alexander Hamilton to palm upon the Convention a monarchial constitution, through the corrupted mazes of funding and banking, stockjobbing and speculating systems, down to the alien and sedition laws, standing army and navy of the present day."[87] Tracing a decade of objectionable policies and their implications, the advertisement for subscriptions suggested how a Republican administration would be different if they won the election of 1800.

In his history of the early United States, Henry Adams noted that "a few broad strokes of the brush would paint the portraits of all the early Presidents . . . but Jefferson could be painted only touch by touch, with a fine pencil, and the perfection of the likeness depended upon the shifting and uncertain flicker of its semi-transparent shadows."[88] Jeffersonians, like the man himself, have too often been slathered with the broad brush of strict constructionism. To understand him and them, one must look carefully and openly at their objections to Federalist policies in the 1790s. They surely were strict constructionists, but to stop there is to do them a disservice. They fought Federalists on constitutional, philosophical, and policy grounds, giving themselves a solid background in what they would need after the Revolution of 1800.[89]

During the debates over the Bank of the United States, the Neutrality Proclamation, and the Alien and Sedition Acts, Jeffersonians—and Jefferson—articulated numerous objections to Federalist policies. Strict construction played a role in their attacks but so did policy disagreements and other concerns. Taken as a whole, these policy objections demonstrate that Republicans were not just objecting to constitutional precedents. In addition to objecting to Federalist policies, they were promoting a vision of America and policies of their own. These policies were just as vital to Jeffersonian politics as was their strict construction of the Constitution.

The proper way to view Jeffersonians in the 1790s, then, is to see them as a developing party finding their identity in the context of a new nation, birthed with an overriding revolutionary concern to defend liberty from the encroachments of government. Although a network of newspapers helped to circulate polemical essays, diversity of thought and a wide-ranging geographical base left Republicans with no intention to, nor mechanism for, dictating policy or ideology to supporters. That said, in questioning the wisdom of Federalist policies in the 1790s, Republicans articulated deep-rooted philosophical concerns over individual liberty and legislative supremacy that sketched their developing political ideology and policies, and charted a potential course for their administrations to come. In the bank debates, Republicans saw economic problems with banks and observed the privileging of merchants and investors at the expense of agrarian concerns. During the proclamation discussions in 1793, Republicans perceived international law being trampled, the will of the American people ignored, legislative superiority subjected to executive desires, and an old ally slighted. Finally, Republicans believed that the Alien and Sedition Acts stifled immigration, interfered with the free exchange in the marketplace of ideas, and violated the link between the people and their government at the heart of republican governance.

Of course, during the 1790s, Republicans also believed that Federalists were unjustly bending the Constitution to their will. But believing in one ideological position does not preclude holding a variety of policy concerns. The Jeffersonians in the 1790s were a diverse group of individuals who held a complex web of ideas that served them well as they assumed the mantle of authority after 1800. The power of the state, the will of the people, the support of agrarian interests, the need to maintain vigilant watch over elected officials: all of these things would be foundations of Republican policy in decades to come.

Notes

I would like to thank the editors of this volume for the invitation to participate in this project and for their guiding hands in the creation of the essay. Librarians at

Washington University and John Burroughs School were as helpful as any I have encountered and also very deserving of my thanks. My colleagues and students at Burroughs have provided me with a friendly and stimulating environment in which to work, and I cannot thank them enough. I would also like to thank my wife and children for tolerating another venture into the 1790s. Finally, I need to tip my cap to Peter Onuf, without whom none of this would have been possible.

1. See U.S. Constitution, art. 1, sec. 8, clause 18; Tenth Amendment.

2. *Annals of Congress,* House of Representatives, 1st Cong., 3rd sess., Feb. 1, 1791, 1941. The literature on party development in this period is voluminous. Among others, see Dumas Malone, *Jefferson and the Rights of Man* (Boston, 1951), esp. chapters 15–17; Stanley Elkins and Eric McKitrick, *Age of Federalism* (New York, 1993), esp. chapter 7; James Rogers Sharp, *American Politics in the Early Republic* (New Haven, Conn., 1993), esp. chapter 2; and the essays in Lance Banning, ed., *After the Constitution: Party Conflict in the New Republic* (Belmont, Calif., 1989), esp. chapters 2–4.

3. For Jackson, see *Annals of Congress,* House of Representatives, 1st Cong., 3rd sess., Feb. 1, 1791, 1941. For Stone, see ibid., Feb. 5, 1791, 1982. For Giles, see ibid., Feb. 7, 1791, 1993.

4. Ibid., Feb. 2, 1791, 1946, 1947–49, 1950.

5. On the press in the early republic, see Donald Stewart, *The Opposition Press of the Federalist Period* (Albany, N.Y., 1969); Carol Sue Humphrey, *The Press of the Young Republic* (Westport, Conn., 1996), chapter 3; Michael Lienesch, "Thomas Jefferson and the American Democratic Experience: The Origins of the Partisan Press, Popular Political Parties, and Public Opinion," in *Jeffersonian Legacies,* ed. Peter S. Onuf (Charlottesville, Va., 1993), 316–39; William David Sloan, "Scurrility and the Party Press, 1789–1816," *American Journalism* 5 (1988): 97–112; and Jeffrey L. Pasley, *"The Tyranny of Printers": Newspaper Politics in the Early American Republic* (Charlottesville, Va., 2001).

6. For examples of these positions, see *Federal Gazette* (Baltimore), Feb. 5, 1791; *Daily Advertiser* (New York), Feb. 10, 1791; *American Daily Advertiser* (Philadelphia), Feb. 16, 1791; *Columbian Centinel* (Boston), Mar. 9, 1791.

7. *National Gazette* (Philadelphia), January 16, 1792, as reprinted from the *American Daily Advertiser* (Philadelphia), Jan. 9, 1792.

8. On Jefferson's opinion on the bank bill, see Malone, *Jefferson and the Rights of Man,* chapter 20. On larger Jeffersonian issues with the bank bill and their connection to previous complaints about centralized power, see Lance Banning, *The Jeffersonian Persuasion: Evolution of a Party Ideology* (Ithaca, N.Y., 1978), chapter 5. Washington also asked Madison for his opinion of the bank. See "To George Washington from James Madison, 21 February 1791," Founders Online, National Archives, Washington, D.C., http://founders.archives.gov/documents/Washington/05-07-02-0232.

9. Thomas Jefferson, "Opinion on the Constitutionality of the Bill for Establishing a National Bank, 15 February 1791," Founders Online, http://founders.archives.gov/documents/Jefferson/01-19-02-0051.

10. On the importance of Jefferson's federalism, see Peter S. Onuf, "Thomas Jefferson, Federalist," in *The Mind of Thomas Jefferson,* (Charlottesville, Va., 2007), 83–98.

See also David N. Mayer, *Constitutional Thought of Thomas Jefferson,* (Charlottesville, Va., 1994), 193–96, and Malone, *Jefferson and the Rights of Man,* 342–50.

11. On the connections between the new bank and the Bank of North America, see Jackson, *Annals of Congress,* House of Representatives, 1st Cong., 3rd sess., Feb. 1, 1791, 1941, and Stone, ibid., Feb. 5, 1791, 1984.

12. Ibid., Feb. 2, 1791, 1944–46. On Madison's thoughts on the constitutionality of the bank as they evolved over time, see Ralph Ketcham, *James Madison* (Charlottesville, Va., 1971), esp. chapter 13; Drew R. McCoy, *The Last of the Fathers* (Cambridge, 1989), 80–83; and Kevin R. C. Gutzman, "A Troublesome Legacy: James Madison and 'The Principles of '98,'" *Journal of the Early Republic* 15, no. 4 (Winter 1995): 569–89.

13. Jackson, *Annals of Congress,* House of Representatives, 1st Cong., 3rd sess., Feb. 4, 1791, 1969–70.

14. Madison, ibid., Feb. 9, 1791, 2011–12.

15. *General Advertiser* (Philadelphia), Feb. 25, 1791. The article responded to "A Constitutionalist" two days earlier in the *Gazette of the United States* (Philadelphia).

16. *New Jersey Journal,* Feb. 15, 1792.

17. For Ames, see *Annals of Congress,* House of Representatives, 1st Cong., 3rd sess., Feb. 3, 1791, 1952–53; for Gerry, see ibid., Feb. 7, 1791, 2000–2004; for Lawrence, see ibid., Feb. 4, 1791, 1965–66; for Boudinot, see ibid., Feb. 4, 1791, 1970–72; for Sedgwick, see ibid., Feb. 4, 1791, 1963.

18. Ibid., Feb. 1, 1791, 1941.

19. Ibid., Feb. 5, 1791, 1981.

20. *New York Daily Gazette,* Feb. 2, 1791.

21. Madison, *Annals of Congress,* House of Representatives, 1st Cong., 3rd sess., Feb. 2, 1791, 1944–46.

22. Malone, *Jefferson and the Rights of Man,* 344–45; Ketcham, *James Madison,* 321.

23. "Draft Veto of the Bank Bill, 21 February 1791," Founders Online, http://founders.archives.gov/documents/Madison/01-13-02-0295.

24. For example, see *Federal Gazette,* June 1, 6, 1793.

25. All Caius quotes in this paragraph are from *National Gazette,* Jan. 16, 1792. See *American Daily Advertiser,* Jan. 9, 1792, for original publication. See *New Jersey Journal,* Jan. 18, 1792, for a reprint.

26. *National Gazette,* Feb. 6, 1792.

27. *New Hampshire Gazette* (Portsmouth), May 19, 1791.

28. *Freeman's Journal* (Philadelphia), May 2, 1792.

29. *Independent Chronicle* (Boston), Aug. 12, 1790, cited in Banning, *Jeffersonian Persuasion,* 151.

30. *National Gazette,* July 4, 1792.

31. *National Gazette,* Sept. 12, 1792.

32. Jefferson, "Opinion on the Constitutionality of the Bill for Establishing a National Bank, 15 February 1791."

33. Ibid.

34. On Jefferson's view of the legislature, see Mayer, *Constitutional Thought,* esp. 127–44.

35. For the questions, see George Washington to "the Cabinet," Apr. 18, 1793, in Harold C. Syrett, ed., *The Papers of Alexander Hamilton* (New York, 1966–87), 14:291–92, 326. On Hamilton's role in the cabinet debate, see Forrest McDonald, *Alexander Hamilton* (New York, 1979), 272–78. For background on the Jeffersonian objections to Federalist foreign policy, see Banning, *Jeffersonian Persuasion,* chapter 8.

36. Every major Philadelphia paper (except the nonpolitical *Pennsylvania Journal*) printed Washington's proclamation in its first issue after he issued the text on April 22, 1793. For the impact of the proclamation on the developing partisan press in the nation's capital and beyond, see Mark Smith, "Crisis, Unity, and Partisanship: The Road to the Sedition Act" (PhD diss., University of Virginia, 1997), chapter 2.

37. *Richmond [Va.] and Manchester Advertiser,* Sept. 12, 1793, reprinted in the *National Gazette,* Sept. 25, 1793.

38. The Pacificus-Helvidius letters have been collected in Morton Frisch, ed., *The Pacificus-Helvidius Debates of 1793–1794* (Indianapolis, 2007). Hamilton published the Pacificus letters between June 29 and July 27, 1793. Madison's Helvidius appeared from August 24 to September 18, 1793. Hamilton's Americanus essays appeared on January 31 and February 7, 1794.

39. James Madison, "Helvidius I," in Frisch, ed., *Pacificus-Helvidius Debates,* 58. On Locke and Hamilton's use of "federative power," see Federalist 75, in Clinton Rossiter, ed., *The Federalist Papers* (New York, 1961), 449–54, and Morton Frisch, "Introduction," in Frisch, ed., *Pacificus-Helvidius Debates,* xi.

40. On waging war, see "Helvidius II," in Frisch, ed., *Pacificus-Helvidius Debates,* 65–73. On receiving ambassadors, see "Helvidius III," in ibid., 74–79. On making and keeping treaties, see "Helvidius III and IV," in ibid., 80–89. On issuing the proclamation, see "Helvidius V," in ibid., 90–98.

41. On the public sphere, see Jürgen Habermas, *Structural Transformation of the Public Sphere,* trans. Thomas Burger (Cambridge, Mass., 1992); Michael Warner, *Letters of the Republic: Publication and the Public Sphere in Eighteenth Century America* (Cambridge, Mass., 1990); Benedict Anderson, *Imagined Communities: Reflections on the Origins and Spread of Nationalism* (1983; reprint, London, 1991); and Craig Calhoun, ed., *Habermas and the Public Sphere* (Cambridge, Mass., 1992).

42. On Jefferson's unwillingness to write for newspapers, see "From Thomas Jefferson to George Washington, 9 September 1792," Founders Online, http://founders.archives.gov/documents/Jefferson/01-24-02-0330. On the closing of Freneau's paper, see Pasley, *"The Tyranny of Printers,"* 73–78.

43. Jefferson to Madison, July 7, 1793, in William T. Hutchinson et al., eds., *The Papers of James Madison: Congressional Series* (Chicago, 1962–77; Charlottesville, Va., 1977–91), 15:43.

44. *American Daily Advertiser,* June 24, 1793.

45. "Opinion on the Treaties with France, 28 April 1793," Founders Online, http://founders.archives.gov/documents/Jefferson/01-25-02-0562-0005.

46. Ibid.

47. Jefferson to Madison, July 7, 1793, in Hutchinson et al., eds., *Papers of James Madison,* 15:43.

48. *National Gazette,* Aug. 10, 1793. Secretarius was originally printed in the *New York Journal.* Truth and A Republican appeared in the *General Advertiser,* May 8, June 25, 1793. See also Philadelphius, *National Gazette,* June 12, 1793. Other letters in this series appeared on June 8, 15, 19, 22.

49. *National Gazette,* Aug. 14, 1793. See also *National Gazette,* June 12, 1793. Other letters in this series appeared on June 8, 15, 19, 22.

50. *American Daily Advertiser,* May 10, 1793.

51. *American Daily Advertiser,* June 22, 1793.

52. Veritas was originally printed in the *National Gazette* and reprinted in numerous papers from Boston's *Argus,* June 18, 1793, to Norfolk's *Virginia Chronicle,* June 22, 1793.

53. *National Gazette,* June 1, 1793.

54. *National Gazette,* June 5, 1793.

55. *National Gazette,* June 12, 1793.

56. Hamilton, "Pacificus I," in Frisch, ed., *Pacificus-Helvidius Debates,* 9.

57. On the road to the Sedition Act, see John C. Miller, *Crisis in Freedom: The Alien and Sedition Acts* (Boston, 1951); James Morton Smith, *Freedom's Fetters: The Alien and Sedition Laws and American Civil Liberties* (Ithaca, N.Y., 1956); and Walt Brown, *John Adams and the American Press: Politics and Journalism at the Birth of the Republic* (Jefferson, N.C., 1995).

58. *Annals of Congress,* 5th Cong., 2nd sess., June 21, 1798, 2011.

59. Ibid., June 19, 1798, 1975.

60. *Aurora* (Philadelphia), July 3, 1798.

61. *New York Journal,* July 4, 1798.

62. On Jefferson's authorship and the method of introduction, see Dumas Malone, *Jefferson and the Ordeal of Liberty* (Boston, 1962), 401–5.

63. Jefferson, Kentucky Resolutions, in Merrill D. Peterson, *The Portable Jefferson* (New York, 1975), 282. See also Malone, *Jefferson and the Ordeal of Liberty,* 383–85.

64. Jefferson, Kentucky Resolutions, 285.

65. Ibid., 287.

66. For a brief recounting of Jefferson's long-held beliefs on the importance of liberty and freedom, see Malone, *Jefferson and the Ordeal of Liberty,* 393–94.

67. On Jefferson and federalism, see Onuf, "Thomas Jefferson, Federalist," 83–98.

68. *Annals of Congress,* 5th Cong., 2nd sess., June 19, 1798, 1982.

69. Ibid., June 21, 1798, 2014, 2021, 2023.

70. *Bee* (New London, Conn.), Jan. 30, 1799.

71. *Annals of Congress,* 5th Cong., 2nd sess., July 5, 1798, 2105–6.

72. Ibid., July 10, 1798, 2140–44.

73. Ibid., July 5, 1798, 2109.

74. Ibid., July 10, 1798, 2162; Madison to Jefferson, May 5, 1798, in Hutchinson et al., eds., *Papers of James Madison,* 17:126.

75. See speeches by John Nicholas and John Allen, *Annals of Congress,* 5th Cong., 2nd sess., July 5, 1798, 2093–165.

76. On Sedition Act prosecutions, see Smith, *Freedom's Fetters.* They included Benjamin Franklin Bache, John D. Burk of the *Time Piece* (New York), Thomas Adams of the *Independent Chronicle,* Charles Holt of the *Bee,* James Callendar of the *Richmond Examiner,* William Duane (who succeeded Bache at the *Aurora*), Abijah Adams of the *Boston Chronicle,* Thomas Cooper of the *Northumberland Gazette* (Sunbury, Penn.), William Durrell of the *Register* (Mount Pleasant, N.Y.), and Anthony Haswell of the *Vermont Gazette* (Bennington), who were all arrested. Thomas Greenleaf of the *Argus* (New York) died of yellow fever in 1798 before he could be arrested, so Federalists targeted his wife, Ann, who continued the paper, and David Frothingham, the editor who helped her.

77. *Aurora,* July 3, 1798.

78. *Centinel of Freedom* (Newark, N.J.), Jan. 1, 1799, reprinted from the Virginia *Argus* (Richmond).

79. *Independent Chronicle,* Oct. 1, 1798.

80. *Bee,* Sept. 4, 1799.

81. *Aurora,* July 18, 1798.

82. *Annals of Congress,* 5th Cong., 2nd sess., June 21, 1798, 2021, 2006, 2027–28.

83. *Centinel of Freedom,* Oct. 2, 1798; Virginia *Argus,* Sept. 8, 1798.

84. *Federal Gazette and Baltimore Daily Advertiser,* Oct. 23, 1798; *Kentucky Gazette,* Aug. 1, 1798.

85. Jefferson's first message to Congress in December 1801 included many of these similar themes. On the transformation of Jeffersonians from opposition party to ruling party, see Noble E. Cunningham, *The Jeffersonian Republicans in Power: Party Operations, 1801–1809* (Chapel Hill, N.C., 1963), esp. chapter 1.

86. *Bee,* Mar. 20, 1799. For other examples, see *Centinel of Freedom,* Feb. 12, 1799; *Independent Chronicle,* Oct. 18, Nov. 1, 12, 1798, Jan. 24, 31, 1799; and *Bee,* Oct. 1, Nov. 21, 1798.

87. The advertisement was printed numerous times; for one example, see *Bee,* Sept. 4, 1799. On Jefferson's connection to Lyon, see "To Thomas Jefferson from James Lyon, 29 November 1800," Founders Online, http://founders.archives.gov/documents/Jefferson/01-32-02-0173.

88. Henry Adams, *History of the United States during the First Administration of America, during the First Administration of Thomas Jefferson* (New York, 1889), 1:277.

89. For previous interpretations of the Jeffersonian mindset in this time period, see Mayer, *Constitutional Thought,* esp. chapters 1–5; Banning, *Jeffersonian Persuasion,* esp. chapter 10; and Forrest McDonald, *The Presidency of Thomas Jefferson* (Lawrence, Kans., 1976).

II The Challenges of Holding Power

5 Thomas Jefferson's Virginian Revolution

Kevin R. C. Gutzman

Thomas Jefferson's unhappy retirement found him often contemplating his achievements.[1] He worked hard to recall them to compatriots' minds and to ensure their impress in posterity's conception of the Revolution. Among other components of this campaign was his sketching the obelisk he hoped would mark his grave.

Jefferson's grave marker would state his name and the dates of his birth and death, and it would list the key roles for which he hoped to be remembered. From among a plethora of things he might have noticed, Jefferson selected three: "Author of the Declaration of American Independence," "[Author] of the Statute of Virginia for Religious Freedom," and "Father of the University of Virginia." The three share numerous attributes. Most significantly, they were central to his project to remake the Old Dominion into a republican society.[2]

If a brilliant writer and architect, Jefferson also deserves renown as a visionary legislator. He envisioned a state radically different from the one in which he was born, and he sketched out a legislative plan that would have gone far toward bringing an egalitarian republic into being. Yet, beyond the achievements mentioned on his gravestone, he was not as successful in having it implemented as historians generally have asserted.

Although Jefferson's chief Virginia public policy aims—independence, a federal union with the other twelve states, enactment of the Virginia Statute for Religious Freedom, and radical reform of Virginia's inheritance law—were met, numerous of his other significant proposals were not adopted. Thus, Virginia by 1826 had not ended slavery, colonized blacks abroad, or made any progress toward these goals; it had not established public education for all free children, as he proposed; it had not adopted his reforms to its criminal penalties; its House of Delegates was still apportioned the English way (geographically), not by population; and the curriculum at the College of William and Mary remained about as steadfastly traditional as ever. Far from a triumph for Jefferson's egalitarian vision, the University of Virginia had been launched on what for many decades would be a path of training the sons of the elite for their positions atop Virginia politics and society—exactly the opposite of what Jefferson had hoped its path would be.

Historians have been mistaken, then, to think of the Old Dominion of Jefferson's day as "Jeffersonian Virginia." Yes, Jefferson deserves credit for drafting the Declaration of Independence. Yes, he drafted the Virginia Statute for Religious Freedom—though it would have lain on the table forever had not his friend James Madison pushed it to enactment nearly a decade after Jefferson failed at that task.[3] Yet he did not participate in drafting the Virginia constitution, and his decades-long push for radical reform to that document came to naught. In light of the strong pressure in Virginia for disestablishment of the Church of England and reforms similar to Virginia's adopted in the revolutionary era in regard to other states' inheritance laws, it seems likely that Virginia's religious disestablishment and inheritance reforms would have happened without him. His proposal for general land distribution led nowhere. Nor did his proposal to make criminal penalties proportionate to crimes succeed. When it came to smaller-bore reforms, he did win relocation of the state capital from Williamsburg to Richmond, and he did persuade the general assembly to use an ancient model for the new state capitol. Still, one struggles to name a significant reform associated with Jefferson's name that would not have been adopted in Virginia more or less at the same time if he had never lived—creation of the oligarchy's university excepted. (John Adams made similar observations about Jefferson's authorship of the Declaration of Independence.)

Furthermore, Jefferson lived to see a new nationalism ascendant in federal politics. Resigned to its advance, he avowed himself pleased that he would not live to see it triumph. He saw it as a negation of the Declaration of Independence. Its triumph would be Jeffersonianism's destruction.

Jefferson's chief concern in the days before independence was to vindicate his vision of the proper relationship between Virginia and federal authority, in this case British authority. For a substantial period of time after the Battles of Lexington and Concord on April 19, 1775, he continued to be dedicated to the hope of reconciliation between the colonies and the British. The reasons are not hard to find.

Jefferson grew up in an Old Dominion contented with life under the Crown. His father, Peter, sat atop his county's social hierarchy. His relatives played key roles in colonial government. When Jefferson entered the House of Burgesses in the 1760s, his cousin Peyton Randolph sat in the speaker's chair, and another cousin, John Randolph, served as the colony's attorney general. By all accounts, Jefferson and John Randolph—several years his senior—got along famously. It must have been painful then for the younger man when in August 1775, he wrote John to wish him well in his relocation to England. Along the way, Jefferson told his departing cousin that he was "looking with fondness toward a reconciliation with Great Britain" and counted himself "sincerely one of those" who "would rather be in dependence on Great Britain, properly limited, than on any other nation on earth, or than on no nation."[4]

Perhaps Jefferson was simply striking an accommodating pose in writing to a loyalist relative. In any event, only a year earlier, he had urged Virginia to assume a quite strident posture. His *A Summary View of the Rights of British America* claimed that Virginia's sole constitutional relationship to the British was through a common monarch, that Virginia's consent was the ground of that relationship, and that George III should remember that the king's duty bound him to satisfy those he denominated "subjects." Not privileges granted by a superior but the rights of Englishmen were Jefferson's concern. "Let those flatter who fear," he advised, "it is not an American art."[5]

A Summary View built on the work of another of Jefferson's burgess-cousins, Richard "Spectacle Dick" Bland. Bland had argued nearly a decade before that Virginia was established by its first settlers through their own efforts and with their own money, that they had come to North America in exercise of a natural right to emigrate (a radical, often-overlooked innovation), and that the English kings' dominion in their colony had been established at the colonists' request: not divine right, in other words, but popular consent accounted for George III's role. Jefferson later credited Bland, whom he called the foremost constitutional authority he had ever known, with outlining the entire American constitutional position in the imperial crisis of 1765–76. Jefferson criticized his senior only for not following the argument all the way to independence.[6]

The Declaration of Independence comes as a kind of anticlimax after *A Summary View of the Rights of British America.* It takes the form of a rhapsody rather than a didactic essay, and its now-hackneyed (John Adams said then-) phrases seem a bit timeworn. In reading it, one notices the divergence from *A Summary View*'s revolutionary (somewhat erroneous) account of colonial history. The similarity comes only at the very end, in the operative part, where Jefferson dutifully echoes Richard Henry Lee in propounding the Virginia Convention's statement that the former colonies "are, and of right ought to be, free and independent states."[7]

The use of the plural "states" is key. It reflects the position laid down in *A Summary View,* the one that would mark Jefferson's thinking about the relationship between Virginia and central authority—first British, next Confederation, in time federal authority—to the very end of his life.[8]

The grounds of this claim are now philosophical rather than historical, perhaps due to the imperative to craft a case equally applicable to thirteen polities with distinct constitutional histories. Schoolboys know those grounds perfectly well, and even members of Congress can sometimes repeat them. Absent are *A Summary View*'s claims that the colonies were founded by the first settlers through their own efforts, with their own money, and without aid from the British government, and yet the Declaration's account of things dovetails perfectly with the prerevolutionary pamphlet. If "all men are created equal," if they are entitled to a government to which they have consented, if "to secure these rights, Governments are instituted among Men, deriving their just powers from the consent of the governed," and if "whenever any Form of Government becomes destructive of these ends, it is the Right of the People to alter or to abolish it, and to institute new Government, laying its foundation on such principles and organizing its powers in such form, as to them shall seem most likely to effect their Safety and Happiness," then Jefferson's warning in *A Summary View* that George III risked losing his role in the colonies' politics rested on natural right.[9]

Jefferson's 1774 pamphlet enunciated an essentially federal view of the imperial constitution in which the Crown exercised a few national powers on behalf of the entire empire, and matters of local concern were reserved entirely to the separate dominions. That George III rejected this schema did not dissuade Jefferson from adhering to it. Rather, he would insist on it, come hell or high water, to the end of his days. This idea of federalism came to be Republican, and thus Virginia, orthodoxy no later than 1794.[10]

Jefferson described the Declaration shortly after penning its first draft as "my political creed in the form of a 'Declaration &c.'"[11]

There is not space to develop the history of Jefferson's federalism here.[12] Suffice to say that although a diplomatic posting to France kept him from direct involvement in drafting or ratifying the U.S. Constitution, his every surviving statement on the question distinguished between the internal matters over which he held that the states ought to retain or had retained control, on the one hand, and the power concerning common interests delegated to the federal government, on the other. Noted occasions on which he iterated this position as an official matter included the 1791 cabinet debate on Alexander Hamilton's bank bill, the Sedition Act crisis of 1798–1801, and his first inaugural address. Analogous private occasions included his 1797 correspondence with Governor James Monroe over the Cabell presentment, the Missouri crisis, and his 1825 "Draft Declaration and Protest." There were numerous others, besides scattered private jottings along the same lines.

Jefferson of course did not stop at federalism. Once independent, Virginia must have a proper republican constitution. Jefferson held adoption of such a constitution to be the keystone of the Revolution, in default of which the Revolution would be wasted effort. "In truth," he claimed at the time, "it is the whole object of the present controversy; for should a bad government be instituted for us in future it had been as well to have accepted at first the bad one offered to us from beyond the water without the risk and expence of contest."[13]

Logically, Jefferson wanted to help draft Virginia's new constitution. That was why he repeatedly asked to be relieved of his duties as a congressman in Philadelphia.[14] In default of that, Jefferson drafted a constitution and sent it to Williamsburg for consideration in his absence.

Broaching the subject with the convention's leadership, Jefferson's friend George Wythe found that "the revision of a subject the members seemed tired of would at that time have been unsuccessfully proposed."[15] Still another Jefferson kinsman, Edmund Randolph, presented Jefferson's proposal to the Virginia Convention's leaders Patrick Henry, George Mason, and Edmund Pendleton. They said it was too late to take up the congressman's handiwork as a whole, but they did use Jefferson's proposed preamble and a few of his other provisions in revising the document that the convention had already written.[16]

Jefferson objected that the Virginia Constitution of 1776 was not properly speaking a constitution at all but merely an ordinance of a legislative body.[17] His second and third drafts reflected his understanding that the people must be brought more directly into the process of constitution-making in providing for popular ratification at the local level, with majority votes of two-thirds of the counties required to put a constitution into effect. Virginia's leading lights rejected this argument, averring that Virginians must have intended for a body empowered to throw off British rule to establish a new government immediately.[18] Historians invariably accept the validity of Jefferson's objection, but the convention leaders' position seems persuasive.

Jefferson's first-draft Virginia constitution, dated no later than June 13, 1776, would have made a thoroughly republican revolution in the Old Dominion.[19] More than simply creating a new government, it incorporated several significant reforms. After a preamble including a list of grievances against George III similar to the one in the Declaration of Independence, it provided that the delegates still would have been elected annually but with a far laxer suffrage qualification. Representation would have been apportioned by population rather than geographically. Senators would have served for life. Capital punishment, very widely applied at the time, would have been reserved for only a few crimes, and tax laws would have been subject to a sunset provision. (Jefferson would always hold that it was an error, ineluctably leading to growth of government, to provide a permanent source of revenue.[20])

Jefferson envisioned a governor with a one-year term ineligible for reelection for five years. With English kings' prerogative powers in mind, he would have deprived his governor of the veto, power to declare war or make peace, power to raise armies, power to coin money, power to regulate weights and measures, power to create courts, power to lay embargoes, power to pardon, and a few other minor powers. All of that authority would have gone to the legislature.

The lower house would have appointed a privy council, which would have shared the executive authority with the governor. The house of representatives would have appointed the supreme court. Jefferson would have erected statewide courts, but the county courts—self-perpetuating strongholds of the colonial aristocracy—would have been essentially unchanged.[21]

Most radically democratic of all was Jefferson's provision that "[fifty] acres of land shall be appropriated without purchase money to every person not owning nor having ever owned that quantity & no other person shall be capable of taking an appropriation." Under this provision, suffrage, though still tied to land, would have been nearly universal among white men, and perhaps even extended to women. Along the same lines, Jefferson envisioned abolition both of primogeniture and of the tradition excluding daughters from inheritance, providing for all children, males and females, to inherit equally.

He also proposed that anyone swearing an intention to live in Virginia for seven years and signing to the constitution would be treated as a "natural born" citizen. An oath of fidelity would have been the only qualification for office.

"All persons," Jefferson wrote, "shall have full & free liberty of religious opinion," and none would have to attend or give financial support to any services. All freemen would have the use of arms. The press would be free. No legislator, administrator, judge, or councilor would receive a salary. Only unanimous agreement of both houses of the legislature could change these provisions. Colonial law would remain in effect until modified.

In short, Jefferson's first draft constitution for Virginia would have reformed the Old Dominion extensively. But draftsman Jefferson was just getting started.

He wrote a second draft making significant changes to the first.[22] It laid out the principle of separation of powers. It initiated the universal American practice of calling the upper house the "Senate." Besides setting a slighter property qualification for voting than under colonial law, it made taxpayers eligible too. When it came to the state senate, Jefferson envisioned a longer term of office, nine years, and election by the lower house. Members would be perpetually ineligible for reelection. All torture would be abolished.

Jefferson shifted election of some local officials from the legislature to the local electorate. He provided for a two-year term limit for Virginia's congressmen, who would be elected by the house of representatives. As in his first draft, Jefferson provided for jury trials in chancery, ecclesiastical, and admiralty cases, and even in contempt proceedings—where only common-law courts had sat with juries before.

Another new provision said that "no person hereafter coming into this country shall be held in slavery under any pretext whatever."

Where the first draft had allowed only a unanimous legislature to change the constitution, this one eased the path to constitutional change by saying that if two thirds of the counties voted for a change, it would become part of the constitution. Finally, it said that two thirds of the counties could ratify the constitution.

Still dissatisfied, Jefferson wrote a third draft incorporating still more changes.[23] It established a one-year term for the governor, who would be ineligible for four years after his term. Where the second draft had made congressmen ineligible for two years after their two-year terms, they now were to be ineligible one year after one-year terms.

The Virginia Constitution of 1776 turned out much differently than Jefferson had hoped. Among his proposals omitted from the final version were population apportionment, separation of church and state, reservation of capital punishment for the worst offenses, lengthy terms for senators, a grant of fifty acres of land to many Virginians, and ratification by popular vote. In the immediate aftermath of the convention, Jefferson lamented the constitution's shortcomings. He spent considerable energy over the following years trying to amend it—which was made particularly difficult by the absence of anything like the amendment provisions in Jefferson's draft constitutions.

Jefferson was notably critical of the new senate, which he bewailed as essentially a smaller version of the House of Delegates.[24] It should be indirectly elected, not elected by the people directly, he argued, because "this first secretion from them is usually crude and heterogeneous. . . . For this reason it was that I . . . thought I had . . . made the Senators . . . perfectly independent of their electors." Senators ought not be reeligible because "if they might be re-elected, they would be casting their eyes forward to the period of election (however distant) and be currying favor with the electors, and consequently dependent on them." Although he thought a nine-year term, with its certainty of eventually having to live under the laws they had made, preferable, he would accept life terms in preference to "a mere creation by and dependance on the people."

Jefferson balanced those notably undemocratic words with an argument against a property qualification for senators. "My observations," he said, "do not enable me to say I think integrity the characteristic of wealth. In general I believe the decisions of the people, in a body, will be more honest and more disinterested than those of wealthy men." A property qualification for voting was not needed either, for "I can never doubt an attachment to his country in any man who has his family and peculium in it." This is why he had favored "extending the suffrage (or in other words the rights of a citizen) to all who had a permanent intention of living in the country."

One feature of the new constitution in particular struck Jefferson as unacceptable. "The other point of equal representation," he said, "I think capital and fundamental." Critics assailed his proposed restriction of capital punishment to cases of homicide; Jefferson must trust mankind more than they. In response, he insisted, "It is only the sanguinary hue of our penal laws which I meant to object to." He would retain punishments "but proportioned to the crime." Death ought to be the penalty for "murther and perhaps for treason," properly defined, while "rape, buggery &c." merited castration, and other crimes should be punished with time working on public facilities such as roads. As "this would be no punishment or change of condition to slaves," he would simply banish them. Once these reforms were made, "Laws thus proportionate and mild should never be dispensed with. Let mercy be the character of the law-giver, but let the judge be a mere machine." Virginians must not allow unaccountable officials to depart from this indulgent scale of punishments.

Since the Virginia Constitution of 1776 lacked a provision for amendment, Jefferson abandoned his project of thorough societal reform via constitution-making. Instead, he would take up his rejected constitutional provisions as discrete legislative proposals. The subject of the Revisal of the Laws, as it came to be known, appears in a letter Pendleton wrote to Jefferson mere days after promulgation of the Declaration of Independence.[25] Perhaps the idea came from Jefferson's hero Francis Bacon, who had proposed a similar project in England.

In October 1776, Jefferson accepted appointment to the legislative committee charged with proposing a republican revision of Virginia's laws. (Pendleton joined him as a member.) Although the committeemen divided the work among themselves, Jefferson took the lead.[26] The work covered the entire sweep of Virginia law. Among the 126 bills the committee finally proposed, the most significant was Jefferson's Bill for Establishing Religious Freedom.[27] Here in mature form Jefferson laid out his position on the proper relationship between church and state.

He began by positing that belief is an "involuntar[y]" response to the evidence presented to one's mind. Attempts to enforce orthodoxy of opinion only "beg[a]t habits of hypocrisy and meanness, and [were] a departure from the plan of the holy author of our religion, who being lord both of body and mind, yet chose not to propagate it by coercions on either." Although he later insisted that he meant by not naming "the holy author of our religion" to leave open an inference that he referred to Muslims' Allah or a Hindu god, Jefferson's language here seems to reflect a political environment shaped by Virginia's official Anglicanism. It is however true enough that even at that early date, Jefferson disbelieved Christian dogma concerning Christ's power.[28]

After its second, operative section, the bill included a final section about the problem of its being solely a statutory enactment susceptible of repeal. While one legislature could not bind a later one, it said, "the rights [t]hereby asserted [were] of the natural rights of mankind," which any act repealing it would violate. In time, later generations of Virginians made both Jefferson's philosophical and operative language parts of their state constitution.

Jefferson's revisal package included other elements related to the Episcopal Church as well. One, bill no. 83, recognized the permanency of that organization's ownership of the lands assigned to it when it was the state church. This bill was never enacted.[29]

Incongruously, Jefferson also drafted a bill for perpetuation of the English policy of punishing Sabbath-breakers, as well as for punishment of anyone who disrupted a religious service. Even more surprisingly, this bill was passed into law in 1786 through the efforts of Delegate James Madison.[30]

The terse statement in Jefferson's draft constitution reserving capital punishment for only the most serious crimes became in the revisal a full-fledged "Bill for Proportioning Crimes and Punishments in Cases Heretofore Capital." Far from the momentous reform some have seen, this bill essentially would have formalized "generally accepted practices concerning capital offenses."[31] Jefferson blamed its ultimate rejection on lawmakers' hesitance to reduce the penalty for stealing a horse, as Virginians loved their horseflesh.

More conspicuous among Jefferson's efforts is bill no. 20, "A Bill Concerning the Course of Descents."[32] As Jefferson had envisioned in 1776, it abolished the traditional discrimination in favor of sons by making all offspring inherit equally. Jefferson did retain some preference for males by, for example, favoring male lines in cases where there were no progeny. Long considered essentially meaningless, this bill was shown in a seminal journal article two decades ago to have been precisely as significant as Jefferson thought.[33]

Various persons' status in the commonwealth formed the general subject of bill nos. 51–56. The first four of these had to do with servants and slaves, while the last two concerned citizenship and aliens. Jefferson famously claimed in his "Autobiography" to have sponsored or cosponsored legislation aimed at cutting off importation of slaves and at gradual emancipation. Scholars such as the editors of Jefferson's papers and his leading biographers, Dumas Malone and Merrill Peterson, traditionally took him at his word, but iconoclastic students of the subject in recent decades have adopted the opposite attitude.[34]

Bill no. 51, "A Bill Concerning Slaves," would have banned importation of slaves into Virginia. It also would have required any freed slave to leave the Old Dominion within a year of being freed, barred blacks from testifying in cases between whites, restricted slaves' travel, and restricted slaves' gun possession. Jefferson later claimed that there was to be an amendment providing for gradual emancipation, but his papers' editors found no evidence of this amendment's ever being written. The version of this bill adopted into law substantially slackened the ban on importing slaves insofar as it concerned those from other states.[35]

Two of Jefferson's bills, nos. 55 and 56, defined citizens and set out legal treatment of aliens.[36] Generally, Jefferson envisioned very liberal criteria for immigration, including that anyone who had lived in Virginia for two years before the bill's adoption, all who arrived thereafter and swore that they intended to live there and would be loyal to the commonwealth, anyone who migrated to Virginia with a parent who became a citizen, and all who migrated thither without parents were citizens until they voluntarily surrendered that status. Jefferson then laid out in detail the process by which a Virginian could exercise the natural right to emigrate underlying *A Summary View* and the Declaration of Independence.

The last major reform initiative outlined in the revisal must be classed as one of the most significant. In bill nos. 79 and 80, Jefferson proposed "the more general diffusion of knowledge" and "amending the constitution of the college of William and Mary."[37] The first of these bills called for setting up a three-tiered system of taxpayer-funded schools to which all free children (the language included females and nonwhites) would have gone for at least three years. At the conclusion of three years, the best in each locale would have been selected to continue at a higher-level school for three more years, and then the best of those would have gone on to William and Mary at taxpayers' expense. Jefferson hoped by this mechanism both to prepare all citizens for meaningful participation in public life and to sift the most able members of society—the "natural aristocracy"—out from among the whole population so that they could hold public offices.[38]

Jefferson's unhappiness with the curriculum and organization of William and Mary was of long standing. His years in Williamsburg profited him most due not to his formal work at the college but to evenings spent in the company of local intellectual luminaries at the governor's palace. Only there did he come to love immersion in the latest currents of European thought. Only there did he become addicted to learning and to membership in the "Republic of Letters."[39]

Jefferson hoped by his legislative proposal to give time spent in William and Mary the potential for being as fruitful as his at the palace had been.[40] He contemplated completely remaking the old school's antique course of study, which he judged highly impractical, into one of more immediate applicability. The school had always been composed of a professor of Hebrew and exegetics, one of theology, two of philosophy in its various branches, a school of Greek and Latin, and an Indian school charged with educating (including Christianizing) its charges. Jefferson would have devoted the commonwealth's college, whose mission had been primarily religious, to the task of "endow[ing] with science and virtue, to watch and preserve the sacred deposit . . . the future guardians of the rights and liberties of their country." To that end, he would have mandated by law that there "be eight Professorships, to wit, one of moral philosophy, the laws of nature and of nations, and of the fine arts; one of law and police; one of history, civil and ecclesiastical; one of mathematics; one of anatomy and medicine; one of natural philosophy and natural history; one of the ancient languages, oriental and northern; and one of modern languages." For the old Indian school, he would have substituted periodic anthropological missions among Indians.[41]

Jefferson's bill failed of adoption in the general assembly. His two years as governor gave him the opportunity to alter his alma mater somewhat, but not as thoroughly as bill no. 80 would have done.[42] That bill's chief importance is in making clear that Jefferson had already begun to envision the University of Virginia, which he would succeed in having the Old Dominion establish four decades later. It also casts light on the egalitarian, republican form Jefferson hoped to see his polity take.

* * *

The late 1770s saw Jefferson called to the governorship. The press of military calamity kept Governor Jefferson from pursuing the legislative reforms to which he had devoted such time and care. In the wake of his unhappy tenure in that post, he took a respite from politics and then headed off for a long stint as American minister to France. For much of the following quarter-century, he held significant federal political office. Still, his republican project for Virginia never left his mind. His ideas of Virginia's proper place in the federal union and of its appropriately republican shape account for much of the content of *Notes on the State of Virginia,* which was written during this time.

The most extensive Jeffersonian commentary on his state's constitution, for example, is the "Constitution" chapter of this, his sole book.[43] In that work, Jefferson based Virginia's constitutional order on his argument in *A Summary View* that Virginia was established by the colonists through their own effort and with their own money, and so their link to the British through the Crown was always entirely voluntary. His twenty-page chapter included eight pages of criticism, generally scoring the constitution for not including all of the provisions he had proposed in regard to suffrage, legislative apportionment, the senate's composition, the separation of powers, popular ratification, and legislative quorums.

Jefferson also devoted extensive attention in his book to the shape, effects, and future of slavery in his homeland. The short of it was that although he thought that blacks' supposed mental dullness and recollection of their longstanding mistreatment at whites' hands, joined to whites' prejudice against them, ruled out a biracial society, the fundamental philosophical commitment spelled out in the second sentence of the Declaration of Independence counted as much in blacks' favor as in whites'. Since blacks had a right to self-government and would never be able to take advantage of it in Virginia, they had to be deported.

We cannot finally resolve the question whether Jefferson really proposed emancipation in the general assembly or was just posing as antislavery to ingratiate himself with a European audience.[44] We might guess, however, that since Jefferson's book appeared less than a decade after he supposedly had, someone would have corrected the record if correction had been in order.

We do know for certain that Jefferson could have done more along these lines. For example, as president, he lit on the policy of nonrecognition for Haiti, whose status as a republic founded by ex-slaves through the Western Hemisphere's only successful slave rebellion struck him as distressingly dangerous. He considered various possible destinations for Virginia's potential African-descended expatriates, but nothing much came of that.

Jefferson's political partner James Madison and his acolyte James Monroe, however, pushed the colonization concept energetically. Madison served for years as president of the American Colonization Society, an influential civic organization. Monroe, for his part, played a significant role in establishing Liberia as a place to which freedmen could be sent. Ultimately, Nat Turner's rebellion provided an opening for Jefferson's grandson Thomas Jefferson Randolph to advocate colonization in the House of Delegates. That long-running debate concluded with the complete and final rejection of the Jeffersonian racial program. Blacks would never be deported en masse from Virginia; instead, the Old Dominion rededicated itself to enforcement of the slave system.[45]

In retirement, Jefferson rebuffed a request that he take the lead in bringing the Old Dominion into the company of states that had abolished slavery.[46] Jefferson said that his ongoing political engagement must be limited, for he was old and not of the current generation. Some judge this rationale disingenuous, criticizing Jefferson for not making abolition of slavery his first priority. Absent from their account is that Jefferson gave a similar justification to his friend Governor John Tyler when Tyler asked that Jefferson return to the House of Delegates to sponsor Tyler's education program.[47] Jefferson's desire to focus on his university project helps account for his demurrals.

As they both expected, Tyler failed. One widely circulated case against their scheme came from former senator and future governor William Branch Giles.[48] Giles filled several columns in the *Richmond Enquirer* with numerous different arguments against Jeffersonian education reform. Giles said that Tyler's proposal would give a board of public education control over the various components of a young man's intellectual nurturance traditionally controlled by his parents. The plan's application only to people whose parents could not afford private tutoring was grossly unjust, Giles continued. In addition, the teachers' wide dispersion across the commonwealth and their organization ("an hierarchy of incorporated pedagogues") meant that they must soon have substantial influence over the state government—a dangerous prospect.

Echoing John Randolph of Roanoke's earlier complaint, Giles noted that the plan really amounted to transferring some people's property to others in the name of education. Where would such a pattern of behavior stop? Besides, Giles added, this program would not benefit the poor overall: parents deprived of farmhand sons for three, six, or—in the case of the best students—nine years would be hard-pressed to make up for their absence. So-called Jeffersonian Virginia never established public primary and secondary schools. Rather, a general program of public education came only during Reconstruction.[49]

Another aspect of Jefferson's legal reform effort into which *Notes on the State of Virginia* provides insight is the provision of his draft constitutions calling for each male Virginian to be given enough of the government's land to bring his holding up to fifty acres. Jefferson's book devotes extensive attention to farmers' peculiar fitness for republican citizenship. Jefferson waxes poetic in considering this "chosen people of God, if ever He had a chosen people, whose breasts" are the special depositories of independent virtue.[50] Joined to his inheritance reforms, the effect of which would be to break up the few gigantic estates whose holders had dominated Virginia's political and economic life from the beginning, this plan promised to make Virginians a people of substantial, though relatively small, landholdings. Throw in President Jefferson's providential Louisiana Purchase, and Virginia republicanism could bloom "to the thousandth and thousandth generation."[51]

One threat to this prospect was the potential that other statesmen would succeed in assimilating the United States to the British constitutional, political, social, and economic model.[52] Here we see the ground for Jefferson's vociferous opposition to Alexander Hamilton's program of the 1790s. Hazily at first, and finally quite clearly, Jefferson discerned that if Hamilton's argument for the constitutionality of the bank bill, the political advice to average men in Washington's "Farwell Address" (which was partly Hamilton's handiwork), and Hamilton's Report on Manufactures were accepted, the republican, peaceful, agrarian, egalitarian vision underlying Jefferson's draft constitution for Virginia and his work on the revisal would never reach fruition. We might note that Hamilton's abolition activity clashed with Jefferson's hopes for Virginia (and America) as well.

Matters reached their nadir in the John Adams years, of course, beginning with the Cabell presentment of 1797, and ultimately with the Quasi-War and Adams's signing the Alien and Sedition Acts into law on Bastille Day 1798.[53] The Virginia and Kentucky Resolutions of 1798 and 1799 and the Report of 1800 are to be understood as defenses of Jefferson's conception of and hopes for the Revolution.[54] His greatest coadjutor, James Madison, who by this time had done yeoman's work in the general assembly pushing many elements of Jefferson's program to passage, essentially shared his vision, as did lesser lights involved in the Republican counterattack. All would be enormously satisfied by the victory of 1800–1801.[55]

Two events during Jefferson's presidency seemed to mark the final victory of his federal vision, which was tightly interwoven with his Virginia vision. First was his triumphant delivery of an inaugural address outlining his party's program. Often unnoticed in this regard is Jefferson's characteristically Virginian insistence that Americans essentially all thought alike when it came to politics—that they were "brethren of the same principle . . . all republicans, . . . all federalists."[56] His agrarian idyll, we might almost say "his republican idyll," depended on the expectation—a characteristically American expectation, due to be thwarted for Jefferson as the Puritans' had been thwarted for them—that there would be consensus, fellow-feeling, and mutual affection.[57]

Like his friend Madison, who foretold in *The Federalist* a time when the population of the United States would have grown so great as to eliminate for poor men the option of settling unclaimed land, Jefferson thought that Thomas Malthus might in the end be proven right even in North America. If in his first inaugural address he had cast his eye forward to descendants of "the thousandth and thousandth generation," Talleyrand and Napoleon added an even wider prospect.

Jefferson's career in federal office assumes a new appearance when seen in light of his Virginia reform career. Jefferson's foreign policy, both in Washington's cabinet and as president, arose from the desire to avoid pushing America—Virginia—down a British path of development.[58] Militarism, perchance war, meant concentration of authority in the general government, diversion of wealth to a connected few, industrialization, and national debt. Better the Embargo than that. Perhaps by its example, America could usher in a new era of free trade and peace.[59] If so, could a republican age be far behind?

Jefferson conceded in his retirement that the events culminating in the War of 1812 had shattered his illusions.[60] America must have economic diversification.[61] Manufacturing could not be left to trading partners in Europe. In other words, President Jefferson had failed to insulate Virginia from the pressures of the outside world.

Jefferson also returned in those years to one of the elements of the revisal of the laws that had not been adopted: establishment of an Enlightenment college in Virginia. Since the dominant Episcopalians would not relinquish control over William and Mary, he would have his own Central College—in time, the University of Virginia.

Jefferson made the most of his opportunity, essentially setting up the curriculum at the Charlottesville school along Jeffersonian lines. Not only did the professorships mirror the model he had envisioned forty years before, but Jefferson as architect made the campus into precisely the "academical village" he thought such a place should be. The buildings' designs, the open vista at one end, the absence of a professor of divinity. . . . Every aspect would serve (as Jefferson hoped the classical architecture he succeeded in showing Americans to adopt for their public buildings would serve[62]) to inculcate enlightened republicanism.

Besides emancipation and precollegiate education, another issue on which Jefferson refused to take a public position during his twilight years was the reform of Virginia's constitution.[63] Yet he continued to think about it. Jefferson had noted several changes that should be made in 1792. Interestingly, while he listed reduction of the number of delegates, a longer gubernatorial term, removal of the governor's election from the general assembly, and various judicial reforms, he said nothing in public about apportionment or suffrage. On the other hand, in an 1816 letter to western Virginia reform leader Samuel Kercheval, Jefferson listed his favorite reform ideas as universal suffrage; population apportionment; popular election of the governor; elected or removable judges; elections for justices, jurors, and sheriffs; ward divisions; and regular constitutional amendment.[64]

Lest it be thought that Jefferson's criticisms of the 1776 convention's handiwork showed him less charitable to others' achievements during the Revolution than to his own, we ought to note that Jefferson saw constitution-making as a science.[65] Virginia's revolutionary leaders had been the founders of a tradition, he said, and so of course had erred here and there.[66] Succeeding framers' efforts benefited from intervening experience, and so predictably other states and the federal union had improved on the Old Dominion's example. Institutions, he insisted, must advance as knowledge advanced, and that meant that updating the constitution should become routine.[67] The passage of time brought progress, so change would be positive.[68] Such rhetoric masked the fact that other than dropping his call for reducing the number of legislators, he had kept his views essentially unchanged since 1776. Amendment did not come until three years after Jefferson's death, and Tidewater refusal to adopt Jeffersonian apportionment reforms helps explain the creation of West Virginia in 1863.

Peter S. Onuf has judged Jefferson virtually suicidal at the end of his life.[69] He says that Jefferson saw his whole world, personal and political, crashing down around him. Chief among the precipitants was the Missouri Crisis, now notable to us as the first major crisis of sectionalism. Jefferson saw it that way too. While most often noted for the metaphor of "a firebell in the night," Jefferson's April 22, 1820, letter to John Holmes stands out for us because Jefferson adds the simile of "the knell of the Union."[70] Here was the reason the crisis, and particularly the so-called Missouri Compromise (which found precious few congressmen actually compromising[71]), "filled [him] with terror": it threatened to undo the federal union of American states for which he had contended as a young man. Congress seemed to Jefferson to have created an inferior tier of states via its decree that any new states carved out of the northern Louisiana Purchase territory would exclude slavery. Where the Atlantic states had made this decision for themselves, the new ones would not. This scheme contradicted the federal vision he had developed as early as *A Summary View.* Unmentioned by Jefferson but doubtless quite troubling to him was that his one-time student President James Monroe had signed all three of the Missouri Compromise bills. Jefferson's federal vision had received a grievous wound from a fellow Virginian, ally, and friend.

Prodded by the Missouri fracas and the additional shocks to the federal system represented by *McCulloch v. Maryland* (1819), *Cohens v. Virginia* (1821), the Tariff of 1824, and John Quincy Adams's inaugural address, Jefferson in 1825 prepared a "Draft Declaration and Protest of the Commonwealth of Virginia, on the Principles of the Constitution of the United States of America, and on the Violations of Them."[72] Here Jefferson said that Virginia and the other states had given the federal government only enumerated powers, that this principle was being violated by the efforts to establish federal roads programs and in other ways, and that Virginia insisted on proper constitutional construction. This final Jeffersonian constitutional blast shows Jefferson still insisting at the very end of his life on the principle central to his first noted public document: that since Virginia's relationship to federal authority was limited and defined, Virginians controlled their own destiny.

This was the essence of Jeffersonianism. Jefferson would go to his grave insisting that the Revolution had awakened people to "the palpable truth, that the mass of mankind has not been born with saddles on their backs, nor a favored few booted and spurred, ready to ride them legitimately, by the grace of God."[73] To a degree, the heat of his last surviving missive came from the threat to his vision of republicanism represented by what he took to be the renascent Federalism of the anti-Missouri impulse. That Federalism stood to him for irresponsible central authority, authority over which local communities could have no influence, authority whose tendency was to seize locals' money despite constitutional systems and elections and to spend it on its own "foreign" favorites, and more. Such authority, as in 1776, would make republican culture such as he had tried to nurture through his Virginia reform efforts impossible. Virtually at his last minute, Jefferson continued animated by the attitude of 1774, 1776, 1797, and 1798, dreaming of resistance.[74] Yet, Jefferson's "Draft Declaration and Protest of the Commonwealth of Virginia" never saw the light of day. James Madison, Jefferson's longtime coadjutor, persuaded him to keep it to himself. As a practical matter, both of his presidential fellows had abandoned the Jeffersonian vision.

Jefferson thus had reason to despair as he neared his life's end. Revolutionary that he was, he died bereft of important allies, his Virginia reforms half-finished and the meaning of independence much in doubt. In the years to come, Virginia would become still less Jeffersonian. The Jeffersonian phase of Virginia's political life had been fleeting, at most. Perhaps a more Jeffersonian way of understanding Jeffersonian Virginia is as a half-completed edifice.

Notes

1. Alan Pell Crawford, *Twilight at Monticello: The Final Years of Thomas Jefferson* (New York, 2008).

2. Kevin R. C. Gutzman, *Thomas Jefferson—Revolutionary: A Radical's Struggle to Remake America* (New York, 2017); Gutzman, *Virginia's American Revolution: From Dominion to Republic, 1776–1840* (Lanham, Md., 2007).

3. Kevin R. C. Gutzman, *James Madison and the Making of America* (New York, 2013), xxi–xxiii.

4. Jefferson to John Randolph, Aug. 25, 1775, in Julian P. Boyd et al., eds., *The Papers of Thomas Jefferson* (Princeton, N.J., 1950–), 1:240–43 (hereafter *PTJ*).

5. Jefferson, "A Summary View of the Rights of British America," July 1774, in *PTJ*, 1:121–35, 134 (quotation).

6. K. R. Constantine Gutzman, "Jefferson's Draft Declaration of Independence, Richard Bland, and the Revolutionary Legacy: Giving Credit Where Credit Is Due," *Journal of the Historical Society* 1 (2001): 137–54.

7. "Resolution of Independence Moved by R. H. Lee for the Virginia Delegation," June 7, 1776, in *PTJ*, 1:298.

8. Kevin R. C. Gutzman, "Thomas Jefferson's Federalism, 1774–1825," *Modern Age* 53, no. 3 (Summer 2011): 74–80.

9. "The Declaration of Independence as Adopted by Congress," July 4, 1776, in *PTJ*, 1:429.

10. Gutzman, *Virginia's American Revolution*, 117.

11. Jefferson to William Fleming, July 1, 1776, in *PTJ*, 1:412–13. Note the "&c.," which indicates that Congress had gone beyond the Virginia Convention's instruction to declare independence and thus arguably beyond its members' writ. No member had been instructed to develop a political theory to which the states would be bound, and so as a legal-constitutional matter, the rest was surplus.

12. For that, see Gutzman, *Thomas Jefferson—Revolutionary*, chapter 1.

13. Jefferson to Thomas Nelson, May 16, 1776, in *PTJ*, 1:292.

14. Jefferson to Thomas Nelson, May 16, 1776, in ibid., 1:292.

15. George Wythe to Jefferson, July 27, 1776, in ibid., 1:476–77.

16. "Editorial Note: The Virginia Constitution," in ibid., 1:331.

17. Ibid., 330.

18. Edmund Randolph, *History of Virginia*, ed. Arthur H. Shaffer (Charlottesville, Va., 1970), 251–52.

19. "First Draft by Jefferson," before June 13, 1776, in *PTJ*, 1:337–45. The material and quotations in the next six paragraphs come from this document.

20. Jefferson to Edmund Pendleton, Aug. 13, 1776; Jefferson to Archibald Stuart, Jan. 25, 1786, in Merrill Peterson, ed., *Thomas Jefferson: Writings* (New York, 1948), 752, 844.

21. For the county courts, see F. Thornton Miller, *Judges and Juries Versus the Law: Virginia's Provincial Legal Perspective, 1783–1828* (Charlottesville, Va., 1994).

22. For this and the next two paragraphs, see "Second Draft by Jefferson," before June 13, 1776, in *PTJ*, 1:347–54.

23. "Third Draft by Jefferson," before June 13, 1776, in ibid., 1:356–64.

24. For this and the next two paragraphs, see Jefferson to Edmund Pendleton, Aug. 26, 1776, in ibid., 1:503–6.

25. Edmund Pendleton to Jefferson, July 22, 1776, in ibid., 1:472.

26. "Editorial Note: The Revisal of the Laws, 1776–1786," in ibid., 2:313. Hereafter, the judgment of the editors of *PTJ* concerning Jefferson's authorship of the revisal bills is accepted. Ibid., 2:320.

27. Jefferson, "A Bill for Establishing Religious Freedom," in ibid., 2:545–47.

28. Ibid., 2:552n3. Jefferson from an early date scorned religious establishment and Christian teaching about Jesus. The classic summary of Jefferson's religious outlook is Merrill D. Peterson, *Thomas Jefferson and the New Nation: A Biography* (New York, 1970), 49–53. Also see Paul Conkin, "The Religious Pilgrimage of Thomas Jefferson," in *Jeffersonian Legacies,* ed. Peter S. Onuf (Charlottesville, Va., 1993), 21. For Jefferson and freedom of conscience, see Gutzman, *Thomas Jefferson—Revolutionary,* chapter 2.

29. Jefferson, "A Bill for Saving the Property of the Church Heretofore by Law Established," in *PTJ,* 2:553–54.

30. Jefferson, "A Bill for Punishing Disturbers of Religious Worship and Sabbath Breakers," in ibid., 2:555.

31. Jefferson, "A Bill for Proportioning Crimes and Punishments in Cases Heretofore Capital," in ibid., 2:492–507, 505n.

32. Jefferson, "A Bill Directing the Course of Descents," in ibid., 2:391–93.

33. Holly Brewer, "Entailing Aristocracy in Colonial Virginia: 'Ancient Feudal Restraints' and Revolutionary Reform," *William and Mary Quarterly,* 3rd ser., 54 (1997): 307–46; for Jefferson's estimation, see Jefferson to John Adams, Oct. 28, 1813, in Peterson, ed., *Thomas Jefferson: Writings,* 1307–8.

34. See particularly Paul Finkelman, *Slavery and the Founders: Race and Liberty in the Age of Jefferson,* 2nd ed. (Armonk, N.Y., 2001).

35. Jefferson, "A Bill Concerning Slaves," in *PTJ,* 2:470–72, 472–73nn.

36. Jefferson, "A Bill Declaring Who Shall Be Deemed Citizens of This Commonwealth"; Jefferson, "A Bill Concerning Aliens," in ibid., 2:476–78, 479–80.

37. Jefferson, "A Bill for the More General Diffusion of Knowledge"; Jefferson, "A Bill for Amending the Constitution of the College of William and Mary, and Substituting More Certain Revenues for Its Support," in ibid., 2:526–33, 535–42.

38. Jefferson to John Adams, Oct. 28, 1813, Founders Online (National Archives), https://founders.archives.gov/documents/Adams/99-02-02-6189.

39. Douglas L. Wilson, "Jefferson and the Republic of Letters," in Onuf, ed., *Jeffersonian Legacies,* 50–76.

40. The best book on Jefferson's career as an education reformer is Jennings L. Wagoner, *Jefferson and Education* (Charlottesville, Va., 2004).

41. Jefferson, "A Bill for Amending the Constitution of the College of William and Mary, and Substituting More Certain Revenues for Its Support," in *PTJ,* 2:535–42.

42. Gutzman, *Thomas Jefferson—Revolutionary,* 210.

43. Thomas Jefferson, *Notes on the State of Virginia,* ed. William Peden (Chapel Hill, N.C., 1954), 110–29.

44. Jefferson's claim is at ibid., 137, but see Finkelman, *Slavery and the Founders,* 145.

45. Alison Goodyear Freehling, *Drift toward Dissolution: The Virginia Slavery Debate of 1831–1832* (Charlottesville, Va., 1982).

46. Jefferson to Edward Coles, Aug. 25, 1814, in Peterson, ed., *Thomas Jefferson: Writings,* 1343–46. See also Suzanne Guasco, *Confronting Slavery: Edward Coles and the Rise of Anti-Slavery Politics in Nineteenth-Century America* (De Kalb, Ill., 2013).

47. Gutzman, *Virginia's American Revolution,* 150–52.

48. The description of Giles's and Randolph's criticism in this and the following paragraphs is from ibid., 154–57.

49. Wagoner, *Jefferson and Education,* 128.

50. Jefferson, *Notes on the State of Virginia,* 164–65.

51. Jefferson, First Inaugural Address, Mar. 4, 1801, Avalon Project at Yale Law School, Lillian Goldman Law Library, http://avalon.law.yale.edu/19th_century/jefinau1.asp.

52. Eric M. Nelson, *The Royalist Revolution: Monarchy and the American Founding* (Cambridge, Mass., 2014).

53. Precisely how cognizant Americans of that period were of French anniversaries has been made clear by David Waldstreicher, *In the Midst of Perpetual Fetes: The Making of American Nationalism, 1776–1820* (Chapel Hill, N.C., 1997), and Simon P. Newman, *Parades and the Politics of the Street: Festive Culture in the Early American Republic* (Philadelphia, 1997).

54. Gutzman, *Virginia's American Revolution,* 113–34.

55. For the short-run nature of the Jeffersonian victory, see ibid., 135–62.

56. Perhaps the foremost Virginian expression of this expectation is John Taylor of Caroline, *A Pamphlet Containing a Series of Letters* (Richmond, Va., 1809).

57. Jefferson, First Inaugural Address. For the agrarian idyll, see Drew R. McCoy, *The Elusive Republic: Political Economy in Jeffersonian America* (Chapel Hill, N.C., 1980).

58. McCoy, *The Elusive Republic.*

59. Peter S. Onuf and Nicholas Onuf, *Federal Union, Modern World: The Law of Nations in an Age of Revolutions, 1776–1814* (Madison, Wis., 1993), and Gutzman, *James Madison and the Making of America.*

60. Jefferson to William Short, Nov. 28, 1814, in Peterson, ed., *Thomas Jefferson: Writings,* 1357.

61. Jefferson to Marquis de Lafayette, Feb. 14, 1815; Jefferson to Benjamin Austin, Jan. 9, 1816, in ibid., 1366, 1370–72.

62. Jefferson to James Madison, Sept. 20, 1785; Jefferson to William Buchanan and James Hay, Jan. 26, 1786, in ibid., 828–30, 845–47.

63. A treatment of the Virginia constitutional reform movement is Robert P. Sutton, *Revolution to Secession: Constitution Making in the Old Dominion* (Charlottesville, Va., 1989).

64. Jefferson to Samuel Kercheval, July 12, 1816, in Peterson, ed., *Thomas Jefferson: Writings,* 1400.

65. Jefferson to Major John Cartwright, June 5, 1824, in ibid., 1492.

66. "This constitution," he wrote in 1781, "was formed when we were new and unexperienced in the science of government. It was the first too which was formed in the whole United States. No wonder then that time and trial have discovered [i.e., disclosed] very capital defects in it." Jefferson, *Notes on the State of Virginia,* 118.

67. Jefferson to Samuel Kercheval, July 12, 1816, in Peterson, ed., *Thomas Jefferson: Writings,* 1401.

68. For Jefferson and time, see Hannah Spahn, *Thomas Jefferson, Time, and History* (Charlottesville, Va., 2011).

69. Peter S. Onuf, *Jefferson's Empire: The Language of American Nationhood* (Charlottesville, Va., 2000).

70. Jefferson to John Holmes, Apr. 22, 1820, in Peterson, ed., *Thomas Jefferson: Writings,* 1433–35.

71. Michael F. Holt, "Coming of the Civil War," lectures, University of Virginia, 1992 (notes in author's possession).

72. See Gutzman, "Thomas Jefferson's Federalism."

73. Jefferson to Roger C. Weightman, June 24, 1826, in Peterson, ed., *Thomas Jefferson: Writings,* 1516–17.

74. "Draft Declaration and Protest of the Commonwealth of Virginia, on the Principles of the Constitution of the United States of America, and on the Violations of Them," Dec. 1825, in ibid., 482–86.

6 Jefferson's Embargo

National Intent and Sectional Effects

Benjamin L. Carp

"The spirit of rivalry, jealousy, and opposition . . . between the southern planters and northern merchants in the United States" was readily apparent to the English traveler John Lambert. He had seen grass growing on the wharves of New York City in April 1808, and he was stunned that Republican merchants would "commit a sort of *commercial suicide*" in support of the Embargo. It was a situation that could not last.[1] Jeffersonians intended the Embargo Act of 1807—an indefinite ban on overseas trade from the United States—as a nationwide response to foreign incursions on American shipping, but many Americans quickly came to see the Embargo and its enforcement as a sectionally divisive measure.

The Embargo of 1807–9 was not just an instance of failed foreign policy but a failure of domestic political mobilization, one that the Republicans expected to succeed because it was a matter of international relations, national independence, and patriotic honor—and therefore should have led to unity. As Peter S. Onuf writes, "The nation Jefferson imagined was united in principle, harmonious in its interdependent interests, homogeneous in character." Jefferson was not the first president to face collapsing support for his policies, but he may have been uniquely disillusioned and repressive in the face of his administration's failure. The new nation learned that successful government policies required careful sectional calibration, lest they yield catastrophic outcomes. The Embargo was an example of a policy so careless and untenable that partisan politics almost failed to contain sectional conflict.[2]

Prior to the drafting of the Constitution, Americans wondered, according to Onuf, "whether or not sectional interests could be both protected and promoted in a more energetic union." Convinced that "sectional differences were intractable," many predicted the formation of separate regional confederacies. The nationalists who drafted the Constitution managed to convince Americans that a balanced federal union "could provide a framework for containing and redirecting sectionalist impulses." Yet lawmakers still worried that forcible federal policies might lead to interstate conflicts and anarchy. While the union seemed durable, they also had to tread carefully, because Americans expected that the rights and interests of particular places and localities would be equally protected under the Constitution. Jefferson's attempt to enforce the Embargo would become one of the first significant tests of these crucial questions.[3]

Jefferson regarded the Embargo as an "experiment" to see whether economic coercion could succeed as diplomatic strategy. Yet the Embargo also required the cooperation of American citizens, and so it inadvertently became an experiment to see whether the union could survive a sectionally divisive federal policy. Jefferson believed that every American, "at the call of the law, would fly to the standard of the law, and would meet invasions of the public order as his own personal concern," a belief that was affirmed for him, James E. Lewis Jr. argues, by the outcome of the Burr Conspiracy. When Americans flew away from the law rather than to its standard, Jefferson was compelled (as the Federalists had been) to use the power of the central government to prod local communities into upholding their responsibility to the people's interest.[4]

Historians have not always been comfortable discussing the sectionalizing tendencies of the Embargo. Henry Adams's influential history characterized the issue as sectionally divisive but also largely driven by personality conflict—particularly the Federalists' hatred of Jefferson. Walter W. Jennings defended the policy's promotion of manufacturing as a boon to the North, while Louis Martin Sears viewed economic coercion as a pacifist alternative to war and played down the resultant sectional conflict; he too was drawn to the conclusion that the Embargo hurt the South as much as the North, thus undercutting contemporary northerners' objections.[5] Since World War II, historians have examined the Embargo by emphasizing the ideologies of statesmen, their practices of partisanship, and questions of transatlantic diplomacy. Linda K. Kerber and James M. Banner analyzed the anti-southern ideology that colored the party politics of certain New England Federalists concerning the Embargo, but Banner doubted that their fears were rooted in reality. Forrest McDonald posited that a rigid Republican ideology had forced Jefferson's exhausted administration into the Embargo policy and guaranteed its failure. In a more focused study, Burton Spivak argued that Jefferson had been "New England's President" in his defense of sailors and commerce, but over the course of 1808 he retreated to an agrarian ideology. Spivak dismissed the New Englanders' "angry" conviction that "a crass sectional plot posed as national policy," and argued that Jefferson's harsh enforcement measures were consistent with his ideological views.[6]

More recently, historians from James E. Lewis Jr. and Garry Wills to Brian Schoen and Dinah Mayo-Bobee have become comfortable with the idea that Jefferson's anti-Federalist and anti-commercial stance had sectional undertones. Scholarship on slavery and foreign policy has helped scholars to understand sectionalism during Jefferson's presidency in new ways—and the Embargo is central to this story. Jefferson may not have hated northerners, but his vision of an agrarian economy carried with it a distrust of northern commerce. His commercial and diplomatic policies threatened the region (particularly New England) with severe disruption. As even Spivak admitted, "The embargo years . . . challenged the merchant class to renounce foreign trade or accept a marginal role in the nation's economic future." Even if we accept Spivak's argument that the Embargo was designed in part to protect northern commercial shipping, the short-term costs were too much for many northerners to bear, and they reacted accordingly.[7]

After the HMS *Leopard* captured the USS *Chesapeake* on June 22, 1807, the U.S. government felt compelled, as a matter of national honor, to respond. Unprepared for war and unable to devise a strategy compatible with the angry national mood, the Republican Congress instituted an indefinite Embargo, prohibiting all American shipments to foreign ports, on December 22, 1807. The Embargo would keep American ships safely in port while diplomats tried to negotiate concessions from the European belligerents (Britain and France) respecting American trade rights. Over the coming months, the Jeffersonians increasingly emphasized the coercive potential of withholding exports from Britain and France.[8]

As diplomacy sputtered, the Embargo also became an instrument for coercing American citizens to obey an unpopular law. Jerry L. Mashaw argues that the Embargo "ultimately required the use of domestic coercive authority that was more aggressive and intrusive than the Federalists' hated Alien and Sedition Acts." By January 9, 1808, Congress had also imposed controls on coasters, whalers, and fishing vessels; New Englanders took note when southern and western representatives defeated Josiah Quincy's motion (supported by many northern Republicans) to protect fishermen from the Embargo. Violation of the Embargo would result in a forfeiture of the ship and cargo (or a fine equal to double their value), plus fines and de facto exclusions from trade. A third law of March 12 extended export restrictions to overland trade, while coasting vessels now had to complete their journeys in four months. Congress passed another pair of laws in April: one authorized the president to suspend the embargo if the diplomatic situation improved, while the other prohibited shipments to the Maine District or Florida without presidential approval, required customs officers to supervise the loading of ships before clearing them, authorized customs collectors and naval ships to seize violators' ships or cargo without a warrant based on suspicion alone, and allowed customs collectors to detain a vessel if they believed it intended to violate the law.[9]

Treasury Secretary Albert Gallatin, the reluctant enforcer of the Embargo, lamented in July 1808 that the diplomatic situation was now too complex to "rouse" Americans' "patriotism and unite their passions and affections." Their selfishness had turned them against the Embargo, and this selfishness manifested as smuggling. He suggested that collectors would have to be "invested with the general power of seizing property anywhere" and detaining suspicious vessels, though he also acknowledged that "such arbitrary powers are equally dangerous and odious."[10] By November, Gallatin had to talk Jefferson down from a "*denunciation* of commerce" in his annual message to Congress: he warned Jefferson that it would "furnish a powerful weapon to the disaffected in the seaports and in all the Eastern States." A few days later, Jefferson asked Gallatin to withhold commercial permits from anyone living in a town that was "tainted with a general spirit of disobedience" unless the merchant could demonstrate that he had never spoken or acted against the Embargo.[11]

In the eyes of many Americans, the administration finally overstepped its authority with the Enforcement Act of January 9, 1809, which proved to be the Embargo's undoing. This act imposed penalties and forfeitures to anyone who aided and abetted in the violation of the Embargo, required permits even to load a ship (which could be denied at a collector's discretion), rewarded informers, protected officials from lawsuits, and imposed a heavy burden of proof on ships claiming that they had faced distress at sea. Finally, this act allowed the president (or designated customs collectors) to use the army, navy, or militia to interdict, seize, and detain violators on land and sea.[12] By the beginning of 1809, therefore, enforcement of the Embargo necessitated increasingly vigorous federal action, which interfered with state, local, and individual prerogatives. Historians have criticized the political effects of such policies—notably, Leonard W. Levy castigated them from a civil liberties perspective—but contemporaries also focused on the economic hardships caused by the Embargo. As Jeremiah Olney, Providence's customs collector, wrote, "the minds of all classes of Citizens are much exasperated by the operations of the *Fatal* Act" of January 9. He resigned soon after.[13]

Opposition to the Embargo took many forms. Political historians have concentrated on the electoral effects of antipathy toward the policy. Federalists and dissenting Republicans were not always able to capitalize on discontent; many 1808 elections occurred before the citizenry felt the full impact of the Embargo. Still, Federalists were able to mobilize voter turnout and reduce Republicans' hold on power, and these effects were largely sectional: Philip J. Lampi notes that Federalists contested every congressional seat north of the Potomac and Ohio in 1808 and doubled their number in Congress but gained much less traction in the South. At the state level, they made gains in New York, New Jersey, Maryland, and Delaware; in spring of 1809, they captured seats in New York and New England. All told, with the exception of New Jersey and Pennsylvania, Federalists gained at least partial control of every New England and mid-Atlantic state. Although Federalists also had some success in the South, it was minimal by comparison, and the Embargo cost the Republicans little popularity in the region. The Embargo, in this way, almost succeeded in sectionalizing the two political parties.[14]

Jefferson's allies dismissed organized opposition to the Embargo as stemming from foreign interests and disaffected Federalists; he claimed that only Republicans truly served the national interest. Soon enough, such comforting self-delusions about "malignant leaders and their deluded followers," as Onuf writes, became more difficult to sustain. Harrison Gray Otis noted the Republican strategy of arguing "that an Essex or a Boston Junto give the cue to the Eastern States, and that the Federalists in those States are our Dupes and tools." Yet the Federalists were capable of flipping the script on the Republicans, to argue that a federal government ought to have as much responsibility toward the northern regions as it did to the South and West. As Senator Timothy Pickering of Massachusetts asked his son-in-law, "Who will believe that Mr. Jefferson, other southern men, and the members from the interiour (some of whom never saw a ship or seaman) are anxiously concerned for the protection of (as I believe Jefferson once called them) their 'sea-faring *brethren,*' against British impresses; when, they are willing that our shipping should be annihilated?" In a letter to Rufus King, Pickering called for "a union of sentiment in the six eastern states" or "a union of Northern Interests" to advocate for better policies.[15]

Sectionalist resentment against the Virginia dynasty became more widespread during the Embargo crisis. Newspaper readers were urged to break free of the "Southern party" and the "fetters of the Virginia Faction" that threatened New England commerce.[16] In September 1808, Thomas Barclay, the British consul general in New York City, remarked on "the jealousy of the Eastern & Northern States" of Virginia's national influence, and their "determination to shake them off." Edmond-Charles Genet, the son-in-law of James Madison's Republican rival George Clinton, wrote that if New Yorkers continued to support Jefferson, they would "perpetuate the Presidency in the hands of Virginia, and . . . consolidate an order of things highly gratifying to the jealousy which the rapid prosperity of New York and of the other commercial states has raised in the bosom of the indolent slave holders of that state." He continued, "The embargo is the undisputed property of a few southern systematic politicians."[17]

It was one thing for a Federalist like Josiah Quincy to deny that the Embargo "was a burden which pressed equally" on the sections. But James Sloan, a New Jersey Republican who had voted for the Embargo and the first two supplementary acts, also decided by November 1808 that the Embargo acted "partially and unequally upon different parts of the country." Representative Orchard Cook of Massachusetts (Maine district) began to fret that Republicans needed to "make some steps to still the Clamours of our state against southern influence." As Brian Schoen notes, congressional debates "quickly degenerated into contests over whose region or interest had suffered most for the nation." Southerners convinced themselves that their sacrifice was greater, because they had supported the Embargo and sacrificed their own profits on behalf of northern shipping interests. "We have suffered, and now suffer," declared Senator William H. Crawford of Georgia, "yet we have not complained." In making such claims, they glossed over northerners' own hardships and underplayed their ability to endure depressed employment by switching to slave labor. When northerners eventually moved for repeal, these self-sacrificing southerners howled their feelings of betrayal.[18]

The administration did its best to mobilize support for the Embargo using the tools of state (from courts to military force) and party (from newspapers to street theater), and the statements of state and local governments. Although the Jeffersonians attempted to affix party labels to the supporters and opponents of the Embargo, a sectionalist interpretation seems just as valid. "Defiance contributed more to party divisions, than partisanship to defiance," historian Reginald C. Stuart argues. The economic interests of northerners, rather than ideology or partisanship, shaped their views. Federalist politicians helped things along: when Senator James Hillhouse of Connecticut wrote that Virginians "have embarked very little in commerce, and consequently feel but little interest in its prosperity, or disposition to protect it," the newspapers printed his words. Jeffrey L. Pasley argues that Federalists, in speeches and print, "focused on appealing to Yankee sectional prejudices in their criticisms of Jefferson, emphasizing the distasteful aspects of southern culture and casting administration policies as indifferent or hostile to New England's economic interests." Whatever their centralizing aspirations, Federalist elites made their appeals with their constituents' local interests in mind; at the same time, Americans of all stripes voiced their grievances in sectional terms. Northern newspapers were particularly fervid venues for criticism of the Embargo. The *New London Gazette,* for instance, mentioned the Embargo in almost every issue while the law was in effect.[19]

Soon after the passage of the Embargo, Senator Timothy Pickering urged, "Nothing but the sense of the commercial states, clearly expressed, will save them from ruin." Federalists spread Pickering's pamphlets so quickly and broadly that New England Republicans felt powerless to counteract them.[20] Complaints had surfaced in March 1808 about the "undue influence which the Southern States have acquired over the hardy, honest and industrious people of New-England." By January 1809, the rhetoric had escalated: "Where is the Yankee," asked the *Newburyport Herald,* "who could bear to be abused and ridiculed by Virginian boys? Beings, suckled by slaves, pampered in indolence, and effeminate by indulgence!—Can New-England, rich in intellect, and knowledge, and wealth . . . support this forever?"[21] New Englanders invoked a particular regional identity in their protests, but discontent could be found throughout the North, especially in New York.

The debate was also not limited, of course, to congressmen and printers. Black voters in New York City, for instance, met to protest the Embargo and support an anti-Jeffersonian ticket in April 1808.[22] Petitions opposing the Embargo came from mercantile communities throughout the United States, particularly in the North. A Boston committee argued that the Embargo intended "to unjustifiably depress an ill fated section of the union, and on their ruin to erect the riches and glory of another part of the nation."[23] Meanwhile, as James H. Broussard writes, "from Virginia to Georgia there was [comparative] silence."[24] By June 1808, a New York merchant wrote that he could no longer be patient waiting for Jefferson's "foolish Experimental Embargo" to end. Even children protested; an orphan girl from Boston presented Jefferson with a bill for lost income. While one petitioner told Jefferson to "Go to Hell," another said the president was "determined on the total destruction of our Commerce especially the Northern states."[25]

The populace mobilized out of doors, deploying practices common to urban street theater of the early republic. As early as January 7, 1808, Boston's unemployed seamen and laborers were parading the streets with a flag at half-mast. In Wells, Maine, on the anniversary of the Embargo's enactment in December 1808, the bells tolled in mourning, the townspeople passed protest resolutions, and the minister composed a funeral dirge that began, "Hark from the South a doleful sound." After the passage of the Enforcement Act, the Boston *Repertory* printed a picture of a coffin for Liberty borne by congressional pallbearers who had opposed the bill, led by Revolutionary War veterans, and trailed by farmers, merchants, artisans, seamen, and laborers.[26]

A Republican author hit back against this trend of funeral processions and handbills and newspapers festooned with coffins. "Hancock" accused the Federalists of using the Embargo protests as a pretense to create "A Division of the States" and therefore "*Anarchy* and *Civil War*" between the North and South. "Would it be pleasing to WASHINGTON," asked the author, "to see the pageantry of a funeral procession, merely to stimulate the citizens to rise in opposition to the acts of the Constituted Authorities?" Republicans resorted to nationalist appeals as prophylaxis against sectionalist stirrings in the North. At the same time, they also attempted to aid suffering constituents with soup kitchens, employment in public works, and other forms of poor relief.[27]

The implementation of Jefferson's Embargo became a maddening problem. Terry Bouton has shown that Pennsylvania farmers defended their communities with "rings of protection" from unpopular state and federal laws in the years 1788–93—these included a series of measures ranging from lenient local officials to violence and road obstructions. Similarly, maritime communities in 1808–9 developed several layers of protection against the federal Embargo. The early customs service was built on a foundation of negotiation and accommodation between officials and local communities. In the spirit of this tradition, merchants under the Embargo took advantage of legal loopholes or an absence of personnel, collaborated with (or bribed) lenient federal officials, intimidated more scrupulous officials, and broke the law outright. Local residents might act as informers for customs officials, but they also might warn smugglers when officials were near. The Jeffersonians attempted to upend cozy relationships between violators and officers, and they simultaneously endowed administrators with more power. Yet violations continued, particularly in the North, to the detriment of the Embargo's success.[28]

So long as they lacked the support of local communities, the Jeffersonians could not successfully enforce the Embargo. Local district attorneys proved to be worthless. Treasury Secretary Albert Gallatin removed the collector of customs at Perth Amboy, New Jersey, for clearing vessels and refusing to allow his papers to be inspected. The customs service also had to replace Federalist officials in New Bedford, Massachusetts, and Oswego and Sackett's Harbor, New York, with Republicans. Jefferson came to believe that loyal partisans would do more to combat smuggling, and he sought out northern Republicans to do the job. Some of the largest northern ports, indeed, had vigorous customs collectors. Massachusetts governor James Sullivan was another staunch supporter of the Republican Party and the Embargo. Yet even he undermined the policy and ran afoul of the Jefferson administration by freely granting licenses for flour imports, which indirectly helped smugglers. Meanwhile, outside of New Orleans and Baltimore, most southern customs collectors were fairly reliable (which was easier when the population was more acquiescent to the Embargo). Smuggling may not have been extensive—but the violations that were publicized in the press and in government reports infuriated Jefferson and helped to set the terms of the debate over the Embargo. And as 1808 wore on, frustrations with the laws led more merchants to violate them.[29]

Because the Embargo had to be enforced locally, it could not help but provoke regional anger. Certainly, many southern merchants violated the Embargo; a Virginia congressman later wrote, "On the southern limit of our territory, the same game was playing to an equal extent." Around New

Orleans and at Savannah and St. Mary's, Georgia; Baltimore; and Edenton, North Carolina, merchants were violating the Embargo. Yet the bulk of the complaints and the traffic came from the areas around Maine, Vermont, and New York. As early as March 1808, Boston collector Benjamin Lincoln reported, "The law is very much evaded and we have no means to prevent it." By the summer, Gallatin observed that "the danger is much greater from New York northwardly, principally from Massachusetts." James Madison would later lament that the northern borderlands were a "world of itself" where the Embargo policy foundered. In the fall of 1808, two hundred men, armed and masked, occupied the Portland, Maine, wharves and loaded two vessels with shipments for export.[30]

Jeffersonian officials quickly found that prosecuting violations of the Embargo would be difficult. Federalist lawyers in New England did their best to disrupt the enforcement of the Embargo using a variety of tactics, including lawsuits against customs officials (for instance, in Boston and Barnstable, Massachusetts) and writs of replevin to recover seized goods. In Massachusetts, Embargo cases decided by a federal judge had a conviction rate of 66 percent, while juries convicted at an 18 percent rate; incidents of jury resistance occurred in a number of localities, particularly in New England and New York. One Massachusetts juror, according to John Quincy Adams, declared, "He never would agree to convict any person under these laws, *whatever might be the facts.*" The chief justice of the Massachusetts Supreme Judicial Court believed that the Embargo was unconstitutional, and the U.S. Supreme Court had to reverse the Massachusetts court three times to provide legal protection for a customs collector.[31]

Supporters and enforcers of the Embargo became poisonously unpopular in merchant communities. John Quincy Adams supported Republicans in the midst of the Embargo; when he returned to his Massachusetts constituents and faced their anger, he became sick to his stomach and was soon forced to resign his seat in the Senate. Lewis Delesdernier, collector of Passamaquoddy, Maine, was ostracized by his neighbors and undermined by faithless subordinates; on November 17, 1808, a local trader battered and wounded Delesdernier's son. Josiah Hook, collector of the Penobscot, Maine, district, was reprimanded for his lack of vigilance even though his conduct had been particularly firm. Joshua M. Smith argues that local complainants had launched a deliberate whisper campaign against him. A diligent officer could face threats of having his house burnt.[32]

Jefferson's administration found that enforcement would require "a veritable war against the violators of the embargo," according to Robert W. Tucker and David C. Hendrickson. Extensive powers of search and seizure, armed forces along the Canadian border, and active (if insufficient and occasionally uncooperative) gunboat squadrons became the tools of enforcement.[33] In the North, armed enforcement led to armed resistance. Some officers were intimidated into inaction (like William Ellery of Newport) or resignation (like Jeremiah Olney of Providence). Locals near Cumberland Head, New York, made several attempts to kidnap their local collector, which seems to have made him a rather timid enforcer. Townspeople seized customhouses in Oswego, Portland, and Providence; tarred and feathered an informer in Portland; disabled customs vessels in the Kennebec River; fired on a revenue cutter in Bath, Maine (in front of cheering crowds); and physically stopped customs officers in Newburyport. A group of women opened the jails in Augusta, Maine. Two customs officials and another man died during a gunfight over smuggling on Lake Champlain. After some smugglers who had murdered a customs guard on Isle au Haut were captured, a crowd dressed as women released most of the prisoners; for those that remained in custody, no witnesses would testify against them.[34] Gallatin began to worry that "the disobedience & resistance which have been encouraged sap the very foundation of our institutions. And I had rather to encounter war itself than to display our impotence to enforce our laws." He came to doubt whether "there was virtue enough in the Eastern people" for the Embargo to succeed, which must have been a blow to Jefferson's vision for the republic.[35]

These acts of violence led to lurid fears that a civil war was in the offing. Much of this talk was partisan gamesmanship, and many refused to take it seriously. Republicans could dismiss Federalist opposition by tarring it with the brush of disunionism. The Richmond *Enquirer* noted the irony of Federalists advocating disunion, claiming that Virginia had not gone nearly as far in its protests against the Alien and Sedition Acts. Meanwhile, John Quincy Adams warned against excessive anti-southern rhetoric: if "people in the different quarters of this Union are not sufficiently drawn together" by ties of nationalism, then crises like the Embargo would "awaken every sleeping ember of jealousy . . . , widen every breach of separation, [and] . . . stiffen coldness into frost." As Onuf has shown, the fear that disparate sectional interests would tear apart the union was fundamental to early American politics.[36]

From the first month that the Embargo was in effect, Governor James Sullivan warned Jefferson that Massachusetts Federalists "talk of a division between the southern and northern States as a matter of course." A New York merchant wrote, "The people of the Eastern states, who may be termed the true Americans of this country, are much dissatisfied with the conduct of the General Government, and appear determined to obtain an alleviation of their sufferings or result to measures which may eventually dismember the union." Federalist leaders could be quite cynical about mobilizing sectionalism for partisan ends, and historian David Hackett Fischer argues that they succeeded too well: while genuine disunionism was ultimately a step too far for most Federalist leaders, the economic hardships of the Embargo did cause popular upheaval in the North. Referring to the Enforcement Act as "the DEATH-WARRANT of New-England Liberty," the *Salem Gazette* announced that the law "leaves but one horrible alternative, Civil War or Slavery." Meanwhile, ardent southern Republicans were all too eager to seize on the shibboleth of Federalist-backed disunion and urge Americans to shun the disloyal opposition.[37]

Jefferson himself, his faith in the "honest patriot" shaken, fed some of the unrest. Hearing reports of smuggling along the Canadian border, he proclaimed on April 19 (the anniversary of the Battles of Lexington and Concord) that residents around Lake Champlain were "confederating . . . for the purpose of forming insurrections against the authority of the laws of the United States" and ordered "such insurgents" to disperse on pain of arrest. Federal officials, and any other local authorities, were enjoined to suppress the rebellion "by all the means in their power, by force of arms, or otherwise." Jefferson's words inflamed the outrage in the borderlands.[38]

Active Republican enforcement also fed northern resentment. When under the Enforcement Act Congress empowered state governors to call out the militia, New Englanders and New Yorkers dug in their heels. Jeremiah Olney noted the "spirit of opposition" in the seaports, which (if the Embargo was not repealed) "will soon pervade the whole extent of Sea Coast." If Congress continued to use the military to enforce the Embargo, he wrote, it would eventually "shake the empire to its centre and deluge this once happy land in Blood." At Sackett's Harbor, merchants refused to sell supplies to soldiers, and local residents ostracized and intimidated the troops. In Oswegatchie (Ogdensburg), New York, the locals intimidated officials and their supporters. In Rhode Island, militia companies declined to muster and the governor refused to call them up. Governor Levi Lincoln of Massachusetts (Sullivan had died on December 10, 1808) appointed militia officers, but the legislature censured him and petitioned Congress for repeal, calling for a constitutional amendment "to give to the Commercial States their fair and just consideration in the government of the Union," probably a reference to the distasteful three-fifths compromise that artificially inflated southern majorities in Congress and the Electoral College. The legislature then adopted resolutions that stopped short of secession but, as Forrest McDonald writes, included "an ultimatum that amounted to a threat to secede." The town meeting of Bath established a committee of safety to warn residents about government enforcement of the law. Connecticut's Governor Jonathan Trumbull wrote to the secretary of war that the president had no authority to direct him; in support, the legislature prohibited state officials from enforcing the Embargo.[39]

Rather than face these challenges to the Constitution, northern Republicans turned against the Embargo. By early 1809, smuggling vessels were departing from ports all over the United States, particularly New York and New Jersey. Although the Jeffersonians made every effort to retain allies in the North, northern statesmen began worrying about the stability of the union and the social order—and their constituents had clearly had enough. The House of Representatives voted to repeal the Embargo on February 3, 1809, largely along regional lines.[40] Henry Adams later regarded the Republicans' capitulation with disgust, seeing it as "a reward for threats of disunion, and conceding to traitors what would have been refused to good citizens"; this was "an evil augury." In the North, the Embargo had kicked up hundreds of dust devils of dissent and resistance, leading to sectional resentment. In the South, a more muted resistance simmered along with a self-sacrificing rhetoric of support for the Jefferson administration. Southern resentment against "commercial States" would resurface many times during the antebellum years.[41]

In retirement, Jefferson was both angry at New England Republicans like Joseph Story and Ezekiel Bacon who turned against the Embargo, and impressed at the New England institutions that had propelled the opposition. He predicted that "as commercial avarice and corruption advance on us from the north and east, the principles of free government are to retire to the agricultural States of the south and west, as their last asylum and bulwark." Over time, his fear of and bitterness toward the Northeast increased, as did his awareness of the power of northeastern resistance. A few years later, in letters to fellow Virginians, he wrote of New England's "little republics" with grudging admiration: "We owe to them the vigor given to our revolution in its commencement in the Eastern States, and by them the Eastern States were enabled to repeal the embargo." Later, advocating for "ward republics" over the "drunken loungers" who hung around county courthouses in the South, he wrote, "How powerfully did we feel the energy of this organization in the case of embargo? I felt the foundations of the government shaken under my feet by the New England townships." Jefferson could not help denigrating them as "this little selfish minority," but he was impressed that their organization "enabled it to overrule the Union."[42]

Eventually, manufacturing would buoy the North (Jefferson would later boast about this, refusing to acknowledge the Embargo's failure), and in this way the net economic consequences of the Embargo may well have been harder on the South than on the North—yet few perceived this at the time, and southern planters were better able to weather the crisis than New England merchants and their employees. New Englanders would step up their anti-southern rhetoric once more during the War of 1812, linking their own political slavery to the plight of southern slaves.[43] The sectionalized debates that surrounded the Embargo and the War of 1812 would ultimately sink the Federalists. But none of this was clear three days before the end of Jefferson's administration, when he reluctantly signed the bill that replaced the Embargo with the Non-Intercourse Act that outlawed trade only with Great Britain and France. In enforcing federal policy, Jefferson had kindled a sectional conflagration, one that northern Republicans hastened to extinguish before Jeffersonian policy destroyed the economy and the political fortunes of the party.

Notes

The author wishes to thank Rachel Knecht, Brian Schoen, and the editors.

1. John Lambert, *Travels through Canada, and the United States of North America, in the Years 1806, 1807, and 1808,* 2nd ed. (1810; London, 1814), 2:63, 74, 364.

2. Peter S. Onuf, *Jefferson's Empire: The Language of American Nationhood* (Charlottesville, Va., 2000), 78; Onuf, "Federalism, Republicanism, and the Origins of American Sectionalism," in Edward L. Ayers et al., *All Over the Map: Rethinking American Regions* (Baltimore, 1996), 116n68; Onuf, "Constitutional Politics: States, Sections, and the National Interest," in *Toward a More Perfect Union: Six Essays on the Constitution,*

ed. Neil L. York (Provo, Utah, 1988), 52; Richard Mannix, "Gallatin, Jefferson, and the Embargo of 1808," *Diplomatic History* 3, no. 2 (April 1979): 151–72.

3. Onuf, "Constitutional Politics," 35–37, 52; Onuf, "Anarchy and the Crisis of the Union," in *To Form a More Perfect Union: The Critical Ideas of the Constitution,* ed. Herman Belz, Ronald Hoffman, and Peter J. Albert (Charlottesville, Va., 1992), 295; Onuf, "Federalism, Republicanism," 36; Onuf, *The Origins of the Federal Republic: Jurisdictional Controversies in the United States, 1775–1787* (Philadelphia, 1983), chapter 7. On local interests and community understanding of law, see Barbara Clark Smith, *The Freedoms We Lost: Consent and Resistance in Revolutionary America* (New York, 2010), and Joshua M. Smith, *Borderland Smuggling: Patriots, Loyalists, and Illicit Trade in the Northeast, 1783–1820* (Gainesville, Fla., 2006).

4. Jefferson, "First Inaugural Address," Mar. 4, 1801, Avalon Project at Yale Law School, Lillian Goldman Law Library, http://avalon.law.yale.edu/19th_century/jefinau1.asp; Onuf, *Jefferson's Empire,* 76–79, 93–98, 117–37; Dumas Malone, *Jefferson the President: Second Term, 1805–1809* (Boston, 1974), 583–84. On the union itself as an experiment, see Paul C. Nagel, *One Nation Indivisible: The Union in American Thought, 1776–1861* (Westport, Conn., 1964), chapter 1. On Jefferson's understanding of the Burr Conspiracy, see James E. Lewis Jr., "'The Strongest Government on Earth' Proves Its Strength: The Jefferson Administration and the Burr Conspiracy," in this volume.

5. Henry Adams, *History of the United States of America during the Administrations of Thomas Jefferson* (1890; New York, 1986), 1230; Walter W. Jennings, *The American Embargo, 1807–1809* (Iowa City, 1921), 98; Louis Martin Sears, *Jefferson and the Embargo* (1927; reprint, New York, 1966), 109–10.

6. Linda K. Kerber, *Federalists in Dissent: Imagery and Ideology in Jeffersonian America* (Ithaca, N.Y., 1970), chapter 2; James M. Banner, *To the Hartford Convention: The Federalists and the Origins of Party Politics in Massachusetts, 1789–1815* (New York, 1970), 84, 99–101; Forrest McDonald, *The Presidency of Thomas Jefferson* (Lawrence, Kans., 1976), 163–65; Burton Spivak, *Jefferson's English Crisis: Commerce, Embargo, and the Republican Revolution* (Charlottesville, Va., 1979), chapter 7, 209–10 (quotations).

7. Spivak, *Jefferson's English Crisis,* 204; James E. Lewis Jr., *The American Union and the Problem of Neighborhood: The United States and the Collapse of the Spanish Empire, 1783–1829* (Chapel Hill, N.C., 1998), 41–48; Garry Wills, *"Negro President": Jefferson and the Slave Power* (Boston, 2003), chapters 11–14; Brian Schoen, "Calculating the Price of Union: Republican Economic Nationalism and the Origins of Southern Sectionalism, 1790–1828," *Journal of the Early Republic* 23, no. 2 (Summer 2003): 173–206; Schoen, *The Fragile Fabric of Union: Cotton, Federal Politics, and the Global Origins of the Civil War* (Baltimore, 2009), 70–72; Dinah Mayo-Bobee, *New England Federalists: Widening the Sectional Divide in Jeffersonian America* (Madison, N.J., 2017); John Craig Hammond and Matthew Mason, eds., *Contesting Slavery: The Politics of Bondage and Freedom in the New American Nation* (Charlottesville, Va., 2011); Doron S. Ben-Atar, *The Origins of Jeffersonian Commercial Policy and Diplomacy* (New York, 1993); Drew R. McCoy, *The Elusive Republic: Political Economy in Jeffersonian America* (Chapel Hill, N.C., 1980), 217–18.

8. Robert W. Tucker and David C. Hendrickson, *Empire of Liberty: The Statecraft of Thomas Jefferson* (New York, 1990), 210; Marie-Jeanne Rossignol, *The Nationalist Ferment: The Origins of U.S. Foreign Policy, 1792–1812,* trans. Lillian A. Parrott (Columbus, Ohio, 2004), 183–86.

9. Jerry L. Mashaw, "Reluctant Nationalists: Federal Administration and Administrative Law in the Republican Era, 1801–1829," *Yale Law Journal* 116, no. 8 (June 2007): 1641–42 (quotation), 1651–53; *Columbian Centinel* (Boston), Jan. 2, 1808. See also Schoen, *Fragile Fabric,* 294n49; Adams, *History of the United States,* 1107–14; Leonard W. Levy, *Jefferson and Civil Liberties: The Darker Side* (Cambridge, Mass., 1963), 105, 112–13; and Douglas Lamar Jones, "'The Caprice of Juries': The Enforcement of the Jeffersonian Embargo in Massachusetts," *American Journal of Legal History* 24, no. 4 (Oct. 1980): 312.

10. Gallatin to Jefferson, July 29, 1808, in Henry Adams, ed., *The Writings of Albert Gallatin* (Philadelphia, 1879), 1:398; Richard Mannix, "The Embargo: Its Administration, Impact, and Enforcement" (PhD diss., New York University, 1975).

11. Gallatin to Jefferson, Nov. 2, 1808, in Adams, ed., *Writings of Albert Gallatin,* 1:423–24; Jefferson to Gallatin, November 13, 1808, in H. A. Washington, ed., *The Writings of Thomas Jefferson* (New York, 1859), 5:386–87; Tucker and Hendrickson, *Empire of Liberty,* 212.

12. Mashaw, "Reluctant Nationalists," 1653–54; Mannix, "Embargo," 268–70.

13. Jeremiah Olney to Gallatin, Jan. 23, 1809, RG 56, M178, Correspondence of the Secretary of the Treasury with Collectors of Customs, 1789–1833 (hereafter Collectors Correspondence), reel 28, f. 192, National Archives, Washington, D.C.; Harvey Strum, "Rhode Island and the Embargo of 1807," *Rhode Island History* 52, no. 2 (1994): 62; Levy, *Jefferson and Civil Liberties.*

14. Bradford Perkins, *Prologue to War: England and the United States, 1805–1812* (Berkeley, Calif., 1961), 159; Philip J. Lampi, "The Federalist Party Resurgence, 1808–1816: Evidence from the New Nation Votes Database," *Journal of the Early Republic* 33 (Summer 2013): 259–60; Harvey Strum, "New Jersey and the Embargo, 1807–1809," *New Jersey History* 116, nos. 3–4 (Fall–Winter 1998): 37–38; David Hackett Fischer, *The Revolution of American Conservatism: The Federalist Party in the Era of Jeffersonian Democracy* (New York, 1965), 84–87, 115–16; James H. Broussard, *The Southern Federalists, 1800–1816* (Baton Rouge, 1978), 108–9. See also Mayo-Bobee, *New England Federalists,* which was published as the present volume was entering production.

15. Onuf, *Jefferson's Empire,* 122–23 (quotation), 131; [Harrison Gray Otis] to [Roger Griswold], Jan. 4, 1809, William Griswold Lane Collection, Yale University, New Haven, Conn., reprinted in Banner, *To the Hartford Convention,* 353–56, 354 (quotation); see also 50–51; Timothy Pickering to [Samuel Pickering Gardner], Dec. 10, 1807, Business Papers (series 2), Gardner Family Papers, Massachusetts Historical Society, Boston, also cited in Rachel Knecht, "'The Absolute Destruction of Their Interest': New England and Jefferson's Embargo" (BA thesis, Tufts University, 2011), 40; Timothy Pickering to Rufus King, Jan. 19, Feb. 26, 1808, in Charles R. King, ed., *The Life*

and Correspondence of Rufus King (New York, 1898), 5:64, 81. See also Spivak, *Jefferson's English Crisis,* 159; and McCoy, *Elusive Republic,* 216–23, 227–30.

16. Brutus, "To the Electors of Lincoln District," *Portland [Maine] Gazette,* Oct. 24, 1808, also cited in Knecht, "Absolute Destruction," 48.

17. Thomas Barclay to John Borlase Warren, Sept. 3, 1808, in George Lockhart Rives, ed., *Selections from the Correspondence of Thomas Barclay* (New York, 1894), 284; [Edmond-Charles Genet], "A Citizen of New-York," in *Communications on the Next Election for President of the United States, and on the Late Measures of the Federal Administration* (New York, 1808), 11–12; Stephen E. Siry, *De Witt Clinton and the American Political Economy: Sectionalism, Politics, and Republican Ideology, 1787–1828* (New York, 1990), 76–79, 105, 138–40, 142–45.

18. Crawford, Senate, Nov. 23, 1808; Quincy, House of Representatives, Nov. 28, 1808; Sloan, House of Representatives, Nov. 29, 1808, in *Annals of Congress,* 10th Cong., 2nd sess., pp. 64, 544, 573; Orchard Cook to John Quincy Adams, Nov. 27, 1808, Adams Papers, Massachusetts Historical Society, also cited in Knecht, "Absolute Destruction," 55; Schoen, *Fragile Fabric,* 70–71, 77–80, 82, 295n66; Mannix, "Embargo," 279–89.

19. Reginald C. Stuart, "Special Interests and National Authority in Foreign Policy: American-British Provincial Links during the Embargo and the War of 1812," *Diplomatic History* 8, no. 4 (Oct. 1984): 322; James Hillhouse to Noah Webster, March 22, 1808, in *Connecticut Herald* (New Haven), Apr. 5, 1808; Jeffrey L. Pasley, *"The Tyranny of Printers": Newspapers Politics in the Early American Republic* (Charlottesville, Va., 2000), 236; Glenn S. Gordinier, "Enterprise and Authority: Southeastern Connecticut Responds to the Jeffersonian Embargo," *Connecticut History* 49, no. 1 (Spring 2010): 35. For more on congressional debates and printed protests, see Mayo-Bobee, *New England Federalists,* chapters 4–5.

20. Timothy Pickering, *A Letter from the Honourable Timothy Pickering . . . Addressed to His Excellency James Sullivan* (Boston, 1808), 11; Banner, *To the Hartford Convention,* 298; Wills, *"Negro President,"* chapters 12–14.

21. *Newburyport [Mass.] Herald,* Mar. 15, 1808, Jan. 17, 1809; Benjamin W. Labaree, *Patriots and Partisans: The Merchants of Newburyport, 1764–1815* (Cambridge, Mass., 1962), 155, 166; Matthew Mason, *Slavery and Politics in the Early American Republic* (Chapel Hill, N.C., 2006), 43–44.

22. *New-York Evening Post,* Apr. 26, 1808; Fischer, *Revolution of American Conservatism,* 99–101, 166–67. See also Mayo-Bobee, *New England Federalists,* 136, 143–45.

23. "Merchants, Mechanics, Traders, and . . . Mariners (Boston)," petition to Thomas Jefferson, December 28, 1808, Thomas Jefferson Papers, series 1, General Correspondence, 1651–1827, Library of Congress, Washington, D.C., http://hdl.loc.gov/loc.mss/mtj.mtjbib019496. See also Robin D. S. Higham, "The Port of Boston and the Embargo of 1807–1809," *American Neptune* 16 (1956): 189–208.

24. Broussard, *Southern Federalists,* 108.

25. "A Merchant" to Jefferson, June 30, 1808, http://hdl.loc.gov/loc.mss/mtj.mtjbib018737; Anonymous to Jefferson, Mar. 29, 1808, http://hdl.loc.gov/loc.mss/mtj

.mtjbib018436; Anonymous to Thomas Jefferson, Oct. 4, 1808, http://hdl.loc.gov/loc.mss/mtj.mtjbib019124, all Jefferson Papers, Library of Congress; "A sitizen" to Jefferson, Aug. 29, 1808, in Jack McLaughlin, ed., *To His Excellency Thomas Jefferson: Letters to a President* (New York, 1991), 21. See also Gautham Rao, "The Creation of the American State: Customhouses, Law, and Commerce in the Age of Revolution" (PhD, University of Chicago, 2008), 303; Rao, *National Duties: Custom Houses and the Making of the American State* (Chicago, 2016), 139–40; Strum, "New Jersey and the Embargo," 26; and Banner, *To the Hartford Convention,* 299n2.

26. *The Diary of William Bentley* (Salem, Mass., 1911), 3:337; *Portland Gazette,* Dec. 26, 1808; see also *Salem [Mass.] Gazette,* Jan. 3, 1809; *Greenfield [Mass.] Gazette,* Jan. 2, 1809; and *Repertory* (Boston), Jan. 17, 1809. For Newburyport, see Labaree, *Patriots and Partisans,* 164–65. See also David Waldstreicher, *In the Midst of Perpetual Fetes: The Making of American Nationalism, 1776–1820* (Chapel Hill, N.C., 1997), and Nicole Eustace, *Passion Is the Gale: Emotion, Power, and the Coming of the American Revolution* (Chapel Hill, N.C., 2008), 394–418.

27. Hancock, "A Cautionary Address to the 'Friends of Order,' in the Northern States," *Independent Chronicle* (Boston), Jan. 19, 1809; Schoen, *Fragile Fabric,* 77–80; James Duncan Phillips, "Jefferson's 'Wicked Tyrannical Embargo,'" *New England Quarterly* 18, no. 4 (Dec. 1945): 472; Harvey Strum, "Smuggling in Maine during the Embargo and the War of 1812," *Colby Library Quarterly* 19, no. 2 (June 1983): 90–91; Paul A. Gilje, *The Road to Mobocracy: Popular Disorder in New York City, 1763–1834* (Chapel Hill, N.C., 1987), 183.

28. Terry Bouton, *Taming Democracy: "The People," the Founders, and the Troubled Ending of the American Revolution* (New York, 2007), chapter 9; Smith, *Borderland Smuggling,* 12–16, 38–41, 43–45; Rao, "Creation of the American State," 282–83, 308–13; Stuart, "Special Interests," 328; Mashaw, "Reluctant Nationalists," 1655, 1664; Herbert Heaton, "Non-Importation, 1806–1812," *Journal of Economic History* 1, no. 2 (Nov. 1941): 189; Amy Bass, "A Matter of Customs," *American Neptune* 58, no. 1 (Winter 1998): 28.

29. Strum, "New Jersey and the Embargo," 20–21; Rao, "Creation of the American State," 322–23, 326–36; Rao, *National Duties,* 141–47; Richard P. Casey, "North Country Nemesis: The Potash Rebellion and the Embargo of 1807–1809," *New-York Historical Society Quarterly* 64 (1980): 42–44; Paul Goodman, *The Democratic-Republicans of Massachusetts: Politics in a Young Republic* (Cambridge, Mass., 1964), 193–94; Jeffrey A. Frankel, "The 1807–1809 Embargo against Great Britain," *Journal of Economic History* 42, no. 2 (June 1982): 291–308; William Jeffrey Bolster, "The Impact of Jefferson's Embargo on Coastal Commerce," *Log of Mystic Seaport* 37 (Winter 1986): 121; Heaton, "Non-Importation," 183–85, 189; Mannix, "Embargo," 199–211, 231–44.

30. Wilson Cary Nicholas to his constituents, [Mar.] 1809, in Noble E. Cunningham Jr., ed., *Circular Letters of Congressmen to Their Constituents, 1789–1829* (Chapel Hill, N.C., 1978), 2:670; Benjamin Lincoln to Gallatin, Mar. 22, 1808, Collectors Correspondence, reel 11, f. 196; Gallatin to Jefferson, July 29, 1808, in Adams, ed., *Writings of Albert Gallatin,* 1:396; James Madison to Richard Rush, Nov. 13, 1823, in

Gaillard Hunt, ed., *The Writings of James Madison, 1819–1836* (New York, 1910), 9:164; J. C. A. Stagg, *Mr. Madison's War: Politics, Diplomacy, and Warfare in the Early American Republic, 1783–1830* (Princeton, N.J., 1983), 41; John D. Forbes, "Boston Smuggling, 1807–1815," *American Neptune* 10 (1950): 144–54; Strum, "Smuggling in Maine," 93; Heaton, "Non-Importation," 187–88; Rao, "Creation of the American State," 304–10; Gene A. Smith, *"For the Purposes of Defense": The Politics of the Jeffersonian Gunboat Program* (Newark, Del., 1995), 108; Mannix, "Embargo," 121–24, 158–68, 174.

31. Jones, "'Caprice of Juries,'" 314, 319, 325–27; Strum, "Smuggling in Maine," 90; Strum, "Rhode Island and the Embargo," 62; Spivak, *Jefferson's English Crisis,* 175–76; Mashaw, "Reluctant Nationalists," 1646, 1663–64, 1677, 1680; Mannix, "Embargo," 183, 266–67.

32. Paul C. Nagel, *John Quincy Adams: A Public Life, a Private Life* (New York, 1997), 174–80; Rao, "Creation of the American State," 314; Smith, *Borderland Smuggling,* 52–58, 62–63; Joshua M. Smith, "'So Far Distant from the Eye of Authority': The Embargo of 1807 and the U.S. Navy, 1807–1809," in *New Interpretations in Naval History: Selected Papers from the Twelfth Naval History Symposium,* ed. William B. Cogar (Annapolis, Md., 1997), 128; Strum, "Smuggling in Maine," 91; Mannix, "Embargo," 234–38, 258–60, 272–77; *New-York Evening Post,* May 4, 1808.

33. Tucker and Hendrickson, *Empire of Liberty,* 223; Smith, *"For the Purposes of Defense,"* 105–8; Mannix, "Embargo," 243–60.

34. Gallatin to Jefferson, Aug. 17, 1808, in Adams, ed., *Writings of Albert Gallatin,* 1:406–7; Mashaw, "Reluctant Nationalists," 1663; Rao, "Creation of the American State," 312–14, 346–47; Strum, "Rhode Island and the Embargo," 61–62; Casey, "North Country Nemesis," 41, 44; Rosemarie Zagarri, *Revolutionary Backlash: Women and Politics in the Early American Republic* (Philadelphia, 2007), 95; *Columbian Centinel,* Aug. 17, 1808; *New-York Evening Post,* Jan. 14, 1809; Jennings, *American Embargo,* 116; H. N. Muller, "Smuggling into Canada: How the Champlain Valley Defied Jefferson's Embargo," *Vermont History* 31, no. 1 (Winter 1970): 14; Strum, "Smuggling in Maine," 92–93; Smith, "'So Far Distant,'" 133–34; Smith, *Borderland Smuggling;* Mannix, "Embargo," 206–9.

35. Gallatin to Madison, Sept. 9, 1808, Founders Online, National Archives, http://founders.archives.gov/documents/Madison/99-01-02-3512; Gallatin to Joseph H. Nicholson, Oct. 18, 1808, in Henry Adams, *The Life of Albert Gallatin* (Philadelphia, 1879), 375.

36. "Things Turned Topsy-Turvy," *Enquirer* (Richmond, Va.), Feb. 14, 1809; John Quincy Adams, *American Principles: A Review of the Works of Fisher Ames* (Boston, 1809), 36–37; Onuf, "Anarchy and the Crisis of Union," 272–302; Kenneth M. Stampp, "The Concept of a Perpetual Union," *Journal of American History* 65, no. 1 (June 1978): 23; Forrest McDonald, *States' Rights and the Union: Imperium in Imperio, 1776–1876* (Lawrence, Kans., 2000), 64; Ronald P. Formisano, *The Transformation of Political Culture: Massachusetts Parties, 1790s–1840s* (New York, 1983), 7, 10, 111.

37. James Sullivan to Thomas Jefferson, Jan. 4, 1808, Jefferson Papers, Library of Congress, http://hdl.loc.gov/loc.mss/mtj.mtjbib018066; Henry Kermit to John

B. Laurence, Feb. 16, 1808, Kermit Family Papers, Mystic Seaport Museum, Mystic, Conn., quoted in Bass, "Matter of Customs," 32–33; *Salem Gazette,* Jan. 17, 1809; Fischer, *Revolution of American Conservatism,* 176–77, 267; Banner, *To the Hartford Convention,* 302–4.

38. Jefferson, "First Inaugural Address"; "A Proclamation," *Vermont Centinel* (Burlington), May 6, 1808; Stuart, "Special Interests," 322; Muller, "Smuggling into Canada," 7–9; Casey, "North Country Nemesis," 38–40; McDonald, *States' Rights and the Union,* 63.

39. Jeremiah Olney to Gallatin, Jan. 25, 1809, Collectors Correspondence, reel 28, f. 193; Rao, "Creation of the American State," 347; Casey, "North Country Nemesis," 45–46; Strum, "Rhode Island and the Embargo," 63; *Boston Gazette,* Feb. 6, 1809; Fischer, *Revolution of American Conservatism,* 159–60; McDonald, *States' Rights and the Union,* 65–66; Mashaw, "Reluctant Nationalists," 1666; Strum, "Smuggling in Maine," 93–94; Malone, *Jefferson the President,* 651–55.

40. Heaton, "Non-Importation," 191; Joseph Story to Edward Everett, n.d., in William W. Story, ed., *Life and Letters of Joseph Story* (Boston, 1851), 1:187; Phillips, "Jefferson's 'Wicked Tyrannical Embargo,'" 475; Spivak, *Jefferson's English Crisis,* 181–91; Banner, *To the Hartford Convention,* 298–306; Schoen, *Fragile Fabric,* 81; Reginald C. Stuart, "James Madison and the Militants: Republican Disunity and Replacing the Embargo," *Diplomatic History* 6, no. 2 (Apr. 1982): 156; Mayo-Bobee, *New England Federalists,* 137–41.

41. Adams, *History of the United States,* 1227, 1236; Schoen, *Fragile Fabric,* 77–82; Nicholas Onuf and Peter Onuf, *Nations, Markets, and War: Modern History and the American Civil War* (Charlottesville, Va., 2006), 286.

42. Jefferson to Henry Dearborn, July 16, 1810; Jefferson to Henry Middleton, Jan. 8, 1813; Jefferson to John Tyler, May 26, 1810; Jefferson to Joseph C. Cabell, Feb. 2, 1816, in Washington, ed., *Writings of Thomas Jefferson,* 5:91, 525, 529, 6:544; McCoy, *Elusive Republic,* 249.

43. Ben-Atar, *Origins of Jeffersonian Commercial Policy,* 167–68; Schoen, *Fragile Fabric,* 78; Rossignol, *Nationalist Ferment,* 185; Mason, *Slavery and Politics,* chapter 2.

7 How the Jeffersonians Learned to Love the State

Consumption, Finance, and Empire in the Madison Administration

Leonard J. Sadosky

> The interests and prosperity of the United States, are not only intimately, but inseparably, connected with trade. The market of the farmer depends greatly upon the merchant and the shipper. . . . Any sudden check to our commerce, whether produced by our own municipal regulations, or the outrages of foreign powers, checks the market and price of produce, so that not only the merchants, but the farmers feel its effects. I scarcely need to recur to the history of the times, when trade was principally suspended in this country, to show how severely the suspension operated upon every class of our citizens, and in every part of the country. . . . This proves the connexion which subsists between the two great agricultural and commercial interests of our country.
>
> —Representative Jonathan Fisk,
> speech in Congress, January 17, 1811

Idiom and Action in Jeffersonian Republican Reality

By the spring of 1801, Albert Gallatin's life had been one defined by a series of regularly and gradually diminishing vistas. Born on the shores of Lake Geneva and in the shadow of the Alps, Gallatin had come of age in the Swiss metropolis, and at age nineteen migrated to the United States. He first settled in Boston, sought fortune on the Maine frontier as a trader, and then migrated to western Pennsylvania. Involved in mercantile concerns and land speculation, he rose in prominence in the community, and eventually was elected to Congress in 1794. A leader in the House of Representatives and a stalwart member of the emerging Jeffersonian Republican movement and party, Gallatin was tapped by Thomas Jefferson to serve as his secretary of the treasury shortly after the Virginian's election to the presidency in 1801. In the course of two decades of adult life, Gallatin had exchanged the sublime brilliance of Lake Geneva and the Swiss Alps for the muted grays and browns of the Maine and Pennsylvania frontiers, and now he turned even those views aside for a place in the nascent federal city that was rising from the estuary that was the lower Potomac. For an eighteenth-century gentleman conditioned to seek out the beautiful and sublime, this life journey could be imagined as something of a disappointment. But Albert Gallatin saw the world very differently from most of his contemporaries. He was where he wanted and needed to be.[1]

It is tempting to write that where his friends and rivals among America's founding generation saw words and ideas, Albert Gallatin primarily saw numbers. But this would be overstating the case. Numbers were second nature to most of America's founding mothers and fathers. George Washington was a skilled surveyor; Thomas Jefferson kept meticulous accounts and mastered the study of mathematics; Abigail Adams played the post-revolutionary bond markets with exquisite acumen; and, of course, Alexander Hamilton was a skilled political economist, eminently comfortable in the world of financiers. In many ways, Gallatin's numeracy as a politician was no more special or distinct than that of dozens of his contemporaries. As lawyers, merchants, planters, and farmers, America's founders were experienced (if not always successful) businessmen. What Gallatin saw that many did not, however, were numbers in motion—numbers as language. Along with Hamilton, Gallatin was one of the few founders who grasped intuitively that the story of the new American nation would be written on balance sheets and ledgers as much as on state papers and newspaper essays.[2]

Numbers—specifically those counting money—defined the early American nation. The success of the American revolutionaries in their war for independence, the adoption of the federal Constitution in 1787–88, and the growth and stability of the new federal government in the 1790s all had a vital fiscal and monetary dimension. During the Revolution, one of the great achievements of the Continental Congress was simply coming up with the money to sustain a war effort. Congress created a circulating medium—the Continental currency—from scratch, issued a variety of debt instruments, and successfully borrowed money from European powers (namely, France and the Netherlands) opposed to Great Britain. Although in the modern popular imagination the Continental currency was an inflation-bedeviled failure akin to the Weimar-era Reichsmark, in the estimation of historians it was, on balance, a success. It allowed the American economy to function and the United States to win its independence. As historian E. James Ferguson demonstrated a generation ago, even as the war was winding down, financial concerns remained paramount to American leaders. The desire to find stable, national sources of revenue for the Confederation was the impetus behind the emergence of the "nationalist" movement in Congress that led the failed push for the impost, the basis for the movement behind the Philadelphia Convention of 1787, and the fuel driving the state- and regime-building of the 1790s.[3]

The actors at the center of this project of American state-building drew on many models, but in terms of financial resources, the regime they most readily emulated was that of Great Britain and the British Empire. By the final quarter of the eighteenth century, Britain epitomized what early modern historians now call a fiscal-military state. Over the course of the eighteenth century, the British state had geared itself for war. It did this not simply by building an enormous navy and a respectable standing army but also by creating institutions to support its preponderant power: regular and systematic taxation; a permanent national debt; and public, private, and hybrid banking and financial institutions from which the state and private interests could draw capital. This interlocking set of institutions, policies, and emergent customs allowed the British imperial state to wage war on a global scale over an extended period of time. Other European powers emulated Britain in whole or in part, and the new United States was a part of this larger phenomenon. Several historians have connected the regime-building activities of the American federal union in the 1780s, 1790s, and early nineteenth century to this wider European trend. A modern state demanded modern financial institutions and policies—both fiscal and monetary.[4]

However, historical movements that have become clear in retrospect were not as evident to contemporaries. Some historians might argue that the bulk of politically active Americans in the 1780s and 1790s lacked the perspective or insight to understand the evolution of modern finance and its connection to state power. A more sympathetic viewpoint is that American statesmen and political commentators of the founding era had the ability to see these connections but perceived them through a different lens and talked about them using a different idiom than twenty-first-century political, diplomatic, and institutional historians do. As political and intellectual historians between the 1960s and 1980s have charted, the idiom of American political debates between the 1760s and 1810s mapped loosely onto English political debates that stretched from the Glorious Revolution through the ministry of Robert Walpole. Rhetorically, a classically republican "country" party defended a predominantly agrarian society against the inroads of a modernizing and liberalizing but corrupt and decadent "court" party. The reality was more complicated. Republican rhetoric was used by nearly every major politically active group and individual during the revolutionary and founding eras. Republicanism's universality tended to obscure the reality that all factions—federalist or antifederalist, Federalist or Republican—were pushing for the emergence of the American union as a modern state. The opposing factions differed over the location, construction, and concentration of power and authority within the American states, the American union, and American society. Each utilized the rhetoric of republicanism to criticize its opponents.[5]

As Americans built new states and a new federal polity under the federal Constitution—seemingly proving the success of the republican political project—republicanism seemed more under threat than ever before. The reality that harsh, definitive choices about the future of the American union confronted policymakers gave classical republican rhetoric increased saliency and bite. Federalists championed American engagement with an Atlantic (and even global) marketplace, under the aegis of federally promoted financial and shipping sectors, while Republicans embraced the producer ethos and championed the primacy of the agricultural sector into the foreseeable future. And when they talked of producers, Republicans meant those who owned and worked the land: farmers and planters. Manufacturing, finance, and the carrying trade were seen as supplementary or ancillary to a producer core. Jefferson authored one of the era's most famous defenses of the producer ethos in *Notes on the State of Virginia,* where he identified the natural state of a good republican citizen to be that of a planter or a farmer: "Those who labour in the earth are the chosen people of God. . . . Corruption of morals in the mass of cultivators is a phænomenon of which no age nor nation has furnished an example." Ignoring the productive labor of the slave, the indentured servant, the hired hand, women, and children, the Jeffersonian producer ethos saw the householder as the primary economic and political unit. Free, adult, male, and white (usually Anglo-Saxon and Protestant, but with a growing number of exceptions), the producer was unencumbered by any dependent status. "Dependence begets subservience and venality, suffocates the germ of virtue, and prepares fit tools for the designs of ambition," Jefferson argued. Independence conveyed virtue and meant that one had the requisite freedom to participate in the life of the polity.[6]

Being a producer thus made one a republican citizen. However, being a consumer made one part of a global community and marketplace. While production was the force animating Jeffersonian ideology, from the turn of the nineteenth century consumption was becoming the driver of Jeffersonian policy. The shift was unacknowledged but very real. Jefferson was, to use a modern turn of phrase, giving the people what they wanted. As much as American politicians, be they Republican or Federalist, talked up the virtues of an agrarian republic that eschewed luxury, sought solace in homespun accoutrements and crafts, and looked abroad only for necessaries, the reality was that American consumers wanted choices and access to foreign products. This had been true throughout the eighteenth century, and it did not change with Jefferson's election to the presidency. In fact, the desire to consume only accelerated and expanded. Americans liked wine and liquor, port and madeira, porcelain and textiles, coffee and tea, sugar and spices, books and furnishings. This consumption required production—the agricultural production of foodstuffs and staples to be sold and exchanged. And this production required preliminary consumption—of land (acquired from extra-national polities, be they foreign or indigenous) and of labor (both enslaved and free). Americans could eschew consumption for a short time to sacrifice for a political goal in the national interest, but they were not going to countenance a massive shift in consumption patterns. They would not permanently alter their desires. The propensity to consume drove Jeffersonian actions in the realm of international relations. Diplomacy, the military establishment, and the federal financial program all worked together to open doors for American producers and consumers, whether through acquiring land, opening markets, or sustaining labor regimes.[7]

The mismatch between rhetoric and reality, between idioms and institutions, has tended to confound scholars who have studied the Jeffersonian movement and the Jeffersonian Republican Party in power.[8] Both in and out of power, Jeffersonians, including and particularly James Madison, could sound like country oppositionists while at the same time acting like precocious, modern state-makers.[9] Madison's administration brought this tendency to a head, pursuing policies that furthered the growth of an American fiscal-military state while continuing to talk (and to a great extent think) like a country opposition movement. In order to understand how Jeffersonians reconciled this apparent contradiction, an understanding of the position, policies, and role of Albert Gallatin is vital.

A Jeffersonian Fiscal-Military State: The Gallatinian Solution

In the 1800s and 1810s, Jeffersonian action looked forward while Jeffersonian discourse looked backward. The Jeffersonians venerated producers while favoring consumers. Claiming fealty to the "Principles of '98"—the spirit of unified opposition to the Federalists during the height of the crisis over the Quasi-War and Alien and Sedition Acts—the Jefferson and Madison administrations nonetheless embarked on a program that solidified the centrality of the federal government in managing diplomatic, military, and fiscal affairs.

While everyone in Jefferson's and Madison's cabinets could talk the talk of agrarian producers, probably no one understood the centrality of consumption to the new American economy better than Gallatin. As secretary of the treasury under both Presidents Jefferson and Madison, he attempted to repurpose the Hamiltonian engine of the federal government and drive the nation toward Republican ends. Rhetorically, the Jeffersonian Republican Party and movement could tend toward simple oppositionism and a vulgar rejection of the Federalist programs of the 1790s. Gallatin, and most of Jefferson's cabinet, sought to temper this rejectionist spirit. Thus, as secretary of state, Madison did not attempt to stifle American trade with Europe but rather tried to promote and expand American trade to nations beyond Federalist-favored Britain. Along similar lines, Secretary of War Henry Dearborn did not undo the Indian diplomacy of Henry Knox; he still sought treaties with the various Indian nations that would convert them to "civilization" and entice them to sell lands. But unlike his Federalist predecessors, who focused on trade and the continental balance of power, Dearborn directed his diplomatic efforts toward acquiring lands to clear the way for new states in the West. Gallatin's financial plans mirrored Dearborn's diplomacy in strategy and spirit.[10]

At the heart of the Gallatinian financial project was Jefferson's promise to eliminate the United States' national debt. While this would consume the bulk of the federal government's revenues during Jefferson's first term, outside circumstances made collecting revenue and paying down the debt relatively easy. The conclusion of the Quasi-War with France by the Adams administration shortly before Jefferson took office produced a sizeable peace dividend. After the Treaty of Mortefontaine (signed in September 1800 and ratified in December 1801), French privateers ceased to prey on American merchantmen. Also in 1800, a British Admiralty Court decision known as the *Polly* case legalized, for all intents and purposes, the American merchants' practice of the "broken voyage." American carriers would offload belligerent cargo in a U.S. port, pay the required duties, and then reload and ship the cargo to another power. As the United States remained neutral in the ongoing Napoleonic Wars, it now had the ability to trade openly with both Britain and France. American trade boomed and so did federal customs receipts. Gallatin explained to Congress in his annual message of December 1802 that the government had taken in $12.2 million in the previous year, over $2 million more than had been budgeted and more than had ever been taken in before. In spending revenue, Gallatin budgeted roughly $10 million in total expenditures, $2.7 million toward the operating expenses of government and the remainder for debt service. He now could, theoretically, get a leg up on Jefferson's desire to pay down the national debt.[11]

The reality proved to be more complicated, due in large part to crises in international relations. Jefferson's desire to pursue overseas operations against the state-sponsored privateers of the North African Maghreb (the so-called Barbary Pirates) had already prevented his desired mothballing of the regular navy. And as Gallatin penned his 1802 message to Congress, a new crisis in international relations began with the closure of the Mississippi River to American commerce by the Spanish official in charge of the port of New Orleans. The Mississippi crisis of 1802–3 would culminate with the July 1803 Louisiana Treaty that transferred the Louisiana Purchase from France to the United States. At a cost of $15 million, the purchase required some creative financing. Gallatin accomplished this by combining a specie payment and a sale of debt instruments, issued under the aegis of the Baring Brothers banking house in London.[12]

Yet just as the challenges of international relations forced Gallatin to embrace creativity with government finance to continue Jefferson's project of paying down the national debt, international developments also provided a salve. With the costs imposed by the Louisiana opportunity, as well as Jefferson and Gallatin's decision in 1801 to cut internal taxes and dismantle pieces of the internal taxation bureaucracy, the federal government now had to find other ways to make up for decreased revenue. It did this through customs duties. Relative peace in the Atlantic world opened the doors to an expansion of commerce conducted from U.S. ports, and a consequent increase in customs revenues. Between the eve of Jefferson's inauguration and the Embargo, American customs duties rose from $9.1 million to $16.4 million per year.[13]

Despite a favorable balance of payments, the challenges to maintaining a budget situation that allowed Gallatin to pay down the debt never disappeared and only increased during the second Jefferson administration. Because of both constitutional restrictions and policy choices, the federal government during the 1800s and 1810s was funded almost entirely through import duties, rather than direct taxes on property, internal duties, or excise taxes. On this revenue, both the funding of the government and the retirement of the debt depended. As the United States' international commerce waxed and waned, so too did Gallatin's ability to reduce the national debt. And the instability of both international relations and international commerce was a constant in these years.

While American ships plied the Atlantic and Caribbean in relative safety during Jefferson's first term, Great Britain and France renewed war in May 1803. Napoleon's armies defeated a succession of British allies and broke British-led coalitions against the French Empire. Although Napoleon lacked the naval superiority that would have allowed him to attempt an invasion of the British Isles, he resorted to waging economic warfare. After the British Privy Council proclaimed a blockade of French trade with its May 1806 orders in council, Napoleon responded with a series of like-minded restrictions known collectively as the Continental System. Subsequent orders in council proclaimed France and its imperial possessions closed not only to Britain and the British Empire but also to Britain's allies and all neutral nations. Napoleon's Milan Decree did essentially the same thing. Both the British and French governments had declared trade with the other illegal. American merchants, who had profited during the peaceful interlude of the early and mid-1800s, now found themselves in the crosshairs of the navies of both great powers. For the Jefferson administration, the problem was twofold. American citizens and property were now at risk; more prosaically, but no less importantly, U.S. customs receipts were also at risk.[14]

By the beginning of 1807, the reality that a world war between the great powers could negatively affect the United States was real. Even before the orders in council of 1806 and 1807, the British government had altered its commercial policies to the detriment of American carriers. In 1805, the British admiralty courts had abandoned the *Polly* precedent of 1800 in the *Essex* decision. The "broken voyage" that U.S. merchants relied on to conduct trade between Europe and the Americas was now illegal again. So, by the end of 1805, American carriers trading out of British colonies were, in the minds of British authorities, violating the law of nations and subjecting themselves to interdiction. Once the orders in council were in place, as was the Continental System, even technicalities became superfluous. While the United States proclaimed its neutrality and the freedom of its merchant ships to go where their owners and captains pleased, for Britain and France these actions rendered American merchantmen de facto belligerents. And for U.S. ships interdicted by the Royal Navy, the dangers of this new order extended beyond the loss of cargo. Crews filled out with sailors who were former Britons and naturalized U.S. citizens were still considered British subjects by the Royal Navy. These sailors were subject to impressment into His Majesty's Service. The emerging international order was threatening Americans' liberty and lives, American merchants' property, and, by extension, the American government's solvency. With the eruption of a full-blown crisis in 1807, the *Chesapeake-Leopard* affair, and the resulting Embargo, Albert Gallatin's ability to keep the finances of the United States on a sound footing was put to the test.[15]

The Embargo undid most of the work Gallatin had done during Jefferson's first term and a half to put the finances of the United States on a sound footing while adhering to Jeffersonian principles. Working with Congress, Jefferson and Gallatin unwound many of the mechanisms of internal taxation the Federalists had put into place. Not only did they sunset the direct taxes enacted in 1798, but they also cut back on the apparatus of internal taxation. Historian Max Edling has argued this was done for multiple reasons—not only to fulfill campaign promises and reduce expenses in the immediate term but also to shift the direction of the federal government for the long term. Gallatin and Jefferson were making it difficult for future administrations to use the collection apparatus mobilized by the Federalists.[16] Regardless of the administration's motive, the reality was that customs duties were now the major source of revenue for the United States. And when the United States cut itself off from international commerce in 1807, the pinch was felt in short order. In a June 1809 report to Congress, Gallatin plainly observed that net revenues for the federal government had fallen from $16 million in 1807 to a little over $10 million in 1808. Needless to say, this was an enormous decline and a severe stressor on the federal budget. By keeping with republican ideals and reigning in the American fiscal-military state, Gallatin had ironically managed to hamstring himself and his government long before his measures limited future administrations. His preferred solution to the problem was ultimately a conventional one. He continued to pay homage to the Jeffersonian idiom but tacked in a more Hamiltonian direction. Gallatin eschewed direct taxation, but he was more willing to embrace debt financing, and he understood that, in the event of war, the federal government would have to take on additional loans. To help finance these loans, a larger national bank was needed. Gallatin began to see that the Bank of the United States, its charter due to expire in 1811, needed not just to be renewed but expanded. And this realization put him on a collision course with much of the Jeffersonian Republican Party.[17]

Idiom's Failure: The Bank and the War

When James Madison took the oath of office as president of the United States in March 1809, the country remained in the midst of a crisis that had brought about the Embargo. During the eight years Thomas Jefferson had occupied the presidency, the transatlantic systems of politics and markets in which the United States was enmeshed had gone from nurturing American growth to putting at risk the security and economy of the union. American commerce had flourished under the brief respite in the world war between revolutionary France on the one side and Great Britain and the continental monarchies on the other. With Napoleon's consolidation of power, rechristening of France as an empire, and resumption of hostilities between the European powers, America's commerce was increasingly threatened. Both British and

French interpretation of the law of nations (contemporary international law and law of the seas) eschewed the definitions of neutrality under which American commerce had flourished early in the decade. U.S.–flagged ships increasingly found themselves facing interdiction and seizure by the navies of the belligerent powers, and, in the case of the operations of Britain's Royal Navy, American sailors risked being impressed into British service. After the *Chesapeake-Leopard* incident in June 1807, many in the United States pressed Jefferson to declare war. The president, however, opted to use commerce as his weapon, and working with Congress, imposed the Embargo—a complete closure of the United States to international trade. After two years of commercial restriction, neither Britain nor France had budged in their strict construction of neutral rights. With the Embargo a failure, the country would chart a different course under President Madison.[18]

Madison and his administration faced two interlocking sets of challenges upon taking office in the spring of 1809—one diplomatic and the other financial. The international order still worked to the detriment of the sovereignty and interests of the United States. This was a reality that Madison and most politically active Americans believed needed to change. Chaos in the realm of international commerce threatened to undo the fiscal labors undertaken by Albert Gallatin and Congress during Jefferson's presidency. With the collapse of the United States' Atlantic commerce, the federal government was taking in far less revenue in customs duties—annual accounts were now back in the red—and the United States was going deeper into debt. This ongoing crisis in the interlocking realms of diplomacy, economics, and finance would define Madison's presidency. On the diplomatic front, even with the end of the Embargo, the United States remained entangled in what amounted to a world war between Europe's two great naval powers: Great Britain and Napoleonic France. By not recognizing neutral status, British orders in council and Napoleon's Berlin and Milan Decrees had effectively closed off the French and British Empires to American commerce. To take the place of the Embargo, Madison and the Jeffersonian Republican Congress opted for a new strategy to attempt to open European and imperial markets—a more targeted program of commercial suspension known as nonintercourse.[19]

Rhetorically, the policy of nonintercourse seemed to return America to its revolutionary roots. During the imperial crisis, the nonimportation of British goods had been an important element of the movement against King

George III's various ministries. The nonimportation of British goods and the manufacture and consumption of domestic wares was a political tool designed to damage British commerce and affect public opinion, as well as serving as a marker of solidarity and a vector of mobilization for the patriot cause. The efficacy of programs of mass commercial discrimination was debatable, but the story of a virtuous people rejecting metropolitan luxury, embracing homespun wares, and thus choosing liberty in everything they did became a key element in revolutionary mythology and the Republican ideal. Since the Jeffersonian program always imagined itself as a recapitulation of the first American Revolution, it was no accident that American efforts to shape the behavior of European sovereigns through altering habits and patterns of domestic consumption became a key pillar of Jefferson's policy from 1807 onward. The Embargo was an extreme effort—it constituted both nonimportation and nonexportation—but it seemed to prove that a totalizing, untargeted approach to limiting consumption had minimal to no effect on changing great-power diplomacy and belligerence. Moreover, it was increasingly unpopular and unenforceable throughout the union.[20]

The Madison administration and Congress therefore turned to a more targeted and limited program of commercial restriction in an attempt to directly alter belligerent behavior. In 1809, the Embargo was replaced with the Non-Intercourse Act. This measure restricted U.S. commerce with just Britain and France, rather than the entire world. While providing an opening for American producers to sell legitimately on the international market after two years of having no legal access whatsoever, the act was not successful in its main goal: forcing Britain, France, or both to alter their regimes of commercial restriction and interdiction. In early 1810, Congress attempted to tweak the United States' commercial regulations to make them more coercive. Madison signed Macon's Bill no. 2 into law on May 14, 1810. As under nonimportation, the United States would allow trade with neutrals but not with the belligerents (France and Britain). Interestingly, barriers to belligerent imports would now be rescinded when one of the powers ceased interdicting American commerce and opened its ports to U.S. commercial shipping—for that power alone. Americans sought to incentivize both nations to abide by the American vision of neutral rights and international commercial regulation. While the Non-Intercourse Act and Macon's Bill both made sense within the logic of the republican idiom—virtuous self-sacrifice could bring corrupt purveyors of luxury to heel; the moves of agricultural producers preceded those of merchant, industrial, and financial capital—in reality, the Americans' actions barely moved the proverbial needle. Despite some limited diplomatic maneuvering by Napoleon and signs from the ministry of Spencer Perceval that they were open to reexamining the orders in council, by the spring of 1812, the diplomacy of commercial restriction had not borne the desired fruit. As a result, President Madison and the Republican Congress took the United States to war against the British Empire on June 18, 1812.[21]

The war had come—but it was not a surprise. The bulk of James Madison's first term as president had been consumed by attempts to resolve challenges resulting from the United States' being a militarily weak, commercially oriented republic in a time of world war. Since the *Chesapeake* incident, American involvement in a war with one or more of the European great powers loomed as an option and a fear for policymakers. But while the president and Congress attempted to guide the United States using policies consistent with Jeffersonian Republican thought and idiom, the secretary of the treasury made use of a set of tools that was not. But these were tools he had no choice but to use. As Albert Gallatin's 1809 report to Congress had made clear, if the United States became involved in a war, expenses would need to be paid by issuing more debt, and this debt would need to be absorbed by creditors. To guarantee this, the existing national bank, the Bank of the United Sates, needed to have its charter renewed and the size of its capital expanded. Even without the war that eventually came, it was already apparent to Gallatin that because of the ongoing European/Atlantic war, as well as the legacy of the Embargo, the federal government needed to be active and vigorous—far more than many in his party would like. It was simply a question of numbers. In 1809 and 1810, funding for the army and navy remained at the same levels it had during the Jefferson administration. But because of the restrictions imposed on American commerce, first by the Embargo and then by nonimportation, tax receipts were insufficient. The expenses for both the army and navy would have to be cut by close to 50 percent. Gallatin proposed a new loan, and in 1810, Congress authorized a new loan of $3.75 million to cover the budget deficit. While the United States still felt like a classical republic, it was thinking once again like a fiscal-military state.[22]

This situation was not ideal, but it was consistent with how Gallatin imagined federal finance could function during an emergency. At the same time, with the economy still not having regained its pace of growth, in 1810 another worry pressed at Gallatin from front and center. The charter of the Bank of the United State was up for renewal. While not the size of the larger and more legendary Second Bank of the United States (1816–36), and certainly far, far smaller than the Federal Reserve System of the twentieth and twenty-first centuries, the First Bank of the United States played an important role in the American economy during the first decades of its existence. While the bank had performed its main duties since the 1790s fairly successfully, many in the American public, especially in the Jeffersonian Republican Party, had never been reconciled to its existence. It continued to be viewed as unnecessary, exploitative, unconstitutional, or some combination of all three. Of course, the tools of the few filled many with suspicion. Distrust of modern financiers and financial instruments, as well as the emerging commercial society as a whole, was part and parcel of country ideology, and thus a large part of received Jeffersonian Republican rhetoric. This idiom came to the fore in the discussions and debate over the potential renewal of the charter of the First Bank of the United States.[23]

As Congress, the administration, and the public contemplated the status of the Bank of the United States during the Eleventh Congress (1809–11), Gallatin had already come down firmly and publicly on the side of renewing its charter. His message of March 1809 presented to Congress the history of the bank, the accepted arguments for both its necessity and constitutionality, and a recommendation for a renewal of its charter, with an increase in the number of shares available for purchase and an increase in operating capital.

In early 1810, in the second session of the Eleventh Congress, both the Senate and the House took up re-charter bills, informed both by Gallatin's report of March 1809 as well as petitions from the stockholders of the bank itself. Both houses convened select committees to consider new charters, but by April, both houses had also moved to postpone further consideration and a final vote on the re-charter until they reconvened in the fall.[24] The proposals being considered by the House and Senate would have been in line with what Gallatin had recommended. Not only would the bank remain a chartered corporation and continue functioning, but the size of its capital would increase substantially. Gallatin's 1809 proposal envisioned a much larger bank; he had estimated that the Bank of the United States needed to be able to support the purchase of government bonds totaling

$20 million in value. While the Senate considered a proposal that would have given the bank $20 million in operating capital (double the $10 million it then had), on the floor of the House, Virginia representative John Love proposed an operating capital of $30 million. A larger national bank fit within the financial framework Gallatin had been using during both of Jefferson's terms as president—paying down the national debt while keeping the nation's options open in the event of war. Throughout this entire period, he remained loathe to ask for new taxation. If war came during Madison's presidency, Gallatin planned to follow the existing practices that both he and Hamilton had engaged in during national emergencies—funding military spending via debt financing. But the key element of Gallatin's plan to put the United States on a secure financial footing in the event of war or other national emergency—a national bank—went down to defeat as the Eleventh Congress drew to a close.[25]

The defeat of the Bank of United States during the presidency of James Madison presents a paradox of sorts. As Madison put the nation on a steadily increasing war footing as the European crisis continued, he also allowed the bank charter to lapse. Why did he go against the wishes of his secretary of the treasury and many of his party in Congress? The answer to this question is complicated. The politics of a national bank had, on the one hand, changed considerably since Alexander Hamilton proposed it twenty years beforehand during the first Washington administration. The bank was one of several items in Hamilton's centralizing agenda that served as a catalyst for the formation of the Jeffersonian Republican opposition. As a member of the opposition in the House of Representatives, Madison had taken the lead in opposing the bank, and his February 1791 speeches against the bank bill would be reprinted and referred to by many congressional Republicans during the re-charter debates in early 1811.[26] But with the Federalists in eclipse, the Republicans now beginning their second decade in power, and the bank having a proven history of providing capital for a (mostly) expanding economy, President Madison was supportive of the charter's renewal. Gallatin was far from being a party of one. That acknowledged, a substantial part of the public—mostly among the Jeffersonian Republican Party—wanted the bank eliminated. They saw it as unconstitutional and believed it to be a nest of foreign influence. They believed it concentrated power in the hands of an eastern financial elite. And in response to pragmatic arguments from Gallatin and others that the bank had provided investment capital and driven economic expansion, they responded that state-chartered banks could do this work just as effectively and with less corruption.[27]

The anti-bank rhetoric that filled the American public sphere in 1810 and into 1811 echoed the rhetoric of the 1790s. Many of those who supported the Jeffersonian Republican Party were generally in favor of eliminating the bank. Holding memories from when Alexander Hamilton had first proposed it in 1791 (and James Madison had opposed it), they believed it malign, unconstitutional, inessential, or some combination thereof. It was not difficult to find bank opponents among those who were part of the Jeffersonian movement and the Republican Party. Congressional debates over the bank resumed in the third session of the Eleventh Congress. While the administration—with Gallatin's voice being the loudest—publicly supported the re-charter, the president spoke little on the subject. As his 1791 speeches against the bank were referenced on the floor of the House, Madison fielded complaints and critiques from bank opponents, and understood that the issue was contentious and divided the Jeffersonian Republicans.[28]

The multifold nature of criticism of the bank offered by rank-and-file Jeffersonian Republicans was epitomized by Samuel Carswell, a Philadelphia merchant subsequently nominated by Madison to serve as commissary general for the army shortly after the start of the War of 1812. An occasional but persistent correspondent of Madison's during his first term, he came out vehemently against the bank's re-charter in early 1811. Shortly after the House voted to table re-charter legislation in late January 1811, Carswell celebrated the bank's de facto defeat as "another triumph of American Virtue, over British corruption & intrigue," since it had "always been under the influence of those who are inimical to the Republican principles of this Government." He noted that the public allies of the bank included former loyalists, as well as friends of the disgraced former vice president Aaron Burr. "An Institution that can receive into it's bosom" such men, "cannot, in it's operation be friendly to this Republic," Carswell opined. Decades after the partisan battles of the 1790s and the ferment of the Revolution, he maintained a political vocabulary and idiom informed by classical republican ideals. Further attacking the bank, he asserted that "no institution, capable of extending it's influence so greatly, as the US Bank was & of establishing that influence, by so powerful a motive, as a sense of dependence in those connected with it, should be suffered to exist in this Country." Defeating the bank decreased dependency and aided the ongoing struggle for independence. In thwarting the bank, Congress and the administration were limiting the power of those who had either actively or passively sought to subvert the American republic and tie its fate to foreign influences. In Carswell's reckoning, such powerful, emotional appeals overrode any considerations of practicality or expediency for supporting the bank's continuation.[29]

Equally potent as the force of ideology and idiom in driving opposition to the bank was the pull of interest and politics. In the spring of 1810, Madison was directly attacked in a series of anonymous essays published in the Baltimore newspaper the *Whig*. A writer using the evocative surname of "Tammany" (the fictitious American Indian leader depicted as a patron saint of America and a connection to the noble virtues of the aboriginal Americans) offered two essays in April 1810 that criticized the Madison administration generally, and Madison in particular. Responding to news that Madison reportedly considered the question of the bank's re-charter to be "settled," Tammany wondered aloud what that really meant. Had Madison returned to the principles he had articulated in Congress in the early 1790s and as the author of the Virginia Resolutions in 1798? If he turned his back on his former mode of thinking, his "fame will be blasted forever," the essayist promised. Furthermore, if Madison embraced the Bank of the United States, he could not claim ignorance of this policy's implications. James Madison knew what he was doing. The only explanation for the president to turn his back on his earlier beliefs was easily understood—"corruption's soul-dejecting arts" had changed Madison. A week later, Tammany pointed to the culprit who had led Madison down the path of corruption: none other than the treasury secretary, Albert Gallatin. A dupe of Britain with a "capacity for business," Gallatin was corruption incarnate. He had fudged and exaggerated the extent of the threat to American finance and the American economy posed by the end of the bank. Gallatin was accused of hosting "dinners upon dinners" at his home to lobby members of Congress to vote for the re-charter—he was a model of "Swiss venality" who was leading Madison "to destruction." Taken together, the Tammany essays offered not just a recitation of classical Republican talking points but a detailed reading of some of the fissures present in Madison's cabinet. They also outlined a path for Madison to come right and embrace the Republican cause by publicly rejecting the bank. The discourses infusing the opposition to the bank were thus multifold—drawing from ideology, policy, and political culture.[30]

With a diverse but potent opposition arrayed against the Bank of the United States, Madison stepped lightly and did not fight hard for its renewal. The president knew that a large number of his party were not with his treasury secretary. After both houses of the Eleventh Congress made the decision to punt at the end of the second session in spring of 1810, it fell to the third session in the winter of 1810–11 for Congress to make a decision on a new charter. Given that the charter of the first Bank of the United States expired on March 3, 1811, this was cutting it close. The bank shareholders submitted a new petition to Congress lobbying for renewal of its charter in December 1810, and they were joined by multiple committees of citizens, mostly from urban seaports like Philadelphia, where mercantile and financial concerns were most keenly felt.[31] But beyond this, the administration allowed Congress to take the lead—and Congress made the decision to kill the bank by allowing the re-charter bill to die. The House of Representatives again voted to table the re-charter legislation (by a single vote) on January 24, 1811. The Senate actually gave the re-charter bill an up-or-down vote on February 20, which ended in a tie. Vice President George Clinton, at odds with the administration, cast a negative vote to defeat the bill. As the session of Congress drew to a close, Gallatin formally requested that Madison allow him to begin winding-down operations by moving federal funds to a variety of state-chartered banks.[32]

As Congress left Washington in the spring of 1811, President Madison and his administration now faced the same wider world of ongoing conflict without a national bank to backstop its finances. While the immediate effect of the lack of a national bank was minimal, as war unfolded the strains on the federal financial system would become apparent again and again by the end of the War of 1812. For the remainder of 1811 and into 1812, as the prospect of war loomed ever larger, Gallatin knew his best bet to fund the federal government and sustain the army and navy was to maintain the tools put in place by Hamilton and maintained by himself over the previous decade, namely national infrastructure and debt finance. Gallatin deployed a multifaceted approach in putting the United States on a footing to cope with the growing international crisis, using continued taxation to generate revenue while using debt financing to keep the war effort afloat. Of course, it was the Gallatinian-Hamiltonian system of finance that would hold the United States together during the War of 1812, not simply Gallatin himself.

In the spring of 1813, he left the United States to join the diplomatic mission seeking to negotiate an end to the war with Great Britain. The American diplomats—John Quincy Adams, joined by Henry Clay and James Bayard—eventually engaged their British counterparts at Ghent, Belgium, and concluded a treaty in December 1814. However, the war that had unfolded over the course of the previous two and a half years had severely tested Gallatin's system of federal finance.[33]

Gallatin's system sustained the United States through *most* of the War of 1812. To be colloquial, his system worked up until it didn't. Fortunately, the limits of the system were reached as Gallatin, along with the other diplomats, were bringing the war to an end. (This was not the first time during the early modern period that wars ended when the financial means to prosecute them were wanting—similar developments had ended the Seven Years' War.)[34]

Keeping the federal government funded during wartime, without a national bank and with minimal new taxes, meant that the administration and Congress leaned heavily on debt financing. The federal government took out its first new loan in 1813, issuing bonds that totaled $16 million in value. This loan, overseen personally by Gallatin before he left on his diplomatic mission, was successful—all the bonds were sold. As Max Edling argues, Gallatin made this loan work because he adopted the proven British practice of selling debt instruments via subscription to small lists. These few subscribers would buy large numbers of bonds, and then would turn around and sell these securities in smaller numbers on secondary markets. Gallatin thus gamed the system by engineering the appearance of securities in multiple markets that tied investors with various amounts of capital to the system. This widespread buy-in among the wealthy mitigated the standard Republican critiques of corruption as well as fear of the financial sector. Gallatin was succeeded at Treasury first by William Jones as interim secretary and then by George W. Campbell in early 1814. It was Campbell who oversaw the more problematic loan issue of 1814. Given the state of the war (now over two years old), the mixed fate of American arms (the United States had successfully defended its own soil but its attempts to invade Canada and force Britain to negotiate had failed), and the moribund nature of the wartime economy, there was less demand for this issue. Of the $10 million in bonds issued, approximately half the subscription was purchased by merchant Jacob Barker. This looked to many like corruption, and the loan was approved by Congress over vocal Federalist opposition. More ominously, the need to pay a higher interest rate to sell all the securities meant that the federal government's credit was worsening. Without a national bank to finance debt purchases, it was an open question as to what extent the system of ad hoc finance could continue. At a minimum, the United States needed an end to the war and a resumption of commerce in order to begin again to fill federal coffers. Ghent and New Orleans came at the perfect time.[35]

American Dynamo: An Empire of Consumption

As far as the Madison administration was concerned, peace came to North America in the nick of time. Word of the Treaty of Ghent, concluded on December 24, 1814, reached North America in mid-February 1815. Peace was embraced by President Madison, Congress, and the population at large. But perhaps no American was happier with the onset of peace than the man charged with guiding the Gallatinian ship-of-state into port, the new treasury secretary, Alexander Dallas, appointed in the wake of George W. Campbell's resignation in September 1814. Dallas's immediate assessment on coming into office was that the finances of the United States remained in dire straits. The loan of 1814 sufficed as a stopgap, but continuing the war into 1815 would have required a new infusion of funds. Dallas requested an additional $40 million for the coming year, to be paid for with new borrowing and a new issue of treasury notes. He also asked for, and received, new taxes—a direct tax, a tax on whiskey, and taxes on manufactured goods were all approved. And that was not all. Dallas asked Congress in October 1814 to charter a new national bank. For Alexander Dallas, there were seemingly no Republican sacred cows that could not be sacrificed for the war effort. The proposed bank was debated heavily in Congress but actually passed the Senate and was under consideration in the House when news of the treaty arrived in Washington. Beyond these financial measures, Congress had approved legislation that would strengthen federal powers in other ways, particularly around the military establishment (for example, state troops could be incorporated into the federal service) and customs enforcement (a new enemy trade act would give customs officers increased powers to interdict smugglers in borderland and frontier regions). While the return of peace rendered many of these measures moot, the Republican majority had shown a willingness to expand the ambit of centralized federal power when faced with the ongoing emergency of the war. It was a habit that the Jeffersonians could never entirely kick.[36]

As 1815 drew to a close, President James Madison sent his annual message to Congress. Even though the United States had been at peace for almost a year, the effects of three years of warfare loomed large. Both in describing the state of the union, and assessing and planning its prospects for the future, Madison seemed to accept the realities that the United States had to embrace the fiscal-military state, and that its economy was rooted in a balance of production and consumption. Indeed, commerce was foregrounded in the message. Madison announced that peace had been made with Algiers and that the Mediterranean would once again be open to American ships without harassment. The peace treaty with Britain had already led to the conclusion of a new commercial accord, so British markets would now be open to American producers and consumers. The northern borderlands were peaceful, although there seemed to be growing unease with the Indian nations in the Southeast. Madison opened the message by assuring Congress and the public that peace was now the standard condition in America once again, and markets long closed to American producers, consumers, and shippers were open.[37]

After reassuring his audience that peace was the new status quo and that the foundations for commerce were strong, Madison proceeded to tie up the many loose ends from the War of 1812 while also describing government actions that could ensure the next national emergency would not be so dire. The process of military demobilization and the institution of a peace establishment was proceeding, although slowly and with difficulty. The Treasury would soon be on a sound footing, although there was a need for a "uniform national currency," and the national debt had ballooned from a prewar figure of $39 million to a whopping $120 million. While the president was hopeful that credit markets would open up in short order, and that economic growth would return, active measures to move the national economy forward could not be discounted. "It is, however essential, to every modification of the finances, that the benefits of a uniform national currency should be restored to the community," Madison asserted. He continued, "If the operation of the State Banks cannot produce this result, the probable operation of a National Bank will merit consideration, and if neither of these expedients be deemed effectual, it may become necessary to ascertain the terms, upon which the notes of the Government (no longer required as an instrument of credit) shall be issued, upon motives of general policy, as a common medium of circulation." Madison was letting Congress and the public know that in order for the American market economy to return to desired levels of growth, the United States might not be able to rely on the happenstance of the invisible hand. A national bank and national currency (made up of specie, paper money, or some combination) might be required in short order. Additionally, the president proposed an increase to the size of the permanent military establishment, expansion of the existing military academy to train officers, spending on a national system of roads and canals, and the creation of a national university. While he concluded his annual message by calling on Americans to remember "the goodness of a superintending providence to which" they were indebted for their current happy situation, the policy proposals he endorsed were designed to make sure the future of the United States was not left to chance. The machinery of state would be embraced in order to ensure future national security and economic growth.[38]

The Fourteenth Congress eagerly picked up the gauntlet that the president had thrown down. Led by Henry Clay of Kentucky and John C. Calhoun of South Carolina, an emerging group of younger Republicans embraced Madison's call. Congress created the Second Bank of the United States in June 1816. Calhoun devised a plan to utilize the revenue "bonus" derived from the new bank to fund Madison's proposed program of internal improvements. A nationally directed system of roads and canals would facilitate the rapid expansion of white settlement (and in the plantation belts, the expansion of the enslaved population as well), a process accelerated by the increased pace of Indian diplomacy and land cessions after the end of the war. The Bonus Bill, as the measure came to be called, would answer Madison's 1815 call while satisfying Jefferson's dream of American expansion into the Mississippi Valley and Gallatin's plans for a national system of internal improvements. The Bonus Bill, however, ran into difficulty as it moved through the legislative process. The emerging bloc of "Old Republicans" adhered to a strict-constructionist, close reading of the Constitution and doubted the Bonus Bill's constitutionality for the same reasons they had opposed the Bank of the United States—powers not explicitly granted to Congress still belonged to the states. Roads and canals were great; the Old Republicans just wanted them planned, funded, and built at the state level. Beyond the constitutional issues, other legislators worried that the Bonus Bill might advantage some states at the expense of others. It passed both houses of Congress late in the Fourteenth Congress's third session but still in time for Madison to sign before he left Washington for his retirement at Montpelier and turned the presidency over to his neighbor and successor, James Monroe. However, on his last day in office, March 3, 1817, Madison vetoed the Bonus Bill. Madison's veto message was economical and clear in its prose. While he approved of the building of roads and canals, in his reading the Constitution simply did not grant this power to the federal government. It was not among the enumerated powers, and thus an amendment to the Constitution would be needed if the federal government was to direct a program of internal improvements.[39]

James Madison's presidency ended in paradox. While presiding over and approving of a postwar expansion of the federal state, Madison's final action as president and last state paper were a rhetorical rejection of this trend and an invocation of classical republican principles. In order to prevent a recurrence of the near-failure of the War of 1812, the administration and Congress had authorized an impressive program of state expansion to buttress the American fiscal-military state. They chartered a new Bank of the United States. They crafted an ambitious plan to provide for a regular army and navy, and planned the expansion of a network of military communication, coastal fortification, and associated defensive infrastructure. Some in Congress saw this as a springboard for state-sponsored expansion. A rising generation of lawmakers recognized no immediate contradiction between federally supported expansion and military preparedness and adherence to the Principles of '98. But Madison did. With the scratch of the presidential pen, he vetoed the Bonus Bill, the centerpiece of nationalist plans for expansion and growth, on his last day in office. For many historians, this is testimony that Madison and many of the so-called Old Republicans he came to stand for rejected the emerging modern state. For a moment, at least, they held it at bay. Of course, in the long run, the modern state came to the United States. So what exactly were the Jeffersonians trying to do?

Considering the sweep of the history of the Jeffersonians in power, from Jefferson's inauguration in March 1801 to Madison's farewell in March 1817, a close look at the policies pursued, institutions built, and actions taken reveals an evolving, modern political movement, increasingly comfortable with the modernizing state. It reveals a movement more than willing to reconcile central state action and authority with its established ideology of decentralization and republicanism, and a political idiom that still treasured virtue and loathed corruption. During both the Jefferson and Madison administrations, the political leadership of the party and the movement embraced state authority and state power not because they were brainwashed into supporting some kind of neo-Hamiltonian project but because it allowed them to pursue the policies that the people who voted for them and who supported them wanted. From the late 1790s through the 1810s, the conflicts in which the United States became embroiled, both on the Atlantic and in North America, were driven by a desire to consume. Consumption had replaced production as America's economic driver. The people, the repository of virtue, wanted access to Atlantic markets and Native American lands. They wanted to purchase land on which to build farms and plantations and, eventually, towns, mills, and factories. The wanted to sell their produce on the open market, and in turn select from a variety of things, both luxurious and mundane, produced by factories in Britain and Europe and harvested from all over the globe. Americans wanted a government that would open the doors to allow them to truck, barter, and trade. Jefferson and Madison, Dearborn and Monroe, Gallatin and John Quincy Adams, all engaged in actions to make that more possible. Madison vetoed the Bonus Bill, but he did not veto the Second Bank of the United States. Unlike the situation of the 1790s and 1800s, the 1810s did not see war followed by more war, but war followed by treaties—treaties with Indian nations to acquire new land and treaties with Britain and other European nations to open the doors of commerce across the Atlantic and beyond.

True, the Bonus Bill veto can be seen as a reassertion by Madison of the Principles of '98 and classical republicanism, but the ends that his party were seeking required the growth of state power to encourage consumption as a central economic driver. As Madison's second term as president wound down, the Jeffersonians still spoke like a political party and a political movement that despised state power. To be sure, as the Missouri crisis would reveal just a couple of years later, Jeffersonians retained an enormous skepticism toward central state authority when directed inward against producers and their ability to organize domestic economies (with all their legally sanctioned inequalities) as they saw fit.[40] But when they looked outward, they could be modern, liberal, and a little bit ruthless. The actions they engaged in and the processes that they were involved in revealed something deeper and perhaps a bit subconscious. By the end of the Madison administration, the Jeffersonians, despite Madison's own anxieties, in many ways had learned to love the state.

Notes

1. An introductory biographical sketch of Albert Gallatin is available in Robert E. Wright and David J. Cohen, *Financial Founding Fathers: The Men Who Made America Rich* (Chicago, 2006), 75–102. For more thorough biographical treatments, see the classic Raymond Walters, *Albert Gallatin: Jeffersonian Financier and Diplomat* (New York, 1957), and the more recent Nicholas Dungan, *Gallatin: America's Swiss Founding Father* (New York, 2010).

2. The American founding generation's thinking on matters of finance and economics is the subject of an extensive literature that continues to grow. For an overview of current thinking, see Thomas K. McCraw, *The Founders and Finance: How Hamilton, Gallatin, and Other Immigrants Forged a New Economy* (Cambridge, Mass., 2012). For the emergence of the American financial sector, see Robert E. Wright, *The First Wall Street: Chestnut Street, Philadelphia, and the Birth of American Finance* (Chicago, 2005), and Wright, *The Origins of Commercial Banking in America, 1750–1800* (Lanham, Md., 2001). For the emerging financial sector's intimate connection with politics, see Brian Phillips Murphy, *Building the Empire State: Political Economy in the Early Republic* (Philadelphia, 2015). For Thomas Jefferson's engagement with financial issues, see Herbert Sloan, *Principle and Interest: Thomas Jefferson and the Problem of Debt* (Oxford, 1995). For Alexander Hamilton, see Stanley M. Elkins and Eric L. McKitrick, *The Age of Federalism: The Early American Republic, 1788–1800* (Oxford, 1995), 77–132; Ron Chernow, *Alexander Hamilton* (New York, 2005); and Wright and Cohen, *Financial Founding Fathers*, 10–25. For Abigail Adams, see Woody Holton, "Abigail Adams: Bond Speculator," *William and Mary Quarterly*, 3rd ser., 64, no. 4 (Oct. 2007): 821–38.

3. E. James Ferguson, *The Power of the Purse: A History of American Public Finance, 1776–1790* (Chapel Hill, N.C., 1960); Ferguson, "The Nationalists of 1781–1783 and the Economic Interpretation of the Constitution," *Journal of American History* 56, no. 2 (Sept. 1969): 241–61.

4. The classic, definitional study of the rise of the British fiscal-military state is John Brewer, *The Sinews of Power: War, Money, and the English State, 1688–1783* (New York, 1989). For the emergence of modern finance and its role in state-making in the mid-eighteenth century, see Matt Schumann and Karl Schweizer, *The Seven Years War: A Transatlantic History* (London, 2008), esp. chapter 3. For the American context, see Max Edling, *A Revolution in Favor of Government: Origins of the U.S. Constitution and the Making of the American State* (Oxford, 2008).

5. For an overview of the rise and consequences of the "Republican synthesis" of the 1960s through 1980s, see Daniel T. Rodgers, "Republicanism: The Career of a Concept," *Journal of American History* 79, no. 1 (June 1992): 11–38. The key studies

from this historiographic moment of republicanism among the political actors of the revolutionary and founding generations are Bernard Bailyn, *The Ideological Origins of the American Revolution* (Cambridge, Mass., 1967); Gordon S. Wood, *The Creation of the American Republic, 1776–1787* (New York, 1969); and J. G. A. Pocock, *The Machiavellian Moment: Florentine Political Thought and the Atlantic Republican Tradition* (Princeton, N.J., 1975).

6. Query XIX, "Manufactures," in Thomas Jefferson, *Notes on the State of Virginia*, ed. William Peden (Chapel Hill, N.C., 1954), 164–65 (quotations). For an overview of the political thinking and experiences that informed Jefferson's own thinking on economic issues in *Notes* and beyond, see Peter S. Onuf, *Jefferson's Empire: The Language of American Nationhood* (Charlottesville, Va., 2000), esp. 160–65; Peter S. Onuf and Leonard J. Sadosky, *Jeffersonian America* (Oxford, 2002), 124–71; and Annette Gordon-Reed and Peter S. Onuf, *Most Blessed of the Patriarchs: Thomas Jefferson and the Empire of the Imagination* (New York, 2017), 45–94.

7. For the importance of consumption as an economic and political force during the eighteenth and early nineteenth centuries, see John Brewer and Roy Porter, eds., *Consumption and the World of Goods* (London, 1993); Richard L. Bushman, *The Refinement of America: Persons, Houses, Cities* (New York, 1993); Laurel Thatcher Ulrich, *The Age of Homespun: Objects and Stories in the Creation of an American Myth* (New York, 2001); and T. H. Breen, *The Marketplace of Revolution: How Consumer Politics Shaped American Independence* (New York, 2004).

8. For a discussion of Jeffersonian political thought and political economy with a focus on its classical republican and agrarian themes, see Lance Banning, *The Jeffersonian Persuasion: Evolution of a Party Ideology* (Ithaca, N.Y., 1980). For Jeffersonian political economy's forward-looking nature, see Joyce Appleby, *Capitalism and a New Social Order: The Republican Vision of the 1790s* (New York, 1993). For a synthesis of the "liberal" and "republican" interpretations, see Drew McCoy, *The Elusive Republic: Political Economy in Jeffersonian America* (Chapel Hill, N.C., 1980).

9. Drew McCoy conceived of the actions of the Jeffersonians during the Jefferson and Madison presidencies as a "sustained Jeffersonian attempt to secure the requisite conditions for a republican political economy." The belief in noble, republican ends caused Jeffersonians to overlook or ignore the implications of their centralizing actions. See *Elusive Republic*, 185–208, 187 (quotation). This essay builds on McCoy's observations as well as those of Max M. Edling in *A Hercules in the Cradle: War, Money, and the American State, 1783–1867* (Chicago, 2014). While McCoy sees the Jeffersonian embrace of the federal state as a means to accomplish immediate, limited republican ends, Edling sees the actions of the Jeffersonians in power as part of a larger sweep of the emergence of modern central state authority in the United States during the eighteenth and nineteenth centuries. This was an ongoing process, elements of which are described in John Lauritz Larson, *Internal Improvement: National Public Works and the Promise of Popular Government in the Early United States* (Chapel Hill, N.C., 2001), and Peter S. Onuf and Nicholas Onuf, *Nations, Markets, and War: Modern History and the American Civil War* (Charlottesville, Va., 2006). I also attempt to describe

elements of these processes of modern state formation in *Revolutionary Negotiations: Indians, Empires, and Diplomats in the Founding of America* (Charlottesville, Va., 2009), particularly 176–215. I should acknowledge that *Hercules in the Cradle* appeared as I was preparing the initial draft of this essay, and I am deeply indebted to the clarity of Edling's argument and interpretation as I refined subsequent drafts. Edling's work also fits squarely into the developmental trajectory outlined by historians and political scientists foregrounding the role and place of emerging modern political and business institutions in shaping American life. See Stephen Skowronek, *Building a New American State: The Expansion of National Administrative Capacities, 1877–1920* (Cambridge, 1982); Theda Skocpol, *Protecting Soldiers and Mothers: The Political Origins of Social Policy in United States* (Cambridge, Mass., 1995); and Richard F. Bensel, *Yankee Leviathan: The Origins of Central State Authority in America, 1859–1877* (Cambridge, 1991).

10. For Jefferson's and Madison's political and commercial diplomacy with the European powers and their empires, see Doron S. Ben-Atar, *The Origins of Jeffersonian Commercial Policy and Diplomacy* (New York, 1993), and James E. Lewis Jr., *The American Union and the Problem of Neighborhood: The United States and the Collapse of the Spanish Empire, 1783–1829* (Chapel Hill, N.C., 1998). For engagement with the Islamic world (primarily in the Maghreb of North Africa), see Robert J. Allison, *The Crescent Obscured: The United States and the Muslim World, 1776–1815* (Chicago, 2000). For Jeffersonian policies toward Native peoples and North America's western borderlands, see Bernard W. Sheehan, *Seeds of Extinction: Jeffersonian Philanthropy and the American Indian* (Chapel Hill, N.C., 1973); Anthony F. C. Wallace, *Jefferson and the Indians: The Tragic Fate of the First Americans* (Cambridge, Mass., 1999); and Onuf, *Jefferson's Empire,* 18–52. For an explanation of the interconnectedness of these two areas of policy, see Sadosky, *Revolutionary Negotiations,* 176–205.

11. Details of federal government revenues, expenditures, and the national debt come from Albert Gallatin to the Senate, Dec. 20, 1802, in U.S. Congress, *American State Papers: Documents, Legislative and Executive, of the Congress of the U.S.* (Washington, D.C., 1832–61), Class 3: *Finance,* 2:5–7. For details of the developments in transatlantic commerce during Jefferson's first presidential term, see Burton Spivak, *Jefferson's English Crisis: Commerce, Embargo, and the Republican Revolution* (Charlottesville, Va., 1979), 12–30; Bradford Perkins, *Prologue to War: England and the United States, 1805–1812* (Berkeley, Calif., 1968), 32–100; and Sadosky, *Revolutionary Negotiations,* 180–89.

12. For details of the negotiation of the Louisiana Purchase, see Alexander DeConde, *This Affair of Louisiana* (New York, 1975), and James Lewis, *The Louisiana Purchase: Jefferson's Noble Bargain?* (Chapel Hill, N.C., 2003). For a discussion of how the purchase and transfer played out on the ground, see Peter J. Kastor, *The Nation's Crucible: The Louisiana Purchase and the Creation of America* (New Haven, Conn., 2004), esp. 35–52. Gallatin informed Jefferson of the details of the financing of the Louisiana Purchase shortly after the details of the treaty were communicated to him. See Gallatin to Jefferson, Aug. 31, 1803, in Henry Adams, ed., *The Writings of Albert Gallatin* (Philadelphia, 1879), 1:145–52.

13. Edling, *Hercules in the Cradle,* 134–35. Expansion of the United States' Atlantic commerce bolstered not only GDP but also the fortunes of free white American men who owned farms, plantations, or manufacturing or mercantile enterprises. Expansion of American power in transatlantic markets, and the concomitant articulation of a modern liberal capitalist regime, came with human costs—particularly the extension of the planation economy and its use of enslaved labor. See James Oakes, *Slavery and Freedom: An Interpretation of the Old South* (New York, 2013); Walter Johnson, *River of Dark Dreams: Slavery and Empire in the Cotton Kingdom* (Cambridge, Mass., 2013); and Joshua D. Rothman, *Flush Times and Fever Dreams: A Story of Capitalism and Slavery in the Age of Jackson* (Athens, Ga., 2014). For a consideration of America's plantation South in its transatlantic context, see Brian D. Schoen, *The Fragile Fabric of Union: Cotton, Federal Politics, and the Global Origins of the Civil War* (Baltimore, 2011).

14. Perkins, *Prologue to War,* 32–100; Spivak, *Jefferson's English Crisis,* 1–30; Sadosky, *Revolutionary Negotiations,* 180–89.

15. For the origins and progress of the *Chesapeake-Leopard* affair, see Spivak, *Jefferson's English Crisis,* 73–101.

16. For the Embargo, see ibid., 102–36. For Gallatin and fiscal policy in response to the Embargo, see Edling, *Hercules in the Cradle,* 135–36.

17. For Gallatin's description of declining revenues year over year from 1807 to 1809, see State of the Finances, Communicated to the Senate, June 8, 1809, in *American State Papers,* 3, *Finance,* 2:365–67. For Gallatin's report calling for a renewal of the charter of the Bank of the United States, explicitly mentioning war financing, see Bank of the United States, Communicated to the Senate, Mar. 3, 1809, in ibid., 2:351–53. For an overview of Gallatin's thinking during this period and on these questions, see Edling, *Hercules in the Cradle,* 136–40. For a detailed discussion of the military financing Gallatin was able to achieve under Jefferson, see J. C. A. Stagg, *Mr. Madison's War: Politics, Diplomacy, and Warfare in the Early American Republic, 1783–1830* (Princeton, N.J., 1983), 130–39.

18. Spivak, *Jefferson's English Crisis,* 102–36.

19. For Madison's policy on nonintercourse, see Perkins, *Prologue to War,* 40–183, and Donald R. Hickey, *The War of 1812: A Forgotten Conflict* (Urbana, Ill., 1995), 17–28.

20. See Benjamin L. Carp, "Jefferson's Embargo: National Intent and Sectional Effects," in this volume.

21. Hickey, *War of 1812,* 17–48.

22. See Gallatin to Madison, May 28, 1810, in Robert A. Rutland et al., eds., *The Papers of James Madison, Presidential Series* (Charlottesville, Va., 1984–), 2:361. Additional details of government finances are in the *PJM* editorial note, as well as Gallatin's 1809 report to Congress. See State of the Finances, Communicated to the Senate, June 8, 1809, in *American State Papers,* 3, *Finance,* 2:365–67.

23. For Gallatin's approach to the First Bank of the United States, see Edling, *Hercules in the Cradle,* 138–45.

24. The House postponed consideration of the re-charter on April 21, 1810; see U.S. Congress, *Journal of the House of Representatives of the United States,* 11th Cong., 2nd

sess., Apr. 21, 1810, 384. The Senate held its final discussions on the bill for the session on April 24; see U.S. Congress, *Journal of the Senate of the United States,* 11th Cong., 2nd sess., Apr. 24, 1810, 499–500.

25. Edling, *Hercules in the Cradle,* 138–45. The House defeated the bank's re-charter with a 65–64 vote for the indefinite postponement of the bill's consideration; see U.S. Congress, *Journal of the House of Representatives of the United States,* 11th Cong., 3rd sess., Jan. 24, 1811, 499–500. The Senate vote was tied, with Vice President George Clinton casting a negative vote to defeat the bill; see U.S. Congress, *Journal of the Senate of the United States,* 11th Cong., 3rd sess., Apr. 24, 1810, 499–500.

26. For Madison's speeches against the bank bill, see "The Bank Bill," [Feb. 2], 1791; "The Bank Bill," [Feb. 8], 1791, in William T. Hutchinson et al., eds., *The Papers of James Madison, Congressional Series* (Charlottesville, Va., 1981), 13:372–82, 383–88.

27. Edward Kaplan, *The Bank of the United States and the American Economy* (Westport, Conn., 1999), 31–33.

28. See Mark Smith, "Beyond Strict Construction: Jeffersonians in the 1790s," in this volume. Representative William Burwell of Virginia invoked Madison's 1791 speeches on two occasions during a floor speech on January 16, 1811. See Burwell, speaking on the Bank of the United States, Jan. 16, 1811, in *Annals of Congress,* 11th Cong., 3rd sess., 588–89.

29. Samuel Carswell to James Madison, Jan. 28, 1811, in Rutland et al., eds., *The Papers of James Madison, Presidential Series,* 3:137–39.

30. "Tammany" to Madison, Apr. 18, 1810 (abstract); "Tammany" to Madison, Apr. 25, 1810, in ibid., 2:304–5, 325. See also Mark Smith, "Beyond Strict Construction: Jeffersonians in the 1790s," in this volume.

31. Congress recorded receiving petitions supporting the re-chartering of the bank from the Chamber of Commerce of Philadelphia, the president and directors of the Bank of New York, and a group of Philadelphia citizens. Dec. 24, 1810; Jan. 8, 31, 1811, in *American State Papers,* 3, *Finance,* 2:453–54, 460, 470. Petitions opposed were received from the legislatures of Pennsylvania and Virginia, and a group of Pittsburgh citizens. Jan. 22, 26, Feb. 4, 1811, in ibid., 2:467, 470, 479.

32. For the Senate vote on the re-charter, see U.S. Congress, *Journal of the Senate of the United States,* 11th Cong., 3rd sess., Feb. 20, 1811, 578. For Gallatin on winding down bank operations, see Gallatin to Madison, Feb. 26, 1811, in Rutland et al., eds., *The Papers of James Madison, Presidential Series,* 3:184–85.

33. For an overview of events of the war during 1813 and 1814, see Hickey, *The War of 1812,* esp. chapters 6, 8.

34. Details of the Madison administration's war financing and administration measures can be found in Edling, *Hercules in the Cradle,* 138–54, and Stagg, *Mr. Madison's War,* 270–303.

35. Hickey, *War of 1812,* 166–67; Edling, *Hercules in the Cradle,* 150–53.

36. Hickey, *War of 1812,* 246–53.

37. James Madison to U.S. Congress, Dec. 5, 1815, Legislative Records of the House of Representatives, RG 233, National Archives, Washington, D.C., reprinted in Jack N. Rakove, ed., *James Madison: Writings* (New York, 1999), 710–18.

38. Ibid.

39. For the Bonus Bill, see Larson, *Internal Improvement,* 82–89. For additional context, see Charles Sellers, *The Market Revolution, 1815–1846* (Oxford, 1994), 70–102, and Daniel Walker Howe, *What Hath God Wrought: The Transformation of America, 1815–1848* (Oxford, 2009), 87–89. For text of Madison's veto, see Madison, "Veto Message to Congress," Mar. 3, 1817, in Rakove, ed., *Madison: Writings,* 718–20. In retirement, Madison believed in a dynamic republican economy. See Drew McCoy, *The Last of the Fathers: James Madison and the Republican Legacy* (Cambridge, 1989), 173–92.

40. For the Jeffersonians and the Missouri crisis, see Onuf, *Jefferson's Empire,* 109–46, and Glover Moore, *The Missouri Controversy, 1819–1821* (Lexington, Ky., 1953).

8 Lower South Jeffersonians

States and the Federal Imagination

Brian Schoen

In the heat of his well-known 1830 debate with Daniel Webster, South Carolina senator Robert Hayne found himself reaching back to the political battles that preceded his political coming of age. He framed much of his argument around a historical interpretation of the respective state and federal governments from the Federalist era through the Jefferson and Madison administrations to the 1820s. Hayne, the former apprentice of Langdon Cheves and rising star of South Carolina politics, hoped to transform a recurring debate over the sale of public lands into a diatribe about how a consolidated federal government had become the "hard taskmaster," the "oppressor" of southern and western agrarians alike. Through indirect taxation, he lamented, northerners had used the federal government to redistribute capital (from land and tariffs) into their region at the expense of Republican majorities elsewhere. Now, with the anticipated repayment of the federal debt, Hayne feared that federal surpluses would further grow the government and weaken his region's relative position. To Hayne and other southeastern planters, federalism had devolved into an exploitative system made possible by states' lapsed dependence on the federal government. As he himself threatened, those states allegedly most exploited, his own South Carolina being chief among them, might have to invoke the cherished "Principles of '98" to nullify federal law.[1]

Webster's responses pointed out the numerous inconsistencies in Hayne's logic and famously highlighted the constitutional effects of the "Carolina doctrine," furthering a concept of perpetual union that became dogma among many American politicians and jurists. But just as Hayne and Webster did, we gain much by looking backward before we jump forward to the nullification crisis and the sectional politics on the horizon. In particular, we should ponder how Hayne and many others from the Deep South came to the conclusion that the federal government hurt rather than helped state and regional interests. The most immediate and important answer, of course, lies in the battle against protective tariffs and antislavery pressures that rose to the surface in the 1820s. This chapter proposes that this conventional and accurate answer has a historical context, one that takes us back to the essence and practice of decentralized, Republican national and state governance in the first decades of the nineteenth century.

That history—let's call it a backstory—begins in the 1790s with what South Carolinians and Georgians believed to be Federalist neglect of their interests. Indeed, a supposed Federalist pariah played a major role in Hayne's semi-mythological political history. Yet, Hayne's fixation on Federalist-minded "consolidation" neglects the reality that many, if not most, of the policies that Lower South secessionists lamented—navigation acts, public land policy, internal improvements, protective tariffs, and especially the Embargo and War of 1812—were inaugurated or expanded by Republican-controlled Congresses and signed into law by Virginia-born presidents. Although Hayne focused his rhetorical flourishes on Federalist shadows, the debate itself and the states'-rights positions that pressured Hayne to pick it up were as much the byproduct of a complex interplay of regional, national, and international dynamics while Jeffersonians were in power.

Between the 1790s and 1820s, Republican political leaders constructively used state and federal apparatuses to meet the perceived needs of their diverse citizenry. Their efforts included centralizing, and in Georgia liberalizing, the sale of public land and (for a time) slaves, furthering a network of internal improvement projects inland, and using policing and militia laws to preserve state security, all of which contributed to a rising cotton empire. Coinciding with an intentional desire by state leaders to standardize civil law, these "bottom-up" reforms led residents to increasingly identify their own interests with the corporate interests of their respective states.[2] At the same time, Republicans in national power after 1800 worked to serve Lower South residents' interests, eventually creating a greater degree of geopolitical and commercial security that culminated in a post–War of 1812 boom and the 1819 Adams-Onís Treaty, which removed Spanish threats from the region. The diminution of external threats and continuation of internal ones (from slaves and Native Americans particularly) created political space for a more virulent states'-rights (but not antigovernment) ideology to develop in the 1820s. Within that context—and facing the prospect of relative economic decline at home and protective tariffs and antislavery actions out of the North—the central state authority came to be seen as an impediment to rather than a facilitator of intrastate and regional advancement. Instead, Lower South agrarians came to believe that their previous success had been the inevitable result of nature, international trade, and intrastate governmental action. Understanding subsequent states'-rights positions requires understanding the domestic *and* international failures and successes of policies that occurred prior to the 1820s.

All politics might be local but in the early national Lower South, local politics were critically informed by international context and developments. The region's first proto-parties coalesced in the wake of a civil war, the American Revolution, in which the enemy had occupied much of Georgia and South Carolina for the final two years of fighting. When the Royal Navy finally evacuated, they left behind a great deal of resentment and took with them a large number of the region's labor force: former slaves. In spite of that, the desperate need for capital led state leaders to allow British merchants to stay, their presence deemed necessary for rebuilding a war-torn economy. British slavers, along with a growing number of New England merchants participating in the transatlantic slave trade, were deemed essential for solving a labor shortage that the British and freedom-loving slaves had created. Thus, during the Confederation era, state politics revolved around questions like debts to these merchants and the treatment of loyalists. Within the region, pro- and anti-British poles shaped both the substance and grammar of politics for much of the early republic, eventually dovetailing with the dichotomies that came to define national politics. As if fears of real and imagined enemies in their midst were not enough, the post-revolutionary settlement left Georgia and South Carolina on the periphery of an American Confederation, precariously adjacent to historic Spanish enemies and Floridians' powerful allies: Native American nations like the Creek, Cherokee, Seminole, and Choctaw. Achieving security on land and robust commerce abroad shaped the region's leaders' generally enthusiastic embrace of the federal Constitution in 1787, after delegates won some important guarantees for slavery.[3]

The messiness of war and peace within southeastern communities and their weakened role within a chaotic British Atlantic also framed the region's response to Federalist leadership. Lowcountry planters and merchants found comfort in the idea and practice of a national power capable of projecting power abroad and willing to work with British merchants to stitch the region back into the world's economy. Even James Jackson, the man who fought the last battle against the British on Georgia soil (and a future Jeffersonian), had to admit that "the southern states are obliged to make use of British vessels" to carry their crops to market.[4] Alexander Hamilton relied heavily on pro-Washington administration South Carolinians and Georgians, like William Loughton Smith, to push his fiscal policies through Congress. Passage of the Jay Treaty depended on the support of Senator James Gunn of Georgia and James Read of South Carolina. South Carolinian Thomas Pinckney's ability to negotiate a favorable southern boundary with Spain and to get duty-free access to the port of New Orleans in the Treaty of San Lorenzo gained wide regional acclaim. Furthermore, Georgia state leaders' disastrous Yazoo and Pine Barrens land speculation deals, made possible by Georgia's inability to successfully control or settle its vast western lands, joined with concerns about Native Americans, could have created a context for a powerful Federalist Party willing to centralize greater power in a national government.[5] Both internal instability and external threats presented Lower South whites with good reasons to side with Federalist "friends of order" over the "friends of liberty" then coalescing in opposition behind Thomas Jefferson. Federalists would continue to provide alluring ideas that informed Lower South politics even after their national demise.[6]

Yet localized responses to internal politics and frustration with federal leadership on critical issues of governance instead drove larger numbers of residents, especially backcountry farmers, into the opposition and eventually the Jeffersonian coalition. Federalist visions of order, dominant on the coast and in towns, generally precluded the full political empowerment of backcountry "ruffians." Malign neglect of or (in Georgia's case) corrupt speculation in western counties provided political leaders like Charles Pinckney and James Jackson ample western constituencies determined to wrest control away from coastal adversaries who they called out as aristocratic "Anglo-men." These men promised westerners state infrastructure, education, courts, pro-developmental policies, and a political voice. Recently empowered western populations and disaffected easterners would provide the grassroots local and state opposition that eventually contributed to Republican national ascendance.[7]

In the West, the Washington and Adams administrations, despite the aforementioned successes, were seen as betraying regional interests. As early as 1790, Washington negotiated with Creek leaders, recognizing their sovereign claims and even placing one of their leaders, Alexander McGillvary, on the federal payroll. An unstable peace emerged until McGillvary's death in 1793, when frontier friction again broke out and war seemed likely. Yet again the Washington administration refused to pick up the sword, restraining more hawkish South Carolinian and Georgian officials and preventing them from participating in treaty negotiations. In 1793, Washington told South Carolina's governor that he believed most Creek wanted peace and that fear of war with a European power dictated negotiation and accommodation rather than force.[8] During John Adams's presidency, federal forces actually removed white encroachers from Cherokee lands. When he later reflected back on his presidency, Adams boasted that unlike his Republican successors, he had "preserved peace with the Indians."[9] Residents of the Lower South borderlands also wanted peace, but on expansionist terms that Federalist presidents proved reluctant to grant.

Washington's and Adams's pragmatic approach showed more nuance than some successors. Yet as Andrew R. L. Cayton showed, Washington's near simultaneous exertion of executive power to force the British from northwestern forts and raise an army to defeat Little Turtle's coalition suggested to Georgians and South Carolinians differential, and for whites detrimental, use of federal power.[10] In the 1790s, Virginians, Pennsylvanians, and New Englanders pressing into northwest territories found a transplanted Georgian rice grandee, Anthony Wayne, and his Legion of the United States clearing the way. Future white Ohioans, Indianans, and Illinoisans profited and made their peace with what Patrick Griffin has called an "American Leviathan."[11] Indeed, Webster's later refutation of Hayne invoked victory at Fallen Timbers, "the epoch of 1794," as evidence for why the national government had been more than fair to westerners and chiefly responsible for clearing the Northwest.[12] South of the Ohio, however, early white settlers would have no epic federal victory to point toward. There, at least until the War of 1812, they encountered what they perceived as a weak, or even possibly obstructionist, national presence.[13] Worse yet, for South Carolinians and Georgians, Washington and Adams appeared as concerned with protecting federal power and Native Americans' rights as extending the questionable property claims of white settlers within expansive southern state borders.

Georgia and South Carolina backcountry farmers covetous of Natives' lands turned to state officials like Jackson (who had lost his congressional reelection campaign to Wayne) and fended for themselves.

If relative beneficence toward southwestern Native Americans alienated would-be inland nationalists, the Jay Treaty convinced others that a conspiracy was afoot, one determined to keep them dependent on Britain. By giving Britain most-favored-nation status, the treaty undermined market diversification efforts that rice and other commodity producers sought, and which Jefferson had previously urged as minister to France. It also nullified state debtor relief laws that had partially shielded regional merchants, planters, and farmers from British creditors. But the treaty was as "onerous" for issues it incompletely dealt with or entirely ignored. Those who geographically and historically had benefited from the British West Indian provisioning trade would be disappointed with the meager concessions. Slaveholders who demanded remuneration for the thousands of slaves who stowed away on British vessels would be appalled with the lack of serious effort on the treaty's behalf. With the cotton revolution only beginning, even the treaty's most beneficial aspects—preserving peace and securing direct trade with Great Britain—rang hollow to most Lower South farmers and planters. Those political leaders within the region who supported it paid the price. Effigies of key treaty supporters Senators Gunn and Read joined those of John Jay at the center of popular discontent.[14]

Nor could South Carolinian Thomas Pinckney's successful negotiation of a southern boundary with Spain in 1795, though heralded, win over southwestern farmers to administration policies. That was partly because the future of the land within that border remained clouded by contested claims between Georgia residents, nonresident and mostly Federalist speculators, and semi-protected Native Americans. Consequently, untrusting Georgia politicians rejected Federalist-sponsored plans to cede western lands to the national government and jealously guarded their states' control over domestic matters. They instead trusted that opposition leaders would better fulfill the expansionist Republican vision for agrarians that Jefferson so poetically trumpeted as "those chosen people of God."[15]

On the other major commercial and security issues within the region—protecting slaves and coasts—states necessarily took the lead due in part to the paltry size of the U.S. Navy. Close proximity to the French West Indies generated particular anxiety, even in inland areas, as a steady stream of refugees from Haiti and the threat of French naval vessels portended to destabilize a slave society still recovering from the aftershocks of the American Revolution. In 1798, Thomas Pinckney's cousin, three-term governor and future Republican state party leader Charles Pinckney, ushered through a defense bill that opened up the state treasury to construct rudimentary gunboats and new forts. Charles Pinckney also suggested a bill making it a capital offense to introduce a "free person of color or slave" from the West Indies into the state. Fearing French slaves and fleets, Pinckney and Georgia's James Jackson joined their North Carolina counterpart in an agreement for mutual aid in the event of an invasion.[16] Importantly, these state executive leaders tasked with preserving order and balancing diverse political interests within their states emerged as the Jeffersonians' chief promoters in 1800, thus blunting pro-administration forces' ability to exploit the uptick in Francophobic sentiment.

The 1800 elections of delegates who would choose presidential electors took place under this cloud of domestic and international concern. Threats of frontier violence remained and the preliminary Treaty of Mortefontaine settling matters with France remained unratified. Like most Americans, Georgians and South Carolinians did not relish the idea of partisanship. Factions, coalescing around personality and particular issues, shaped political culture much more than any party loyalty. Fortunately for Thomas Jefferson, the ascendant factions in Georgia and South Carolina, led by popular former governor Charles Pinckney and sitting governor James Jackson, mobilized enough support and legislative votes to throw their states into the Jeffersonian-Republican column. Pinckney even delayed taking his seat in the U.S. Senate to remain in Columbia to lobby votes for Jefferson, a move ensuring a break with his extended family, most of whom supported the candidacy of his older cousin, Federalist Charles Cotesworth Pinckney and John Adams. In the end, the younger Pinckney's efforts worked, and South Carolina's electors threw the election the Republican way. Pinckney took credit for the victory, though not the debacle created when Aaron Burr and Thomas Jefferson tied.[17]

The personal politics surrounding these state "chieftains" mattered, but importantly both of these men's rise to state and national power depended on their own ability to convince residents that neither Adams's nor Hamilton's policies (nor those of their elitist Lowcountry Federalist supporters like Charles Cotesworth Pinckney) served regional interest. Fears of Haitian revolutionaries might have blunted criticism of the Alien Acts, but the Sedition Act was widely panned, especially at a time when many Lower South residents decried a coastal press they believed had been controlled by Anglo-men. (By the 1820s, one of the few victims prosecuted under the Sedition Act, British émigré [via Philadelphia] Thomas Cooper, would use his presidency of the University of South Carolina to encourage a generation of states'-rights theorists.) Particularly appalling, in 1798 concerns about national defense led the Federalist-controlled Congress to pass a direct property tax on land, houses, and slaves. Although carefully designed by Federalists to ensure, as Carolina Federalist Robert Harper claimed, that the "burden is made to fall on those who are able to bear it, and on every one in proportion to his ability," voters believed it a burdensome indication of Adams's failure.[18] For these reasons, Jefferson's election was welcomed by the region's Republican editors as a blow for "the rights and liberties of his fellow citizens" and against those "advocating standing armies . . . [who] call the liberty of the press, licentiousness; [and] ridicule the sovereignty of the people."[19] Hayne and other future states'-rights leaders would later turn back to this moment as the time when the Principles of '98, as outlined in Thomas Jefferson and James Madison's Virginia and Kentucky Resolutions, became fixed principles of party.

It would be tempting to see the "Revolution of 1800" as the tipping point toward states'-rights ideology and an abandonment of nationalizing potential. Yet underneath that rhetoric, the continued realities of the Southeast led citizens to accept and at times even demand stronger, more forceful national action directed toward accomplishing the expansionist goals Federalists had resisted.

Lower South Jeffersonians eagerly joined a national coalition and hoped federal patronage would expand their personal and political interests. Having successfully served out his term as governor, James Jackson headed to Washington and joined fellow representative Abraham Baldwin to make sure that Georgians, and specifically western Georgians, received their share of federal appointments. He repeatedly urged Jefferson to replace Adams's supporters with party loyalists, including suggesting future party leader William H. Crawford as a circuit judge. Jackson had mastered patronage politics as governor, using a stronger administrative state to ensure ample state revenue for a variety of state-level initiatives and a loyal political following.[20]

Jefferson's victory and his return to Congress gave him better spoils to offer. Charles Pinckney also sought the rewards of political combat, earning himself the position of U.S. minister to Spain. Neither man, nor the neighbors they left back home, desired to curtail the power or prestige of the federal government. Indeed, they would have likely agreed with historian Bethel Saler, who has keenly observed that though Jefferson "did pare down the national government, his contribution lay not in dismantling the central state but in reconceptualizing its sphere of operation."[21] Regional supporters like Pinckney and Jackson sought to use the strength of a rebalanced, purportedly more equitable federal system of states to achieve regional goals of greater commercial opportunity and increased security from Spanish and Native American threats. One example would be an 1803 law that urged federal officials to help enforce state bans on the admission of "negro, mulatto, or other persons of colour," including such bans passed in the Lower South to inoculate slaves from West Indian notions of freedom.[22]

In at least one other area, the Old Southwest, Republican control actually extended central state authority. More trusting of Republican leadership, in 1802 Georgia finally handed over its vast western lands to the federal government in exchange for cash and Jefferson's pledge to press Indians within the state's borders for more land cessions. On this score, the Virginia dynasty of Jefferson, Madison, and James Monroe appeared as an upgrade to Federalist precursors. Still, results would be mixed, gradual, and, in comparison to developments in the Northwest, incomplete. Jefferson's Indian agent in the Southwest, Benjamin Hawkins (an Adams appointee), continued to be derided by southeasterners as overly sympathetic to civilized Indian nations. As William Harrison used the threat of U.S. Army troops and Kentucky and Virginia militia to force the treaty cession of most of Indiana and Illinois, Hawkins hosted Creek and Cherokee dignitaries on his scientifically run plantation. Their embrace of the booming cotton economy helped Indian groups survive, and in a few cases thrive, within their semi-protected lands, despite the drop-off of the deerskin trade. Jefferson's civilization project included a coercive element, namely driving Native Americans deeper into debt and forcing them to sell land to pay if off. But through the eyes of land-hungry whites, peaceable coercion was slow and uneven. Unlike in the Northwest, prior to 1810 it netted only one major land cession—5 million acres of Choctaw land via the Treaty of Mount Dexter in 1805.[23]

A related and ultimately politically divisive challenge for national Republicans emerged over the continuing effects of Georgia's early chaotic land policy. In the 1790s, corrupt state officials granted, and then retracted, massive tracts of land to competing companies, many of them constituted of nonresident speculators, including the New England Mississippi Land Company (NEML). James Jackson and his "anti-Yazoo" faction's opposition to those grants had been instrumental in his own and Republicans' rise within the state. The issue gained new national prominence after the 1802 cession brought much of that land under federal control. In 1803, Jefferson's special commission of three cabinet members, Secretary of State James Madison, Treasury Secretary Albert Gallatin, and Attorney General Levi Lincoln, agreed with Georgian Republicans that speculators' titles could not be legally supported, but that "the interest of the United States and the tranquility of those who thereafter may inhabit the territory" suggested setting aside 5 million acres of federal land for those speculators. By 1804, NEML agents began exerting tremendous pressure on Congress for a compensation law.[24]

With almost united support from New England politicians and Federalists, the bill passed the Senate by a two-to-one vote. In the House, however, it encountered stiff resistance from southern Republicans, led by Virginian John Randolph, who believed it to be a federal endorsement of corruption and in violation of Georgia's honor and states' right to remedy her own mistakes. Compensation for NEML investors continued to divide Jeffersonians within the House—generally along sectional lines. Unable to find relief, they enlisted the aid of recent Republican convert John Quincy Adams and sued in federal court. In the landmark *Fletcher v. Peck* (1810) decision, Chief Justice John Marshall and four other judges ruled that because Georgia was a "member of the American Union" and not a sovereign, independent state, her attempt to repeal the original grant represented a breach of the Constitution's contract clause—previously interpreted as only applying to private citizens. Jefferson appointee South Carolinian William Johnson agreed with the verdict, but his concurring opinion preserved what he thought to be a state's reserved right to seize individual property for the public good. In retirement, Jefferson lamented Marshall's "twistifications . . . in the late Yazoo case," but practically speaking the decision cleared the way for the compensation that his successor had believed politically necessary. In early 1814, over the stiff opposition of Old Republicans, including Georgia's George Troup, the House finally passed a compensation bill. War concerns along with a reminder from Mississippi's territorial delegate that settlement of the Southwest necessitated resolving the matter shifted enough Republican votes. Federal action restored order within Georgia and the southeastern lands but with a bitter legacy, one prominently felt by the heirs to James Jackson's mantle as state party leaders: George Troup and William H. Crawford.[25]

In terms of greater geopolitical security, Jefferson and Madison would more aggressively use federal power to acquire land from the Spanish and French, but with deceptively mixed results for the Old Southeast. Crucially, their friend James Monroe had—with some help from Charles Pinckney in Spain—used geopolitical circumstances to pry Louisiana from France's Napoleon with Spanish acquiescence. Yet the original objects of the administration's desire—and that of Pinckney and the Southeast—had been East and West Florida. On that point, Monroe, Pinckney, and two subsequent ministers singularly failed. Furthermore, when word leaked that Monroe's mission had entailed a pledge of $2 million without clear congressional approval, Jefferson's administration was charged with incompetence and abuse of executive power. White settlers, most from Georgia, South Carolina, or Louisiana, continued to drift into Spanish-controlled lands.[26]

Although not inhabited by many Spaniards, the Floridas were acutely significant for Georgians and South Carolinians, and not just for the lands in which some had started to invest. Under foreign control they provided supply lines and a haven for escaped slaves, marooned communities, and hostile Indians, each of which challenged state authorities across a very porous border. Spanish sovereignty presented roadblocks to port access that would take cotton crops abroad. Furthermore, the possibility of a British takeover could not be dismissed, especially with the presence of financial interests like the Forbes Company at a time when the two nations were frequently on opposite sides in the Napoleonic wars. By 1810, Madison's agents on the ground, including former Georgia governor George Mathews, allied with Anglo-American settlers to take matters into their own hands. Inspired by other instances of Spanish colonial revolts, they encouraged Anglo-American settlers to do likewise, hoping that it would compel Spain to cede land to the United States. Aided by a large number of U.S. settlers and claims that West Florida had actually been part of the Louisiana Purchase, these efforts gained traction from Baton Rouge to Mobile. The outbreak of war with Britain and settlers' declarations of independence gave Madison the pretext to attempt annexation of West Florida in the spring of 1813.[27]

In East Florida, however, the case was weaker. Without assurances from Madison of U.S. military support, Mathews turned to Georgia's current governor, David Mitchell, who, though irritated that he had not been made privy to any administration plans, ordered his state militia to be at the ready. Upon hearing the full extent of Mathews's plan—ironically from British minister Augustus Foster and Indian agent Benjamin Hawkins—Madison repudiated them. With American filibusters still there but without federal sanction, "a political and military" stalemate produced an escalation of undeclared "guerrilla war" that involved the Spanish, Native Americans, fugitive slaves, and Georgia militias. Madison may have been willing to also unleash militias into eastern Florida but sought Senate approval first. It was not forthcoming, as northern senators believed it unconscionable to risk a two-front war for Georgia and South Carolina interests. As Gallatin, a commissioner charged with negotiating the end of the war with Britain would write, a "Southern" scheme that risked war with Spain would "disgust every man north of Washington." The demands of an armed conflict with a stronger enemy over vast oceans and an expansive border understandably took national precedence, but for Lower South whites, Spanish Florida remained a haven for escaped slaves and provided an alliance for Native Americans.[28]

Taken as a whole, the War of 1812 would be a defining moment for southeasterners' views of governance, though the legacy would be complicated. The causes of the war remain a contested point of historiography, with some historians treating it as a war of conquest for western lands and others affirming Madison's public claims that it fought to preserve "free trade and sailors' rights." It was surely a war rife with Anglophobia, an obvious point recently driven home by Lawrence A. Peskin.[29] In the Southeast, commercial needs, landed hopes, and Anglophobia all contributed to hawkish sentiments. The bitter legacy of the American Revolution had created deep hatred of the English, a hatred that redoubled when they heard stories of British liberation of slaves living in coastal regions. British orders in council had curtailed regional desires for commercial diversification, and there were no small number of sailors from the region. For complicated reasons, Lower South representatives proved to be among the most virulent defenders of

Jefferson's most extensive use of federal power, the 1807 Embargo. When commercial warfare appeared to have failed, they aggressively pushed Madison toward war.[30]

Within the region, the war effort led to thousands of enlistments—including Hayne's as regimental captain—an expansion of coastal defenses, and, in South Carolina at least, one of the nation's highest property tax burdens per white capita in the country. This last measure (surprising in light of subsequent southern tax policy) was necessary to pay for defenses and to meet federal tax quotas, a policy that most Republican-controlled southern states responded to but which Federalist-leaning New England balked at.[31] The two states saw little direct military action, though British raids on St. Mary's and the Cumberland Islands late in the war liberated some slaves, and the war seriously curtailed trade. In all, the region wanted but received little federal support, most of which necessarily went to the Canadian border and the naval war. Leaders in Washington, D.C., like John C. Calhoun and William Crawford, who witnessed firsthand the shortcomings of the national war effort, afterward urged greater federal preparedness and reform, but residents more isolated from the war's immediate terrors remained less convinced. Consequently, under the umbrella of national patriotism and sacrifice, the fighting and financing of the war actually reinforced a sense of local and regional pride, one that could minimize the role of the federal government in many minds, not unlike what Alan Taylor suggests happened to white Virginians.[32]

The federal military played a much more important role further west, though there too state militias and their leaders seized the headlines. Prior to the war, approximately a third of the nation's military had been posted in New Orleans. They had helped put down the 1811 German coast slave insurrection, and led by General William Claiborne, would occupy Mobile. Yet other aspiring military leaders, like Carolina-born Andrew Jackson, continued to criticize federal neglect of the southern borderlands. In 1812, when Jackson arrived in Natchez with militiamen, he was instructed that the U.S. government did not need and would not pay for their services. Civil war within the Creek Nation transformed into attacks against white settlers and slaves and then full-blown war in 1813. As the major-general of the Tennessee militia, Jackson and his 2,500 militia and 500 allied Indians exacted a crippling blow on the Red Sticks at Horseshoe Bend in March 1814. Only afterward would Jackson get his coveted U.S. army commission and the authority to treat with the defeated Creek. The subsequent Treaty of Fort Jackson netted the largest tangible geopolitical result of the War of 1812: the cession of 23 million acres of Creek lands, including most of the future state of Alabama, to the U.S. government. Georgians had hoped to get more lands in their borders awarded, but still the return of peace and trade after the war triggered a cotton and land boom into the western country that would allow many southern planters and farmers to gain considerable wealth.[33]

Although the Fort Jackson negotiations and the climactic Battle of New Orleans would take place under the authority of the U.S. government, Jackson and his subsequent campaign biographers shaped the story as one in which a great leader led do-it-yourself western and southern militias to victory over a challenge that the federal government had ignored. In truth, the history was considerably more complicated. Jackson placed recent arrivals to the march, the U.S. 39th Infantry, at the center of his attack. Indeed, the previous December, 1,200 members of the U.S. 3rd Infantry, led by General Ferdinand Claiborne (a veteran of the Battle of Fallen Timbers), had defeated a large force of Creeks at the seldom-mentioned Battle of Holy Ground. Yet Jackson's victories and image better fit a growing southern populist sentiment stressing that a republican people at arms did not need a strong federal state to win exacting victories. State militias would do. When taken to its extreme, this idea allowed South Carolinian nullifiers to contemplate armed resistance to federal law and a President Jackson and Congress they no longer trusted.[34]

Prior to that, however, Jackson's rogue efforts along with continued diplomatic pressure by the Monroe administration granted the Southeast one additional and critical victory. Between 1816 and 1818, Jackson's raids into Spanish territory took out a fort manned by escaped slaves and towns occupied by Spanish, Creek and Seminole Indians, and two British merchants, one of which Jackson summarily executed. This threatened an international crisis and the derailment of Monroe's secretary of state, John Quincy Adams's ongoing negotiations for the purchase of the Floridas. Ultimately, however, Adams and Monroe used it, and the question of the border with Texas, as leverage to finally pry the Floridas from Spain. Removing the Seminole threat would require a second war in the 1830s, but the Southeast had achieved a long sought after geopolitical security. By 1821, the federal government had delivered to the region greater commercial opportunity through peace with Britain, more lands for whites, and greater political security. Yet few residents fully appreciated what a government generally "out of sight" had managed to accomplish. Instead, by the 1820s, they embraced a cotton-centric, free-trade political economy that stressed that only state initiatives (which remained robust) were necessary to support what appeared to be the natural ascendance of cotton.[35]

Ironically, the greater security achieved by Jeffersonians in the War of 1812, the Creek Wars, and the Transcontinental Treaty likely weakened the region's bonds to a stronger federal government. States that had long cried for greater federal protection needed it less. A postwar cotton boom empowered Lower South residents to believe that their long-suffering economies had finally blossomed during peace. The postwar commercial boom and emergence of an inland cotton empire had made growers increasingly dependent on the very British who had long served as the Jeffersonian bugaboo. By the 1820s, regional fears of overdependence on Great Britain gave way to a belief that healthy interdependence had been achieved. Although Carolinians had been instrumental in bringing the war about, afterward Hayne could downplay that and declare it had been fought "for the protection of Northern shipping and New England seamen."[36] A war that southern Republicans had forced on many New Englanders became, especially after the Hartford Convention, a proof of South Carolinians' and Georgians' own benevolent sacrifice. The threat of higher federal protective tariffs—a place in which the federal government clearly came into sight—was thought to threaten free trade. As fears of war subsided, more passive nationalists within the region gradually began to edge out, or wear down, those among them who continued to argue for more strength at the federal center.[37]

Greater external security did not, however, alleviate concerns about slavery's instability within the region. The demands of a rejuvenated global market and slave owners' desire for profits exacted untold damage to slaves' bodies. Black emancipations in the North and Latin America increased the number of free black sailors entering Lower South ports. The first controversy over Missouri's entrance as a slave state suggested that northern Republican allies might not be fully trustworthy. A second one, sparked by northerners' rejection of states' rights to control the entrance of free black citizens, inspired the aged Charles Pinckney, one of the last founders still in public service, to rise before the House and declare the measure unconstitutional. In March 1821, Pinckney's final congressional speech urged the need to protect slavery and avoid "destroy[ing] that Union on which not alone depend our own existence as a free, a powerful, or a happy people."[38] During Pinckney's life he and his state and region had turned to the federal government to serve its interests, restore order on the frontier, pass treaties, and empower commerce.

Although fighting a similar political battle a decade later, Pinckney's son-in-law Robert Hayne struck a tone different from Pinckney in his verbal assault on federal "consolidation." In Hayne's view, a lecherous central government had been feasting on wealth generated by southern planters (one might more accurately say their slaves) and western public lands. Without a clear foreign threat and at a time when federal debt appeared headed toward extinction, the government—and especially a northern majority in Congress—he contended, now wished to foster western dependence as part of a corrupt bargain premised on federal internal improvements and an uncharitable land policy. Without much of a legacy of federal internal improvements, especially compared to those states benefiting from the Cumberland and other national roads, South Carolina in particular had few positive illustrations of national work projects to point toward. Georgians, by contrast (and this could help explain their different approach to nullification), continued to rely on the national apparatus to negotiate peace with Indians and build roads through their lands, until Jackson's own tragically underfunded federal removal policy went into effect in the 1830s.[39] Indeed, by the late 1820s, in the context of relative economic decline, even these federal roads appeared to some to have become pathways for the outmigration of their citizens, forcing southeasterners into a tough calculation about whether to support expansion or undermine it to keep people and capital at home.[40] Under this context, Hayne and other nullifiers had come to believe that the decentralized Jeffersonian-Republican union had morphed into a northeastern-centered union reminiscent of Federalist times.

History had provided a tangled set of ironies that states' righters sought to exploit for political gain within and outside of their region. Of course, what they were reluctant, even incapable, of admitting was that this current state of affairs had emerged within the Jeffersonian coalition and largely at the insistence of constituents who demanded that the government do more for them, in part based on their own experiences during the War of 1812 and in the aftermath of the Panic of 1819. Either willfully or unwittingly, self-proclaimed Jeffersonian proponents of states' rights like Hayne proved to have short and selective memories.

Notes

1. Herman Belz, ed., *The Webster-Hayne Debate on the Nature of the Union* (Indianapolis, 2013), 5, 8; Daniel Feller, *The Public Lands in Jacksonian Politics* (Madison, Wis., 1984).

2. Milton Sydney Heath, *Constructive Liberalism: The Role of the State in Economic Development in Georgia to 1860* (Cambridge, Mass., 1954); Laura F. Edwards, *The People and Their Peace: Legal Culture and the Transformation of Inequality in the Post-Revolutionary South* (Chapel Hill, N.C., 2009).

3. Sylvia Frey, *Water from the Rock: Black Resistance in a Revolutionary Age* (Princeton, N.J., 1991); Jerome Nadelhaft, *The Disorders of War: The Revolution in South Carolina* (Orono, Maine, 1981); George R. Lamplugh, *Politics on the Periphery: Factions and Parties in Georgia, 1783–1806* (Newark, Del., 1986).

4. Jackson, House Debates, May 13, 1790, in Helen E. Veit, Charlene Bangs Bickford, and Kenneth R. Bowling, eds., *Documentary History of the First Federal Congress* (Baltimore, Md., 1994), 13:1259.

5. Thomas Abernathy, *The South in the New Nation, 1789–1819* (Baton Rouge, La., 1961), 136–68; Lamplugh, *Politics on the Periphery.*

6. Thomas Slaughter, *The Whiskey Rebellion: Frontier Epilogue to the American Revolution* (New York, 1988), successfully employs this useful dichotomy to explain the proto-parties that emerged in the 1790s. George C. Rogers Jr., "South Carolina Federalists and the Origins of the Nullification Movement," *South Carolina Historical Magazine* 71, no. 1 (Jan. 1, 1970): 17–32.

7. Rachel N. Klein, *Unification of a Slave State: The Rise of the Planter Class in the South Carolina Backcountry, 1760–1808* (Chapel Hill, N.C., 1992), 149–202, 238–68; Lamplugh, *Politics on the Periphery.*

8. Washington to Governor William Moultrie, Aug. 28, 1793, in John C. Fitzpatrick, ed., *The Writings of George Washington* (Washington, D.C., 1931), 33:73–74.

9. Daniel H. Usner, "'A Savage Feast They Made of It': John Adams and the Paradoxical Origins of Federal Indian Policy," *Journal of the Early Republic* 33, no. 4 (2013): 629–32, 632 (quotation).

10. Andrew R. L. Cayton, "'Separate Interests' and the Nation-State: The Washington Administration and the Origins of Regionalism in the Trans-Appalachian West," *Journal of American History* 79, no. 1 (June 1, 1992): 39–67.

11. Patrick Griffin, *American Leviathan: Empire, Nation, and Revolutionary Frontier* (New York, 2008).

12. Daniel Webster, speech, Jan. 20, 1830, in Belz, ed., *Webster-Hayne Debate,* 18.

13. Jeffrey Pasley, "Midget on Horseback," *Common-Place* 9, no. 1 (Oct. 2008), http://www.common-place.org/vol-09/no-01/pasley/.

14. John Herald Wolfe, *Jeffersonian Democracy in South Carolina* (Chapel Hill, N.C., 1940), 71–81; Lamplugh, *Politics on the Periphery,* 127–28, 141n34; Schoen, *Fragile Fabric,* 36–37, 282n39.

15. Thomas Jefferson, *Notes on the State of Virginia,* query XIX, in Merrill D. Peterson, ed., *Thomas Jefferson: Writings* (New York, 1984), 290.

16. George Terry, *A Study of the Impact of the French Revolution and the Insurrections in Saint-Domingue upon South Carolina, 1790–1805* (Columbia, S.C., 1975); Marty D. Matthews, *Charles Pinckney: Forgotten Founder: The Life and Times of Charles Pinckney* (Columbia, S.C., 2004), 93–95.

17. Pinckney to Thomas Jefferson, Oct. 12, 1800; n.d.; Nov. 22, 1800, in James Bain, Jr., "South Carolina in the Presidential Election of 1800," *American Historical Review* 4, no. 1 (Oct. 1898): 111–20; Joanne B. Freeman, *Affairs of Honor: National Politics in the New Republic* (New Haven, Conn., 2002).

18. Quoted in Robin L. Einhorn, *American Taxation, American Slavery* (Chicago, 2008), 194.

19. Klein, *Unification of a Slave State,* 259.

20. Heath, *Constructive Liberalism,* 134; George R. Lamplugh, "Oh the Colossus! The Colossus! James Jackson and the Jeffersonian Republican Party in Georgia, 1796–1806," *Journal of the Early Republic* 9, no. 3 (Fall 1989): 320–21, 325–26.

21. Bethel Saler, "An Empire for Liberty, a State for Empire," in *The Revolution of 1800: Democracy, Race, and the New Republic,* ed. James J. Horn, Jan Ellen Lewis, and Peter S. Onuf (Charlottesville, Va., 2002), 361.

22. Brian Schoen, "Positive Goods and Necessary Evils," in *Contesting Slavery: The Politics of Bondage and Freedom in the New American Nation,* ed. John Craig Hammond and Matthew Mason (Charlottesville, Va., 2012), 166–67.

23. Adam Rothman, *Slave Country: American Expansion and the Origins of the Deep South* (Cambridge, Mass., 2007), esp. 42, 56–58; Anthony F. C. Wallace, *Jefferson and the Indians: The Tragic Fate of the First Americans* (Cambridge, Mass., 1999), 206–40; Daniel H. Usner Jr., "American Indians on the Cotton Frontier: Changing Economic Relations with Citizens and Slaves in the Mississippi Territory," *Journal of American History* 72, no. 2 (Sept. 1, 1985): 297–317.

24. C. Peter Magrath, *Yazoo: Law and Politics in the New Republic; Case of Fletcher v. Peck* (Providence, R.I., 1966), 36.

25. Ibid., 88–99. On "twistifications," see "Thomas Jefferson to James Madison, 25 May 1810," Founders Online, National Archives, Washington, D.C., http://founders.archives.gov/documents/Jefferson/03-02-02-0362.

26. Peter S. Onuf, *Jefferson's Empire: The Language of American Nationhood* (Charlottesville, Va., 2000); James E. Lewis, *The American Union and the Problem of Neighborhood: The United States and the Collapse of the Spanish Empire, 1783–1829* (Chapel Hill, N.C., 1998); J. C. A. Stagg, *Borderlines in Borderlands: James Madison and the Spanish-American Frontier, 1776–1821* (New Haven, Conn., 2013).

27. Stagg, *Borderlines in Borderlands,* esp. 81–82, 207.

28. Ibid., 87–133, 132 (quotation).

29. Lawrence A. Peskin, "Conspiratorial Anglophobia and the War of 1812," *Journal of American History* 98, no. 3 (Dec. 1, 2011): 647–69. For a recent summary of this vast debate, see Jasper M. Trautsch, "The Causes of the War of 1812: 200 Years of Debate," *Journal of Military History* 77 (Jan. 2013): 273–93.

30. Brian Schoen, "Calculating the Price of Union: Republican Economic Nationalism and the Origins of Southern Sectionalism, 1790–1828," *Journal of the Early Republic* 23, no. 2 (July 1, 2003): 173–206. See also Benjamin Carp's essay in this volume.

31. Einhorn, *American Taxation, American Slavery,* 220; Richard Sylla and John Joseph Wallis, "The Anatomy of Sovereign Debt Crises: Lessons from the American State Defaults of the 1840s," *Japan and the World Economy* 10, no. 3 (July 1, 1998): 281.

32. Alan Taylor, *The Internal Enemy: Slavery and War in Virginia, 1772–1832* (New York, 2013).

33. Rothman, *Slave Country,* 116–17.

34. Fred Anderson and Andrew Cayton, *Dominion of War: Empire and Liberty in North America, 1500–2000* (London, 2005), chapter 5.

35. Brian Balogh, *A Government Out of Sight: The Mystery of National Authority in Nineteenth-Century America* (Cambridge, 2009).

36. Belz, ed., *Webster-Hayne Debate,* 57.

37. Nicholas Greenwood Onuf and Peter S. Onuf, *Nations, Markets, and War: Modern History and the American Civil War* (Charlottesville, Va., 2006); Brian Schoen, *The Fragile Fabric of Union: Cotton, Federal Politics, and the Global Origins of the Civil War* (Baltimore, 2009), chapter 3; Rothman, *Slave Country,* 175.

38. Robert Pierce Forbes, *The Missouri Compromise and Its Aftermath: Slavery and the Meaning of America* (Chapel Hill, N.C., 2009); Matthews, *Forgotten Founder,* 136–37 (quotation).

39. Angela Pulley Hudson, *Creek Paths and Federal Roads: Indians, Settlers, and Slaves and the Making of the American South* (Chapel Hill, N.C., 2010); Richard E. Ellis, *The Union at Risk: Jacksonian Democracy, States' Rights, and Nullification Crisis* (New York, 1987).

40. James D. Miller, *South by Southwest: Planter Emigration and Identity in the Slave South* (Charlottesville, Va., 2002).

III Jefferson and Madison

9 Apocalypse Now

Thomas Jefferson's Radical Enlightenment

Andrew Trees

> Alliances holy or hellish, may be formed and retard the epoch deliverance, may swell the rivers of blood which are yet to flow, but their own will close the scene, and leave to mankind the right of self government.
>
> —Thomas Jefferson to the Marquis de Lafayette, November 4, 1823

Let us leave aside the rivers of blood for now and turn to the place where any scholar would naturally begin a piece on the Enlightenment and Jefferson's politics—the majestic and, most importantly, indigenous North American moose. On January 7, 1786, while serving as U.S. minister to France, Thomas Jefferson sent a request to John Sullivan of New Hampshire. He asked Sullivan to send to Paris the "skin, the skeleton, and the horns of the Moose, the Caribou, and the Original or Elk . . . but most especially those of the moose."[1] He gave detailed instructions about how he wanted the animal prepared, asking Sullivan "to leave the hoof on, to leave the bones of the legs and of the thighs if possible in the skin, and to leave also the bones of the head in the skin with the horns on, so that by sewing up the neck and belly of the skin we should have the true form and size of the animal." He claimed that such a specimen would be "more precious than you can imagine." At first glance, Jefferson seems far too interested in securing the moose when his attention should have been focused on negotiating commercial treaties, but that is only because we tend to privilege the political issues of the time instead of studying Jefferson through the lens of his lifelong and passionate engagement with the Enlightenment. The two projects were more closely related than they might first appear, and Jefferson's search for a moose was as much a political and even national project as an Enlightenment one.

The larger issue that lay behind his effort to secure a moose was a long-running debate about what sort of promise America held. According to George Louis Leclerc, Comte de Buffon, the leading French naturalist of the time, the unhealthy climate of America led to degeneracy so that animals were smaller and weaker than those in Europe, including the human animal. Buffon claimed that American Indians were "small and feeble" as well as "more timid and cowardly." (Frontiersmen who had fought the Indians would undoubtedly have argued the point).[2] Although he did not explicitly say that the same degeneracy was afflicting Europeans who had emigrated to America, the implication was there for anyone to see. In this case, spreading Enlightenment knowledge and nation-making went hand in hand for Jefferson. The size of the moose was intended as a definitive rebuttal of Buffon's theory of American degeneracy. In fact, the importance of disproving Buffon's theory played a large role in Jefferson's only published book, *Notes on the State of Virginia.* At the heart of that work was Jefferson's careful refutation of Buffon's theory, involving long lists comparing the relative sizes of animals from America and Europe. His most important examples were the moose and the mastodon. (Jefferson believed the mastodon was not extinct and still lived undiscovered in the western part of the continent.) The quest for a moose, skin and all, was nothing less than an attempt to refute the idea of America as a land of degeneracy and inferiority so that the Enlightenment ideal of advancing knowledge and the political project of launching a new nation became virtually indistinguishable from one another.[3]

I have to admit to a weakness for any story involving a founding father and moose bones rattling across the ocean, but this particular story offers a good vantage point to begin to understand Jefferson and the Enlightenment. The tale shows how ostensibly political matters could quickly become entangled in Enlightenment debates (and vice versa). Even more important, the story of the moose suggests the central role of the Enlightenment in Jefferson's life.

At first glance, viewing Jefferson through the lens of the Enlightenment does not seem to get us very far in understanding him. Virtually every educated and well-read American of that generation was influenced by the Enlightenment to one degree or another, so it seems a label without much interpretive power. This likely explains why the topic of Jefferson and the Enlightenment has largely become a neglected backwater among Jefferson scholars.[4]

But it is a mistake not to take Jefferson's involvement with the Enlightenment seriously, even (or perhaps especially) when considering his politics. In fact, the Enlightenment was at the core of Jefferson's own self-image in a more significant manner than it was for most of his contemporaries, even those who fashioned themselves as followers of the Enlightenment.[5] Let us look simply at his self-presentation. When asked about his heroes, Jefferson always named three of the towering giants of the Enlightenment: Sir Francis Bacon, Sir Isaac Newton, and John Locke. And consider Monticello. Jefferson devoted a good portion of his life to modeling and remodeling it into an architectural masterpiece, reflecting not only his own design but also his vision of man's place in the world. What was a visitor's first experience of Monticello when he entered the house? The entranceway was a miniature natural history museum filled with a variety of artifacts Jefferson had collected.[6] Given how meticulous he was about planning every aspect of Monticello, this was not a haphazard development. The entranceway was an important declaration of who Jefferson was, how he saw himself, and how he wanted others to see him. Jefferson's *Notes on the State of Virginia* was a classic Enlightenment text, blending everything from natural history to anthropology to his own scientific theories on race.[7] Even his official, public life showed a similar bent. Jefferson's letters are littered with complaints about holding office and about how he would like nothing better than to retire to Monticello.[8] There was one office, though, that Jefferson did not complain about holding—the presidency of the American Philosophical Society for a term that lasted seventeen years (he was a member for forty-seven years). If all of that was not proof enough, his tombstone acts as a final reminder. From a lifetime filled with accomplishments, he chose to include three:

Author of the Declaration of American Independence
of the Statute of Virginia for religious freedom
Father of the University of Virginia

All three reflect his deep commitment to the Enlightenment and its principles.

I do not mean to belabor Jefferson's obviously impeccable Enlightenment credentials. These are well-known examples, and no scholar would disagree that the Enlightenment influenced Jefferson. When we take that commitment as seriously as Jefferson did, though, it begins to have significant explanatory power for the man, his thinking, and his actions. Additionally, by seeing him first and foremost as a man of the Enlightenment, we begin to see him as he saw himself. I want to suggest, however, that we pursue this line of inquiry in a particular way. Typically, scholars focus on his younger years. Through close examination of his library and his literary commonplace book (and always noting the handicap imposed by the Shadwell fire, which destroyed his early books and papers), historians try to establish the key works that shaped Jefferson's thinking. I believe this is a misguided approach for one simple reason: Jefferson was so widely read and so obviously engaged with the intellectual ferment of the time that it is overly simplistic to suggest that a few books can be privileged over all the rest. In addition, reader response theory has undermined any simplistic notion of ideas being transferred from book to brain without serious distortion.[9] To understand what the Enlightenment meant to Jefferson, instead of looking inward we are better off looking outward and seeing how Jefferson actively attempted to apply the Enlightenment to real-world problems and policies.

Of course, even the question of the Enlightenment's meaning or purpose can quickly become hopelessly mired in pedantic hair-splitting. In fact, to speak of the Enlightenment in the singular is already to impose a fiction over a complicated and even contradictory, not to say riotous, movement. It is a convenient and even a necessary fiction. One cannot stop every time one mentions the Enlightenment to enumerate all of its variations. But we need to acknowledge the simple fact that there was no single Enlightenment. The Scottish Enlightenment was different in many respects from the French Enlightenment. And even these categories are too broad (as a juxtaposition of Jean-Jacques Rousseau and Voltaire quickly reveals).

Even so, most key figures agreed on a few basic principles: a belief in man's reason and his ability to understand his world and even improve it, and also a belief in certain natural rights for mankind, such as the right to self-government. Yet even these basic principles quickly led to disagreement. For instance, how much self-government? How much improvement? Were women capable of self-government? What place did God have in all of this, if any? So, instead of attempting to define the slippery concept of the Enlightenment and to synchronize it with the inscrutable process of what trace, if any, a book leaves in a man's mind when he reads, let us look instead at Thomas Jefferson, practitioner of the Enlightenment. This Jefferson is less opaque than he is usually depicted as being.[10] In fact, this Jefferson is refreshingly concrete and literal-minded.

That is not to say that the Enlightenment magically explains a figure as notoriously complex as Jefferson. All individuals are complicated and contain within them multiple and often contradictory identities. Jefferson was also a Virginian, a politician, a father, and a slave owner to name only a few of the roles that contributed to his sense of who he was. But the preeminent role he himself always had at the forefront of his mind and tried to live up to was as a man of the Enlightenment. When possible, he tried to reason and act in a way that was consistent with what he believed were Enlightenment principles. When it wasn't possible, he tried at least to rationalize actions in a way that helped them seem to conform to Enlightenment principles. And he did not abandon this approach when facing a particularly difficult situation. *He embraced it even more tightly.* Because of this, Jefferson's attempts to apply the Enlightenment to the American political world were often far more radical and less pragmatic than his contemporaries. This proved to be both liberating and horrifying. It could lead to visions of unfettered freedom spreading across the globe and the generations, or it could lead to visions of blood-soaked rivers that threatened to wipe out the very people who were supposed to be enjoying the gift of freedom in the first place.

In some cases, Jefferson's Enlightenment beliefs helped him throw off the dead hand of the past in ways that greatly benefited America—the liberating aspect of his radical commitment. Although much of this essay focuses on the dark turn that Jefferson's radical Enlightenment could take, it is worth briefly listing some of the most notable accomplishments on the positive side of the ledger. Leaving aside the Declaration of Independence, whose opening paragraphs are as eloquent and influential a statement of Enlightenment political principles as any of us are ever likely to read, Jefferson struck numerous monumental blows for the Enlightenment project of liberating mankind from a corrupt and corrupting *ancien régime.* He was the author of the Virginia Statute of Religious Freedom, which firmly separated church from state and erected a wall of protection around an individual's right to believe as he chooses. The influence of the statute spread not only to other states but across the Atlantic. Jefferson also proposed bills abolishing entail and primogeniture, tearing down two of the primary obstacles to the aristocracy of talent that Jefferson hoped would replace the hereditary aristocracy.[11] Jefferson's land ordinance of 1784 was equally significant in offering a vision of a free land for a free people, even if the more famous Northwest Ordinance of 1787 later obscured it from view.[12] These accomplishments alone would be enough to establish him as the great American champion of liberal Enlightenment political principles. And they were all largely done by the mid-1780s, long before what most of us think of as the main phase of his political career. In cumulative effect, they went a long way toward tearing down the old order and allowing a new one to take its place.

In other instances, though, Jefferson's Enlightenment principles led him astray in ways that look profoundly misguided to us today. That is the inescapable nature of Jefferson's deep commitment to the Enlightenment: it stands at the heart of both his soaring ideal of a liberal, free society and his dark vision of a desolated earth flowing with "rivers of blood." The very same Enlightenment mindset that led to a string of outstanding liberal accomplishments could, under the wrong circumstances, lead to a far more grim and even tragic outcome. What we tend to forget after the passage of so much time is the messiness associated with any radical restructuring, even one as generally good in its influence as the Enlightenment. Jefferson's radical commitment to Enlightenment principles did not always lead to what we would think of as "enlightened outcomes." Indeed, some of Jefferson's biggest political and social blind spots were the result of his attempts to hold fast to his ideal of "enlightened" politics.[13]

Most often, Jefferson blundered when he attempted to impose an abstract clarity on the messiness of political life, even turning to mathematical calculation to parse difficult issues, perhaps most famously with the U.S. Constitution. Jefferson was not part of the Constitutional Convention, and he had a number of reservations about its handiwork. On a broader philosophical level, he also rebelled against the idea of a permanent constitution binding not just his generation but all future generations of Americans. Calling it "self-evident," he wrote Madison "'*that the earth belongs in usufruct to the living*': that the dead have neither powers nor rights over it."[14] There were many reasons for Jefferson's strong feelings on this issue, including personal ones, but there was also a key Enlightenment principle at stake: self-government. How could a people claim to be self-governed if they were in fact laboring under a form of government established long before they were born? For anyone associated with drafting or ratifying the Constitution, this thought would have likely struck him as taking an abstract principle to an absurd extreme. For Jefferson, though, practical considerations were easily swept aside in the face of the larger Enlightenment principle of self-government.

Of course, the question still remained: how long should the Constitution remain in effect? Only a man supremely confident in the power of enlightened reason would even attempt such a calculation. Jefferson was such a man. After an elaborate series of assumptions involving the age of maturity, the average lifespan, births, and deaths, Jefferson proposed that a law (and a debt) should not be allowed to extend beyond nineteen years because that was the length of a generation according to his computations. Jefferson's earnest attempt to calculate the length of a generation was a testament to his commitment to Enlightenment reason as a tool to improve society, but it also revealed how far astray that reason could lead him. Even though Jefferson was out of the country during the convention and ratification debates, he would have known how difficult the process was and how close it came to failure. His calculations revealed not only a man confident that the knottiest problem was susceptible to enlightened reason but someone so dedicated to an abstract Enlightenment principle—every generation should be free of the dead hand of the past—that he was willing to ignore practical problems associated with its strict application. As he wrote confidently to one correspondent, "Only lay down true principles, and adhere to them inflexibly. Do not be frightened into their surrender by the alarms of the timid."[15]

This proudly declared inflexibility was apparent in one of Jefferson's most misguided presidential decisions—the Embargo Act of 1807, which banned all exports from the United States in a futile attempt to force Great Britain (and, to a lesser extent, France) to stop seizing American ships. Part of the larger Jeffersonian vision of enlightened nations in harmony was an insistence on free trade. His attempt to strictly uphold this abstract principle while Great Britain and France were at war revealed both inflexibility and a willingness to ignore practical realities; the Embargo's main effect was to devastate the American economy.

Abstract calculation reared its head again when Jefferson discussed Shays's Rebellion. Writing to William Stephens Smith, John Adams's son-in-law, Jefferson offered a ringing endorsement: "What signify a few lives lost in a century or two? The tree of liberty must be refreshed from time to time with the blood of patriots and tyrants. It is it's natural manure." Most of the political elite, particularly men from New England, were horrified by the rebellion and worried that it signaled the start of anarchy if they could not strengthen the national government. Jefferson took entirely the opposite point of view, calling the rebellion "honourably conducted," the antithesis of an anarchical breakdown in society. For him, it was tied not only to the goals of the American Revolution but to the Enlightenment itself because self-government, the freedom of man to live under a political system of his choosing, was at the core of his Enlightenment beliefs. In the letter to Smith, there is another, less famous passage that is for our purposes even more striking. In it, Jefferson offers an arithmetic of revolution. "God forbid we should ever be 20. years without such a rebellion," he wrote, claiming that it would be a sign of "lethargy" and "the forerunner of death to the public liberty." Then he turned to his calculations: "We have had 13. States independant 11. Years. There has been one rebellion. That comes to one rebellion in a century and a half for each state. What country ever existed a century and a half without a rebellion? And what country can preserve it's liberties if their rulers are not warned from time to time that their people preserve the spirit of resistance?"[16]

The mathematical precision with which he addressed the question is once again indicative of his "enlightened" approach to political problems, as well as how that approach could lead to disturbing conclusions. Reducing Shays's Rebellion to a question of math allowed Jefferson to distance himself from the messiness of the events themselves, which was a typical rhetorical maneuver for him. More deeply, though, the calculation revealed his attempt to reduce that very messiness to an orderly system, as if the problem was as susceptible to Enlightenment methods as the refutation of Buffon. But the calculation came with its own cost: by removing the rebellion from the gritty reality of fighting and bloodshed, and lifting it to the level of abstraction, it allowed Jefferson to discuss all of this without any reckoning of the human cost, the death and suffering that were invariably a part of any revolution, no matter how noble. When earlier Enlightenment thinkers had endorsed the right to rebellion, they usually did so reluctantly, recognizing that the price inherent in a rebellion was great enough to make it a choice of last resort.[17] But Jefferson's abstract calculations shifted that perspective dramatically. Instead of a reluctance to endorse rebellion, Jefferson exhibited an enthusiasm for it. Indeed, he clearly thought that too few revolutions were far worse than too many.

Jefferson's characteristic move from messy reality to abstract principle—his "enlightened" approach, as I am calling it—led to a number of his most extreme statements. The best example of this was Jefferson's deep and ongoing support of the French Revolution even after the worst of the atrocities had occurred. In a 1793 letter to William Short, a close friend of Jefferson's who served as a diplomat to France during the French Revolution, Jefferson's Enlightenment commitments led to an epistolary blood-letting on a grander scale than one will come across in virtually any other founder. Jefferson spoke of the early efforts to establish a constitutional monarchy as a failed "experiment," already casting events into the language of science and justifying as an "absolute necessity . . . expunging that officer." This was a convoluted way to refer to the grim business of decapitating Louis XVI, and it revealed Jefferson's penchant for escaping from the bloody particular into the abstract (and euphemistic) language of "expunging an officer." According to Jefferson, the issue was of world-changing importance. As he famously (or perhaps infamously) wrote, "Rather than it should have failed, I would have seen half the earth desolated. Were there but an Adam and an Eve left in every country, and left free, it would be better than as it now is." One would be hard pressed to come across a bloodier apocalypse than that.[18]

My point is not to condemn Jefferson for this statement but to understand why he would make it. And what I want to argue is that this bloody-minded remark, far from being in opposition to his usual Enlightenment mindset, was deeply tied to his Enlightenment beliefs. Not only that, but when he made this type of statement, he was thinking in an "enlightened" fashion, at least as he conceived it. Paradoxical as it may seem, the same underlying ideas and manner of thinking that gave shape to his greatest liberal achievements—religious freedom, the abolishment of entail, the Declaration—also gave rise to his most intemperate, even illiberal remarks. The same Jefferson who spoke so eloquently about life, liberty, and the pursuit of happiness could also casually calculate rebellions per state or imaginatively desolate the earth so that a single perfectly free Adam and Eve could be left to recreate society in harmony with natural law.

Let us delve more deeply into the letter to Short to see how enlightened thinking could be turned to such ends. Jefferson claimed that "the liberty of the whole earth was depending on the issue of the contest."[19] Our first instinct is to see that as a gross exaggeration used for effect to persuade Short to stop sending reports back to the United States criticizing the violent course of the French Revolution. With a wider lens, though, this statement made sense in the context of Jefferson's vision of a free and peaceful world of enlightened self-government. For Jefferson, individual freedom was not something that existed in a state of nature; rather, it was something that could only exist within the framework of a nation, and not just any nation but one founded on the principle of self-government. And these governments themselves could not be sustained in a hostile environment but depended for their existence on a community of like-minded governments, a more perfect union of free nations, if you will.[20] This is why Jefferson placed so much importance on the French Revolution. If it succeeded in establishing a republican government, the French Revolution would not just improve the lot of the French people (at least those still alive); it would also improve the lot of other republican governments, including the United States. Indeed, it would bring the world one step closer to Jefferson's idealized vision of a world of self-governing nations in harmony and at peace because all were guided by the same principles. Similarly, the failure of the French Revolution threatened to set back the cause of self-government around the world. Jefferson believed in this vision so completely that he was quite willing to be bloodthirsty in its achievement, because nothing less than the core Enlightenment goals of individual liberty and self-government were at stake.

This apocalyptic vision cannot be dismissed as a stray remark in the heat of the moment. Even long after he had retired from the scene, he still thought in blood-soaked terms when he envisioned the success or failure of republican government on a global scale. As he wrote to the Marquis de Lafayette, "Alliances holy or hellish, may be formed and retard the epoch deliverance, may swell the rivers of blood which are yet to flow, but their own will close the scene, and leave to mankind the right of self government."[21] Within this broader framework, Jefferson's extreme remarks were a testament to how deeply he embraced the core Enlightenment principle of free men coming together in free societies and how much he was willing to sacrifice to achieve that goal.

I do not want to argue that the Enlightenment was the only influence on Jefferson's thinking in this or any other instance. His life experience, including his years in France, had predisposed him to support the French Revolution, especially when coupled with his dislike of the British. This bias was further buttressed by the role that the French Revolution played in the politics of the early republic. But the keystone of all of this was his core Enlightenment commitments, which were made long before the rancorous politics of the early republic reared their head.[22]

Of course, Jefferson did not fancy himself some sort of enlightened despot who could decree the fates of untold millions in order to achieve his more perfect union. In keeping with his Enlightenment belief in the importance of self-government, he justified his apocalyptic prescription on the firm and unwavering support of the people. The notion of "the people" recurred like a drumbeat throughout the letter to Short and was used to defend the radical and bloody turn the French Revolution had taken. Not only did he claim that "the Nation was with them [the Jacobins] in opinion," but he went on to claim that the people "were now generally Jacobins."[23] In truth, the Jacobins were clearly in the minority, especially the farther one got from Paris, but that fact, if freely acknowledged by Jefferson, would have posed severe problems for his entire rationale. The crucial element for justifying any revolution was not how much blood was shed but whether it had the support of the people. Not to take into account the bloodshed may seem at best willfully naive and at worst heartless, but within the context of Jefferson's understanding of Enlightenment political ideals, the people were the crucial element to the formulation. As long as their will was being obeyed, Jefferson was willing to tolerate all manner of violent destruction. More than that, he believed that achieving self-governing nations would necessitate bloodshed, which he considered worth the cost. These extreme statements have long served as a bone of contention between supporters and detractors of Jefferson, but both sides miss the larger point from Jefferson's own point of view. For Jefferson, the bloodshed was not the primary issue. The primary issue was that any revolution needed to have the support of the people if it was to conform to the essential elements of enlightened self-government that he believed in so fervently.

Reinforcing his argument (and putting fairly intense pressure on Short to temper harsh statements he had made about the Jacobins), Jefferson claimed that the "sentiments" he was expressing were "really those of 99 in an hundred of our citizens." Short's views, according to Jefferson, "would be extremely disrelished if known by your countrymen." Excepting a few men of high office or of great wealth, Jefferson wrote that "this country is entirely republican," and that the French Revolution has "given the coup de grace to their [the monarchical party] prospects."[24] In America, as in France, the people were aligned on the side of France, according to Jefferson. In fact, he rhetorically imposed virtual unanimity on the entire American population, despite dealing with one of the most controversial and divisive issues of the day. Jefferson was always most comfortable when he could confidently assert that he was speaking for "the people."

One should not neglect Jefferson's obvious political maneuvering in this letter. The French Revolution was a key flashpoint in the early republic, and both sides viewed its interpretation as a crucial element in furthering their own prospects. For Jefferson, Short's letters criticizing the revolution were a serious political problem, especially since they were having an influence on Washington. And Jefferson was willing to offer a glimpse of the iron fist in the velvet glove if Short failed to adopt the proper interpretation. Jefferson continued, "I know your republicanism to be pure, and that it is no decay of that which has embittered you against it's votaries in France, but too great a sensibility at the partial evil by which it's object has been accomplished there."[25] Although offering Short an easy retreat from his earlier criticisms of the Jacobins, Jefferson's letter did so in a way that made it clear Short had no other alternative. To continue to criticize the Jacobins would mean that his republicanism was not "pure," that he would be aligning himself against "the people," and as we have seen, Jefferson was willing to consider extreme measures against anyone or anything lined up against "the people."

Of course, Jefferson recognized that his reliance on the people came with its own hazards. Noting that the Jacobin terror had led to the death of innocent victims (although he minimized the numbers), Jefferson acknowledged that the people were a blunt instrument: "It was necessary to use the arm of the people, a machine not quite so blind as balls and bombs, but blind to a certain degree." But Jefferson was willing to give the people wide latitude in such a situation. As he wrote in his letter to Smith on Shays's Rebellion, "the people can not be all, and always, well informed. The part which is wrong will be discontented in proportion to the importance of the facts they misconceive." Far worse from Jefferson's standpoint was not the potential ignorance or violent actions of the people; rather, it was the potential for no action at all: "If they remain quiet under such misconceptions it is a lethargy, the forerunner of death to the public liberty."[26] The spread of self-government was a dynamic process that could advance *or* decay. Part of Jefferson's willingness to go to extremes to support the French Revolution (imaginatively depopulating each nation to a single Adam and Eve) was his desire to prevent that decay. The more self-governing societies that existed, the easier it would be for them to maintain their freedom, and the more likely self-government would spread to other nations. But the opposite also held true, which is why Jefferson viewed the potential failure of the French

Revolution as a disastrous setback not simply for France but for America, and indeed for the Enlightenment cause of self-government in general.

But Jefferson's views also meant that the arena of politics was extremely difficult for him to navigate because politics by its very nature means disagreement. Most of the founders struggled with this to some degree, and nearly everyone in the early years of the nation felt a need to decry the slightest sign of political parties forming.[27] But this problem was more acute for Jefferson because of his "enlightened" conception of politics. Jefferson was most comfortable when he could confidently claim to represent the voice of the people. In this context, if sharp political disagreement was difficult, life in the political minority was almost untenable, which is why Jefferson engaged in elaborate verbal contortions in an effort to prove that, even in the minority, he still represented the people. These contortions have frequently led critics to lampoon Jefferson for his hypocrisy, which is a facile judgment (who is not guilty of hypocrisy to some degree?) and does nothing to help us understand the cause of Jefferson's contortions. A more productive approach is to unpack the alleged "hypocrisy" in order to understand why the political maneuvering demanded of all political leaders proved particularly troubling for him and led to such maladroit gambits from a man who could be such an eloquent spokesman.

What we find are a series of verbal habits that Jefferson used to escape any imputation that he and his "party" were in the minority, a consistent rhetorical sleight of hand that was not so much hypocrisy as it was a necessity given Jefferson's views. If all political legitimacy stemmed from the people, Jefferson's place in the minority would mean, in effect, that he himself was the illegitimate political usurper. We should not be surprised that Jefferson found ways of avoiding that conclusion. For example, writing to John Taylor in June 1798, when the tide was running against the Republicans, particularly in New England, Jefferson attempted to disassociate the staunch Federalism of the region from the underlying republicanism of the people. Calling the Federalist elite in New England a "reign of witches," he believed that "their spells" would "dissolve" with "the people recovering their true sight, restor[ing] their government to it's true principles."[28] Again, what is striking in the context of Jefferson's commitment to the centrality of the people was his explicit attempt to drive a wedge between their support of the Federalists and their actual views. Federalist elites were "witches" casting "spells," a group, in other words, holding onto the people's support through tricks. This trope allowed Jefferson to maintain the view that the American people as a whole remained true to republican self-government—that they were still Jeffersonians at heart if they could only free themselves from the Federalist elite's spells. Jefferson trotted out this explanation numerous times, particularly in the late 1790s when the tide was so often running against him.

He also commonly used religious language to dismiss Federalist opposition, referring to "apostates" and "heresies," a surprising choice of words for a man who penned the Statute of Religious Freedom (and offering a linguistic trace of the near religious devotion Jefferson had for Enlightenment principles).[29] At times, he even attempted to remove—at least rhetorically—the Federalist elite from America altogether by claiming that they were a "faction composed of English subjects residing among us."[30]

The medical language of sickness also came easily to hand as a way of maintaining Jefferson's faith in the people, even as they opposed him politically. He referred to political opposition as "gangrene" and "a taint."[31] After the anxious days waiting for a resolution to the election of 1800, Jefferson described the political division as a kind of sickness, writing that it was a "frenzy & delusion, like an epidemic gained certain parts," and contrasting it, as always, with the fundamental soundness of the people: "The residue remained sound & untouched, and held on till their brethren could recover from the temporary delirium."[32] Once the Federalist threat receded, Jefferson could again be magnanimous on the subject of political difference. As he famously wrote in his first inaugural address, "Every difference of opinion is not a difference of principle. We have called by different names brethren of the same principle. We are all republicans: we are all federalists."[33] Given the bitterness of the election of 1800, Jefferson's tolerance is striking, but that tolerance was always based on the unrivaled supremacy of the Republican Party—for Jefferson, the only true representatives of enlightened self-government. On the eve of the War of 1812, when a revitalized Federalist Party reemerged, Jefferson easily fell back into old habits, claiming that "the republicans are the *nation.*" Just as with the French Revolution, the political disagreement was tied to a much larger, indeed a world historical battle for Jefferson, who believed that "the last hope of human liberty in this world rests on us."[34] Jefferson always grew somewhat hysterical when the political tide threatened to overwhelm him, but his grandiose statements make sense within the context of his belief about how enlightened self-government would spread, or fail to spread, around the globe.

His commitment to these principles exerted a seminal influence on his view of how the nation should organize itself politically so that every citizen was involved in government. Proposing an even finer division than county government, Jefferson suggested "wards of such size as that every citizen can attend, when called on, and act in person," which would give "every citizen, personally, a part in the administration of the public affairs."[35] One can imagine Jefferson's proposed divisions multiplying until self-government becomes literalized with each freeholder as the political head of his own property. What could provide a better foundation for liberty than a farmer who owned his land, a belief also reinforced by the prevailing republican ideologies of the day. In this case, Enlightenment liberalism and republicanism found common ground so to speak—and that common ground was privately owned plots of land. Of course, this vision necessitated a great deal of land, which brings us to the most important decision of Jefferson's presidency, the purchase of the Louisiana Territory. In this situation, Jefferson found himself on the horns of a dilemma. On the one hand, his long-stated constitutional views suggested that the president did not have the power to double the size of the country with a stroke of his pen. On the other hand, that land would provide true liberty and independence to "generations" yet unborn. We should not be surprised that the more abstract principle of liberty triumphed over the inconvenient hurdles imposed by the actual Constitution.

As always when Enlightenment principles were at stake, apocalyptic visions of despair were lurking beneath the surface. The gift of land to generations unborn was ideally supposed to lead to an unfolding empire of liberty with independent farmers both self-governing and also tied firmly to the union. The long interregnum of triumphant Jeffersonians helped hide a simple truth: politics inevitably involves conflict. And despite Jefferson's vision of a unified national voice where all share the same principles (indeed, a state replicating on a national scale harmonious family relations based on bonds of affection), those political differences were frequently going to be a matter not simply of policy but of principle.[36]

Unsurprisingly, the eruption of apocalypse in the midst of Jefferson's Edenic garden was the result of the group that was always the most problematic for the Jeffersonian vision of independent freeholders—slaves. The inaptly named "era of good feelings" came to a shuddering halt for Jefferson when he was faced with the Missouri crisis, which forced Americans to wrestle with the question of whether or not to allow slavery in the western territories. (The issue was temporarily settled by the Missouri Compromise, which admitted Missouri as a slave state but prohibited slavery in the former Louisiana Territory north of the latitude line 36′ 30″.)

In his famous letter to John Holmes in 1820 discussing the crisis, Jefferson immediately reverted to the same apocalyptic language that inevitably recurred at moments when he feared the vital principles of the Enlightenment were threatened. Calling it an "act of suicide on themselves and of treason against the hopes of the world," Jefferson saw the crisis in world historical terms, similar to his letter to Short about the French Revolution. For Jefferson, the proposed compromise was not just a setback for his Enlightenment vision, but its complete abnegation and annihilation: "I regret that I am now to die in the belief that the useless sacrifice of themselves, by the generation of '76. to acquire self government and happiness to their country, is to be thrown away by the unwise and unworthy passions of their sons, and that my only consolation is to be that I live not to weep over it."[37] Why would Jefferson take such an extreme view of what was, in the context of the time, a reasonable political compromise to the intractable problem of slavery? For Jefferson, the issue went beyond where slavery would be allowed. It touched on the most fundamental Enlightenment principle: self-government. By removing the ability of new territories to decide the issue of slavery for themselves, the compromise was nothing less than a dilution of the very concept of each new state having full and equal rights with all of the original states. Even with an issue as deeply problematic as slavery, each state (and, for that matter, each individual) should have the right to choose for itself. For Jefferson, this was a foundational principle going back to the Revolution itself when Americans had refused to accept subordinate colonial status.

What is striking about the letter for the purposes of this essay is Jefferson's characteristic attempt to shift out of the messy particulars of political conflict into abstract, and indeed almost mathematical, speculations. In this case, Jefferson relied not on arithmetic but on geometry—the drawing of a line. He wrote that "a geographical line, coinciding with a marked principle, moral and political, once concieved and held up to the angry passions of men, will never be obliterated; and every irritation will mark it deeper and deeper."[38] The combination of a political principle with a geographical line would, Jefferson believed, be a kind of permanent mark that could never be erased, a prediction largely vindicated by the course of events. The kind of unified political voice that Jefferson projected even during times of the most intense political divisions in America would become an impossibility if the line was drawn. The harmonious family would be sundered from itself.

Of course, there was no escaping the fact that slavery represented an insoluble dilemma for a man who championed the Enlightenment ideals of liberty and self-government. To "weep" over the compromise while ignoring slavery was impossible. Jefferson himself acknowledged the problem to some degree, writing, "We have the wolf by the ear, and we can neither hold him, nor safely let him go. Justice is in one scale, and self-preservation in the other." For someone who was willing to imaginatively depopulate the earth so that citizens could stand perfectly free, he conspicuously refused to do that for African Americans. Instead, Jefferson's solution was twofold. In the first place, much as he relied on euphemism to hide the ugly fact of the French king's beheading, Jefferson was forced into odd circumlocutions. He claimed that "the cession of that kind of property, for it is so misnamed, is a bagatelle which would not cost me a second thought, if, in that way, a general emancipation and *expatriation* could be effected."[39] One could hardly come up with a word better designed to minimize the problem of slavery than "bagatelle," as if the entire issue was little more than a housekeeping problem.

But slavery could not be shoved aside as easily as the horrors of the French Revolution, which occurred on the other side of the Atlantic. Expatriation was obviously an impossibility. Not only had the black population grown too large, but most had no desire to go to Africa. Jefferson's Edenic vision of independent yeoman farmers could never escape the original sin of slavery. Instead, Jefferson took refuge in abstract Enlightenment reasoning as an escape from the insoluble problem posed by slaves. In contrast to the Missouri Compromise, Jefferson argued that the solution lay in allowing the unrestrained expansion of slavery: "Their diffusion over a greater surface would make them individually happier and proportionally facilitate the accomplishment of their emancipation; by dividing the burthen on a greater number of co-adjutors."[40] Instead of geometry or arithmetic, the solution this time lay in chemistry. An old adage going back to Greek times is that "the dose makes the poison." In the case of slavery, Jefferson offered dilution as the solution, the idea that slavery, if spread widely enough, would in effect lead to the eventual disappearance of the peculiar institution. Of course, this "solution" ignored the central difference of slavery in the United States versus most other slaveholding powers in the hemisphere: the size of the slave population was growing through natural reproduction. Jefferson himself was perfectly aware of this, although his proposal is one more illustration of his flight from messy particularity to neat abstraction when faced with difficult political circumstances.[41]

We are a long way from the American moose—or are we? The centrality of the Enlightenment to Jefferson's thoughts and actions is a kind of through-line that helps give coherence to the notoriously inscrutable Virginian, a paradoxical and yet perhaps more understandable Jefferson. This Jefferson could wax rhapsodic about liberty and self-government but also rain rhetorical devastation on a vast scale to achieve that vision. He could hold dear the principles of liberty and freedom, even as he relied on the labor of slaves. And in an ironic twist, it was his commitment to enlightened reason, with its escape from the intractable particular to the soothing abstraction, that allowed him to cling to such seemingly diametrically opposed ideals. His commitment to the Enlightenment directly shaped not just his political ideals but also the very policies he attempted to put into place to enact those ideals. In this way, his "enlightened" approach to politics served as the gateway both for his triumphant liberal achievements and for his dark and apocalyptic visions of cleansing rivers of blood.

Notes

1. "From Thomas Jefferson to John Sullivan, 7 January 1786," Founders Online, National Archives, Washington, D.C., http://founders.archives.gov/documents/Jefferson/01-09-02-0145.

2. These passages come from volume 5 of Buffon's *Histoire Naturelle* (1766), as quoted in Keith Stewart Thomson, "Jefferson, Buffon and the Moose," *American Scientist* 96, no. 3 (May–June 2008): 200–202. Thomson also serves as the source for Jefferson's great moose hunt.

3. There is a fitting coda to the story, according to Thomson. By the time Jefferson was attempting to secure the moose, Buffon had already changed his mind about

American degeneracy. Another American had beaten Jefferson to the punch—several conversations with Benjamin Franklin had convinced Buffon that his theory was wrong and needed to be changed. Still, Jefferson thought physical proof was important, so he sent poor Sullivan scampering after moose bones, a task Sullivan (and likely Mrs. Sullivan) would happily have avoided. The juxtaposition with Franklin and his approach does highlight a certain aspect of Jefferson's engagement with the Enlightenment that differed significantly from the Philadelphian's. Franklin chose an informal and pragmatic approach, and counted on Buffon's open-mindedness as a man of science to change his views when presented with countervailing evidence. Jefferson chose a more formal, written, and abstract method, wanting to prove definitively not just to Buffon but to the larger Enlightenment public that Buffon's theories were incorrect. What is interesting about this approach is that it differs so radically from Jefferson's typical political methods. In politics, he rarely liked to write for a public audience, preferring to work through private letters to trusted individuals. I think this speaks to his commitment to the Enlightenment, which was powerful enough to overcome his general reluctance to write directly for a public, undifferentiated audience. And just so that we do not leave our poor moose *in media res,* I am happy to report that it did eventually arrive, although Buffon was away when Jefferson had it delivered so that the Virginian did not have the pleasure of a grand unveiling.

4. While virtually no serious scholar would disagree with the importance of the Enlightenment for Jefferson, very little recent work on Jefferson focuses on that area of his life, and it is almost entirely absent from recent biographies. The exceptions are Maurizio Valsania, *The Limits of Optimism: Thomas Jefferson's Dualistic Enlightenment* (Charlottesville, Va., 2011), and the work of Peter Onuf. See, for example, Onuf, "Liberty to Learn," in *The Mind of Thomas Jefferson* (Charlottesville, Va., 2007), 169–78.

5. John Adams and James Madison shared something of the same spirit but confined their attention more narrowly to the realm of politics. Benjamin Franklin is the only other founding father of Jefferson's stature to have a similar commitment. Even in this case, though, there are differences. Once possessed of enough wealth, Franklin divested himself of his businesses to embrace the role of enlightened scientist full-time. In addition, his own scientific bent was in a more practical vein than Jefferson's (as was most of Franklin's life experience), hence not only his famous kite experiment but his invention of the eponymous Franklin stove. Jefferson tended more to abstraction, which had some crucial implications for his politics as we will see. Finally, Franklin was more comfortable playing a role (as evidenced most vividly with his donning a coonskin cap in Paris to the delight of his French hosts). Jefferson struggled to maintain a facade of authenticity, which makes him a more conflicted figure. See Jay Fleigelman, *Declaring Independence: Jefferson, Natural Language, and the Culture of Performance* (Stanford, Calif., 1993). As an aside to my aside, I do not mean to be derogatory by calling it a facade. All of us maintain similar facades. See Erving Goffman, *The Presentation of Self in Everyday Life* (New York, 1959). As T. S. Eliot wrote in "The Love Song of J. Alfred Prufrock": "There will be time / To prepare a face to meet the faces that you meet."

6. This was not as unusual as it now seems to us. See Joyce Robinson, "An American Cabinet of Curiosities: Thomas Jefferson's Indian Hall at Monticello," *Winterthur Portfolio* 30, no. 1 (Spring 1995): 41–58.

7. Again, the contrast with other founders is instructive. Many of them published essays and even books on political topics, but virtually none of them attempted anything like Jefferson's *Notes.* In stark contrast, Jefferson wrote little for public consumption on the subject of politics (although he explored the subject frequently and extensively in private letters).

8. Of course, this can be attributed at least partially to the republican rhetoric of the time, which demanded that politicians reluctantly agree to hold office, rather than actively seek it out.

9. For an excellent example of the strange ways that books and readers can interact, see Carlos Ginzburg, *The Cheese and the Worms: The Cosmos of a Sixteenth-Century Miller,* trans. John and Anne Tedeschi (Baltimore, 1992).

10. It is a virtual cliché of scholars to see Jefferson as a mystery that cannot be solved. After years spent studying Jefferson, Merrill Peterson considered him "an impenetrable man." Peterson, *Thomas Jefferson and the New Nation: A Biography* (New York, 1970), viii. Joseph Ellis titled his biography, *American Sphinx: The Character of Thomas Jefferson* (New York, 1998). Henry Adams famously wrote, "A few broad strokes of the brush would paint the portraits of all the early Presidents with this exception, and a few more strokes would answer for any member of their many cabinets; but Jefferson could be painted only touch by touch, with a fine pencil, and the perfection of the likeness depended upon the shifting and uncertain flicker of its semi-transparent shadows." Adams, *History of the United States during the First Administration of America, during the First Administration of Thomas Jefferson* (New York, 1889–91), 1:188.

11. Peterson notes that these questions would likely have been settled in the same manner without Jefferson's assistance but that "Jefferson's bills capped the development and exalted the principle of freehold tenure." Peterson, *Thomas Jefferson and the New Nation,* 113.

12. See Peter Onuf, *Statehood and Union: A History of the Northwest Ordinance* (Bloomington, Ind., 1992).

13. Although I believe Jefferson was more prone to this than the other founders because of his deeper commitment to the idea of the Enlightenment, all of the founders were susceptible to one degree or another. See Gordon Wood, "Conspiracy and the Paranoid Style: Causality and Deceit in the Eighteenth Century," *William and Mary Quarterly,* 3rd ser., 39, no. 3 (July 1982): 402–41. Wood persuasively argued that the Enlightenment belief in causality helped to make Great Britain's prerevolutionary measures seem far more coherent and sinister than they actually were.

14. "To James Madison from Thomas Jefferson, 6 September 1789," Founders Online, http://founders.archives.gov/documents/Madison/01-12-02-0248. For an excellent account of this letter and its significance for Jefferson, see Herbert Sloan, "'The Earth Belongs in Usufruct to the Living,'" in *Jeffersonian Legacies,* ed. Peter Onuf (Charlottesville, Va., 1993), 281–315.

15. Jefferson to Samuel Kercheval, July 12, 1816, in J. Jefferson Looney et al., eds., *The Papers of Thomas Jefferson: Retirement Series* (Princeton, N.J: Princeton University Press, 2005–), 10:220–28.

16. "From Thomas Jefferson to William Stephens Smith, 13 November 1787," Founders Online, http://founders.archives.gov/documents/Jefferson/01-12-02-0348. For the seminal importance of Shays's Rebellion to many of the founders, see Robert Gross, ed., *In Debt to Shays: The Bicentennial of an Agrarian Rebellion* (Boston, 1992).

17. Most theorists at that time viewed revolution as a last resort, although John Locke and Frances Hutcheson argued for a lower threshold, arguing that the people no longer owed allegiance to a government once the magistrate had violated the contract that brought it into being. See Ronald Hamowy, "Jefferson and the Scottish Enlightenment: A Critique of Gary Wills's *Inventing America: Jefferson's Declaration of Independence*," *William and Mary Quarterly*, 3rd ser., 35, no. 4 (Oct. 1979): 503–23.

18. "From Thomas Jefferson to William Short, 3 January 1793," Founders Online, http://founders.archives.gov/documents/Jefferson/01-25-02-0016. The quote is so incendiary that it serves as the keystone of Conor Cruise O'Brien's book-length diatribe against Jefferson, *The Long Affair: Thomas Jefferson and the French Revolution, 1785–1800* (Chicago, 1998).

19. "From Thomas Jefferson to William Short, 3 January 1793," Founders Online, http://founders.archives.gov/documents/Jefferson/01-25-02-0016.

20. For the key role of the nation in Jefferson's political philosophy, see Onuf, *The Mind of Thomas Jefferson*, 10.

21. "From Thomas Jefferson to Marie-Joseph-Paul-Yves-Roch-Gilbert du Motier, Marquis de Lafayette, 4 November 1823," Founders Online, http://founders.archives.gov/documents/Jefferson/98-01-02-3843.

22. His hostility toward the British had its own mutually reinforcing motives: his personal dislike of being indebted to British merchants, the experience of the American Revolution, the willingness of Federalists to yoke the American experiment to Great Britain and its trade, and ultimately a belief that a government with a hereditary monarchy and aristocracy were not forces for the spread of enlightened self-government but forces for its retardation.

23. "From Thomas Jefferson to William Short, 3 January 1793," Founders Online, http://founders.archives.gov/documents/Jefferson/01-25-02-0016.

24. Ibid.

25. Ibid.

26. "From Thomas Jefferson to William Stephens Smith, 13 November 1787," Founders Online, http://founders.archives.gov/documents/Jefferson/01-12-02-0348.

27. The one exception to this is perhaps Aaron Burr. Despite his elite pedigree, he was far more comfortable with the grubby reality of politics than virtually any other leading founder, which partly explains why so many other founders were uncomfortable with him.

28. "From Thomas Jefferson to John Taylor, 4 June 1798," Founders Online, http://founders.archives.gov/documents/Jefferson/01-30-02-0280.

29. "From Thomas Jefferson to Philip Mazzei, 24 April 1796," Founders Online, http://founders.archives.gov/documents/Jefferson/01-29-02-0054-0002.

30. "From Thomas Jefferson to Horatio Gates, 30 May 1797," Founders Online, http://founders.archives.gov/documents/Jefferson/01-29-02-0322.

31. "From Thomas Jefferson to Stevens Thomson Mason, 27 October 1799," Founders Online, http://founders.archives.gov/documents/Jefferson/01-31-02-0190; "From Thomas Jefferson to Archibald Stuart, 14 May 1799," Founders Online, http://founders.archives.gov/documents/Jefferson/01-31-02-0094.

32. "From Thomas Jefferson to Nathaniel Niles, 22 March 1801," Founders Online, http://founders.archives.gov/documents/Jefferson/01-33-02-0346.

33. "Thomas Jefferson, First Inaugural Address, 4 March 1801," Founders Online, http://founders.archives.gov/documents/Jefferson/01-33-02-0116-0004.

34. "From Thomas Jefferson to William Duane, 28 March 1811," Founders Online, http://founders.archives.gov/documents/Jefferson/03-03-02-0378.

35. Jefferson to Samuel Kercheval, July 12, 1816, in Looney et al., eds., *The Papers of Thomas Jefferson: Retirement Series,* 10:220–28.

36. For Jefferson's conception of a union based on bonds of affection, see Andrew Trees, *The Founding Fathers and the Politics of Character* (Princeton, N.J., 2003), 13–44.

37. "From Thomas Jefferson to John Holmes, 22 April 1820," Founders Online, http://founders.archives.gov/documents/Jefferson/98-01-02-1234.

38. Ibid.

39. Ibid.

40. Ibid.

41. Of course, there was an even more radical solution to the problem of slavery. If Jefferson was willing to imaginatively depopulate the earth to leave men free, he was also ready to dehumanize blacks in an attempt to uphold his Enlightenment ideals in the face of an American slavery with which he himself was deeply implicated. His commitment to Enlightenment ideals of equality and justice should have helped lift him out of his racial prejudices to at least some degree. Instead, he used Enlightenment reasoning to move beyond mere prejudice to an early version of scientific racism. In *Notes on the State of Virginia,* he catalogued a wide range of "the real distinctions which nature has made" between the two races. According to Jefferson, they were less beautiful because of "that immoveable veil of black" and also "in reason much inferior." In the end, he judged that they were "inferior to the whites in the endowments both of body and mind." Jefferson, *Notes on the State of Virginia,* ed. William Peden (Chapel Hill, N.C., 1982), 138–43. This "enlightened" racism offered a glimpse of the "scientific" racism that would emerge so prominently in the twentieth century. The scandal of slavery at the center of the American project of freedom and equality could be finessed if one could make the argument that blacks were somehow not part of the human race. Even in his personal relations with slaves, Jefferson's behavior was likely influenced by the Enlightenment. Eighteenth-century physiologists, believed that a man should not

waste his energy through masturbation and thought that it was healthier for a man to use a female as a sexual outlet. Andrew Burstein has argued that this medical belief quite possibly served as Jefferson's justification for having sexual intercourse with Sally Hemings. Andrew Burstein, *Jefferson's Secrets: Death and Desire at Monticello* (New York, 2005), 151–90.

10 "The Strongest Government on Earth" Proves Its Strength

The Jefferson Administration and the Burr Conspiracy

James E. Lewis Jr.

Over the summer and fall of 1806, the projects and movements of Aaron Burr, Thomas Jefferson's former vice president, emerged as a subject of great concern in newspapers, correspondence, and conversations across the country. Increasingly, these accounts identified Burr as the prime mover behind a conspiracy either to launch an unsanctioned attack on Spanish Mexico or to divide the federal union at the Appalachian Mountains. For months, each new mail seemed to bring fresh reports of men being recruited, boats being built, and supplies being procured along the West's rivers. Whether Burr's designs actually encompassed either of the goals that were ascribed to him, or whether they extended only as far as settling an immense land purchase beyond the Mississippi River, was unknown at the time and remains unclear two centuries later. But it was precisely because his true intentions were "enveloped in mystery," as a number of his contemporaries lamented, that they seemed so threatening.[1] At a time of great tensions with Spain over the Louisiana Purchase and of fragile ties between East and West, the rumors and reports about Burr's projects and movements generated both a sense of national crisis and an expectation of federal action.

The Jefferson administration clearly viewed this activity with great concern. Between late October and late December 1806, Jefferson and his cabinet met on at least six occasions to shape their response to the crisis. They adopted measures that involved each of the four cabinet secretaries and the postmaster general and included a presidential proclamation, issued on November 27. Nonetheless, their response surprised many due to its limits. The president did not send eastern army troops over the mountains to intercept Burr's men. He did not rush eastern naval vessels to New Orleans, Burr's presumed target. He did not call Congress into a special session or even press it to move quickly against Burr's projects when it did meet in early December. He did not even order all of the federal marshals and district attorneys in the West to arrest and bring to trial Burr and Burr's men. Some Republicans, including at least one cabinet member, quietly worried that the administration response would prove inadequate to the crisis. Many Federalists openly denounced "proclamation-warfare." Rather than sending copies of the proclamation west with one express rider, a Federalist editor argued, the president "had better sent them by *one thousand expresses,* with orders to deliver them from the mouths of their muskets."[2] Many Federalist newspapers reprinted an essay that condemned the president's apparent belief "THAT THE GREAT SECRET OF GOVERNMENT IS TO LET EVERY THING TAKE ITS OWN COURSE."[3]

As the crisis abated, Jefferson trumpeted the ease with which a potentially dangerous internal threat had been defeated as proof of the wisdom of his political principles. In public messages and private letters, he framed the Burr Conspiracy as a test of one of the most questionable assertions of his first inaugural address: that the United States, despite its limited armed forces and decentralized state apparatus, was "the strongest Government on earth" because it was "the only one where every man, at the call of the law, would fly to the standard of the law, and would meet invasions of the public order as his own personal concern."[4] Beginning in late December 1806, much of the news about the crisis that reached Washington seemed to support this view. In western Virginia, a militia company mobilized to arrest a group of Burr's men at Blennerhassett Island on the Ohio River, arriving a few hours too late. In southern Ohio, state officials seized Burr's boats and supplies on the docks; Kentucky officials adopted similar laws, but too late to be effective. Across the trans-Appalachian West, moreover, men who had engaged to join Burr abandoned their plans; as a result, in central Tennessee, Burr had to leave behind three of the five boats he had had built for lack of men. As Jefferson explained to the Marquis de Lafayette after the crisis, "a simple proclamation informing the people of these combinations, and calling on them to suppress them[,] produced an instantaneous *levee en masse* of our citizens wherever there appeared anything to lay hold of, & the whole was crushed in one instant."[5]

Following some of his presidency's earlier challenges, such as the election crisis of 1800–1801 and the Mississippi crisis of 1801–3, Jefferson had written similarly boastful letters for domestic and, especially, European correspondents—letters that projected back onto those crises a confidence in the people's commitment to federal and republican principles that had not always determined his course as events had unfolded. Had he merely done the same with the Burr crisis? A close examination of the measures that the administration proposed, adopted, and rejected shows that Jefferson's principles did shape the response to this crisis. But the principles that constrained his and his advisors' measures in the fall of 1806 were much more complicated than the ones that he would later proclaim had been vindicated by the conspiracy's failure—that the people could be trusted to "meet invasions of the public order as [their] own personal concern," and the states could be relied upon "as the most competent administrations for our domestic concerns."[6]

By the time the cabinet first met to discuss the Burr crisis in late October 1806, the prospect of Burr leading "a *revolution* party on the western waters" had appeared in newspapers, letters, and conversations intermittently for nearly eighteen months.[7] Over the winter of 1805–6, Jefferson had received confidential warnings about Burr's disunionist designs in both anonymous and signed letters. During the summer of 1806, Burr's plans and movements had again risen to public consciousness, prompted in part by a series of articles in a Kentucky newspaper claiming that the men behind the so-called Spanish Conspiracy of the 1780s and 1790s were connected with Burr in a new separatist plot. For months, the administration barely responded to these public and private reports. Then, in the early fall of 1806, letters reached the nation's capital from upstate New York, western Pennsylvania, and southern Ohio that described the recruiting of men, the building of boats, and the purchasing of supplies on a large scale and linked that activity to Burr.

In late October, Jefferson met three times with "the four Heads of Departments"—Henry Dearborn (War), Albert Gallatin (Treasury), James Madison (State), and Robert Smith (Navy)—to consider how to address the growing crisis in the West. On October 22, they reviewed the available information about Burr and decided that he seemed to be engaged in "a scheme of separating the Western from the Atlantic States, and erecting the former into an independent Confederacy." Equally worrisome, James Wilkinson, the highest ranking general in the U.S. Army and the governor of the immense Louisiana Territory, was reported to be "engaged with [Burr] in this design." At this initial meeting, the cabinet agreed "unanimously" to send "confidential letters" to the governors or district attorneys of most of the western states and territories "to have [Burr] strictly watched," and if he "committ[ed] any overt act unequivocally," to arrest and try him. It also decided to dispatch gunboats up the Mississippi to Fort Adams, just above the border with Spanish West Florida, "to stop by force any passage of suspicious persons going down [the river] in force." But it left open the question of "what [was] proper to be done as to [Wilkinson]."[8]

Two days later, the cabinet met again, turning its attention to dangers approaching New Orleans from downriver. It decided, again unanimously, to strengthen the naval detachment at New Orleans, both by sending captains Edward Preble and Stephen Decatur "to take command of the force" there and by reinforcing the port with the brig *Argus* and eight gunboats from Charleston, Norfolk, and New York. The cabinet also agreed to warn the governors of the Orleans and Mississippi Territories and the commanding army officer at New Orleans "against any surprise of our ports or vessels." And it decided to send John Graham, who was in Washington preparing to return to his post as secretary of the Orleans Territory, "through Kentucky on Burr's trail, with discretionary powers to consult confidentially with the governors, and to arrest Burr if he has made himself liable." Once again, the cabinet "postponed" a decision on Wilkinson, though it agreed to empower Graham to replace him as the governor of the Louisiana Territory without further orders.[9]

The next day, the cabinet "rescind[ed]" nearly everything it had agreed upon in the two previous meetings. Graham's mission remained unchanged. And letters would still warn the territorial governors and the commanding officer at New Orleans "to be on their guard." But the letters to the western governors and district attorneys to watch, arrest, and try Burr were cancelled, and all of the planned naval movements were revoked. The cabinet decided to abandon most of its initial decisions, according to Jefferson's notes on the meeting, in response to a new mail delivery "from the westward" in which "not one word [was] heard . . . of any movements by Col. Burr." In the cabinet's thinking, the "total silence of the officers of Government, of the members of Congress, [and] of the newspapers" proved that, whatever his intentions, Burr had "committ[ed] no overt act against the law."[10]

Over the next few weeks, new information from the West forced further adjustments in the administration's response. In early November, Jefferson informed his son-in-law that "Burr [was] unquestionably very actively engaged in the westward in preparations to sever that from this part of the Union."[11] Five days later, the cabinet sat again. It decided to order Wilkinson to seek a temporary, peaceful solution to the border dispute with Spain and to move most of his troops, the bulk of the army in the West, from Natchitoches on the frontier to Fort Adams on the Mississippi. That the army might, in fact, be needed against Burr's men and boats remained unstated in Dearborn's orders, perhaps because the cabinet still had not decided whether the general could be trusted. The arrival of a set of confidential dispatches from Wilkinson on November 25 dispelled most of the remaining doubts, and the cabinet met the same day to discuss the new information. It decided to send letters and orders to various state and federal civil and military officials at seven points along the Ohio and Mississippi Rivers from Pittsburgh to New Orleans urging the seizing or stoppage of men, boats, and supplies. These letters would say nothing about a disunionist plot, however. The stoppages were to be made only if "reasonable ground[s]" existed to link those detained to "a military enterprise against any of the territories of Spain."[12] The cabinet also decided that the president should issue a formal proclamation.

Jefferson's November 27 proclamation charged Americans, in and out of government, to act in appropriate ways to check the unsanctioned expedition. It "enjoin[ed] all officers, civil and military, of the United States, or of any of the States or Territories, . . . [to prevent] the carrying on such expedition or enterprise by all lawful means within their power." It also "command[ed] all persons whatsoever engaged or concerned . . . to cease all further proceedings," and "enjoin[ed] all faithful citizens who have been led without due knowledge or consideration to participate in the said unlawful enterprises to withdraw . . . without delay." And it "require[d] all good and faithful citizens" to aid "in the discovery, apprehension, and bringing to justice of all such offenders."[13] Neither the proclamation nor the president's annual message to Congress five days later, however, mentioned Burr by name or described the conspiracy as anything more than a plan "to carry on a military expedition against the territories of Spain."[14] And neither indicated that the administration had done anything to defeat these "unlawful designs" before the proclamation.[15] The only hint that something other than an "enterprise . . . against a foreign nation" might be—or might have been—afoot appeared in the annual message. There, the president urged Congress to consider a new law analogous to those passed in the 1790s giving the government "powers of prevention" in cases of military expeditions directed against foreign powers. "Would [such laws] not be as reasonable and useful," Jefferson asked, "where the enterprise preparing is against the United States?"[16]

On December 19, the cabinet met for the last time regarding the Burr crisis. News of the impact of its earlier measures—the Graham mission, the official letters, the public proclamation—in the West had not yet reached Washington. As such, the cabinet, as Jefferson noted, still waited "with anxiety to see what exertions the western country will make in the first instance for their own defence." Even as the president insisted that his "confidence in [westerners was] entire," however, the cabinet devised new plans based on the possibility that Burr and his men might "escape" the countermeasures along the Ohio. It decided to instruct the Orleans and Mississippi territorial governors and the commanding naval officer at New Orleans to concentrate as much force as possible—regular army, territorial militia, and gunboats—above Fort Adams. Further measures, including quickly dispatching troops and ships from the East, were agreed upon in case Burr's troops defeated even this force and "[got] possession of N. Orleans."[17]

A number of considerations constrained the administration's response to the Burr crisis over the summer and fall of 1806. Some were principled; others were not. Uncertain information about Burr's plans and movements clearly played a critical role. Many of the earliest warnings seem to have been discounted because the sources were either anonymous or Federalists. It took the arrival of letters from men whom Jefferson knew and trusted in the early fall of 1806—letters consisting not merely of vague suspicions, moreover, but of specific accounts of conversations and actions—before the cabinet was willing to consider any steps against Burr. Its efforts to evaluate the available information were also influenced by the absence of reports from sources that should have divulged major developments. Apparently, none of the federal government's dozens of officers in the West except Kentucky district attorney Joseph Hamilton Daveiss, a Federalist, had reported any concerns. "Through the months of September October and November," Dearborn later informed Wilkinson, "a deep silence so far pervaded the Western States that no information was received from any public character."[18] Concerned that the lack of information from the West might have been the result of efforts by the conspirators to intercept the mail, the administration even decided to send "a confidential agent" to investigate and rectify delays in the western mails in mid-December.[19] Postmaster General Gideon Granger dispatched the agent along the route through Nashville to New Orleans with orders "to expedite the mails, to correct all errors, [and] to remove the disaffected and substitute others in their place."[20]

The administration's response to the Burr crisis seems to have been limited, as well, by its hesitance about employing what might have been a crucial tool: General Wilkinson and the western army. When Federalist presidents had turned to the army to quell the Whiskey and Fries's Rebellions in the 1790s, Jefferson had expressed great discomfort about "arming one part of our society against another."[21] But his hesitance to use the army against the Burr Conspiracy may have derived as much from doubts about Wilkinson's, and even the troops', loyalties as from this principle. The administration had long worried that Wilkinson and Burr were "too intimate"; Dearborn had even cautioned the general "to keep [Burr] at arms length" more than a year before the October cabinet meetings.[22] Throughout the summer and fall of 1806, everything from newspaper articles and private letters to confidential disclosures presented Wilkinson and the troops under his command as crucial to Burr's plans. It took more than a month after the first cabinet meeting before the administration seemed sufficiently confident of the general's loyalty to entrust him with an important role in defeating the conspiracy. Then, a pair of letters from Dearborn to Wilkinson in late November and early December charged the general with deploying the newly concentrated land and naval forces "in such manner as will most effectually intercept and prevent any unlawful enterprize either on New Orleans or elsewhere."[23]

Jefferson's principles played a clearer role in constraining his response to the Burr crisis in two other areas. They seem to have formed the leading obstacle to adopting any of the cabinet's plans for using ships and gunboats from the East to protect New Orleans. At its second discussion of the crisis, the cabinet had agreed to send eight gunboats and one brig to New Orleans "if . . . the appropriations shall be found to enable us."[24] Jefferson attributed the rescinding of these orders the next day to the absence of new information about Burr in that day's mail. A late December letter from the secretary of the navy to the president, however, suggests that scruples about the budget may have played a larger role. Making clear that he thought that more should have been done earlier to thwart Burr, Robert Smith regretted that, due to "the limitations of existing Statutes" and the House of Representatives' criticisms of unappropriated expenditures "at their last Session," the administration had been unable to send the vessels in October, a step that, in his view, would have left the country with nothing to fear from Burr.[25] Replying to Smith, Jefferson made clear that, even if the news from the West showed that Burr had met with "no effectual opposition" on the Ohio, he would still consider it necessary to ask Congress for "an immediate appropriation for a naval equipment" before sending ships and gunboats from eastern ports to retake New Orleans.[26]

The principle that most constrained the administration's response to the Burr crisis, however, was Jefferson's insistence that the federal government could enforce only laws that had been enacted through the procedures in the Constitution. Many Republicans agreed; many Federalists did not. This dispute, unlike earlier political battles over the meaning of the "necessary and proper" and "general welfare" clauses, turned not on the construction of the Constitution but on the idea that some laws inhered in the existence of the government, even without constitutional or congressional action. Jefferson and other Republicans rejected this idea of a common law of crimes, insisting that nothing was illegal that had not been made illegal by a specific act. Many Federalists accepted this idea, arguing that the federal government needed to treat as criminal all actions that threatened its existence, even when no specific act had been adopted.[27]

At some point in the midst of or soon after the late October cabinet meetings, Madison investigated the existing laws and decided that the government had no legal recourse if Burr's plan was to attack the United States. "It does not appear," Jefferson had noted at the end of Madison's list of relevant laws, "that regular troops can be employed, under any legal provision agst *insurrections*—but only agst expeditions having foreign Countries for the object."[28] "The question will be," Jefferson explained to a Republican editor just days before issuing his proclamation, "whether we have authority legally to oppose [Burr's project] by force."[29] His suggestion in his annual message that Congress needed to pass a law before he could arrest those preparing an assault on the United States rankled Federalists. "It is a self evident truth," a writer in a leading Federalist newspaper remarked, "that every nation is under a moral obligation to provide for its self preservation, and as a consequence, that it has a right to make use of all proper means necessary to that end." Even without a specific law, Federalists asserted, the president was "invested with the power & of course the means of *preventing* any insurrection or enterprize on the public peace or safety."[30]

The impact of the administration's principled rejection of a common law of crimes on its response to the Burr Conspiracy seems to have been extensive. Madison's list of the relevant laws is undated, but he may have prepared it when charged with writing instructions for western governors and district attorneys to have Burr "arrested and tried for treason, misdemeanor, or whatever other offence the [overt] act may amount to."[31] Learning that there was no law against merely preparing to levy war against the United States may have fueled the cabinet's decision to cancel those letters. A month later, the Republican rejection of a common law of crimes almost certainly led the administration to present Burr's activities solely as an enterprise against Spanish possessions in both the presidential proclamation and the orders and letters to officials along the Ohio and Mississippi Rivers. And it definitely produced the paragraph in the annual message, written by Madison, that urged Congress to enact legislation making such enterprises illegal when directed against the United States. Around the time of the final cabinet meetings about the Burr crisis in late December, Jefferson secretly prepared a draft bill along these lines and sent it to a congressional ally, requesting that he "copy the within & burn [the] original."[32] Not until the last days of the session, in early March 1807, did Congress pass an act that authorized the use of federal forces against such insurrections.

For more than seven weeks after the proclamation and annual message, the administration said little to the public or even to Congress about the Burr crisis. Then, on January 22, 1807, the president delivered a lengthy message to the legislature that addressed the most persistent questions by "disclosing Burrs treasonous Projects and the Measures taken by the Government to defeat them."[33] The message described Burr's plans, leaving no doubt that they included dividing the union. And it detailed the administration's response, demonstrating its competence in a time of crisis. In it, Jefferson highlighted the role of the people and the states in defeating the conspiracy.

In its contents and its timing, this message served Jefferson's didactic purposes by showing the efficacy of the government when administered on his principles.

Popular and congressional pressure to know more about Burr's projects and the administration's response had built throughout December and finally exploded in January. Newspaper editors lamented the uncertain state of affairs even as they published any scrap of information that might help their readers make sense of events. Finally, in mid-January, Representative John Randolph decided to force the president's hand. On January 16, the Virginia Quid offered a resolution calling on the president for information about "any illegal combination of private individuals against the peace and safety of the Union," as well as about "the measures which the Executive has pursued and proposes to take for suppressing or defeating the same."[34] According to a Randolph supporter, the resolution "met with the most violent opposition."[35] Fifteen congressmen spoke, most against at least part of the resolution. Some insisted that it suggested "a want of confidence in the President."[36] Others opposed a clause that required Jefferson to provide information about his future plans for defeating the conspiracy. When that clause was removed by Randolph, both parts of the resolution passed fairly easily.

Unlike the annual message, which included input from most of the cabinet, the January 22 message came "from Mr. Jefferson's own hand."[37] By far the longest special message of Jefferson's presidency, it provided a full account of events supported by a few key documents. In it, he answered, at least implicitly, most of the questions that had been raised in newspaper articles and essays, private letters and conversations, and, of course, the congressional debate over Randolph's resolution. Jefferson focused on the two broad subjects included in the resolution: the nature and scope of the "illegal combination" in the West and the "measures" adopted by the administration to defeat it.[38] Working within a framework that had been established by the resolution, Jefferson shaped his account of the conspiracy to suit his own purposes.

Much of the message unfolded as a chronological narrative told from the administration's point of view. This history began in September 1806, when Jefferson had "received intimations" of a plot in the West that was "unlawful and unfriendly to the peace of the Union" and whose "prime mover . . . was Aaron Burr." By late October, new information had suggested the outlines of the plan, but it was "still so blended and involved in mystery that nothing could be singled out for pursuit." In this context, Jefferson reported, the administration had decided to send a trusted agent "to investigate the plots," to meet with federal and state officials in the West, and, "with their aid," to do whatever appeared "necessary to discover the designs of the conspirators, arrest their means, [and] bring their persons to punishment." Around the same time, Jefferson had directed that warnings be sent to the army and navy commanders in the Southwest and to "the governors of the Orleans and Mississippi Territories." In late November, the administration had received a full disclosure of Burr's plans, including his efforts to corrupt the army, from Wilkinson. When combined with "some other information" that had arrived at about the same time, Burr's intentions had finally seemed clear.[39]

"Burr's general designs," according to the message, were never simple. He had "contemplated two distinct objects"—"the severance of the Union . . . by the Alleghany Mountains" and "an attack on Mexico." These objects could "be carried on either jointly or separately," and either one could be effected "first, as circumstances should direct." At the same time, Burr had announced another object that was "merely ostensible," settling what Jefferson described as "a pretended purchase of a tract of country on the Washita claimed by a Baron Bastrop." The land was to "serve as the pretext for all his preparations, an allurement for such followers as really wished to acquire settlements . . . [,] and a cover under which to retreat" if his true goals were frustrated. With his three objects in mind, Burr had begun recruiting men, building boats, and purchasing supplies. But, as Jefferson explained, Burr had quickly discovered that a division of the union was impossible. Westerners would not "consent" to "its dissolution," and his resources were too small "to effect it by force." As such, he had shifted his focus to New Orleans, where he intended to "plunder the bank . . . , possess himself of the military and naval stores, and proceed on his expedition to Mexico."[40]

In late November, according to the president's narrative, the administration's efforts had shifted from investigating to defeating Burr's plans. With the new information, Jefferson noted, "it was first possible to take specific measures" to thwart the conspiracy. Accordingly, the proclamation had been issued and orders had been sent "to every interesting point on the Ohio and Mississippi" to mobilize the army, navy, and militias and to alert state and federal authorities. Even before these new orders had arrived, the cabinet's confidential agent had unfolded Burr's plans to the governor of Ohio, who had joined with the legislature "to crush the combination." As the agent and proclamation had worked to counteract the conspiracy in the Ohio valley, Wilkinson had begun to prepare New Orleans for Burr's arrival. In closing his narrative, Jefferson admitted that Burr's plot was not yet defeated and that an express rider had been sent to the West with further letters and orders as recently as late December. But he asserted that, given the seizures at Marietta and other efforts along the river, the small band of "fugitives from the Ohio, with their associates from the Cumberland, [could] not threaten serious danger."[41]

Jefferson's account highlighted the role of the people and the states in checking, if not yet crushing, Burr's treason. The federal government was not entirely missing from his account. He had issued a proclamation; his secretaries had sent orders to various civil and military officials; his agent had followed Burr through the West; and the army had, as Jefferson asserted about the much-suspected General Wilkinson, acted "with the honor of a soldier and fidelity of a good citizen." But these measures had served principally to disabuse westerners, in and out of government, of the idea that Burr's project was either innocent or approved. Burr's disunionist scheme had failed principally because westerners had proven unshakeable in their "attachment . . . to the present Union." Even in New Orleans, where the loyalty of the largely creole population had seemed doubtful to many, the citizens had "manifest[ed] unequivocal fidelity to the Union and a spirit of determined resistance to their expected assailants," according to the president. And Burr's planned invasion of Spanish Mexico had been crippled when state officials in Ohio and Kentucky, acting on information from John Graham, had moved "with a promptitude, an energy, and [a] patriotic zeal" against it. In the end, Burr had been left with what Jefferson described as a small group of "ardent, restless, desperate, and disaffected persons" who could not possibly accomplish any of his designs.[42]

Delivered midway through the session, the message had to address why Jefferson had not already communicated with Congress about the crisis. "For some time," he explained, he had expected reports from the West that would have allowed him to "lay before the Legislature the termination as well as the beginning and progress of this scene of depravity." But only recently had he received information—some of it since the adoption of Randolph's resolution—that "brought us nearly to the period contemplated." Of course, Congress and the public had wanted to know what was happening in the West when everything was still uncertain and unfolding, not when everything was resolved. Earlier information might have allowed Congress to act to meet the crisis. But it is clear that Jefferson did not want much congressional action. The only measure that he had requested from Congress in the first half of the session—a time when Burr and his men were on the move and anxiety was at its peak—was to empower the federal government to meet insurrections against the United States in the same way that it could meet expeditions against foreign powers. In the January message, Jefferson asserted that he had "indulged" his desire to wait for the resolution of events on the Ohio before reporting to Congress precisely "because no circumstance had yet made it necessary to call in the aid of the legislative functions."[43]

Some of Jefferson's closest advisors worried that he had taken on himself the full burden of meeting the crisis. His former personal secretary, Virginia representative William A. Burwell, later acknowledged that he had been "struck with the magnitude of the responsibility of the P[resident]."[44] Within the cabinet, Secretary Smith seems to have repeatedly pushed Jefferson to involve Congress in suppressing the conspiracy. In late December, a few days after the final cabinet meeting on the Burr crisis, Smith again urged the president to take more drastic steps to "[arrest] the progress of this insurrection by all the means within our power." He suggested immediately sending Congress a confidential message with "all the letters in [Jefferson's] possession conveying any information respecting the movements & designs of Col Burr." The message, Smith argued, should ask Congress to suspend the writ of habeas corpus and pass an immediate appropriation "to send promptly a competent naval force into the Mississippi and the adjacent waters."[45] Smith did not think that the ships could arrive in time to prevent an assault on New Orleans. But he believed that, by "lay[ing] the subject before C[ongress]," the president could "let them take the responsibility upon themselves."[46] Instead, Jefferson decided to wait another month for news from the West that would show whether Burr's men had met with "effectual opposition at either Mariette or Cincinnati" before sending a message to Congress.[47]

Delaying his communication to Congress as long as possible helped Jefferson avoid what one senator described as "censure, & perhaps contempt" over his decision to take on himself what seemed to many to be an almost-personal responsibility for thwarting the conspiracy.[48] But Jefferson did not view himself as the only one active against it, as Burwell and Smith seemed to think. Over the course of the congressional session, Jefferson had grown increasingly confident that the conspiracy would be crushed by the people and states of the West. Through the Graham mission of late October and the proclamation, orders, and letters of late November, Jefferson had ensured that the public along with state and territorial officials knew that Burr was not secretly supported by the administration. With that knowledge, the people and their local governments would bear primary responsibility for thwarting Burr's activities. Over time, Jefferson became more and more certain that they would prove that the United States was "the strongest Government on earth."[49]

Meeting the lingering crisis with this uncertain source of strength dictated a delay in reporting the administration's response to Congress. If its fruits were not already apparent, then Jefferson's critics would see only its limits—the failure to send eastern troops and eastern ships to the West and the refusal to arrest Burr on the basis of a common law of crimes. The president's "apparent inactivity," as even Burwell put it, would inspire widespread attacks on "the apathy of the govt."[50] Jefferson needed to wait in order to see if his confidence in the loyalty of westerners and the exertions of the state governments, as well as in the fidelity of Wilkinson and the army, produced the expected results. In late December, after receiving the much-anticipated news of the seizure of most of Burr's boats at Marietta, Jefferson informed one senator that he "had no doubt the conspiracy would be crushed, extensive as it was, with little trouble & expense to the United States."[51] The longer he delayed a communication to Congress and the more time he gave for favorable reports to arrive from the West, the easier it became to defend his decision to defeat the conspiracy with means that involved "little trouble & expense" for the federal government. The Randolph resolution forced him to involve Congress before the western states and people had "finish[ed] the matter" in a way that defended "the honor of popular government" and, in doing so, undermined "all arguments for standing armies."[52] But, by emphasizing the role of the people and the states, Jefferson ensured that his message taught this lesson even though the crisis was not yet done.

Jefferson's message on the Burr Conspiracy has always been viewed as significant. Biographers and historians have treated it as either an honest statement of his understanding of the Burr Conspiracy at that moment or a deliberate effort to manipulate congressional and popular opinion about

Burr, the conspiracy, the administration, and himself. But Jefferson's purposes were much larger—justifying not only his governance of the country but the government itself and the principles that he wished it to embody. The message proclaimed a genuine threat to the union and yet announced that there was no real danger. Jefferson's critics saw these claims as contradictory; the president did not. In a republican government, the emergence of a threat, he believed, would always generate the popular response necessary to defeat it. Jefferson used the message to frame the conspiracy—its nature, its extent, and its failure—in a way that taught this lesson. It was a lesson that Jefferson himself seems to have learned over the course of the crisis. And it was a lesson that would serve him poorly in the last year of his presidency, when the public and the states too often ignored or rejected the "call of the law" in the form of the Embargo.

In the weeks and months after sending the January 22, 1807, message to Congress, Jefferson wrote a number of letters clarifying the lessons it taught. "A conspiracy which, in other countries, would have called for an appeal to armies," he explained to the governor of Ohio, had been "given the mortal blow" by "the hand of the people," "prov[ing] that government to be the strongest of which every man feels himself a part." The suppression of the conspiracy also provided "a happy illustration . . . of the importance of preserving to the State authorities all that vigor which the Constitution foresaw would be necessary, not only for their own safety, but for that of the whole."[53] Writing to Lafayette months later, Jefferson boasted that "nothing has ever so strongly proved the innate force of our form of government as this conspiracy."[54] "The government which can wield the arm of the people," he insisted in another letter on the lessons of the conspiracy in early June, "must be the strongest possible."[55] With these letters to domestic and foreign correspondents, like the much-publicized message to Congress, Jefferson sought to make the Burr crisis teach the wisdom of Jefferson's vision of republican government—decentralized, nonmilitarized, and limited. "On the whole," he concluded, "this squall, by showing with what ease our government suppresses movements which in other countries requires armies, has greatly increased its strength by increasing the public confidence in it."[56]

While Jefferson described his January message to Congress as "a faithful narrative of [Burr's] conspiracy," it did not include everything that he believed on the subject, and he did not believe everything that he included in it.[57] Its account of the administration's response was misleading in a number of ways. It ignored all of the warnings that Jefferson had received about Burr before September 1806. It stated that orders had gone out to the territorial governors and the military commanders in the Southwest to "be on their guard against surprise" in late October, but only one letter, to the commanding officer at New Orleans, seems to have actually been sent.[58] Most importantly, it said nothing about all of the things that the cabinet had decided to do and then abandoned as it reacted to the reports of Burr's plans and movements. Rather than try to justify why the instructions to the western governors and district attorneys to have Burr arrested had been cancelled, rather than try to explain why the redeployment of naval vessels from the East to New Orleans had been rescinded, Jefferson simply omitted those decisions from his history. The principles that guided those reversals were complicated, controversial, and, to some extent, subsumed within the principles that his public recasting of the administration response upheld. By omitting the strong measures that the cabinet had ultimately abandoned, however, Jefferson suggested that it had always believed that making sure that the states and people of the West had correct information—through the proclamation, the Graham mission, and a few well-directed letters—would suffice to defeat Burr's plans. Instead, the president seems to have come to this view only gradually, after retreating from more energetic steps that had once seemed appropriate but had challenged other principles.

Notes

1. Members of Congress, executive officials, and even ordinary citizens, including Abigail Adams, used this phrase (or a close variant) to describe Burr's plans in the winter of 1806–7. I discuss the administration's response to the Burr crisis at greater length in my book *The Burr Conspiracy: Uncovering the Story of an Early American Crisis* (Princeton, N.J., 2017). I would like to thank Joanne Freeman and Johann Neem for putting together this volume and for organizing the celebration that launched it. And I would like to recognize Peter Onuf's tremendous contributions to my life through his scholarship, his prodding, his advice, and his friendship over the past twenty-five years.

2. [Stephen C. Carpenter], *People's Friend and Daily Advertiser* (New York), Dec. 30, 1806.

3. Clinton-Jeffersonianus, "A Speck of War; or, The Good Sense of the People of the Western Country," *New-York Evening Post,* Jan. 7, 1807. The title of this satirical essay came from Jefferson's annual message, which had justified the decision not to expand the army and navy in a time of domestic crisis and foreign tension on the grounds that "were armies to be raised whenever a speck of war is visible in our horizon, we never

should have been without them." Jefferson, "Sixth Annual Message," Dec. 2, 1806, in James D. Richardson, comp., *A Compilation of the Messages and Papers of the Presidents, 1789–1907* (Washington, D.C., 1897–99), 1:410 (hereafter *CMPP*).

4. Jefferson, "First Inaugural Address," Mar. 4, 1801, in *CMPP,* 1:322.

5. Jefferson to the Marquis de Lafayette, May 26, 1807, in Paul Leicester Ford, ed., *The Works of Thomas Jefferson [Federal Edition]* (New York, 1904–5), 10:410 (hereafter Ford).

6. Jefferson, "First Inaugural Address," Mar. 4, 1801, in *CMPP,* 1:322, 323. Over the past two centuries, countless historians and biographers of Burr and Jefferson have examined the administration's response to the Burr crisis in the fall of 1806. Some have seen it as too much, others have viewed it as too little, and a few have treated it as just right. See, in particular, Thomas Perkins Abernethy, *The Burr Conspiracy* (New York, 1954); Merrill D. Peterson, *Thomas Jefferson and the New Nation: A Biography* (New York, 1970); Dumas Malone, *Jefferson the President: Second Term, 1805–1809* (Boston, 1974); Milton Lomask, *Aaron Burr: The Conspiracy and Years of Exile, 1805–1836* (New York, 1982); Peter S. Onuf, *Jefferson's Empire: The Language of American Nationhood* (Charlottesville, Va., 2000), 131–37; Nancy Isenberg, *Fallen Founder: The Life of Aaron Burr* (New York, 2007); and David O. Stewart, *American Emperor: Aaron Burr's Challenge to Jefferson's America* (New York, 2011). These judgments have frequently depended on the author's assessments of both Burr's intentions—how great a threat did he really pose?—and Jefferson's character—would he exploit popular fears to crush, or even have killed, a political rival? As such, they tend to stress the role of the political and the personal rather than the principled in the administration's response.

7. "Queries," *United States' Gazette* (Philadelphia), July 27, 1805.

8. Jefferson, memorandum, Oct. 22, 1806, in Franklin B. Sawvel, ed., *The Complete Anas of Thomas Jefferson* (New York, 1903), 246–47 (hereafter *Anas*).

9. Jefferson, memorandum, Oct. 24, 1806, in ibid., 247–48.

10. Jefferson, memorandum, Oct. 25, 1806, in ibid., 248. There is no evidence that Madison actually sent the agreed-upon letters to either the governor of the Orleans Territory or the acting governor of the Mississippi Territory.

11. Jefferson to Thomas Mann Randolph, Nov. 3, 1806, in Andrew A. Lipscomb and Albert Ellery Bergh, eds., *The Writings of Thomas Jefferson [Definitive Edition]* (Washington, D.C., 1905–7), 18:250 (hereafter L&B).

12. Jefferson, memorandum, Nov. 25, 1806, in *Anas,* 249. See also TJ's memorandum of the same date recording who was to write what to whom in Thomas Jefferson Papers, Library of Congress, Washington, D.C.

13. Jefferson, "Proclamation," Nov. 27, 1806, in *CMPP,* 1:404.

14. Jefferson, "Sixth Annual Message," Dec. 2, 1806, in ibid., 406.

15. Jefferson, "Proclamation," Nov. 27, 1806, in ibid., 404.

16. Jefferson, "Sixth Annual Message," Dec. 2, 1806, in ibid., 407.

17. Jefferson to William C. C. Claiborne, Dec. 20, 1806, in Ford, 8:328–29. This letter was neither finished nor mailed; Jefferson referred to it in his memorandum of

the cabinet meeting as "containing the sum of the orders agreed to be sent." Jefferson, memorandum, Dec. 19, 1806, in *Anas,* 251.

18. Henry Dearborn to James Wilkinson, Jan. 21, 1807, Letters Sent by the Secretary of War Relating to Military Affairs, Records of the Office of the Secretary of War, reel 3, National Archives, Washington, D.C. (hereafter LSMA).

19. Daniel Smith to Andrew Jackson, Dec. 19, 1806, in John Spencer Bassett, ed., *Correspondence of Andrew Jackson* (Washington, D.C., 1926–35), 1:157.

20. Gideon Granger to Jefferson, Feb. 22, 1814, in J. Jefferson Looney et al., eds., *Thomas Jefferson Papers: Retirement Series* (Princeton, N.J., 2004–), 7:206.

21. Jefferson to James Madison, Dec. 28, 1794, in L&B, 9:296.

22. Dearborn to Wilkinson, Aug. 24, 1805, James Wilkinson Papers, Chicago History Museum Research Center.

23. Dearborn to Wilkinson, Nov. 27, 1806, LSMA. Wilkinson's actions with respect to the Burr Conspiracy have produced at least as much debate as Jefferson's or even Burr's. There is no solid, scholarly biography of the general; the most useful accounts of his role can be found in broader works. See, in addition to histories of the Burr Conspiracy, Theodore J. Crackel, *Mr. Jefferson's Army: Political and Social Reform in the Military Establishment, 1801–1809* (New York, 1987).

24. Jefferson, memorandum, Oct. 24, 1806, in *Anas,* 247.

25. Robert Smith to Jefferson, Dec. 22, 1806, Thomas Jefferson Papers, Library of Congress. Due to illness, Gallatin missed the cabinet meeting where the naval orders were rescinded. But a letter he wrote to Jefferson the same afternoon suggests that Gallatin, at least, thought that it was possible to send one cutter, perhaps a gunboat, and sixty sailors to New Orleans within the existing naval budget; see Gallatin to Jefferson, Oct. 25, 1806, ibid. This letter raises the possibility that Jefferson used the appropriations issue to block Smith's more energetic approach to the crisis.

26. Jefferson to Smith, Dec. 13, 1806, in L&B, 10:331.

27. For the idea of and battle over a federal common law of crimes, see Kathryn Preyer, "Jurisdiction to Punish: Federal Authority, Federalism and the Common Law of Crimes in the Early Republic," *Law and History Review* 4 (1986): 223–65; Robert C. Palmer, "The Federal Common Law of Crimes," *Law and History Review* 4 (1986): 267–323; and Stephen B. Presser, "The Supra-Constitution, the Courts, and the Federal Common Law of Crimes: Some Comments on Palmer and Preyer," *Law and History Review* 4 (1986): 325–35.

28. Jefferson, note on Madison to Jefferson, [Oct. 30, 1806], in James Morton Smith, ed., *The Republic of Letters: The Correspondence between Thomas Jefferson and James Madison, 1776–1826* (New York, 1995), 3:1454. Jefferson docketed the memorandum with this date.

29. Jefferson to William Duane, Nov. 24, 1806, Thomas Jefferson Papers, Library of Congress.

30. "President's Message," *New-York Evening Post,* Dec. 11, 1806.

31. Jefferson, memorandum, Oct. 22, 1806, in *Anas,* 247. In preparing this list, Madison was doing work that presumably would have been done by Attorney General

John Breckinridge, but Breckinridge was in Kentucky (where he died early in the congressional session).

32. Jefferson to John Dawson, Dec. 19, 1806, Thomas Jefferson Papers, Library of Congress. For Madison's contribution to the annual message, see Madison to Jefferson, [Nov. 16, 1806], in Smith, ed., *Republic of Letters,* 3:1459. For the congressional debate and final act, see *Annals of Congress,* 9th Cong., 2nd sess., 217–18, 328, 673, 1286.

33. George Clinton to Edmond Charles Genet, Jan. 24, 1807, AHMC—Edmond Charles Genet Papers, New-York Historical Society.

34. John Randolph, speech, Jan. 16, 1807, *Annals of Congress,* 9th Cong., 2nd sess., 334, 336. The Quids, under John Randolph's leadership, had broken from Jefferson and most congressional Republicans during the preceding sessions over foreign policy and other issues.

35. James M. Garnett to James Hunter, Jan. 17, 1807, Garnett-Mercer-Hunter Family Papers, Library of Virginia, Richmond.

36. Samuel Taggart to John Taylor, Jan. 19, 1807, in "Letters of Samuel Taggart, 1803–1814," *Proceedings of the American Antiquarian Society,* new ser., 33 (1923): 207. For the House debate, see *Annals of Congress,* 9th Cong., 2nd sess., 334–59.

37. Samuel Latham Mitchill to Catharine Mitchill, Jan. 22, 1807, in "Dr. Mitchill's Letters from Washington, 1801–1813," *Harper's New Monthly Magazine,* April 1879, 751.

38. Jefferson, special message, Jan. 22, 1807, in *CMPP,* 1:412.

39. Ibid., 412–13.

40. Ibid., 414.

41. Ibid., 414–15.

42. Ibid., 413–16.

43. Ibid., 412.

44. William A. Burwell, memorandum, [ca. late 1808], in Gerard W. Gawalt, ed., "'Strict Truth': The Narrative of William Armistead Burwell," *Virginia Magazine of History and Biography* 101 (1993): 126.

45. Smith to Jefferson, Dec. 22, 1806, Thomas Jefferson Papers, Library of Congress.

46. Burwell, memorandum, [ca. late 1808], in Gawalt, ed., "'Strict Truth,'" 126.

47. Jefferson to Smith, Dec. 23, 1806, in Ford, 10:331. Jefferson told Smith that he wanted to wait twelve days for the western mail, but it would take almost a month before he sent his message to Congress.

48. William Plumer, diary, Jan. 16, 1807, in Everett Somerville Brown, ed., *William Plumer's Memorandum of Proceedings in the United States Senate, 1803–1807* (New York, 1923), 577.

49. Jefferson, "First Inaugural Address," Mar. 4, 1801, in *CMPP,* 1:322.

50. Burwell, memorandum, [ca. late 1808], in Gawalt, ed., "'Strict Truth,'" 126.

51. Plumer, diary entry, Dec. 27, 1806, in Brown, ed., *William Plumer's Memorandum of Proceedings,* 544.

52. Jefferson to Charles Clay, Jan. 11, 1807, in L&B, 11:133.

53. Jefferson to Edward Tiffin, Feb. 2, 1807, in ibid., 147.

54. Jefferson to Lafayette, July 14, 1807, in ibid., 278. See also his similar letter of the same date to Pierre Samuel Dupont de Nemours, in ibid., 275–76.

55. Jefferson to Isaac Weaver Jr., June 7, 1807, in ibid., 221.

56. Jefferson to Claiborne, Feb. 3, 1807, in ibid., 151.

57. Jefferson to James Bowdoin, Apr. 2, 1807, in ibid., 185–86.

58. Jefferson, special message, Jan. 22, 1807, in *CMPP,* 1:413.

11 Taking Root Deeper Than Ever

Jeffersonians and Slavery

Christa Dierksheide

In the summer of 1822, two years after graduating from Middlebury College in Vermont, Daniel Pierce Thompson journeyed southward to see Thomas Jefferson's brainchild, the University of Virginia in Charlottesville. After meeting Jefferson and being invited to dine at Monticello, Thompson, who was later a Vermont jurist, legislator, and sometime novelist, queried the ex-president on a wide range of subjects, including slavery. Jefferson described the antislavery policies that he and other patriots, including James Madison and Patrick Henry, had advocated in the years after the Revolution. For many, the slave trade and the plantation slavery it spawned constituted an archaic system that retarded moral, economic, and political development and posed a direct threat to the survival of the union. These leaders advocated gradual emancipation schemes—the "improvement" of slavery with an eye toward ending it—because they imagined a future empire without slaves, a world in which legitimate commerce and free labor encouraged the unimpeded progress of the new nation within the Atlantic system.[1]

In his conversation with Thompson, Jefferson declared that "Mr. Madison thought, we all thought," that congressional prohibition of the transatlantic slave trade in 1808 represented real progress toward abolition as "a great desideratum of giving slavery its death-blow, or the blow at least under which the institution could only linger a few years to perish from the land." But, Jefferson admitted, "we soon found ourselves sadly mistaken." "When the time arrived on which all had counted for its rapid decline," he related, "we saw it taking root deeper than ever." Thus, just four years before his death, Jefferson was keenly aware that the antislavery narrative—firmly rooted in Enlightenment doctrine—he had helped script for the federal union had inadvertently laid the foundation for a new and more powerful proslavery argument in the nineteenth century. He lamented that while his antislavery policies and actions—including the abolition of the slave trade—sought to unleash democratic forces that would ensure the march toward the end of slavery, the new "democrats" that he helped empower became an "influential class" that mobilized support *for* slavery rather than against it. But to unravel the mystery of how Jeffersonian antislavery ultimately became the foundation of later proslavery ideas, we need to first define and unpack the various stages that encompassed what I call "antislavery amelioration"—the founders' idea of the gradual erosion of slavery and incremental progress toward abolition and emancipation. Only by understanding the discrete components of Jeffersonian antislavery and their implications can we begin to solve the mystery of how these components became critical to later southern—and Democratic-Republican—proslavery.[2]

Although several historians have considered Jefferson's antislavery ideas and policies, none has examined how the two particular strategies of "repatriation" and "diffusion" ultimately became critical aspects of the proslavery arsenal in the South, and, specifically, within Jefferson's own party. The usual narrative has been that Jefferson's antislavery proposals of the post-revolutionary era were ultimately eclipsed by his turn toward proslavery in the nineteenth century. Traditionally, Jefferson's "diffusion" policy—which he advocated most vociferously during the Missouri crisis of 1819–20—has been interpreted as signaling a sea change in his attitudes toward slavery. But instead, Jefferson remained firmly committed to antislavery principles throughout his life. A gradual emancipation scheme, which encompassed several "ameliorative" stages, including "diffusion" and "repatriation," was the most expedient and humane way to resolve the pressing slavery issue, he believed. Still, when slavery threatened the peace and security of the fledgling American nation, Jefferson, as well as other prominent members of his party, revised their "enlightened" antislavery narrative; they qualified many of the "stages" that would lead gradually toward abolition. Inadvertently, these qualifications later laid the groundwork for proslavery positions that would become crucial tenets of Jeffersonian Republicanism: "colonization" of free blacks and insurgent slaves to Africa and the "diffusion" of slaves westward, particularly through the internal slave trade, as a means of entrenching and perpetuating the "peculiar institution." In order to highlight the significance and protean nature of these two Jeffersonian policies, this chapter shows that, ironically, Enlightenment doctrine lay at the core of two emerging narratives of progress: Jeffersonian antislavery and later southern proslavery.[3]

An "Enlightened" Antislavery Narrative

After 1776, many Americans, particularly in the northern states and Upper South, believed that the continuation of slavery jeopardized the American experiment. Because a number of patriots reasoned that the new nation would not succeed so long as whites and blacks occupied the same country, national progress could only be ensured in the absence of slavery. As Patrick Henry wrote, until Virginians could "abolish this lamentable Evil," they should do "everything we can . . . to improve it" and "treat the unhappy victims with lenity, & it is the furthest advance we can make toward Justice." As Henry and others intimated, antislavery amelioration encompassed several gradual stages that would eventually culminate in emancipation and the removal of the African "people" from the federal union. First, the transatlantic commerce would be abolished by the federal government. Second, individual slave owners would ameliorate their slaves' moral and physical conditions on plantations. And lastly, *all* enslaved Africans would be emancipated and repatriated to their "homeland" outside of the United States. This antislavery narrative drew heavily on the Enlightenment belief in the common origin of humankind and suggested that the great task of the revolutionary age was to free man from the tyrannical forces—slavery, monarchy, and despotism—that had caused his degeneracy. Thus, the idea of an ameliorative end to slavery undergirded that very core Enlightenment idea of progress that human history is the history of human betterment.[4]

Patriots' calls to end slavery became much more urgent after 1776 not simply because it was a moral "evil" but because it threatened the viability and legitimacy of the new nation-building project on the international stage. America's status as a legitimate "treaty-worthy" nation in the eyes of the world was jeopardized by continued slave-trading and slave-owning. In order to gain entrance to the European states system, patriot leaders had to transform a provincial slaveholding outpost into a legitimate and independent trading partner and diplomatic ally in the Atlantic family of nations. No powerful, commercial nation in Europe would want to engage with a second-rate state that might soon be overpowered by an imperial power like

Spain or France, patriots reasoned. "Citizens," Jefferson declared in 1806, "would withdraw . . . from all further participation in those violations of human rights which have been so long continued on the unoffending inhabitants of Africa" in order to promote the "morality, the reputation, and the best interests of our country." For the new nation to become as civilized as Europe, America's commerce and institutions had to resemble those of its new counterparts across the Atlantic. Thus, both the transatlantic slave trade and slavery had to be eradicated in favor of free trade and free labor.[5]

Jefferson and others suggested that slavery could be "improved" on individual plantations at the same time that the institution was being weakened by a restricted—and later prohibited—transatlantic slave trade. He believed that planters should mitigate the moral and physical "evils" to which slaves were subjected and prepare them for their ultimate freedom outside of the United States. Similarly, the inimical relationship between masters and their slaves could also be assuaged, allowing slave owners to contemplate emancipation schemes without the threat of slave revolts. On his plantations in Virginia, Jefferson sought to "improve" his slaves' condition, telling a young Edward Coles that until slavery could be abolished in future time, "My opinion has ever been that, until more can be done for them, we should endeavor, with those whom fortune has thrown on our hands, to feed and clothe them well, protect them from all ill usage, require such reasonable labor only as is performed voluntarily by freemen, & be led by no repugnancies to abdicate them, and our duties to them."[6]

After slavery had been eroded by the abolition of the slave trade and "improved" through amelioration schemes on plantations, then planters would consent to free their chattel. But this freedom would be immediately followed by colonization, or "repatriation," as many white elites termed it. Because so many Americans conceived of enslaved Africans and white Americans as distinct and homogenous "peoples" or "nations," expelling one "people"—slaves—was the only way to avoid genocidal race war and the destruction of the union. In 1803, Virginia agriculturist John Taylor of Caroline mused that "if England and America would erect and foster a settlement of free negroes in some fertile part of Africa," slavery and the slave trade "might then be gradually re-exported, and philanthropy gratified by a slow re-animation of the virtue, religion, and liberty of the negroes." Colonization measures were nation-building measures that only gained traction after the end of the war with Britain precisely because the new American nation was threatened by the continued presence of a "foreign" African nation in its midst.[7]

But the antislavery amelioration espoused by Jefferson and his co-patriots in the two decades immediately following the Revolution was ultimately turned on its head. Several domestic exigencies in the first decades of the nineteenth century demonstrated that Jefferson's Enlightenment vision of progress and the antislavery policy that promoted it had failed. Instead, when faced with local or sectional crises, such as the Gabriel Prosser rebellion in Richmond in 1800 or the Missouri crisis in 1819–20, Jefferson and members of his own Democratic-Republican Party swiftly departed from the "repatriation" of an entire African "people" as the only solution to the slavery problem. Since the preservation of the union was always paramount, co-partisans revised their own policies—no matter how immoral or proslavery they might be—in order to assure the survival of the republican experiment in the first few decades of the nineteenth century.[8]

Colonization: "Repatriation" and the "Receptacle"

Beginning with a "repatriation" scheme that he first sketched out in his *Notes on the State of Virginia* in the 1780s, Jefferson believed that the colonization of all American slaves and the establishment of their own "nation" somewhere in the Atlantic littoral was the ultimate solution to the "problem" of bondage in America. In keeping with his commitment to the goal of liberal progress and to antislavery amelioration as the process by which that objective might be reached, Jefferson thought that "an establishment to which the people of color of these states might from time to time be colonized" was the "most desirable measure which could be adopted for gradually drawing off this part of our population most advantageously for themselves as well as for us." Yet when faced with actually deploying such a colonization policy early in his presidency, Jefferson formulated a corollary. When insurrection threatened public safety and posed a threat to white property in Virginia, Jefferson embraced a punishment of "exile" and deportation for violent and insurrectionary slaves.[9]

Such a threat arrived in the summer of 1800, when the enslaved blacksmith Gabriel Prosser conspired to stage a military-style invasion of Richmond. Prosser threatened to burn the capital and imprison or kill all its white inhabitants. After one conspirator was captured, he evinced little regret, instead claiming, "I have nothing more to offer than what General Washington would have had to offer, had he been taken by the British and put on trial. I have adventured my life in endeavoring to obtain the liberty of my countrymen [blacks], and am willing to sacrifice in their cause."[10] In this conspirator's statement lay precisely what Jefferson and his contemporaries feared: a violent and united community of blacks who sought to overthrow and decimate whites. Yet, at the same time, the precise opposite of this insurrectionary conspirator was also present in Richmond. Two loyal slaves, Pharoah and Tom, had disclosed Prosser's plot to their master, Mosby Sheppard, allowing violence to be averted and the conspirators to be captured.[11]

Whites in Richmond and Virginia's legislators were in an uproar over the conspiracy. The threat of revolt had been so proximate that Governor James Monroe declared it to be "unquestionably the most serious and formidable . . . of its kind."[12] But as a more "enlightened" alternative to the execution of Prosser and twenty-six of his co-conspirators, President Jefferson suggested that the Virginia assembly consider adopting a deportation law to "remove" the offenders. Jefferson urged Monroe and lawmakers to "stay the hand of the executioner" since "the other states & the world at large will for ever condemn us if we indulge a principle of revenge, or go one step beyond absolute necessity." He recommended instead that the conspirators be sent to a "fort & garrison of the state or of the Union, where they could be confined" until the legislature could "pass a law for their exportation."[13] In 1801, the Virginia General Assembly did adopt a resolution to "purchase lands without the limits of this state, to which persons obnoxious to the laws or dangerous to the peace of society may be removed." Monroe believed that such an acquisition of land "in the vacant western territory of the United States" was suggested by "motives of humanity" as an alternative to the hangman's noose.[14]

But Jefferson instead suggested sending the insurgent blacks beyond the "limits" of the union. He was convinced that those "persons who brought on us the alarm, and on themselves the tragedy, of 1800" should be exiled to a "receptacle" elsewhere in the Atlantic world. The "West Indies offer a more probable & practical retreat for them," since the sugar islands were already "inhabited . . . by a people of their own race & color," he wrote. Indeed, Jefferson suggested, "nature seems to have formed these islands to become the receptacle of the blacks transplanted into this hemisphere." Jefferson imagined most of West Indian slave society, as nodes of chaos and violence, to be on the verge of insurrection. Only in Saint-Domingue had "blacks . . . established into a sovereignty" and "organized themselves under regular laws & government." And even there they posed a threat. Exiled American blacks "might stimulate & conduct vindicative or predatory descents on our coasts." What Jefferson wanted—and what many Virginians hoped for—was to have these "exiles" banished from Virginia forever.[15]

In the summer of 1802, Jefferson could think of no better way to accomplish this goal than to deport the insurrectionists across the Atlantic. He proposed sending them to Africa, to "the English Sierra Leone Company." Begun as a fledgling settlement for black loyalists in 1787 by the British abolitionist Granville Sharp, the colony became the St. George's Bay Company in 1799, and finally the Sierra Leone Company in 1800. The company's mission, supported by abolitionist members of the Clapham sect in London, including William Wilberforce and Zachary Macaulay, was, in Jefferson's mind, "the express purpose of colonizing blacks to that country [Africa]." Jefferson asked a leading Federalist and the U.S. minister to Britain, Rufus King, to "enter into conference with persons private and public as would be necessary to give us permission to send thither" slaves "guilty of insurgency." Deporting slaves to Sierra Leone, Jefferson reasoned, would allow Virginians to "gradually" draw "off this part of our population": rebellious slaves. The "exile" of blacks to Africa might render their "sojournment and sufferings here a blessing in the end to that country," he stated.[16] King wrote to Henry Thornton, the president of the Court of Directors of the Sierra Leone Company, asking for permission to send to Sierra Leone those Virginia "Negroes that from time to time shall be emancipated in that State together with those whose residence in Virginia might prove injurious to the subordination of the slaves."[17]

Thornton balked at the prospect of his colony being flooded with rebellious American slaves. But King tried to reassure a concerned Wilberforce, promising that the exiles "will include our most meritorious slaves and . . . will not be idle and vicious" as "they would not possess sufficient influence over their associates to become Leaders in the Scheme of Insurrection."[18] Of course, what neither Jefferson nor King realized was that Wilberforce and Macaulay did not see Sierra Leone as a "receptacle" for insurgent slaves. Rather, they saw it as a free-labor experiment in Africa; they envisioned it as a counterpoint to the barbarity of the slave trade that plagued Africa's western coasts and an alternative to the slave-based sugar empire of the West

Indies. Sierra Leone was for members of the Clapham sect a first foray into the wilds of Africa, an initial step in the civilizing process that might "improve" Africa and include it in a global free-market society.[19]

Jefferson did not realize that British lawmakers and members of the Sierra Leone Company had already experimented with a similar policy of deportation, sending rebellious blacks to the new colony in Africa. As a result of the Second Maroon War in Jamaica in 1795, those maroons who surrendered to British troops (numbering around six hundred) were deported to Nova Scotia to quell the threat of rebellion on the island. However, the British government soon rethought the choice of settlement, and former maroons were sent to Freetown, Sierra Leone, in 1800. According to the acting American chargé d'affaires in London, Christopher Gore, the "establishment" at Sierra Leone "sufferd much from the maroons, who have been permitted to go there from Jamaica." Indeed, the Court of Directors, Henry Thornton among them, "consider that the rise of their Colony has been rather impeded, than advanced by the Blacks from Nova Scotia." Problems caused by the entrance of the maroons had destabilized the new colony to such an extent that the directors had to petition Parliament for funds and troops to "keep in check the restless, and disturbed spirits already there" and prevent the colonists from seeking to "revolt, & overturn the existing Government." Because the policy of introducing a foreign and formerly rebellious cohort of slaves was already seemingly wreaking havoc in Sierra Leone, the directors were reluctant to potentially exacerbate the situation with the importation of yet another group of rebellious slaves from America. "I do not think there is much reason to hope, that an incorporation of the Blacks of the U. States with those at Sierra Leone, can be reconciled, in the minds of the Directors, to the safety, and prosperity of the establishment," Gore advised Jefferson.[20]

Jefferson's proposal for a "receptacle" for insurgent Virginia slaves differed from the broader repatriation schemes he had articulated in his *Notes* several decades before. Still, his desire to expatriate blacks living on American soil continued to loom large in his imagination, even in the wake of the Prosser conspiracy. All blacks, Jefferson believed, especially those whose "degraded condition" had been ameliorated by benevolent masters, would one day be sent outside of the United States to form their own legitimate and civilized "people." But Jefferson's proposal for a "receptacle" for rebellious bondsmen and free blacks was an important amendment to his repatriation policy. This scheme entailed sending a limited number of blacks, all of whom exhibited violent and barbaric tendencies, to a remote outpost, not to become a legitimate nation but to be severed from Virginia forever. In short, Jefferson maintained a firm commitment to the future emancipation and expatriation of all Virginia slaves, but in moments of exigency, such as the Prosser conspiracy in Richmond, Jefferson's first recourse was not repatriation but deportation and exile.[21]

The contrast and tension between "receptacle" and "nation" reveals just how ill-suited—and unrealistic—Jefferson's Enlightenment narrative of liberal progress was to solving the slavery problem in America. To achieve his goal of creating peaceful, racially homogenous "peoples" through gradual emancipation, Jefferson had to identify all American blacks as a coherent nation, as a bounded population that could be pried out of America and then relocated to Africa. But this was inherently problematic. While Jefferson imagined that it was the transatlantic slave trade—particularly the horror of the Middle Passage—that created blacks' collective sense of themselves as Africans, the opposite was in fact the case. The slave trade actually diffused Africans throughout the Atlantic world, rather than bringing them together as a distinct polity. Moreover, many of the slaves whom Jefferson identified as "African"—including his own bondspeople—were creoles, having lived on American shores for generations. And Jefferson's "enlightened" suggestion that blacks were an innately sovereign, "independant" people on the other side of the Atlantic was undercut by another suggestion, albeit an offensive one, that also drew on the Enlightenment: blacks were "inferior to the whites in the endowments both of body and mind." As Andrew Trees suggests in this volume, Jefferson's application of Enlightenment ideas to racial theory inadvertently allowed him to harden prejudice and retard the very social progress that was supposed to be a central tenet of the Enlightenment. It was this suggestion of inferiority that most deeply influenced the American colonization movement, which overwhelmingly sought to erect a lesser black "colony," rather than a sovereign African state.[22]

Jefferson's actions in the wake of the Gabriel Rebellion allowed many southerners to revise the narrative of liberal progress and gradual antislavery of which repatriation was a crucial step. Instead of viewing colonization as a step toward the eradication of slavery, Jefferson's own actions demonstrated how colonization—now interpreted as "deportation"—could actually strengthen the "peculiar institution" by removing its greatest threat, the free black and insurgent slave population. As a result, Jefferson's co-partisans, both in the North and South, began to advocate the colonization of only a fraction of blacks in America rather than the repatriation of the entire population to Africa. Unintentionally, Jefferson's new policy of deportation allowed his cohorts to use such a strategy to strengthen, rather than erode, slavery in America.[23]

Antislavery and Proslavery "Diffusion"

Despite Jefferson's actions after the Prosser Rebellion of 1800, he continued to believe that the repatriation of an African people was the only way to fulfill his commitment to liberal progress. But with the prospect of the union's expansion westward, Jefferson began to advocate a complementary policy, called "diffusion," that would help make repatriation more feasible and ultimately lead to the extinction of slavery. Jefferson recognized that slave owners would only consent to repatriation if the threat of slave rebellions was quelled in the South and the concentrated population of slaves somehow diluted. But if slaves were spread westward, either through the domestic slave trade or whites' migration with their chattel in tow, he reasoned, then the reduced number of slaves in eastern states—at least in the Upper South—would allow planters to enact gradual abolition laws. Between the 1790s and the Missouri crisis, diffusionists who hailed from both Federalist and Republican camps advocated the "diffusion" of slavery westward as a step toward eradicating the institution.[24]

That slavery could "diffuse" to new states in the West and thereby hasten gradual emancipation in the old states in the East may seem implausible in hindsight. Reassurances from Jefferson that "spreading them over a greater surface, will dilute the evil everywhere" seem ludicrous now that we know that the "peculiar institution" was both a modern and self-regenerating system. Even Jefferson's fellow antislavery advocate the Marquis de Lafayette was skeptical, despite experimenting with gradual emancipation schemes on his own plantation in Cayenne in the 1780s. "Are you Sure, My dear Friend, that Extending the principle of Slavery to the New Raised States is a Method to facilitate the Means of Getting Rid of it? I would have thought that By Spreading the prejudices, Habits, and Calculations of planters over a larger Surface You Rather Encrease the difficulties of final liberation," the marquis asked his old friend. But Jefferson endorsed the "dissemination" of slavery because he was convinced, like other Democratic-Republicans and

Federalists, that the U.S. slave population would remain static without fresh supplies of African captives brought through the transatlantic slave trade. In other words, if the slave population did not increase, then spreading their fixed numbers over a greater geographical space did not seem so far-fetched.[25]

Diffusion first seemed like a viable plan to weaken slavery during the latter 1790s, when congressional leaders debated the organization of the new Mississippi Territory. Several restrictionists, including Republican Albert Gallatin of Pennsylvania, Federalist George Thacher of Massachusetts, and Republican Joseph Varnum of Massachusetts, argued that slavery should be banned in the new territory, just as it had been in the Northwest Territory, citing slavery as a moral evil that violated the natural rights upon which the new nation was founded. But diffusionists argued that the spread of slaves westward would actually be a more viable way of gradually eradicating slavery. Virginia Republican William Giles suggested that "if the slaves of the Southern States were permitted to go into the Western country, by lessening the number in those [eastern] States, and spreading them over a large surface of country, there would be a great probability in ameliorating their condition, which could never be done whilst they were crowded together as they now are in the Southern States." Highly concentrated slave populations, southerners believed, drastically increased the threat of slave insurrection. By contrast, the promise of the reduction of slaves' numbers in the South through diffusion westward would ensure that "in time it might be safe to carry into effect the plan which certain philanthropists have so much at heart"—the "emancipation of this class of men." In the end, leaders from both parties voted for a pro-diffusionist policy in the new Mississippi lands. While "foreign" slaves would be banned, planters could bring slaves to the new territories from within the United States.[26]

In 1803, President Jefferson lobbied Congress to implement a territorial bill that included this policy of diffusion. Relying on Kentucky Republican John Breckinridge as one of his primary political operatives, Jefferson sought to convince Congress that diffusion was a great panacea—it would keep the prospect of a future end to slavery alive, solve the problem of an increasing slave population in the eastern states, and satisfy expansionists who believed that slavery was the only way to successfully colonize the West. But diffusion as a stepping stone to future emancipation would only remain plausible if Louisiana was prevented from importing new slaves from Africa or the West Indies. Surprisingly, most congressional leaders supported a ban on the international slave trade to Louisiana, the prevention of foreign planters from entering the territory with their slaves, and the prohibition of South Carolina or Georgia slave dealers from selling new slave imports to eager Louisiana buyers. These regulations would have the effect of both "domesticating" the Louisiana Territory and cordoning off the area from potentially incendiary outside influences in the Caribbean. As Senator Breckinridge warned, "unless we mean to aid the destruction of our Southern states, by laying the foundation for another St. Domingo," then the importation of foreign slaves into Louisiana must be outlawed. With peace and security so tenuous in the overextended republic, policymakers were eager to do all they could to prevent a devastating slave rebellion from being unleashed in Louisiana.[27]

But even if the banning of international influences—including slaves—was a critical part of the new diffusion policy for Louisiana, it was less certain whether or how U.S. slaves might enter the new territory. The majority of Federalists and Democratic-Republicans favored some way to send "domestic" slaves westward, either through an internal slave trade or by allowing white settlers to bring their chattel with them. However, James Hillhouse, a Federalist senator from Connecticut, proposed that any adult slave carried by an American into the Louisianas would be emancipated after living in the territory for one year. And younger slaves would receive their freedom when they came of age. Yet this proposal for more explicit gradual emancipation, which echoed the Northwest Ordinance, was defeated by seemingly antislavery Federalists like Timothy Pickering and John Quincy Adams, as well as more predictable proslavery Republicans like Ohioan John Smith. But this did not mean that congressmen, even those Republicans who represented planter interests in states like North Carolina and Kentucky, were not in favor of some sort of restriction on the spread of slavery to Louisiana. In fact, lawmakers who stood the most to gain from a domestic slave trade to the West—mostly in Upper South states that lacked cotton or sugar as cash crops—actually voted to ban such a commerce in 1803. Nonetheless, believing that the security and economic viability of Louisiana rested on the presence of slavery, at least initially, both factions voted in favor of the requirement that new slaves be accompanied by owners who intended to reside in the new territory. Slavery would expand and spread westward, but only against the backdrop of very stringent regulations. Still, the policy of diffusion passed by lawmakers in 1803—which was later repealed in

1805—represented the last time that that a bipartisan agreement to restrict slavery was reached, and the last time that diffusion was deployed with intended antislavery outcomes.[28]

Until 1819, diffusion was widely embraced by politicians of all stripes as a means of controlling and ultimately abolishing slavery while mitigating the threat to geopolitical and economic interests in the West. But the Missouri crisis fundamentally changed the slavery question, thus also altering the definition of diffusion. The crisis that was unleashed when Missouri threatened to become a slave state in the union through popular sovereignty "irrevocably changed the orientation of the slavery expansion quandary," transforming what was "a problem of the West" into a "crisis that defined and divided a free North from a slave South." Northern restrictionists, now composed largely of Federalists, sought to reinvent themselves as a sectional antislavery party that functioned as the true repository of the founders' antislavery beliefs and republican principles. Proslavery southerners, on the other hand, largely banding around the Democratic-Republicans, viewed themselves as the protectors of an institution that had been sanctioned for centuries, first under the aegis of the British Empire and then under the terms of the U.S. Constitution. In the process of remaking themselves—and their party—southerners also transformed slavery from a state issue into a national one. And they reimagined the future of slavery. Instead of the "peculiar institution" being ameliorated and diffused toward eradication, slavery would now be a permanent presence in the South and West.[29]

Jefferson, for whom the Missouri crisis was a "fire bell in the night," placed the blame squarely on the shoulders of northern restrictionists. He saw the Missouri question as "a mere party trick." The "leaders of federalism, defeated in their schemes of obtaining power by rallying partisans to the principle of monarchism," he wrote to Charles Pinckney in 1820, "have changed their tack, and . . . are taking advantage of the virtuous feelings of the people to effect a division of parties by a geographical line." Restrictionists, Jefferson believed, sought to use the slavery question to garner power, to pit supposedly proslavery against antislavery, to set section against section and divide the union. But even if northern Federalists sought to style themselves as the antislavery party by promoting the restriction of slavery, Jefferson responded that efforts to contain the institution were far from moral. For the previous two decades, during the debates about slavery's expansion into the western territories, southerners—and many northerners—had agreed that a concentrated slave population in the East translated into more brutal conditions for bondspeople and an increased threat of rebellion. In Jefferson's eyes, diffusion was the only moral recourse, since spreading slaves across the continent ameliorated their condition and alleviated the threat of race war. Through their migration westward, slaves' "happiness will be increased, & the burthen of their future liberation lightened by bringing a greater number of shoulders under it." Jefferson believed that diffusion would dilute slavery and erode support for the institution, thereby convincing slave owners in the West to emancipate their bondspeople in future time.[30]

Crucially, Jefferson's belief that slavery must be allowed to spread if there was to be any hope for future emancipation represented a minority viewpoint in the South by the time of the Missouri crisis. While Jefferson had always championed antislavery diffusion as part and parcel of party ideology, the irony was that his best intentions actually produced a more proslavery South. As a result of the Missouri issue, his co-partisans took an antislavery diffusion policy and turned it around. No longer would expansion and diffusion lead to gradual emancipation. Instead, diffusion would result in the extension of slavery westward and the continued presence of the peculiar institution in the Atlantic states. Proslavery—the belief in slavery's permanence and in its function as a vital link between eastern and western economies—was a new argument galvanized by the Missouri crisis. For southern Democratic-Republicans, proslavery diffusion alleviated the threat of slave revolt in the South by "draining" bondspeople to the West in addition to allowing slave owners to capitalize on a burgeoning market for slave-grown cotton. Thus, the narrative of liberal progress and commitment to gradual abolition that Jefferson had laid down at the American founding was eclipsed by a new commitment to proslavery.[31]

In many ways, the change from a policy of antislavery diffusion to proslavery diffusion reflected new ways of thinking about American slavery in the nineteenth century. For Jefferson and other like-minded patriots, an "enlightened" narrative of liberal progress, and the antislavery diffusion that undergirded it, was predicated on some important assumptions. The first was that slavery was an archaic institution incapable of being sustained without the transatlantic slave trade. What made the slave population climb in the southern states between 1776 and 1808 was a robust slave trade with Africa and the West Indies, Jefferson reasoned. A second assumption was that slavery posed a direct threat to an extremely fragile union of states. Since the two races had a naturally inimical relationship that could never be reconciled, race war and disunion would be the inevitable future outcome if slavery continued in America. Jefferson himself predicted "doom" if Americans did nothing about the slavery problem. White Americans in the "whole South" would "fall . . . in the ruin of their people or in the overthrow of their republican liberties, in consequence of the inevitable workings of that most unfortunate institution," he warned.[32]

But the two assumptions that buttressed the antislavery diffusion policy promoted by Jefferson and many of his peers were rejected by the 1810s and 1820s. Without the transatlantic slave trade, the American slave population was not contracting, as Jefferson had prophesied. Instead, the population self-reproduced its numbers—from about 1.13 million in 1810 to nearly 2 million by 1830. This seemed to indicate that the peculiar institution was a modern system rather than an archaic one. And the genocidal race war that Jefferson believed would be unleashed should slavery continue to expand in America seemed like a mere chimera. Thomas Roderick Dew, a proslavery critic of Jeffersonian antislavery, was one of the first southerners to revise Jefferson's definition of slavery as a "state of war." Dew asserted there was no real antipathy between the races—it was a "monstrous error" to suppose that "every slave in the slave-holding country" was "actuated by the most deadly enmity" that would lead him to "murder and assassinate" whites. Instead of plotting or executing violence against whites, Dew argued, "the slave . . . generally loves his master and his family." Through the process of amelioration, the enmity between the races had been permanently assuaged, Dew argued.[33]

Dew suggested that the "boisterous passions" that Jefferson had described had been muted and transformed into familial ties of sympathy. Slaves' "domestication"—their inclusion within a household—constituted concrete evidence that white Virginians had progressed from the "hunting into the shepherd and agricultural states." For Dew, the ownership of enslaved people allowed hunter-gatherers to be transformed from "savage and brutal" beings into matriarchs and patriarchs whose households were defined by "kindness and benevolence" toward all dependents, including slaves.[34]

Democratic Republicans' new adoption of "diffusion" as part of a coherent proslavery ideology, as well as the marginalization of repatriation schemes to Africa, opened the door to the American slave system's explosive growth in the antebellum era. After the Missouri crisis, the unrestricted expansion of the peculiar institution undergirded the creation of new slaveholding states in the West as well as the "improvement" and progress of established states on the Atlantic coast. And slaves' "condition"—which whites interpreted as improving over time—was inextricably linked to the progressive condition of the union. As the West was opened, millions of acres of these newly "empty" lands were sold to profit-seeking speculators and settlers whose new investments were backed by British capital. Usually it was the enslaved who "settled" these new lands—they cut down forests, drained swamps, and created fields for cultivation. This "civilization" of the western landscape was a brutal task, but the forced migration of enslaved laborers through the domestic slave trade—nearly 1 million men, women, and children were sold to buyers in the Deep South—assured that new planters' insatiable demand for slave labor was never wanting. Slaves, as laborers and as commodities, became central to the credit economy of the vast American cotton empire, fueling the industrialization of Britain and making America one of the leading capitalist economies in the world by 1860.[35]

Conclusion: War and Epochal Change

Jefferson firmly believed that adhering to Enlightenment policies, including antislavery, would always lead to "enlightened outcomes." Rather than departing from his principles as slavery expanded and grew more entrenched in the South throughout his lifetime, Jefferson instead clung to Enlightenment ideas as his only polestar in a world that he did not foresee, governed by forces that he did not recognize. Despite burgeoning proslavery sentiment among his southern peers, Jefferson continued to advocate his "stale and thread-bare" proposals, rooted in the Enlightenment, to end slavery. As Andrew Trees demonstrates in this volume, Jefferson's Enlightenment thinking led him toward a radical, Manichean vision of good and evil that pushed him to prophesize large-scale destruction—even apocalypse—should his narrative of liberal progress be ignored. Jefferson stubbornly declared that the end of slavery was inevitable—the "hour of emancipation is advancing in the march of time." It would come in one of two ways: through a majority decision by slave owners to consent to free their human property and send them to Africa, or "by the bloody process of St Domingo, excited and conducted by the power of our present enemy." Like his observations about revolutionary Europe in the 1820s, Jefferson suggested that an end to slavery likely would not be a peaceful or immediate turn of events. Indeed, "rivers of blood" might also flow in the federal union, in a great race war fought between whites and blacks, which would decimate one of the two "nations" that occupied the same soil.[36]

But the vision of good and evil, the binary of slavery and freedom, that Jefferson's radical Enlightenment led him to imagine prevented him from comprehending the unintended consequences of his own antislavery ideas. For Jefferson, there was only one narrative of liberal progress in America: the erosion of slavery and tyranny. But even if Jefferson's Enlightenment may have introduced and circulated the possibility of equality and liberty for all humankind, he could not comprehend that this did not mean such notions would be universally embraced or applied in the nineteenth century. In reality, many proslavery southerners, including many of his own co-partisans, eschewed Jefferson's "enlightened" narrative, substituting a new version in its place. Also viewing themselves as children of the Enlightenment, southerners formulated a new script for national progress and created their own "improved" vision of the modern world, a world built on the presence of an "ameliorated" slave regime.[37]

Notes

1. Daniel Pierce Thompson, "A Talk with Jefferson," *Harper's New Monthly Magazine,* May 1863, 833–35; Thomas Jefferson, *Summary View of the Rights of British America* [1774], in Merrill D. Peterson, ed., *Jefferson: Writings* (New York, 1984), 106; Peter S. Onuf, *Jefferson's Empire: The Language of American Nationhood* (Charlottesville, Va., 2000), 6–7; David Brion Davis, *Slavery and Human Progress* (New York, 1984). On the concept of "amelioration" as the mitigation of social and political evils, including slavery, see Christa Dierksheide, *Amelioration and Empire: Progress and Slavery in Plantation America, 1770–1840* (Charlottesville, Va., 2014).

2. Thompson, "A Talk with Jefferson"; Merrill D. Peterson, *The Jefferson Image in the American Mind* (New York, 1960), 480; Thomas Jefferson, "Thoughts on Lotteries, ca. 20 Jan. 1826, 20 January 1826," Founders Online, National Archives, Washington, D.C., http://founders.archives.gov/documents/Jefferson/98-01-02-5845.

3. Peter Onuf refers to Jefferson's "later antirestrictionist, proslavery posture" in *Jefferson's Empire,* 11. See also Paul Finkleman, "Thomas Jefferson and Slavery: 'Treason against the Hopes of the World,'" in *Jeffersonian Legacies,* ed. Peter S. Onuf (Charlottesville, Va., 1993), 181–221, and William W. Freehling, "The Founding Fathers and Conditional Antislavery," in *The Reintegration of American History: Slavery and the Civil War* (New York, 1994), 12–33.

4. Patrick Henry, Speech to the Virginia House of Burgesses, Jan. 18, 1773, Granville Sharp Papers, reel 1, New-York Historical Society.

5. Eliga H. Gould, *Among the Powers of the Earth: The American Revolution and the Making of a New World Empire* (Cambridge, Mass., 2012), 14–47; Christa Dierksheide, "'The Great Improvement and Civilization of That Race': Jefferson and the 'Amelioration' of Slavery, ca. 1770–1826," *Early American Studies* 6, no. 1 (Spring 2008): 165–97; Thomas Jefferson, "Sixth Annual Message," Dec. 2, 1806, *Annals of Congress,* Senate, 9th Cong., 2nd sess., 11–16.

6. "Thomas Jefferson to Edward Coles, 25 August 1814," Founders Online, http://founders.archives.gov/documents/Jefferson/03-07-02-0439.

7. Arator [John Taylor of Caroline], *Being a Series of Agricultural Essays, Practical and Political* (Richmond, Va., 1803), 74.

8. Philip D. Morgan, "Ending the Slave Trade: A Caribbean and Atlantic Context," in *Abolitionism and Imperialism in Britain, Africa, and the Atlantic,* ed. Derek R. Peterson (Athens, Ohio, 2010), 110; Dierksheide, *Amelioration and Empire,* 1–33.

9. "Thomas Jefferson to John Lynch, 21 January 1811," Founders Online, http://founders.archives.gov/documents/Jefferson/03-03-02-0243.

10. Quoted in Philip D. Morgan, *Slave Counterpoint: Black Culture in the Eighteenth-Century Chesapeake and Lowcountry* (Chapel Hill, N.C., 1998), 667.

11. Mosby Sheppard to James Monroe, Aug. 30, 1800, in *Journal of the Senate of the Commonwealth of Virginia* (Richmond, Va., 1801), 26. Pharoah and Tom were emancipated as a result of their demonstration of loyalty; they also adopted the name "Sheppard." James Sidbury, *Ploughshares into Swords: Race, Rebellion, and Identity in Gabriel's Virginia, 1730–1810* (New York, 1997), 107.

12. Monroe to Jefferson, Sept. 15, 1800, in Stanislaus Murray Hamilton, ed., *The Writings of James Monroe* (New York, 1900), 3:208–9.

13. "Thomas Jefferson to James Monroe, 20 September 1800," Founders Online, http://founders.archives.gov/documents/Jefferson/01-32-02-0097.

14. "Thomas Jefferson from James Monroe, 15 June 1801," Founders Online, http://founders.archives.gov/documents/Jefferson/01-34-02-0274.

15. "Thomas Jefferson to James Monroe, 24 November 1801," Founders Online, http://founders.archives.gov/documents/Jefferson/01-35-02-0550.

16. Jefferson to Rufus King, July 13, 1802, Thomas Jefferson Papers, Library of Congress, Washington, D.C.

17. Rufus King to Henry Thornton, Apr. 30, 1803, ibid.

18. Rufus King to William Wilberforce, Jan. 8, 1803, ibid.

19. For more on the importance of Africa to Anglo-Americans, see Philip Stern, "'Rescuing the Age from a Charge of Ignorance': Gentility, Knowledge, and the British Exploration of Africa in the Later Eighteenth Century," in *A New Imperial History: Culture, Identity and Modernity in Britain and the Empire, 1660–1840,* ed. Kathleen Wilson (Cambridge, 2004), 115–35.

20. "Thomas Jefferson from Christopher Gore, 10 October 1802," Founders Online, http://founders.archives.gov/documents/Jefferson/01-38-02-0434.

21. Onuf, *Jefferson's Empire,* 178–82.

22. On the tension in American colonizationists' thinking between a black "nation" or "colony," see Nicholas Guyatt, *Bind Us Apart: A Prehistory of "Separate but Equal"* (New York, 2015); Guyatt, "'The Outskirts of Our Happiness': Race and the Lure of Colonization in the Early Republic," *Journal of American History* 95 (Mar. 2009): 986–1011; Thomas Jefferson, *Notes on the State of Virginia,* ed. William Peden (Chapel Hill, N.C., 1982), 138–43; and Andrew Trees, "Apocalypse Now: Thomas Jefferson's Radical Enlightenment," in this volume.

23. Matthew Mason, *Slavery and Politics in the Early Republic* (Chapel Hill, N.C., 2006), 112–13.

24. John Craig Hammond, *Slavery, Freedom, and Expansion in the Early American West* (Charlottesville, Va., 2007), 36, 44–45; Onuf, *Jefferson's Empire,* 185–86.

25. Jefferson to Lafayette, Dec. 26, 1820; Lafayette to Jefferson, July 1, 1821; June 1, 1822, in Gilbert Chinard, ed., *Letters of Lafayette and Jefferson* (Baltimore, 1929), 402, 407, 409.

26. *Annals of Congress,* 5th Cong., 2nd sess., 8:1306–10; Adam Rothman, *Slave Country: American Expansion and the Origins of the Deep South* (Cambridge, Mass., 2005), 22–27, 213.

27. Notes on Administration of Louisiana Territory, 1803; Jefferson to Albert Gallatin, Oct. 29, Nov. 9, 1803, Jefferson Papers, Library of Congress; Hammond, *Slavery, Freedom, and Expansion,* 37; Everett S. Brown, "The Senate Debate on the Breckinridge Bill for the Government of Louisiana," *American Historical Review* 22, no. 1 (1917): 349, 354.

28. George William Van Cleve, *A Slaveholders' Union: Slavery, Politics, and the Constitution in the Early American Republic* (Chicago, 2010), 218–19; Hammond, *Slavery, Freedom, and Expansion,* 44–45.

29. Hammond, *Slavery, Freedom, and Expansion,* 151. On the Missouri crisis and the slavery question, see Mason, *Slavery and Politics,* 177–212; Van Cleve, *Slaveholders' Union,* 225–66; Robert P. Forbes, *The Missouri Crisis and Its Aftermath: Slavery and the Meaning of America* (Chapel Hill, N.C., 2007); Sean Wilentz, *The Rise of American Democracy: Jefferson to Lincoln* (New York, 2005), 218–35; and Leonard Richards, *The Slave Power: The Free North and Southern Domination, 1780–1860* (Baton Rouge, La., 2000), 52–82.

30. "Thomas Jefferson to John Holmes, April 22, 1820," Founders Online, http://founders.archives.gov/documents/Jefferson/98-01-02-1234; "Thomas Jefferson to Charles Pinckney, September 30, 1820," Founders Online, http://founders.archives.gov/documents/Jefferson/03-07-02-0439; "Thomas Jefferson to John Holmes, 22 April 1820," Founders Online, http://founders.archives.gov/documents/Jefferson/98-01-02-1234.

31. Hammond, *Slavery, Freedom, and Expansion,* 165; William W. Freehling, *The Road to Disunion,* vol. 1, *Secessionists at Bay, 1776–1854* (New York, 1990), 150–57; Drew R. McCoy, *The Last of the Fathers: James Madison and the Republican Legacy* (New York, 1989), 253–322.

32. Dierksheide, *Amelioration and Empire,* chapter 1; Thompson, "A Talk with Jefferson."

33. "Slave Population, 1810, 1830," Historical Census Browser, University of Virginia, Geospatial and Statistical Data Center, http://mapserver.lib.virginia.edu/collections/stats/histcensus/index.html; Thomas R. Dew, *Review of the Debate in the Virginia Legislature of 1831 and 1832* (Richmond, Va., 1832), 6, 66, 113; Peter S. Onuf, "Domesticating the Captive Nation: Thomas Jefferson and the Problem of Slavery," in *Jefferson, Lincoln, and Wilson: The American Dilemma of Race and Democracy,* ed. Thomas J. Knock and John Milton Cooper Jr. (Charlottesville, Va., 2010), 34–60.

34. Dew, *Review of the Debate,* 36–37.

35. Walter Johnson, "King Cotton's Long Shadow," *New York Times,* Mar. 31, 2013; Joshua D. Rothman, *Flush Times and Fever Dreams: A Story of Capitalism and Slavery in the Age of Jackson* (Athens, Ga., 2012); Walter Johnson, *River of Dark Dreams: Slavery, Capitalism, and Imperialism in the Mississippi Valley's Cotton Kingdom* (Cambridge, Mass., 2013); Calvin Schermerhorn, *The Business of Slavery and the Rise of American Capitalism* (New Haven, Conn., 2015).

36. "Thomas Jefferson to James Heaton, 20 May 1826," Founders Online, http://founders.archives.gov/documents/Jefferson/98-01-02-6127; "Thomas Jefferson to Edward Coles, 25 August 1814," Founders Online, http://founders.archives.gov/documents/Jefferson/03-07-02-0439.

37. Dierksheide, *Amelioration and Empire,* conclusion.

12 The Constitutional Statesmanship of James Madison

Richard Samuelson

In the fall of 1814, William Wirt visited President James Madison, finding him "miserably shattered and woe-begone. . . . He looked heart-broken. His mind is full of the New England sedition."[1] The sacking of Washington, D.C., not long before was probably also on his mind. Things soon changed. The war ended with no territorial loss to the United States, and General Andrew Jackson's smashing victory in New Orleans gave Americans a surge of patriotism. Meanwhile, the Hartford Convention, with its hints of secession, destroyed the Federalist Party. Yet Madison hardly felt vindicated. Events had made a hash of the Republican program.[2]

Madison's seventh annual message revealed a transformed Republican vision. The union needed a standing army, a "peace establishment," for "notwithstanding the security for future repose which the United States ought to find in their love of peace and their constant respect for the rights of other nations, the character of the times particularly inculcates the lesson that, whether to prevent or repel danger, we ought not to be unprepared for it." Moreover, it needed "a liberal provision for the immediate extension and gradual completion of the works of defense, both fixed and floating." Beyond that, the federal government required additional war powers to ensure that the military could act promptly and effectively: "With this subject is intimately connected the necessity of accommodating the laws in every respect to the great object of enabling the political authority of the Union to employ promptly and effectually the physical power of the Union in the cases designated by the Constitution." In addition, "the embarrassments arising from the want of an uniform national currency" made a national bank necessary.[3] The president also asked Congress to encourage manufactures: "Experience teaches that so many circumstances must concur in introducing and maturing manufacturing establishments." To foster manufacturing establishments, he pointed to the tariff: "Adjusting the duties on imports to the object of revenue the influence of the tariff on manufactures will necessarily present itself for consideration." And he promoted internal improvements, noting their economic benefits and adding that they would also help bind the union together: "The political effect of these facilities for intercommunication in bringing and binding more closely together the various parts of our extended confederacy."[4]

These prescriptions represented a rejection of significant parts of the Republican program of the 1790s and early 1800s. In essence, Madison endorsed what would become known as the "American System" of Henry Clay as the means of sustaining republican government despite the failure of his fondest hopes.

Limited Government and the Politics of Peace

To understand the transformation of Madison's vision and the challenge he faced at the end of his presidency, one should consider his point of departure. Madison is often contrasted with Thomas Jefferson as the more sober of the pair. There is some truth in the idea, and yet it is worth remembering that Madison endorsed a fairly radical program. He and Jefferson had been partners in this radical project. They believed that the short list of powers explicitly granted to the federal government under the Constitution were sufficient. America's "compound republic" represented a bold new departure in republican politics.[5]

What, pace Madison, distinguished America's compound republic from republics of old? In Federalist 10, Madison argued that large republics were better than small. They would make majority tyranny unlikely: "Extend the sphere, and you take in a greater variety of parties and interests; you make it less probable that a majority of the whole will have a common motive to invade the rights of other citizens." In sum, "in the extent and proper structure of the union, therefore, we behold a republican remedy for the diseases most incident to republican government."[6] Note that Madison highlighted the "proper structure of the union" along with the extended sphere. Federalism and a strictly limited federal government were closely related in Madison's mind.

Creating an extended republic, in contrast with the small republics of the ancient world and of medieval Italy, was for Madison the *primary* means of reconciling wisdom with consent. In Federalist 51, he argued that "a dependence on the people, is, no doubt, the primary control on the government," but in his view, the people could only be depended on in an extended republic. Factions would wreck a small republic, and, as he noted in Federalist 10, "the vicious arts, by which elections are too often carried" would succeed. By contrast, "in the large [rather] than the small, republic, it will be more difficult for unworthy candidates" to win. In an extended republic, "the suffrages of the people being more free, [they] will be more likely to centre on men who possess the most attractive merit, and the most diffusive and established characters."[7] Large republics, Madison expected, would elect better men than would small republics. These men would discern "the true interest of their country" and not merely negotiate among groups.[8] Checks and balances, a feature virtually absent from his Virginia plan proposed at the federal convention, were "auxiliary precautions." The extended republic was primary.

This extended republic featured a limited federal government. Majority tyranny was less likely in an extended republic, Madison thought, because most issues upon which a majority could be assembled in Congress would be, in fact, good for the republic in general—"the true interest of their country." If the list of federal powers expanded, however, it would be easier for leaders in Congress to create bills that pleased several minority factions, combining them together to produce bills to gain a majority in the House, subverting the design Madison outlined in Federalist 10.

What kind of thing was an extended republic? Small republics regulated human life intimately, as in ancient Sparta. In a classic republic, the laws actively enforced a particular way of life. In an extended republic, by contrast, they did not. That was partly a practical necessity. The kind of community present in a small republic was impossible in a geographically large and populous land. Relatedly, ancient and medieval republics often had aristocrats and kings. Modern republics would not.[9] They also would have no religious establishment. In the *Spirit of the Laws,* Montesquieu argued that republics were suited to small territories and monarchies to larger lands, but he also suggested a confederation of republics might govern a larger territory. As Colleen Sheehan notes in *The Mind of James Madison,* Madison took Montesquieu's suggestion and transformed it into his vision of the American federal republic.[10] Such a regime could remain republican only if its central powers were few and clearly defined.

Expand federal power and the union would be transformed from a compound republic to an extensive nation in need of, as Montesquieu noted, a monarchy. Madison made that point in the "Report of 1800," his most considered response to the political fights of the late 1790s. According to Madison, "the obvious tendency and inevitable result of a consolidation of the States into one sovereignty, would be to transform the republican system of the United States into a monarchy." Why?

> One consequence must be, to enlarge the sphere of discretion allotted to the Executive Magistrate. Even within the legislative limits properly defined by the Constitution, the difficulty of accommodating legal regulations to a country so great in extent and so various in its circumstances has been much felt, and has lead to occasional investments of power in the Executive, which involve perhaps as large a portion of discretion as can be deemed consistent with the nature of the Executive trust. In proportion as the objects of legislative care might be multiplied, would the time allowed for each be diminished, and the difficulty of providing uniform and particular regulations for all be increased. From these sources would necessarily ensue a greater latitude to the agency of that department which is always in existence, and which could best mould regulations of a general nature so as to suit them to the diversity of particular situations. And it is in this latitude, as a supplement to the deficiency of the laws, that the degree of Executive prerogative materially consists.

Expanding the number of objects of federal concern would, of necessity, "enlarge the sphere of discretion allotted to the Executive." It would be unjust and arbitrary to apply a uniform code across a large, diverse land once the federal government regulated more than those few objects suited to such uniform regulation. The result would be government by executive discretion, rather than by legislation made by the people's elected representatives. Montesquieu was correct: consolidated national power tended toward monarchy in a large territory.[11]

From this perspective, the Federalist agenda, or what Madison understood to be the Federalist agenda, did in fact represent a turn to monarchy.[12] Monarchical corruption would follow from the expansion of federal power:

"The patronage of the Executive would necessarily be as much swelled in this case as its prerogative would be in the other." That would corrupt elections, for "this disproportionate increase of prerogative and patronage must, evidently, either enable the Chief Magistrate of the Union, by quiet means, to secure his re-election from time to time, and finally to regulate the succession as he might please; or, by giving so transcendent an importance to the office, would render the elections to it so violent and corrupt, that the public voice itself might call for an hereditary in place of an elective succession."[13] Hence, Madison, Jefferson, and their friends reasoned, Alexander Hamilton was a "monocrat." Monarchy was the logical political result of his program.

Madisonian government was national in scope but limited in its legal reach. On many issues, of course, the federal government simply had no power.[14] Even within those areas that belonged to the sphere of the federal government's authority, the constitutional grant of power was to use that power in a particular way. In *A Government Out of Sight,* Brian Balogh notes that the federal government in its sphere was present but seldom seen.[15] In Madison's view, that was part of the constitutional mandate. It was the constitution the people ratified, the means necessary to preserve the "compound" nature of the republic. Beyond that it was the best means to ensure that the people, rather than a governing class, ruled. To switch to a more active approach would be to point back toward monarchy and aristocracy, to a regime of leaders and followers. Such a change would represent, from Madison's perspective, a change of regime in the Aristotelian sense of the term.

Madison reasoned that this republic would be a commercial republic. To grasp this dimension of Madison's thought it might help to consider the French turn in his thought. Since Douglas Adair's path-breaking work in the 1950s, Madison's argument for an extended republic has been connected with David Hume.[16] There is much to this argument, but there may also be a French connection to Madison's ideas. As Colleen Sheehan notes, French thinkers like the Marquis de Condorcet and Jean-Jacques Bathélemy were important in Madison's studies. A close reading suggests that Voltaire was also significant in Madison's hopes.[17] Toward the end of Federalist 10, Madison writes that "a religious sect, may degenerate into a political faction in one part of the confederacy." The remedy? "The variety of sects dispersed over the entire face of it must secure the national councils against any danger from that source."[18] Similarly, in Federalist 51, Madison argued that "in a free government, the security for civil rights must be the same as that for religious rights. It consists in the one case in the multiplicity of interests, and in the other, in the multiplicity of sects. The degree of security in both cases will depend on the number of interests and sects."[19]

Madison often made this connection between the multiplicity of sects and the enjoyment of religious liberty, sometimes, as in Federalist 51, comparing the two explicitly.[20] Why? And why mention religion at all in Federalist 10 and 51? It might have to do with Voltaire's influence.[21] In a famous passage in his *Letters from England,* Voltaire wrote, "Take a view of the Royal Exchange in London, a place more venerable than many courts of justice, where the representatives of all nations meet for the benefit of mankind. There the Jew, the Mahometan, and the Christian transact together, as though they all professed the same religion, and give the name of infidel to none but bankrupts." He continued a few sentences later: "If one religion only were allowed in England, the Government would very possibly become arbitrary; if there were but two, the people would cut one another's throats; but as there are such a multitude, they all live happy and in peace."[22] Madison was fond of that passage and often quoted it.[23] Note that Voltaire combines religious liberty, religious pluralism, and commerce in one short anecdote. Given liberty and the security of property of all kinds, it would be, pace Voltaire, "as though they all professed the same religion," however individuals worshiped God in their congregations and at home. Presumably the law left each citizen free to manage his business in accord with his conscience too. In dealing with others, only the rules of the exchange would apply.

Madison followed Voltaire's logic. In his essay on "Property," Madison noted that "government is instituted to protect property of every sort. . . . This being the end of government, that alone is a *just* government, which *impartially* secures to every man, whatever is his *own.*" And in that essay Madison emphasized a man's property in his conscientious beliefs: "He has a property of particular value in his religious opinions."[24] A good regime secured one's real property and the property one has in religious beliefs. Civil society, the realm of both commercial and religious action, was independent of government; indeed, good government would secure liberty in those realms. It provided the framework in which men could pursue happiness; it did not tell them how to act in the day-to-day business.

This republican regime would train a particular sort of citizen. Classically, small republics had employed religion to train men in virtue, as in Sparta. They had also had mixed feelings about commerce. Madison's republic, by contrast, was both extensive and emphatically commercial. Self-interest, rightly understood, would produce republican sentiment and the patriotism necessary to secure the union, Madison thought, but it could only do so in a government that was not "consolidated."[25] This regime would foster what much of America became in the nineteenth century—a nation of joiners.

The Snake in Madison's Garden

There was one major problem with this republican vision. There were other nations in the world. Madison thought American economic might would be enough to ensure markets and peace. In fact, the problem of the American republic's relations with other nations were the shoals upon which his vision broke. Long ago Drew R. McCoy pointed to this dimension of Madison's statecraft. Republican farmers were not slothful. On the contrary, they worked hard and produced surplus crops. They would need markets or their hard work would soon go to waste, and in time their work ethic would atrophy. That left Americans in some respects dependent on other nations as markets for their goods.[26]

How could Madison ensure access to markets? The Jay Treaty submitted to British misbehavior in exchange for commercial access. The Federalist alternative to such a treaty was to make war to secure markets. That was the old madness, the Federalist "heresy."[27] War would, moreover, concentrate power in federal hands and teach American citizens to be soldiers and not citizens. Submission was a return to colonial dependence.

In Madison's scheme, commercial interest and commercial coercion provided an alternative approach that was neither war nor submission. He put it this way in a 1794 speech: "Measures of moderation, firmness, and decision . . . were now necessary to be adopted, in order to narrow the sphere of our commerce with those nations who see proper not to meet us on terms of reciprocity." The choice of terms is highly suggestive. "Narrow the sphere of our commerce" with the British and they will fall into line. Remaining outside the republic of commerce was no more an option for Britain than it was for America.[28] Mutually assured commercial destruction would render war moot. No army, navy, or bank would be necessary. To serve commercial goals without warmongering, commercial coercion would be sufficient. Historian J. C. A. Stagg described Madison's logic, noting that Britain was:

> vulnerable to the risks of diplomatic isolation, while the social strains created by war threatened upheaval at home. Indeed, Madison did not entirely dismiss the possibility that Britain would suffer the loss of its trade from a combination of rival European powers and undergo internal revolution as a consequence, which would bring in its aftermath another republic in the concert of nations. Thus, in a period when Madison believed the progression of events was toward freer trade and freer governments, Britain would, . . . be hard pressed to maintain its 'monopolizing' practices of the past.[29]

Madison was confident that Britain would have to surrender to American commercial restrictions, for "her merchants would feel it. Her navigation would feel it. Her manufactures would feel it. Her West-Indies would be ruined by it. Her revenue would deeply feel it. And her government would feel thro' every nerve of its operations." To be sure, he recognized, "we too should suffer in some respects, but in a less degree, and, if the virtue and temper of our fellow citizens were not mistaken, the experiment would find in them a far greater readiness to bear it." Moreover, it was a low risk policy: "Of all the objections which Mr. Madison had heard suggested against the resolutions, the most extravagant and chimerical was the idea of a war with Great-Britain as a consequence of them."[30] The Atlantic trade system, like the stock exchange in Voltaire's account, would provide security against misbehavior.

Madison's vision looked beyond America's troubles with Britain to an international regime of peace. Ultimately, Madison hoped that war would cease to be a tool of public policy. In a 1792 essay on "Universal Peace," he proclaimed, "had Rousseau lived to see the constitutions of the United States and of France, his judgment might have escaped the censure to which his project has exposed it." The French and American constitutions were proofs of progress. The essay ended by noting that the republican international regime, rightly executed, would be "the only hope of UNIVERSAL AND PERPETUAL PEACE."[31] The American system, Madison thought, was part of a larger worldwide movement.[32] There were two sources of war: "one flowing from the mere will of the government, the other according with the will of society itself." The former kind of war could be eradicated by a republicanizing "reformation in governments," removing power independent of the people as the French had done.[33] The second source of war could "only be controlled by subjecting the will of the society to the reason of the society, by establishing permanent constitutional maxims of conduct, which may prevail over occasional impressions, and inconsiderate pursuits." Madison sought to ensure that the people, and only the people, "whose toils and treasures are to support its burdens, instead of the government which is to reap its fruits," may declare war. Borrowing a page from Jefferson, Madison also made a generational argument: ensure that "each generation should be made to bear the burden of its own wars, instead of carrying them on, at the expense of other generations."[34] Roughly two years earlier, Madison had argued to Jefferson that "debts may be incurred for purposes which interest the unborn, as well as the living: such are the debts for repelling a conquest, the evils of which descend through many generations."[35] In pursuit of a more rational world order, Madison changed his mind. Forcing the people to calculate the tangible cost of each war would make them averse to war in general. "Were all nations to follow the example," he noted, "the reward would be doubled to each; and the temple of Janus might be shut, never to be opened more." Hence, he added, "had Rousseau lived to see the rapid progress of reason and reformation, which the present day exhibits, the philanthropy which dictated his project would find a rich enjoyment in the scene before him."[36]

Just as a multiplicity of sects could tame religious conflict, and an extended republic could solve the riddle of faction, so too did Madison hope that economic interest could be used to end war as a tool of policy. That was the logic of the Embargo of 1807–9.[37] Faced with acts of war by both Britain and France, Madison and Jefferson tried the ultimate trade restriction: a full embargo, halting all American foreign trade, not only with the belligerents but with all nations. Newspaper essays defending the Embargo, almost certainly from Madison's pen, suggested that "it is singularly fortunate that an embargo, whilst it guards our essential resources, will have the collateral effect of making it to the interest of all nations to change the system which has driven our commerce from the ocean."[38] In other words, the Embargo fostered the project of universal and perpetual peace. Historian Irving Brant notes that Madison's language here repeats "almost verbatim" his argument from 1794.[39] If the Embargo had worked, it would have created a new and better international order. Moreover, it would have meant that a radically limited federal government could function effectively; neither a national bank nor a system of roads and canals would have been necessary.[40] Domestic manufactures would not be necessary, as it would always be possible to import them.

Could Madison's constitutional scheme survive if the Embargo failed? That was an open question. Since at least Henry Adams, historians have noted that the Embargo squeezed Great Britain; the trouble was that it hurt the United States more.[41] Moreover, Americans were not the nation Madison hoped they were. He believed that "we will flinch from no sacrifices which the honor and good of the nation demand from virtuous and faithful citizens."[42] Events demonstrated that Madison was mistaken. To function, the Embargo seemed to require the Spartan virtues that Madison's commercial republicanism foreswore. That contradiction dashed Madison's highest constitutional hopes. The federal government would have to be more powerful. Making it so without subverting republican self-government was the challenge of Madison's last year as president.

The Bank, the Bonus Bill, and the People

Experience taught Madison that the U.S. government needed more powers than he had thought. But he did not conclude that Hamilton had been correct and he and Jefferson wrong in the fundamental sense.[43] Instead, Madison sought to cabin constitutional change in order to preserve his republican vision. That explains why he vetoed the Bonus Bill and signed the second Bank of the United States into law.

The Bonus Bill veto is more obviously congruent with Madison's constitutional ideal. When experience demonstrates that the government needs a power the people have not given, according to Madison, the people must amend the Constitution to add the needed power.

The way Madison vetoed the bill is also worth noting. Since the end of his term was the end of the legislative session, he could have exercised a pocket veto. Instead, he vetoed and penned a detailed veto message as his last official act as president. As he was retiring from public life that day, the veto message is, in a sense, his valedictory.

Why veto the bill? After all, a congressional majority considered the bill constitutional, otherwise they would not have approved it. But that was not a sufficient reason for their interpretation to prevail.[44] "The legislative powers vested in Congress are specified and enumerated in the eighth section of the first article of the Constitution," Madison wrote, "and it does not appear that the power proposed to be exercised by the bill is among the enumerated powers, or that it falls by any just interpretation within the power to make laws necessary and proper for carrying into execution those or other powers vested by the Constitution in the Government of the United States." Such a power could not be assumed "without a latitude of construction departing from the ordinary import of the terms strengthened by the known inconveniences which doubtless led to the grant of this remedial power to Congress." Neither the meaning of the terms nor the purposes for which the people gave Congress the power to regulate "commerce among the several states" would admit such a construction. Similarly, he argued that relying on congressional authority "to provide for the common defense and general welfare" would "be contrary to the established and consistent rules of interpretation, as rendering the special and careful enumeration of powers which follow the clause nugatory and improper." Allowing such a construction "would have the effect of giving to Congress a general power of legislation instead of the defined and limited one hitherto understood to belong to them."[45] To assume plenary power over "the general welfare" would render the people's grant of specific powers to the federal government moot. Even the supremacy clause, stating that "this Constitution, and the Laws of the United States which shall be made Pursuance thereof . . . shall be the supreme Law of the Land," only applied to those areas in which the people had given the federal government legitimate power.[46] Absent such logic, the Virginia Resolutions were anticonstitutional. Clearly if the U.S. Constitution had limits, an unconstitutional law was not binding or the constitutional enumeration of powers would, in practice, be meaningless. To allow the federal government to be the judge of its own powers was to allow it to be the judge in its own case, always an invitation to arbitrary power.

Irving Brant, the distinguished Madison biographer, downplayed Madison's strict construction, arguing that Madison did not really want internal improvements: "Had Madison's repeated recommendations of a federal system of roads and canals been based upon imperative economic necessity or the urgent requirements of humanity, the constitutional authority probably would have seemed as adequate to him as it did in the cases of the national bank and the scourge of smallpox."[47] Yet it is worth remembering the amendment process looked very different to Madison in 1817 than it would have to Brant, writing shortly after the New Deal. In the first Congress, Madison pushed through the ten amendments that became the Bill of Rights. The Eleventh Amendment, overturning a Supreme Court decision the people thought mistaken, was added to the Constitution in 1794, and the Twelfth Amendment, to ensure that the crisis of the election of 1800 would not be repeated, passed in late 1803. That is why Madison said "as experience might suggest" when he called amendments "the safe and practicable mode of improving" the Constitution. Based on Madison's own experience, it was not unreasonably difficult to amend the Constitution when warranted.[48]

Constitutional forms mattered to Madison. In his veto message, he explained, "I am not unaware of the great importance of roads and canals and the improved navigation of water courses, and that a power in the National Legislature to provide for them might be exercised with signal advantage to the general prosperity." That said, if the Bonus Bill was constitutional, "no adequate landmarks would be left by the constructive extension of the powers of Congress as proposed in the bill." And it was important to preserve such landmarks. If existing constitutional grants of power needed to be altered, the amendment process was the "safe and practicable mode of improving it [the Constitution] as experience might suggest."[49] That conclusion was consistent with what Madison had said in his seventh annual message. Madison noted the importance of internal improvements, for "no objects within the circle of political economy so richly repay the expense bestowed on them," but, he added, "it is a happy reflection that any defect of constitutional authority which may be encountered can be supplied in a mode which the Constitution itself has providently pointed out."[50]

The amendment process served an important republican function. Jefferson suggested that no constitution should last longer than a generation—nineteen years.[51] Each generation, he thought, should explicitly ratify the Constitution under which it lived. Periodic re-ratification was not only a matter of constitutional legitimacy; it would also have been an educative process, reminding the people that they are the ultimate sovereigns, endowed with the right to decide which powers governments may and may not exercise, and that, as Jefferson put it in his *Summary View of the Rights of British America,* "kings are the servants, not the proprietors of the people."[52] What was true of kings was true of all government employees, elected or appointed. Madison thought Jefferson's scheme would deprive the Constitution of the considerable advantages that time and veneration conferred upon it.[53] Periodic amendment would serve many of the same purposes as Jefferson's proposal but with less danger of destabilizing the regime.

Madison not only embraced the amendment process as the constitutional means of constitutional change but explicitly rejected the most plausible alternative to the amendment process, creative reinterpretation, as well. He wrote Henry Lee in 1825:

> I entirely concur in the propriety of resorting to the sense in which the Constitution was accepted and ratified by the nation. In that sense alone it is the legitimate Constitution. And if that be not the guide in expounding it, there can be no security for a consistent and stable, more than for a faithful exercise of its powers. If the meaning of the text be sought in the changeable meaning of the words composing it, it is evident that the shape and attributes of the Government must partake of the changes to which the words and phrases of all living languages are constantly subject. What a metamorphosis would be produced in the code of law if all its ancient phraseology were to be taken in its modern sense.[54]

Constitutional meaning must be constant over time. Note the language Madison used in his letter to Lee: "If the meaning of the text be sought in the changeable meaning of the words composing it," and if the "changes to which" "all living languages are constantly subject" were followed, it would attack the idea that ratification by the people made the Constitution legitimate; it would subvert the people's government. Pretending to follow the Constitution but, in fact, changing the meaning of the words in it endangers the people's right to consent to the laws. Amendments were the republican remedy for the diseases incident to strict construction. Recall Madison's language in Federalist 43: "The express authority of the people alone could give due validity to the Constitution."[55] That was simply an elaboration of the doctrine of 1776—that government derives its just powers from the consent of the governed.

Given that conclusion, why did Madison not call for a bank amendment in 1816? Why did he sign the second Bank of the United States into law? The answer might have something to do with the sovereignty of the people and the nature of a government based on consent. No one, not even James

Madison, had the right to tell the American people that they were wrong about a constitutional matter when, as Madison noted, they and all three branches of the government had weighed in repeatedly on a particular question. Discussing the bank, President Madison waved aside "the question of the constitutional authority of the Legislature to establish an incorporated bank," for, he argued, it was "precluded in my judgment by repeated recognitions under varied circumstances of the validity of such an institution in acts of the legislative, executive, and judicial branches of the Government, accompanied by indications, in different modes, of a concurrence of the general will of the nation."[56] To contradict the prevailing interpretation, and one that had been followed for a generation, by all three branches of the federal government and supported by "the general will of the nation," however misguided one person might hold that interpretation to be, would be to subvert the principles of 1776 by suggesting that voters—as well as just about everyone in government—were too stupid to understand the Constitution's true meaning. Were this to be a republican constitution, as opposed to an aristocratic one, the people's view could not be dismissed out of hand.

Madison's constitutionalism was dialectical. It was a matter of principle that the United States was a nation of equal citizens. To be a citizen is to have political responsibilities. For that reason, the common views of citizens of the meaning of the constitution must carry heavy constitutional weight. On the other hand, constitutional interpretation cannot roll over for the majority's opinion. And, Madison realized, certain opinions, should constitutional interpretation follow them, would themselves in time subvert the practice of republican self-government. Constitutional statesmanship entailed a negotiation between the most reasonable understanding of the Constitution and the common popular view. That was a matter both of principle and of practice: "Public opinion sets bounds to every government, and is the real sovereign of every free one."[57] To give life to the principle of consent, the beliefs and opinions of the American people, and longstanding practices and precedents, had to get their due. If the people believed a given interpretation was correct, statesmen had to tread lightly if they disagreed. One of Edward Coke's legal maxims was, "unless things are done according to custom, and the usage of the majority, they will neither be approved nor seem to be right."[58]

The context of Madison's change on the bank is also worth noting. Constitutionally speaking, 1816 was not 1791. In 1791, the Constitution was new, and therefore any decision might open a window to an ever more expansive interpretation. In 1816, by contrast, the direction of constitutional interpretation was already bound by some precedents. Allowing a bank to be constitutional without an amendment had a different implication in 1816 than it had in 1791.[59] It had already been deemed constitutional in the past. The First Congress passed it, and President George Washington signed it. By 1816, constitutional interpretation deferred to their view. A bill for internal improvements did not have the same constitutional support nor the same history, Madison implied. Hence he signed one and vetoed the other. Both actions were part of his effort to preserve Republican constitutionalism in light of the experience of four Republican administrations. It was an effort to preserve Jeffersonian constitutionalism.

At the end of his Republican career, Madison endorsed both a bank and internal improvements, indeed most of what became Clay's American System. Madison now supported domestic manufactures. That represented a significant change. Given a dangerous world, and given the lack of national unity on display during the war, the federal government needed powers that facilitated war-making. As he noted in his seventh annual message, it also would be prudent to create a national system of roads, canals, and the like to foster commercial and other forms of exchange throughout the republic, promoting American unity. Even so, his hopes for Enlightened Constitutional republicanism and a more peaceful world remained intact.

Postscript

Although the Federalist Party was dead, there was still one powerful Federalist in office—Thomas Jefferson's cousin John Marshall. Marshall's opinion in *McCullough v. Maryland* (1819) horrified Madison. In Madison's view, it left no limits to federal power: the "high sanction given to a latitude in expounding the Constitution which seems to break down the landmarks intended by a specification of the Powers of Congress." Madison rejected Marshall's suggestion that "the specified powers vested in Congress . . . are sovereign powers, and that as such they carry with them an unlimited discretion as to the means of executing them." Marshall had recapitulated Hamilton's argument that in areas in which the people allotted power to the federal government, it was fully sovereign, with complete discretion to determine what means might be employed in pursuit of legitimate constitutional ends.

Instead, Madison held "that a limited Govt. may be limited in its sovereignty as well with respect to the means as to the objects of his powers; and that to give an extent to the former, superseding the limits to the latter, is in effect to convert a limited into an unlimited Govt."[60] By implication, he was saying that America should not look to the experience of nations across space and time to understand the authority to regulate "commerce . . . among the several states." On the contrary, they should look to what the people who ratified the Constitution understood by that grant of power. To claim that the authority to regulate interstate commerce was a "sovereign" power, Madison held, was to open it to abuse. It was a free invitation to obliterate the powers reserved to the states.

In 1791, Madison had worried about allowing "implications, thus remote and multiplied," until no limitations were left on federal power.[61] In Madison's opinion, Marshall opened up the Constitution to exactly that danger, smuggling the idea of "sovereign" power into American constitutionalism. Such an idea was for Madison a rejection of the principles of 1776, as it seemed to reject the idea that the people gave only limited powers to the federal government. Critics of his reasoning cried "necessity," but Madison thought the argument was weak. Once again he pointed to amendment as the proper republican remedy: "The presumption which ought to be indulged is that any improvement of this distribution sufficiently pointed out by experience would not be withheld."[62] If the people cannot be trusted to amend the Constitution when necessary, they are unfit for self-government. In 1819, as in 1817 and throughout his Republican career, Madison refused to concede defeat in his political and philosophical fights with Hamilton and his Federalist friends. Although chastened by the failure of the Embargo and the embarrassments of the War of 1812, Madison kept the Jeffersonian faith.

Notes

1. Wirt quoted in Henry Adams, *History of the United States during the Administrations of Thomas Jefferson and James Madison* (New York, 1986), 2:1070.

2. Ibid., 1:162.

3. "If the operation of the State banks can not produce this result, the probable operation of a national bank will merit consideration." James Madison, "Seventh Annual Message," Dec. 15, 1815, in Galliard Hunt, ed., *The Writings of James Madison* (New York, 1900), 8:249. See also Madison to Jefferson, Oct. 10. 1814, in ibid., 8:231.

Page references are to the PDF version available via Liberty Fund's Online Library of Liberty.

4. Madison, "Seventh Annual Message," Dec. 15, 1815, in ibid., 8:247–52

5. Federalist 51, in *The Federalist,* ed. Charles R. Kesler (New York, 1999), 320.

6. Federalist 10, in ibid., 78, 79.

7. Federalist 51, 10, in ibid., 319, 77; Samuel Kernell "'The True Principles of Republican Government': Reassessing James Madison's Political Science," in *James Madison: The Theory and Practice of Republican Government,* ed. Samuel Kernell (Stanford, Calif., 2005), 92–125. I discovered this article while working on final revisions to this essay; it draws a similar conclusion, finding that Federalist 51 is unusual in the Madison corpus. Kernell notes that Madison went to the Constitutional Convention with a particular model in mind, but "he left Philadelphia with something quite different in hand." And he wrote Federalist 51 to "to dress up the Constitution in familiar principles in order to reassure delegates . . . [at] state ratifying conventions." In addition, he sees little evidence that Madison "in his subsequent writings . . . seriously revised his theoretical concerns." Kernell, "'The True Principles of Republican Government,'" 94, 95.

8. Federalist 10, in Kesler, ed., *The Federalist,* 76.

9. On the definition of a "republic," see Federalist 10, 14, 39. In Federalist 63, Madison lists Carthage and Sparta as "republics." Ibid., 76, 95, 236–37, 383.

10. Colleen Sheehan, *The Mind of James Madison: The Legacy of Classical Republicanism* (New York, 2015).

11. Madison, "Report on the Resolutions," House of Delegates Session, 1799–1800, in Hunt, ed., *Writings,* 6:194–95.

12. See his essay on "Consolidation," Dec. 5, 1791, in Jack Rakove, ed., *Madison: Writings* (New York, 1999), 498.

13. Madison, "Report on the Resolutions," House of Delegates Session, 1799–1800, in Hunt, ed., *Writings,* 6:195. See also "Consolidation," Dec. 5, 1791, in Rakove, ed., *Madison: Writings,* 498–500.

14. Even Hamilton denied that the federal government had the police power. Madison might not have believed he meant it, however. Hamilton wrote, "A corporation may not be erected by congress, for superintending the police of the city of Philadelphia, because they are not authorized to *regulate* the *police* of that city." Hamilton, "Opinion on the Constitutionality of the Bank," Feb. 23, 1791, in Joanne B. Freeman, ed., *Hamilton: Writings* (New York, 2001), 616.

15. Brian Balogh, *A Government Out of Sight: The Mystery of National Authority in Nineteenth-Century America* (Cambridge, 2009). Michael Greve draws different implications but makes a similar argument in *The Upside Down Constitution* (Cambridge, Mass., 2012).

16. Douglas Adair, "'That Politics May Be Reduced to a Science': David Hume, James Madison, and the Tenth Federalist," *Huntington Library Quarterly* 24, no. 4 (Aug. 1957): 342–60.

17. Colleen Sheehan, *James Madison and the Spirit of Republican Self-Government* (Cambridge, 2009).

18. Federalist 10, in Kesler, ed., *The Federalist,* 79.

19. Federalist 51, in ibid., 321.

20. "I confess to you, sir, were uniformity of religion to be introduced by this system, it would, in my opinion, be ineligible; but I have no reason to conclude, that uniformity of government will produce that of religion." Madison, "Speech in the Virginia Ratifying Convention in Defense of the Constitution," June 6, 1788, in Rakove, ed., *Madison: Writings,* 360–61. "Happily for the states, they enjoy the utmost freedom of religion. This freedom arises from the multiplicity of sects, which pervades America, and which is the best and only security for religious liberty in any society. For where there is such a variety of sects, there cannot be a majority of any one sect to oppress and persecute the rest." Madison, "Speech in the Virginia Ratifying Convention on Taxation, a Bill of Rights, and the Mississippi," June 12, 1788, in Rakove, ed., *Madison: Writings,* 381.

21. Kernell also connects Madison's "extended sphere" with Voltaire in "'The True Principles of Republican Government,'" 104ff.

22. Voltaire, *The Works of Voltaire,* trans. William F. Flemming (New York, 1901), 19, part 2:218.

23. Ralph Ketcham, *James Madison: A Biography,* (Charlottesville, Va., 1990), 166.

24. Madison, "Property," Mar. 29, 1792, in Rakove, ed., *Madison: Writings,* 515.

25. Madison, "Consolidation," Dec. 5, 1791, in Rakove, ed., *Madison: Writings,* 498ff.

26. Drew R. McCoy, *The Elusive Republic: Political Economy in Jeffersonian America* (Chapel Hill, N.C., 1980).

27. For Madison's use of the term "heresy" in a political context, see, for example, Madison to Jefferson, July 13, 1791, in Hunt, ed., *Writings,* 6:71.

28. Madison, "Speech on Discriminating Duties," Jan. 3, 1794, in ibid., 6:112.

29. J. C. A. Stagg, *Mr. Madison's War: Politics, Diplomacy, and Warfare in the Early American Republic, 1783–1830* (Princeton, N.J., 1984), 16.

30. Madison, "Commercial Discrimination," Jan. 14, 1794, in William T. Hutchinson et al., eds., *The Papers of James Madison, Congressional Series* (Charlottesville, Va., 1977–91), 15:183–95.

31. Madison, "Universal Peace," 1792, in Rakove, ed., *Madison: Writings,* 505–8; Sheehan, *Mind of James Madison,* 39ff.

32. Armin Mattes makes a parallel argument: "The assumption of an interdependence between a nation's domestic system and its place in the world" was essential to both Madison and Hamilton. Mattes, *Citizens of a Common Intellectual Homeland: The Transatlantic Origins of American Democracy and Nationhood* (Charlottesville, Va., 2015), 104. Mattes notes that this reading explains why an essay on perpetual peace fits into Madison's concerns in his "party press" essays. Ibid., 124.

33. Madison, "Universal Peace," 1792, in Rakove, ed., *Madison: Writings,* 505, 506. In an essay a little over two weeks later, Madison redefined republican government to suit his idea here. He describes three types: "government operating by permanent military force," "government operating by corrupt influence," and "a government, deriving

its energy from the will of the society, and operating by the reason of its measures, on the understanding and interest of society." He added that "such are the republican governments which it is the glory of America to have invented." Madison, "Spirit of Governments," Feb. 20, 1792, in Rakove, ed., *Madison: Writings,* 510–11.

34. Madison, "Universal Peace," 1792, in ibid., 506.

35. Madison to Jefferson, Feb. 4, 1790, in ibid., 475.

36. Madison, "Universal Peace," 1792, in ibid., 507. McCoy, *Elusive Republic,* 128, suggests Madison's ambition was a bit more sober. America's "juster government" would mean "less need of soldiers either for defence against dangers from without, or disturbances from within."

37. See Benjamin L. Carp, "Jefferson's Embargo: National Intent and Sectional Effects," in this volume.

38. Dumas Malone, *Jefferson the President: Second Term* (Boston, 1974), 488; Irving Brant, *James Madison* (Indianapolis, 1941), 4:402.

39. Brant, *James Madison,* 4:402.

40. Madison did not leave much of a paper trial regarding the constitutionality of the Embargo. Kevin Gutzman notes that Madison had long interpreted the Constitution this way: "One of Madison's goals for the U.S. Constitution in 1787 had been to empower the federal government to conduct trade wars of exactly this type. The power to regulate commerce with foreign nations arguably extended to an embargo power." Gutzman, *James Madison and the Making of America* (New York, 2012), 299. Yet there is clearly a difference between regulating commerce, or even cutting off commerce with nations at war, and cutting off all foreign commerce.

41. For Adams's account of the Embargo, see Adams, *History,* 1:1031–48, 1115–26.

42. Quoted in Brant, *James Madison,* 4:403.

43. Recall that in his seventh annual message he did not concede that wars are an inevitable element of political life. The need for defense was, he stated, peculiar to his times: "The character of the times particularly inculcates the lesson that, whether to prevent or repel danger, we ought not to be unprepared for it." Madison, "Seventh Annual Message," Dec. 15, 1815, in Hunt, ed., *Writings,* 8:250.

44. John Lauritz Larson suggests that a case could be made that Madison was incorrect here. Larson, *Internal Improvement: National Public Works and the Promise of Popular Government in the Early United States* (Chapel Hill, N.C., 2001).

45. Madison, "Veto Message," Mar. 3, 1817, in Hunt, ed., *Writings,* 8:283.

46. U.S. Constitution, art. VI, para. 2.

47. Brant, *James Madison,* 6:417.

48. Jack Rakove argues that because the amendment process is so difficult to follow, in fact, "substantive 'amendments' have taken place outside the formal place outside the formal parameters of Article 5." Rakove, "Ticklish Experiments: The Paradox of American Constitutionalism," in *America and Enlightenment Constitutionalism,* ed. Gary McDowell and Jonathan O'Neill (New York, 2006), 224.

49. Madison, "Veto Message," Mar. 3, 1817, in Hunt, ed., *Writings,* 8:284.

50. Madison, "Seventh Annual Message," Dec. 15, 1815, in Hunt, ed., *Writings,* 8:251.

51. Jefferson to Madison, Sept. 6, 1789, in Merrill D. Peterson, ed., *Jefferson: Writings* (New York, 1984), 959–64.

52. Thomas Jefferson, *Summary View of the Rights of British America,* in ibid., 121.

53. Madison to Jefferson, Feb. 4, 1790, in Rakove, ed., *Madison: Writings,* 473ff.

54. Madison to Henry Lee, June 25, 1824, in Hunt, ed., *Writings,* 9:120. Madison worried that the result of such a turn would be that constitutional argument would result in constitutional partisanship: "The Constitution itself . . . must be an unfailing source of party distinctions."

55. Federalist 43, in Kesler, ed., *The Federalist,* 245.

56. Madison, "Veto Message," Dec. 15, 1815, in Hunt, ed., *Writings,* 8:241. Madison made this statement when vetoing a bank bill, arguing that this particular bank would not serve the ends for which a bank was needed, not that a bank was per se unconstitutional. In 1816, Congress sent him a better bill.

57. Madison, "Public Opinion," Dec. 19, 1791, in Rakove, ed., *Madison: Writings,* 500. For a contrasting perspective, see Leonard J. Sadosky, "How the Jeffersonians Learned to Love the State: Consumption, Finance, and Empire in the Madison Administration," in this volume.

58. Edward Coke, *Selected Writings of Sir Edward Coke,* ed. Steve Shepherd (Indianapolis, 2003), 1:97n9.

59. Ralph Ketcham suggests similarly that Madison thought that the direction of constitutional interpretation was more plastic in the 1790s than it was in 1816. Ketcham, *James Madison,* 610. Madison thought that "the bank, the tariff, and other national measures could, in 1816, be undertaken without loosening 'all the bands of the constitution.'"

60. Madison to Spence Roane, Sept. 2, 1819, in Hunt, ed., *Writings,* 8:320–22.

61. Madison, "Speech in Congress Opposing the National Bank," Feb. 2, 1791, in Rakove, ed., *Madison: Writings,* 486.

62. Madison to Spence Roane, Sept. 2, 1819, in Hunt, ed., *Writings,* 8:320–22. In this context it is worth recalling Hannah Arendt's comment in *On Revolution:* "The great, and, in the long run, perhaps the greatest American innovation in politics as such was the consistent abolition of sovereignty within the body politic of the republic, the insight that in the realm of human affairs sovereignty and tyranny are the same." Arendt, *On Revolution* (New York, 1963), 153.

Afterword

ANDREW BURSTEIN

Coursing through this volume is the spirit of engagement and intellectual rigor taught by Peter S. Onuf, whose students are featured in these pages. What characterizes an Onufian approach to historical analysis? First, it demands that one distinguish visionary principles from the actual conduct of politics. In his rich body of scholarship over four decades, Onuf has forcefully questioned the sentimental assumptions ascribed to the founders. Over his career, he shifted emphasis from the ostensible uniqueness of American political thought and republican ideology toward a more comprehensive understanding of unheralded agents of change, compromised builders of institutions, and covert advocates of empire. In short, he clarifies how history unfolds from a ground-level perspective.

To see the political culture of the United States as a composite of unintended effects is to acknowledge the irrationality of political life. In *The Origins of the Federal Republic* (1983), Onuf shows that states' reticence to use arms to defend their territorial claims did as much to promote a strong central governing authority as did republican principles. In *Jefferson's Empire: The Language of American Nationhood* (2000), he portrays a Jefferson who envisioned a productive and "affectionate" interdependence among self-governing states, yet who alienated New Englanders and contributed to a deepening sectionalism. "He imagined northerners as foreigners," Onuf writes in assessing how, amid the Missouri crisis in 1820, the rhetorical contortionist ex-president communicated, in some of his most extravagant language, why he believed his northern, southern, and western countrymen might cherish the "bonds of union" even as they acquiesced to a temporary dissolution of their compact. The same inveterate optimist delighted in the notion of an "independent empire" on the Pacific coast with something approximating mutuality of feeling across the Continental Divide.[1]

Onuf's exposition of Jefferson's thinking on slavery, the "captive nation" idea, presented blacks and Indians as two peoples effectively "at war" with the American republic. No more racist than the majority of his peers, Jefferson responded to the natural philosophy and crude science embraced by eighteenth-century intellectuals. He saw slaves as "a people without a country." In an online response to a review of *Jefferson's Empire,* Onuf writes, with reference to a famous phrase in *Notes on the State of Virginia:* "Jefferson may have had a 'suspicion' that blacks were inferior, but he was absolutely certain that they were *different,* and this is why it was so critical to him that emancipation be followed by colonization." Peter Onuf's Jefferson has a powerful sense of national community—Jefferson's definition of "belonging" lies at the core of his political thought.[2]

Irony and paradox assuredly figure into the Onufian construct of American history. The common thread in his work across the years is his fascination with unauthorized forms of engagement, a dissenting tradition, and the existence of ambivalent actors who helped chart America's early development alongside (or in the shadow of) the purposeful, larger-than-life founders. Onuf's perspective is broad but never haphazard in the attention he gives to the public dissemination of new ideas and the distillation of republican values over time. He treats the early republic in ways that put to the test Jefferson's own theory of political generations, which "extend[ed] the duration of a majority's rule until the moment when survivors were outnumbered by those subsequently born."[3]

In spatial terms, Onuf reconstitutes the prism through which Jefferson, in a deservedly heralded 1801 letter to the English scientist-theologian Joseph Priestley, imagined "the great extent of our Republic." Onuf follows that majestic construct as far as it stretches our understanding of interactions among the states and complicates the narrative thread pursued by generations of historians in debating the grand tug of war between the forces of consolidation and disunion. As the reigning interpreter of "republican empire," Peter Onuf has redefined how scholars perceive all that flowed from Jefferson's self-determined "Revolution of 1800."[4]

Jeffersonians in Power takes up several Onufian themes in attempting to remove some shadows and shine some light on an emergent national identity.

If a single question permeates this volume it is, How does a political interest that comes into power on the strength of its pronounced distrust of power proceed to govern? One way is to exploit fear, to forecast the dire effects if the governing party is undone—and this is what widely publicized letters and the flow of pamphlets, speeches, and sermons effectively did in the early republic by sustaining a well-rehearsed symbolic vocabulary that had found its footing in the Revolution.

Because language in itself manifests power, let us explore animating features of the revolutionary American vocabulary and grammar of republicanism, as it can be gleaned from the preceding chapters. We know that a morally tinged republican language exploded in the 1760s and 1770s and enlarged as each decade passed and the next political generation was reared. In his 1817 biography of Patrick Henry, one of the most ambitious among the new *littérateurs,* Marylander William Wirt attributed the growth of a distinct language of popular resistance to the slow disavowal of Anglo-American consanguinity: "This transition of feeling is most interestingly marked [in] epithets," Wirt wrote. "Our kind and indulgent mother" progressively became an "unnatural parent—cruel stepmother—proud, merciless oppressor—haughty, unfeeling, and unrelenting tyrant." Henry's "language of passion was perfect," the biographer adjudged, with its "exuberance of appropriate thoughts, of apt illustrations." Each "happy phrase" that formed spontaneously was "some image fresh from Nature's mint," serving as a dynamic counterpart to the animated script of Henry's more typographically inclined peers.[5]

We know better now how our historical memory was shaped by visceral imagery, thanks to Robert G. Parkinson's delineation of the rhetorical boundaries within which the "American people" of 1775–76 resided. His rendering of the dramatic stories that circulated at this time explains the power over the colonial mind of ideas about the unusual cruelty inflicted by "savage" Indians and unfeeling German mercenaries. Because Jefferson and his colleagues brooded over this intelligence, it found its way into the Declaration of Independence. The "swarms" of crown appointees who "harass our people and eat out their substance" could only be resisted by bold, uncowering, independent minds. "Harass," in Samuel Johnson's *Dictionary,* meant "to weary; to fatigue," with the added implication of "waste; disturbance." The emphasis is on forcing submission, which could be accomplished either by arms or by overcoming the spirit.[6]

Republicans' collective self-definition—their normative grammar of politics—never ceased to emphasize the reliable "spirit" of "the people." It was writ in passionate as well as *com*passionate language, posing a virtuous, artless, guileless citizenry against decidedly hostile forces. After independence was won, the rhetorical enemy was the ghostly Tory—whether real or not, a conniving, exploitative class that held itself apart. Republicans were ever sensitive to the "intrigue" and "designs" of the willful, the wicked who, as Samuel Adams warned, "employ every art to soothe the devoted people into a state of indolence, inattention and security, which is forever the forerunner of slavery." Once again, the popular spirit had to be maintained, held aloft. In his 1797 inaugural address, President John Adams stated that American national pride was "justifiable" when it arose from "conviction of national innocence, information, and benevolence"—a strange trio at first glance until one grasps the meaning of "innocence" as a lack of artifice, and "information" as intellectual objectivity that joins the nation's parts in fashioning a harmonious community. This language is consistent with the assertions Parkinson provides from the likes of George Wythe in protesting incursions on American soil (all harassment that was "unprovoked"). Always, deconstruction of the opposition centered on exposing indefensible motives.[7]

As the late Kenneth Cmiel observed, freedom in Revolution-era America, as tied to language, "generated a liberating self-control" that distinguished civilized ideals from uncivilized impulses and connected individual rights with community purposes. Policies that threatened liberty were "obnoxious"; the "honorable spirit" of a deserving people naturally inclined to "loyalty and affection" under good government but rebelled against "coarse" treatment, "violent measures," and "insult and humiliation" that aimed to relegate them to a "tame submission." Americans "renounced" what would defeat their noble spirit; they exhibited "fortitude" when they perceived an attack on their just rights. This vocabulary resonated well into the nineteenth century.[8]

The language is certainly unsubtle, and often didactic. As every rising scholar of the early republic learns, the nation's forefathers and -mothers maintained a purposive dialogue with history by leaving a deliberate paper trail. They politicized polite society. Aiming to exhibit propriety without pomp, they committed to the archive an abundance of texts, each of which took a stab at civic eloquence. The ever-relevant classical ethic and hefty Old Testament warnings about avarice and pride buttressed constitutional interpretation to stretch the already tested nerves of political actors. Each administration from George Washington's forward fixed its sights on an opposition political interest whose maximal threats justified decisive, nation-preserving actions that might otherwise be seen as demagogic, grasping, or dismissive of minority rights. Government went on the defensive.

From Washington's startled reaction to any sign of dissent once Alexander Hamilton convinced him to clothe the office of chief executive in virtual robes of royal dignity; to President Jefferson's willful acceptance of rumors that his former vice president, Aaron Burr, aimed to sever the tramontane West; to President Andrew Jackson's (whether or not accurately recorded), "The Bank is trying to kill me but I will kill it," administrations reacted to a ruinous opposition almost as though they could not do without one. In each case, the governing figure professed that he exhibited benignity in office while insisting that American liberties and institutions were under fire.[9]

The ominous game of republican politics, a rhetorical competition with palpably real consequences, was about more than claiming the moral high ground. Preserving emotional stability—sanity even—was a vital part of the game. In building a satisfying lexicon that would enable him and his allies to diagnose political ills, Jefferson uniformly cast Republicans as "enthusiastic," "buoyant," "healthy," and "firm," whereas Federalists, like Tories, were "timid" men whose "languid fibres" made them worshipful of unmediated authority. This taxonomy made it possible for Jefferson to conclude, "I am not among those who fear the people," as he wrote self-importantly, and with his enemies in mind, to Virginia attorney Samuel Kercheval in 1816. Jefferson put his mind at rest when he described the Federalist interlude as a time of "delusion" leading to his "Revolution of 1800."[10]

On the subject of religious life, as John Ragosta explains, Jefferson stood for secular government while doing nothing to interrupt religious practice across the nation. In public addresses, so as to mollify the faithful, the president moved easily from statements of principle to blanket references to God by using such terms as "an overruling providence," "that infinite power," "the beneficent Being," and the pronoun "Him." The Republican perspective that flowed from the activism of Jefferson, James Madison, and a host of Virginia dissenters in the 1780s made possible the "nonsectarian monotheism" that continues to direct government policy on religious expression in public venues, so that "In God We Trust" performs a purely ceremonial function. Religious extremism had to be neutralized.[11]

In his first inaugural address, Jefferson stressed the "bitter and bloody persecutions" of religious intolerance, which, as president, he vowed to overcome once and for all. It was "the agonising spasms of infuriated man" that rent societies apart; it was "equal and exact justice to all men, of whatever state or persuasion, religious or political," which alone invited "harmony and affection," while "the support of state governments in all their rights" quelled "anti-republican tendencies." This vilification of "anti-republican tendencies" amid comments on the rights of conscience is merely a rhetorical coup, an attack on the Hamiltonian centralizers. It is no less indicative of a core problem facing the first Republican chief executive: Was it really possible, in the atmosphere that existed, for Americans to be of "one heart and one mind," as Jefferson rhapsodized, without the suppression of dissenting opinions? The state of partisanship, within and across the states, was menacing in 1801. And "partisanship" meant just that: partial reach, not a unifying embrace; it was a centrifugal force, not a binding one.[12]

Jefferson wanted to have it both ways, arguing that if people felt content within their states and in no way "harassed" (to revisit his painful expression in the Declaration) by the national government, they would feel somehow freer to identify with, and consent to, the remaining powers assigned to that government. To the Georgia legislature in his second year as president, Jefferson reiterated, "State rights, and State-sovereignties, as recognised by the constitution, are an integral and essential part of our great political fabric. they are bound up by a common ligament with those of the National government, and form with it one system, of which the Constitution is the law and the life. A sacred respect to that instrument therefore becomes the first interest and duty of all." But states' rights, as we all know, were as likely to pull the union apart as to cement it. The president's call for unity was a rhetorical dodge.[13]

This over-optimistic, if understandable, construction was certainly not new for Jefferson. He had been assuaging the recipients of his familiar letters for many years. Loath to expose his personal thoughts about religion, aware of how easy it was to unleash the "agonising spasms of infuriated man," he so comfortably resorted to the word "sacred" when he would underscore his sense of conviction that one might assume his doing so meant more to him than it did: "sacred" was a useful (and one might say mildly enticing) modifier that he knew appealed more to some than to others. His draft of the Declaration held that truths were "sacred and undeniable," a coupling the committee edited down to "self-evident." To his lifelong friend John Page, a devout Episcopalian, he regularly used religious metaphors to soften his prose. Protesting luxury-loving Londoners, he romanced this friend: "Would a missionary appear who would make frugality the basis of his religious system, and go thro the land preaching it up as the only road to salvation, I would join his school tho' not generally disposed to seek religion out[side] of the dictates of my own reason." He would never "bow to the shrine of intolerance," he wrote elsewhere.[14]

Religious intolerance was for him synonymous with the "dogma" uttered in a clamor by "excitable" and "high-toned" clerics whose pretended piety repelled him. He privileged the thoughtful determinations of "free and discriminating minds," which flowed from the same political character that he imagined all "firm" republican citizens embodied. He was convinced that as the animating code words of republicanism demystified the polity, so would the quiet independence of the unbiased parishioner demystify Christianity and consign it to its proper place—that is, to lodge in the sympathy-enriched imagination. What else explains Jefferson's capacity to envision the harmonious intersection of Unitarians and evangelicals? Peter Onuf puts it this way: "Jefferson admired the evangelicals' democratic theology and ecclesiology. . . . Rather than supposing a fundamental opposition between the Unitarians' reasonable religion and the revivalists' heartfelt faith, Jefferson envisioned their ultimate convergence." Reducing "democratic" sects to their common themes, he removed power from the equation. Indeed, though he was critical of theological willfulness, Jefferson always hoped his America would be seen as a redemptive force in the world.[15]

As Mark Smith tells us, the emerging Jeffersonian critique of established power was two-sided in that its domestic agenda—diminishing the influence of "pampered" stock-jobbers, resistance to national "consolidation"—was matched by a concern with the moral implications of a retreat from the Franco-American partnership that had helped secure American independence. Fearing the implications of Hamilton's plan for a national bank, Madison offered a strict constructionist argument: The bank was not "necessary to the government," and the Constitution did not authorize Congress to charter a corporation.[16]

As the fractious 1790s carried forward, the Republicans' lexicon was set in place. A heightened consciousness of limited, enumerated powers meant that the word "federalism" could not contain within its meaning concentrations of wealth. It was to be defined as Jefferson famously broadcast in his first inaugural, when he insisted that republicans were federalists, that Republicans and Federalists were "brethren of the same principle." Again, as Onuf frames the issue, "Jefferson did not privilege 'republicanism' over 'federalism' (as we may), nor would he be willing to distinguish or dissociate these 'principles.'" He ignored contentious divisions when it suited him, assuming that his opinions were moderate even when they might not have been. Like some of his other rhetorical maneuvers, the republican-federalist sleight of hand was near impossible to pull off.[17]

Here is the link between the two suggestive essays by Mark Smith and Benjamin L. Carp. In defending the French Revolution when its excesses were indefensible, Jefferson resorted to a weak hyperbole. His most damaging words (as they live on in the historical imagination) were those to William Short, who had been his private secretary and confidant in Paris until 1789. "I would have seen half the earth desolated," Jefferson wrote in defense of revolutionary violence, as Andrew Trees also argues in this volume. "Were there but an Adam & an Eve left in every country, & left free, it would be better than as it is now." Jefferson praised Lafayette for "exterminating the monster of aristocracy, and pulling out the teeth and fangs of it's associated monarchy." Monsters and witches left Jefferson to his fevered imagination, perceiving a more conspiratorial force than existed in the political darkness. After Louis XVI was guillotined, Madison similarly fretted over "spurious" reports of the king's innocence. Partisanship fed a frenzied spirit of resistance. The Adam and Eve reference (ridiculous when refracted through a modern lens) serves us best as a reminder that revolutionary republicanism required efforts to rebuild once a corrupt structure was felled and artifice removed. That, at least, would be a friendly reading of Jefferson's letter to Short.[18]

In his fine, provocative essay, Carp explores the unintended "commercial suicide" of the Embargo. He exposes the fragility, if not insubstantiality, of the language Jeffersonians had heretofore relied on to advance their causes—that sanguine conceptualization of what happened when power was delivered into the hands of a truly republican administration. The Embargo was coercive, whether regarded as a negotiating strategy abroad or a restrictive policy at home. It had the effect of deepening criticism of Virginia's lock on the presidency, which was extended after Madison's election in 1808.[19]

The same conundrum applies to the political tone accompanying commercial diplomacy. There could be no longer a clear moral dichotomy between English and French interests. The French Revolution had led to Napoleon, who was never to be trusted, and French privateers committed depredations comparable to those of British frigates. The Jeffersonians maintained a largely neutral posture in their discussions of commercial considerations, but they rarely went beyond highlighting, in less distinct terms than before, matters of "justice" and "fairness." Situating the right values in the person of James Madison, the *National Intelligencer* assured that he would "pursue the straight line of honest policy, without being led astray by the false lights of sinister ambition." His distinctive "calmness and sobriety," evidenced on the public stage since the Constitutional Convention, were vintage republican traits.[20]

Writing in the Boston *Patriot* newspaper, John Quincy Adams, a seemingly unlikely convert to the Republican administration and a vocal proponent of the Embargo, continued to take aim at those on both sides of the Atlantic who downplayed the moral challenge: "fanatics" who abided "scandalous calumnies," others who exhibited "malignant passions," all who advocated submission to British power. Opposing the administration was nothing short of "contempt for America," wrote Adams. The same gentleman's father, the Federalist second president, willfully prepared for the *Patriot* letters that excoriated the late Alexander Hamilton and the "British faction" that the New Yorker had commandeered (it was reprinted in the demonstratively titled *Anti-Monarchist, and Republican Watchman*).[21]

One would think such testimony might do the trick. It did not. Throughout the Embargo period, fed up Federalists employed the Jeffersonian weapons of states' rights and nullification in contemplating principled resistance to the Embargo. Reaction across New England was rich and damning, as Carp demonstrates by way of several colorful quotes from regional newspapers; resistance came from merchants in New Orleans, Savannah, and elsewhere too. With Treasury Secretary Albert Gallatin resorting to the term "disobedience" to describe such broad opposition, the moral high ground was ceded. Language no longer served Jeffersonian policy as it had during the clear-cut partisan battles of the 1790s.[22]

Power proved more than the Jeffersonians could deftly manage. The emergence of "schism" within the administration party temporarily reduced the authority of Jefferson's particular language of inevitability. New York Republicans had had enough of Virginia puppeteering, and DeWitt Clinton would come close to defeating Madison in 1812. Outdistanced by a rapidly expanding Republican newspaper network, unreconstructed Federalists who had grossly limited political speech during their reign in the 1790s toyed now with their own equivalent of the Kentucky and Virginia Resolutions by protesting the drift toward one-party tyranny. By the Treaty of Ghent, Jeffersonians had won their war of words, and yet even after the Federalists imploded as a viable political party, Jefferson never stopped fearing their resurgence, believing that a salivating monocrat was always waiting in the wings—waiting for the honest republican to let down his guard.[23]

On the formidable subject of slavery, Christa Dierksheide is interested in the concept of "amelioration," drawn from Enlightenment ideas of incremental progress toward a calmer, better balanced world. In 1798, William Short, Jefferson's intimate at the time he was most absorbed in advancing the ideas he expressed in *Notes on Virginia,* wrote his former mentor a forceful letter. In it he introduced a refined theory of "amelioration," a gradual emancipation plan in which slaves would remain attached to the land in serf-like form, educated and prepared for a productive free life elsewhere. A more directed effort would remove females from those places where the slave population was most dense. Short reminded Jefferson that "the purchasing all the female slaves at once, wch. would cost less than the same number of males, is purchasing in fact all future generations instead of one only." The facts of procreation did not have to be taught to Jefferson, whose mathematical precision led him to calculate to the last shilling, last inch, last ounce, and who kept a farm book containing the details of every life he exercised power over as a financial investment. Somehow, Jefferson was able to combine a cold-blooded penchant for discipline with the conviction that he possessed comprehensive knowledge of all that took place on his farms. In claiming mastery, and motivated by a concept of union that did not doubt the foreignness of the Africa-descended in his midst, he never had cause to question his own humanity.[24]

Jefferson and his various correspondents attached some form of the word "ameliorate" to the condition of unfortunates: orphans, Indians, or "the affairs of men" generally. But, as Jefferson admitted in retirement and Dierksheide lays out, slavery took deeper root after passage of the 1808 law that brought the international trade in human beings to an end in the United States. This was a failure of the optimistic script Jeffersonians were trained to deploy. Once again, Jeffersonian words failed, and Jefferson turned to a different sort of rationale for a nation persisting half-slave and half-free. That rationale centered on an inherited definition of liberty and equality that would not change with the times. During the Missouri crisis, Jefferson refused to believe for a minute that the northern legislators who would restrict slavery in would-be states were capable of negotiating honestly. Their so-called principles were a ruse, he asserted. *They* were the passion-filled reactionaries who would dictate terms to new states without granting those states the same rights that adhered in the original states. Jefferson's axiomatic embrace of "mild" government ultimately dictated a static view of *self*-government.[25]

Amelioration, or gradualism, never really had a chance, if one looks at the subjective path Jeffersonian neology took as the expansion of cotton and sugar production responded to market forces and slaves were transported to the Deep South and Southwest. It was "knowledge" that Jefferson generally referred to whenever he used the word "diffusion" before 1800, and occasionally afterward. It was, most curiously, the African American mathematician Benjamin Banneker, son of a slave, who pleaded with Jefferson when secretary of state to engage "the most active diffusion of your exertions" in the promotion of some measure of justice for the enslaved. In 1810, Jefferson was speaking of breeding merino sheep when he recommended the "diffusion of the race . . . as fast as their increase shall permit."[26]

The species of "diffusion" that came to the fore in the Missouri debate was meant to mollify southern elites as it modified growth patterns among the slave population in the southeastern states. Typifying congressional reaction to the Jeffersonian position, Pennsylvanian William Darlington, a physician, argued as Jefferson did in his draft of the Declaration of Independence that King George III had foisted slavery on America against the will of its colonial legislatures, just as future generations of westerners would indict Congress if it countenanced the further spread of the "desolating evil." Said Darlington for the record: "If we suffer this pernicious population to ramify and diffuse itself throughout the new states to be formed in our territories, their citizens will one day direct their agonized views to the proceedings of this body. . . . Will any gentleman of Virginia or Maryland say, that it would not have been a happy circumstance for their own states if the early settlers had been prevented from introducing slaves among them?"[27]

Dierksheide develops the fallacy of antislavery "diffusion" by charting the rhetorical shift to proslavery diffusion. With no humanistic theory to rationalize racialism, Missouri's defenders of slavery aimed to make free black settlement illegal in the new state. As Adam Rothman has starkly exposed, it was not just Virginians with slaves to sell but well-heeled northerners too who saw opportunities. Surplus humans were "driven like cattle," in the words of one contemporaneous observer. Next, the twisted logic of proslavery took a religious turn, finding in biblical injunctions to practice industry, loyalty, and honorable submission a way to rationalize slave ownership as long as masters mercifully tended to their slaves' needs and encouraged them to exercise religion. Jefferson's states'-rights argument stood rigidly throughout the Missouri crisis, tapping the language and ostensible spirit of the federal Constitution—an uncomfortable massaging of political reality. Because of this, Jefferson's effusiveness as a writer, his obvious erudition, are no longer enough to offset his twenty-first-century reputation as a founder with insufficient moral courage.[28]

This, then, was the revolutionary inheritance that Republicans of the Jeffersonian period sought to codify, and eventually lost control of, by enlarging on the emotive script first introduced by Jefferson. Theirs was a manner of political expression that denied an interest in—indeed, expressed a revulsion to—the exercise of unjust power. Its most obvious source of rhetorical authority was the third president's magnanimously framed first inaugural address.

From his days as a student, Jefferson developed a conception of friendship that extended from individual relationships to the larger community. The nature of friendship enveloped his prescriptive vocabulary on all levels of engagement and ultimately informed his confidence as a political actor. He drew from his literary-philosophic models—the Ciceronian ethos, Lord Bolingbroke's intellectual challenge to conformity, Adam Smith's *Theory of Moral Sentiments,* and Laurence Sterne's politics of sympathy and generosity, to name some of the most prominent sources—a method of public engagement. The enlightened humanism Jefferson channeled in this way imbued him with prophetic pretensions.[29]

Here was Jefferson as a chief proponent of the republic of letters and the purveyor of an American ethos that cast the United States as a sanctuary. Rational friendship extended a healthy national psychology, and rational dialogue kept dangerous passions at bay. The work of Jay Fliegelman shines a light on Jefferson in the midst of an "elocutionary revolution" that "made the credibility of arguments contingent on the emotional credibility of the speaker." The outwardly impassive Virginian sought nothing so much as to win the emotional argument over constituent powers within the republic. In this effort, he resorted to an inflated rhetoric when required, sometimes disregarding his own strict constructionism (as in the acquisition of Louisiana) and abandoning hallowed principles (in his acceptance of the French Revolution at its most violent and in his cynical refusal to empathize with black republicans in Haiti). But the distinctiveness of Jefferson's brand of optimism, when the subject was his nation's capacity to recover affectionate bonds, overshadowed morose predictions about conflicts over which the United States exercised little meaningful control.[30]

It remains impossible for the student of history to ignore the failure of the Jeffersonian script to prevent alienation of significant parts of the commonwealth, even as the Federalist Party disintegrated. The mask of feigned unity between North and South was going to come off. The Embargo and, most explosively, slavery upset the prescriptive language of "harmony and affection" that announced Jefferson's arrival in Washington in 1801. And yet, the progressive spirit and inherent unselfishness of the "sovereign people" became a staple of democratic political discourse in the middle decades of the nineteenth century, morphing eventually into what we know as the doctrine of American exceptionalism.

Jefferson was the progenitor of that assertive vocabulary when he pronounced America "the world's best hope" on the day of his inauguration. He never doubted the correctness of his course, especially when it embraced a patriotic idiom. Jefferson's allure as a stylist as well as his power over historical narrative is what keeps him ever in the public eye. In political speech, he is the eternal flame, as I set forth in my recent book, *Democracy's Muse.*[31] For a man universally described as modest, performing only at the dinner table or private salon, an inner ardor spreads like wildfire across the page; his letters and published writings are overflowing performances.

As Peter Onuf has clarified for us over the course of his academic career, politics, like celebrity, is performative. It is performance built on—and realized through—mastery of a language of persuasion. The Jeffersonian manner of friendship may have been advanced through the exercise of creative faculties, through good-hearted, often sardonic engagement with affairs of the moment, but, as Onuf writes in "Making Sense of Jefferson," political friendship was skillfully worked by the third president when he orchestrated dinner gatherings for those legislators he wanted to "talk up" so as to advance the Jeffersonian order. In applying his personal rules of friendship to executive functions, he subtly fashioned a hierarchy of power within his party. One tends to assume that friendship is democratic in nature, but in politics that is rarely the case.[32]

Jefferson's people consistently mocked themselves by creating unrealistic expectations of political life. The high-flying phrases of the Declaration of Independence—led by "all men are created equal"—made it difficult for politicians to acknowledge the inherent limitations of republican theory. A cult of celebrity was indulged as well, beginning but not ending with George Washington. It was a similar kind of adulatory behavior as that reserved for monarchies. The irony was lost on all.

The middle ranks of men, among them Jefferson's mythical yeomen, were supposed to be something other than banal in their concerns and aspirations. Americans' dignified commonness was meant to differentiate this people from a morally deficient Old World. But commonness in republican America, like "the common good," was almost immediately superseded by the power of class envy. The fully realized republican was supposed to bear the marks of a Washington or a Jefferson, who were constructed by their eulogists and biographers as leaders impervious to accolades, oblivious to charisma, engaged in the pursuit of unselfish aims, and maintaining spotless virtue.

Republicanism did not have to be torn asunder by slavery; there were other inherent contradictions sufficient to do the job. The Jeffersonians, in their rhetorical rejection of power, put up an impossible target to aim at. Their world was, self-evidently, a melodrama seeking to become an epic poem.

Notes

1. Peter S. Onuf, *The Origins of the Federal Republic* (Philadelphia, 1983); Onuf, *Jefferson's Empire: The Language of American Nationhood* (Charlottesville, Va., 2000),

113–18, 117 (quotation). The language of nationhood, with an emphasis on Jefferson's justifications for a republican empire at odds with George Washington's centrally defined vision, is newly developed in Onuf, *Jefferson and the Virginians: Democracy, Constitutions, and Empire* (Baton Rouge, La., 2018), chapter 4.

2. Onuf, *Jefferson's Empire,* chapter 5, 149 (quotation); "Reply to Holly Brewer, by Peter Onuf," H-SHEAR, Jan. 17, 2001, copy in author's possession.

3. Peter S. Onuf, "Every Generation Is an Independant Nation': Colonization, Miscegenation, and the Fate of Jefferson's Children," in Onuf, *The Mind of Thomas Jefferson* (Charlottesville, Va., 2007), 216; from an essay originally published in *William and Mary Quarterly,* 3rd ser., 56 (2000): 155–72.

4. Jefferson to Priestley, Mar. 21, 1801, in in Julian P. Boyd et al., eds., *Papers of Thomas Jefferson* (Princeton, N.J., 1951–), 33:293–94 (hereafter *PTJ*).

5. William Wirt, *Sketches of the Life of Patrick Henry* (1817; reprint, Hartford, Conn., 1832), 91, 94, 102–3. On the contemporaneous reaction to the style, substance, and assertive nationalism in Wirt's biography, and the range of expectations from revolutionary models, see Carolyn Eastman, *A Nation of Speechifiers: Making an American Public after the Revolution* (Chicago, 2009), 17–29, and Scott E. Casper, *Constructing American Lives: Biography and Culture in Nineteenth-Century America* (Chapel Hill, N.C., 1999), 46–67.

6. Robert G. Parkinson, "Friends and Enemies in the Declaration of Independence," in this volume; Samuel Johnson, *A Dictionary of the English Language* (Philadelphia, 1813). With an alternative spelling, "harass" is defined as "to tire or make feeble," in Reverend Francis Allen's *A Complete English Dictionary* (London, 1765).

7. Thomas Gustafson, *Representative Words: Politics, Literature, and the American Language, 1776–1865* (New York, 1992), 204; Andrew Burstein, *Sentimental Democracy: The Evolution of America's Romantic Self-Image* (New York, 1999), 189.

8. Kenneth Cmiel, *Democratic Eloquence: The Fight over Popular Speech in Nineteenth-Century America* (Berkeley, Calif., 1990), chapter 1, 26 (quotation); Burstein, *Sentimental Democracy,* chapters 3–5.

9. John E. Ferling, *The First of Men: A Life of George Washington* (Knoxville, Tenn., 1988), 376, 389, 447–52; Nancy Isenberg, *Fallen Founder: The Life of Aaron Burr* (New York, 2007), 307–9, 315; Mark R. Cheathem, *Andrew Jackson, Southerner* (Baton Rouge, La., 2013), chapter 17.

10. Andrew Burstein, *Jefferson's Secrets: Death and Desire at Monticello* (New York, 2005), 48–54, 199–205.

11. Andrew Koppelman, *Defending American Religious Neutrality* (Cambridge, Mass., 2013); John A. Ragosta, *Wellspring of Liberty: How Virginia's Religious Dissenters Helped Win the American Revolution and Secured Religious Liberty* (New York, 2010); Ragosta, "A Religious Republican and a Republican Religion," in this volume; Gregg L. Frazer, *The Religious Beliefs of America's Founders: Reason, Revelation, and Revolution* (Lawrence, Kans., 2012), chapter 5; Andrew Burstein and Nancy Isenberg, *Madison and Jefferson* (New York, 2010), 117–19.

12. First Inaugural Address, in *PTJ,* 33:148–52.

13. Ibid.; Jefferson to the Georgia Legislature, Jan. 15, 1802, in ibid, 36:377–78.

14. Andrew Burstein, *The Inner Jefferson: Portrait of a Grieving Optimist* (Charlottesville, Va., 1995), 140; Burstein, *Jefferson's Secrets,* chapter 9; Jefferson to Edward Dowse, Apr. 19, 1803, in *PTJ,* 40:236.

15. Peter S. Onuf, "Thomas Jefferson and American Democracy," in *Seeing Jefferson Anew: In His Time and Ours,* ed. John B. Boles and Randal L. Hall (Charlottesville, Va., 2010), 21.

16. Mark Smith, "Beyond Strict Construction: Jeffersonians in the 1790s," in this volume.

17. Burstein and Isenberg, *Madison and Jefferson,* 221–23, 234–40, 264–68; Peter S. Onuf, "Thomas Jefferson, Federalist," in Onuf, *The Mind of Thomas Jefferson,* 87.

18. Burstein and Isenberg, *Madison and Jefferson,* 254–57.

19. Benjamin L. Carp, "Jefferson's Embargo: National Intent and Sectional Effects," in this volume.

20. *National Intelligencer* (Washington, D.C.), July 13, 1808.

21. [John Quincy Adams], *American Principles: A Review of the Works of Fisher Ames* (Boston, 1809), 7, 19 (quotations); *Anti-Monarchist, and Republican Watchman* (Northampton, Mass.), Aug. 23, 1809.

22. Carp, "Jefferson's Embargo," page 138.

23. Burstein and Isenberg, *Madison and Jefferson,* chapter 12. On the role of newspapers in exacerbating party contention, see Jeffrey L. Pasley, *"The Tyranny of Printers": Newspaper Politics in the Early American Republic* (Charlottesville, Va., 2001).

24. Short to Jefferson, Feb. 27, 1798, in *PTJ,* 30:151–52. On mastery, see Annette Gordon-Reed and Peter S. Onuf, *"Most Blessed of the Patriarchs": Thomas Jefferson and the Empire of the Imagination* (New York, 2016).

25. Onuf, *Jefferson's Empire,* chapter 4.

26. Banneker to Jefferson, Aug. 19, 1791, in *PTJ,* 22:50; Jefferson to William Jarvis, Dec. 5, 1810, in J. Jefferson Looney et al., eds., *Papers of Thomas Jefferson: Retirement Series* (Princeton, N.J., 2004–), 3:239–40. Federalist newspapers of the time of Jefferson's accession to the presidency invariably gave "diffusion" the same positive gloss, generically as "diffusion of information," but also "to diffuse correct & salutary notions of the principles of our government." *Alexandria [Va.] Advertiser,* Jan. 16, 1801. See also "the diffusion of political *light,*" in *Columbian Centinel* (Boston), Jan. 17, 1801. Also noteworthy, the *Federal Gazette* (Baltimore), on May 7, 1801, reprinted a letter promoting "the diffusion of knowledge amongst the African race, by unfettering their thoughts and giving full scope to the energy of their minds."

27. *Village Record* (West Chester, Penn.), July 12, 1820.

28. Adam Rothman, *Slave Country: American Expansion and the Origins of the Deep South* (Cambridge, Mass., 2005), chapter 5, 201 (quotation). Merrill D. Peterson neatly synthesizes the political maneuvers of Speaker of the House Henry Clay, who though a proponent of diffusion on the order of Jefferson, seeking a practical means to "lighten the fears of emancipation in overcrowded southern states" and advance the cause of colonization, acted to preserve the torn union through compromise, yet he cared little

for the plight of free blacks in Missouri. See Peterson, *The Great Triumvirate: Webster, Clay, and Calhoun* (New York, 1987), 60–66.

29. In general, see Burstein, *Inner Jefferson,* chapters 2–6, and Hannah Spahn, *Thomas Jefferson, Time, and History* (Charlottesville, Va., 2011), chapter 3. I am especially influenced in this arena of thought by Maurizio Valsania, *The Limits of Optimism: Thomas Jefferson's Dualistic Enlightenment* (Charlottesville, Va., 2011), which demonstrates how Jefferson's deep anxieties coexisted with unbanishable dreamy projections. Valsania writes, "Jefferson's philosophy was consistently an unstable compound of progressive and conservative, forward and backward, universal and particular, optimistic and despondent beliefs and discourses" (138).

30. Jay Fliegelman, *Declaring Independence: Jefferson, Natural Language, and the Culture of Performance* (Stanford, Calif., 1993), 2 (quotation). Fliegelman's is a close study of Jefferson's rhythmic cadence, musical elements, points of emphasis, and adaptations from literary sources.

31. Andrew Burstein, *Democracy's Muse: How Thomas Jefferson Became an FDR Liberal, a Reagan Republican, and a Tea Party Fanatic, All the While Being Dead* (Charlottesville, Va., 2015).

32. Peter S. Onuf, "Making Sense of Jefferson," in Onuf, *The Mind of Thomas Jefferson,* 19–49. This was originally published under the title "The Scholars' Jefferson," in the *William and Mary Quarterly,* 3rd ser., 50 (1993): 671–99.

Contributors

Andrew Burstein is the Charles P. Manship Professor of History at Louisiana State University. He is the coauthor, with Nancy Isenberg, of *The Problem of Democracy: The Presidents Adams Confront the Cult of Personality* (2019) and *Madison and Jefferson* (2010). He is also the author of *Democracy's Muse: How Thomas Jefferson Became an FDR Liberal, a Reagan Republican, and a Tea Party Fanatic, All the While Being Dead* (2015), *Jefferson's Secrets: Death and Desire at Monticello* (2005), *The Inner Jefferson: Portrait of a Grieving Optimist* (1995), and several other books pertaining to political and cultural history.

Benjamin L. Carp is Associate Professor and holder of the Daniel M. Lyons Chair in American history at Brooklyn College of the City University of New York. He is the author of *Defiance of the Patriots: The Boston Tea Party and the Making of America* (2010) and *Rebels Rising: Cities and the American Revolution* (2007); he is co-editor, with Richard D. Brown, of *Major Problems in the Era of the American Revolution, 1760–1791: Documents and Essays,* 3rd edition (2014).

Christa Dierksheide is Brockman Foundation Jefferson Scholars Foundation Professor and Associate Professor of History at the University of Virginia and a Senior Fellow at the Robert H. Smith International Center for Jefferson Studies, Monticello. She is the author of *Amelioration and Empire: Progress and Slavery in Plantation America, 1770–1840* (2014).

JOANNE B. FREEMAN is Professor of History and American Studies at Yale University, and a co-host of the American history podcast BackStory. She is the author of *Affairs of Honor: National Politics in the New Republic* (2001), *Alexander Hamilton: Writings* (2001), *The Essential Hamilton: Letters and Other Writings* (2017), and *The Field of Blood: Violence in Congress and the Road to Civil War* (2018).

KEVIN R. C. GUTZMAN, JD, PhD, is Professor and former Chairman in the Department of History at Western Connecticut State University and author of five books, including *Thomas Jefferson—Revolutionary* (a book club selection), *James Madison and the Making of America* (a book club main selection), *Virginia's American Revolution: From Dominion to Republic, 1776–1840,* and two bestsellers in American constitutional history (one of them a book club main selection). Publications in which his scholarly articles have appeared include the *Journal of Southern History, Journal of the Early Republic, Virginia Magazine of History and Biography, Review of Politics,* and *Journal of the Historical Society,* among several others.

JAMES E. LEWIS JR. is a Professor of History at Kalamazoo College. He has written extensively on the foreign policy, politics, and political culture of the early republic. His most recent book is *The Burr Conspiracy: Uncovering the Story of an Early American Crisis* (2017).

JOHANN N. NEEM is Professor of History at Western Washington University. He is the author of *What's the Point of College?* (2019), *Democracy's Schools: The Rise of Public Education in America* (2017), and *Creating a Nation of Joiners: Democracy and Civil Society in Early National Massachusetts* (2008).

MARTIN ÖHMAN is a researcher at the Department of Historical Studies at Gothenburg University, Sweden. His articles have appeared in *Diplomatic History,* the *Journal of the Early Republic,* and *Early American Studies.* He is currently working on a project financed by the Swedish Foundation for Humanities and Social Sciences that focuses on the mobilization of associations of "friends of industry" from the end of the Napoleonic Wars to the Civil War era.

ROBERT G. PARKINSON is Associate Professor of History at Binghamton University and the author of *The Common Cause: Creating Race and Nation in the American Revolution* (2016). His current project is a study of the 1774 massacre on Yellow Creek entitled *The Heart of American Darkness: Savagery, Civility, and Murder on the Eve of the American Revolution.*

John A. Ragosta, a historian and lawyer, was an international trade attorney before returning to academia. He has taught history and law at the University of Virginia, George Washington University, and Hamilton, Oberlin, and Randolph Colleges. Currently a Fellow at Virginia Humanities and a historian at the International Center for Jefferson Studies at Monticello, he is the author of *Religious Freedom: Jefferson's Legacy, America's Creed* (2013) and *Patrick Henry: Proclaiming a Revolution* (2017).

Leonard J. Sadosky (1972–2018) was the author of *Revolutionary Negotiations: Indians, Empires, and Diplomats in the Founding of America* (2009) and, with Peter S. Onuf, *Jeffersonian America* (2002). He co-edited the collection *Old World, New World: America and Europe in the Age of Jefferson* (2010).

Richard Samuelson is Associate Professor of History at California State University, San Bernardino. He is the editor of *The Political Writings of James Otis.* He is completing an edition of John Adams's *Defence of the Constitutions* and *Discourses on Davila,* and a book, *John Adams and the Republic of Laws.*

Brian Schoen is Associate Professor of History at Ohio University. He is the author of *The Fragile Fabric of Union: Cotton, Federal Politics, and the Global Origins of the Civil War* (2009) and co-editor of *Between Sovereignty and Anarchy: The Politics of Violence in the American Revolutionary Era* (2015) and *The Old South's Modern Worlds: Slavery, Region, and Nation in the Age of Progress* (2011).

Mark Smith is currently the Chair of the History Department and the Robert Sortland Chair in American Studies at John Burroughs School in St. Louis. He has published work in the *History Teacher, American National Biography,* and the *Pennsylvania Magazine of History and Biography.*

Andrew Trees is the author of *The Founding Fathers and the Politics of Character* (2005) and is a Visiting Assistant Professor at Roosevelt University.

Index

"Account of Louisiana, An" (Jefferson report), 57n47
Adair, Douglas, 266
Adams, Abigail, 149
Adams, Abijah, 102n76
Adams, Henry, 69, 96, 129, 140, 218n10
Adams, John: on American national pride, 286; on Butterfield's acceptance of British terms at Cedars, 24; drafting of Declaration of Independence, 18, 26; on Dunmore's African American regiment, 30; and election of 1800, 184; and the Enlightenment, 217n5; exhortation to colonists after Cedars, 26; and intelligence about German mercenaries, 18; on loss of Canada, 25–26; and Lower South westerners, 182
Adams, John Quincy: and abolition of slavery, 253; and compensation for NEML investors, 187; diplomatic mission to end War of 1812, 166; and Embargo Act, 137, 291; on sectional interests, 138; and Spanish Florida, 8, 191
Adams, Samuel, 19, 25, 286
Adams, Thomas, 102n76
Adams-Onís Treaty, 8
African Americans: collective sense of themselves as Africans, 250; Dunmore's regiment, 30; Jefferson's views of abilities of, 117, 250; slaves and free, 186, 192–93. *See also* slaves and slavery
agrarian economy. *See* yeomen and yeoman ideal
Alien and Sedition Acts: constitutional objections to, 91–92; Lower South sentiment, 185; policy-based objections to, 92–96; prosecutions under, 94, 102n76
American Colonization Society, 118
American degeneracy, 200, 217n3
American exceptionalism, 295, 296
"American people, the": based on exclusion, 15, 31–32; Federalists policies as not serving, 80, 81; inherent unselfishness of, 295; Jeffersonian Republicans as party of, 5, 211–12; Jefferson's confidence in, 209, 223–24; Madison's belief in willingness of, to sacrifice, 271; as more honest than that of wealthy, 112; reliable "spirit" of, 286; response

"American people, the" (*continued*) to Embargo Act, 131; role in extended republic, 263–64; and spread of slavery, 254; strength of federal government due to, 8, 223, 288; as supporters of law, 129; will of, as supreme, 8, 87, 90, 92, 108, 124n11, 273, 275
"American System," 262–63
Ames, Fisher, 84
Arendt, Hannah, 281n62
Argus (brig), 95, 102n76
armed forces: and Burr Conspiracy, 223, 225, 226, 228–30, 233, 239n25; and defense of states' territorial claims, 283; funding of, 162, 165; Jefferson's views about using, 237–38n3; navy, 154, 183; standing army, 1, 169, 262, 280n36; state militias, 190, 191, 223, 233; and War of 1812, 190
Arnold, Benedict, 23, 24
Atlantic states, fear of expansionism, 44
Atlantic system of trade: after Revolutionary War, 40, 155, 175n13; collapse of, 158; as security against misbehavior, 269
Austin, David, 65

Bache, Benjamin Franklin, 92, 94, 102n76
Bacon, Ezekiel, 140
Bacon, Sir Francis, 113, 201
Bailey, Jeremy D., 69
Baldwin, Abraham, 185
Balogh, Brian, 4, 266
Bank of North America, 84
Bank of the United States: charter renewal, 161–62, 163–65, 176n25, 176n28, 176n31; considered constitutional over time, 276; constitutional objections to, 82–83, 85; effectiveness of, 162; as hindering American economic development, 81; opposition of rank-and-file Jeffersonian Republicans to, 1, 82–87, 161, 162–64, 176n28; policy-based objections to, 83–87; as wealth transfer, 85–86
Banneker, Benjamin, 293
Banner, James M., 129
Barbary Pirates, 154
Barclay, Thomas, 133
Barker, Jacob, 166
Bartlett, Josiah, 17, 18, 25
Bathélemy, Jean-Jacques, 266
Battle of Fallen Timbers, 182
Battle of Holy Ground, 191
Bayard, James, 166
Bedel, Thomas, 23, 24, 25
Bee (newspaper), 93, 102n76
"Benedict Arnold" (pseudonym), 94
"Bill Concerning Slaves, A" (Virginia), 115
"Bill Concerning the Course of Descents, A" (Virginia), 114
"Bill for Proportioning Crimes and Punishments in Cases Heretofore Capital" (Virginia), 114
Bland, Richard "Spectacle Dick," 107
Bonus Bill, 169–70, 271–73
Boston Chronicle, 102n76
Boudinot, Elias, 84
Bouton, Terry, 135–36
Boyd, Julian Parks, 37n52
Brant, Irving, 271, 272
Breckinridge, John, 49, 252, 253
"broken voyages," 154, 156
Broussard, James H., 135
Buffon, Comte de (George Louis Leclerc), 200, 216–17n3
"Bunker's Hill Man, A" (pseudonym), 90
Burk, John D., 102n76
Burr, Aaron, 219n27

Burr Conspiracy: availability of information about, 222, 227, 228; cabinet decisions about, 224–26, 227; and Federalists, 229–30; and Jefferson's belief in American people's cooperation with law, 129; Jefferson's message to Congress, 230–34, 235–37; Jefferson's response to, 8–9, 222–23, 226–27, 228–29, 235–37, 237–38n3, 239n25; and Madison, 224–26, 229, 230, 238n10, 239n31; objectives of, 222, 225, 232, 238n6
Burstein, Andrew, 221n41
Burwell, William A., 176n28, 234
Butterfield, Isaac, 23–24

Cabell presentment of 1797, 120
Caius, 85
Calhoun, John C., 169, 190
Campbell, George W., 166, 167
Campbell, William, 29
Canada, 23, 25–26
capital punishment: in Revisal of the Laws, 114; in Virginia constitution, 110, 112, 113, 114
Carleton, Guy, 23
Carswell, Samuel, 163–64
Carter, Landon, 30
Caughnawaga, 23
Cayton, Andrew R. L., 182
Cedars stockade incident, 23–27
Centinel of Freedom (newspaper), 95
Cherokee, 23–26, 27, 32, 36n37, 182, 186
Chesapeake-Leopard affair, 130, 156, 158
Cheves, Langdon, 178
Christianity, 73, 75n3, 114, 125n28
churches: incorporation of, 64–65, 76n16; ownership of land in Revisal of the Laws, 114; on public land, 67. *See also* religion, freedom of
citizenship, 111, 115, 275
Claiborne, Ferdinand, 191
Claiborne, William, 190
classism, and Bank of the United States, 84, 85, 86
Clay, Henry, 166, 169, 262–63, 298–99n28
Clinton, DeWitt, 292
Clinton, George, 133, 165
Cmiel, Kenneth, 286
Coke, Edward, 275
College of William and Mary, 106, 115
commerce: Atlantic system, 40, 155, 158, 175n13, 269; as cause of war, 268; and depression of late 1790s, 48, 49; and discriminatory duties, 46, 52; factors necessary for, 44; Federalist championing of Atlantic/global marketplace, 151; with France, 41, 44–45, 46, 48, 51, 56n39, 154; international, as vital to economy, 148; and Jay Treaty, 5–6, 46–47, 48, 51–52, 181, 183, 268; during Jefferson presidency, 154, 155–56, 157–58; Madison's assumption about efficacy of commercial coercion, 268–69, 279n32; during Napoleonic Wars, 154, 155–56, 157–58; nonintercourse policy, 158–60; opening of Mediterranean to, 168; as original objective of Monroe-Livingston mission, 38; and protection of property, 267; realignment as necessary for genuine independence, 40–41; regulation of interstate, 277; with Spain, 42–46, 47–48, 55n20; yeomen's need for, 268. *See also* Embargo Act (1807); Louisiana Purchase
Committee of Five, 18. *See also* Declaration of Independence
Committee on the Cedars Cartel, 26–27
"common cause," using exclusion to create, 15, 16–21, 30–31, 34n10, 34n12

"common good," Federalists as party of, 5
Condorcet, Marquis de, 266
Confederation era, conditions in Lower South during, 180
Congregational Church, 69–70, 72
Connecticut, 60, 69–71
Connecticut Courant (Watson), 35n27
Constitution: amendment process, 272–73, 274, 277, 280n48; as basis of objections to Alien and Sedition Acts, 91–92; as basis of objections to Bank of the United States, 82–83, 85; as basis of objections to official prayer proclamations, 61–62; as basis of objections to Washington's Neutrality Proclamation, 88; constancy of meaning over time, 274; and Embargo Act, 280n40; and financial stability, 150; Jeffersonian Republicans as strict constructionists, 80, 82; and Jefferson's belief in self-government, 74, 204–5, 213, 273; Lower South support for, 180; and Madison's Bonus bill veto, 169–70, 271–72; ratification of, 278n7; as source of party distinctions, 281n54; states and contract clause, 187; states' regulation of religion, 61, 68; and use of armed forces during Burr Conspiracy, 229; and will of people, 275. *See also* strict constructionism
consumers, to Jeffersonian Republicans, 152, 168, 171
Continental Army, recruitment of Native Americans into, 25
Continental Congress: actions of, while considering independence, 25–26; committee to write Declaration of Independence, 25–26; effect of Cedars news on, 25–27; and German mercenaries as proxies of George III, 16–21, 34n10, 34n12; and Native Americans as proxies of George III, 16–17, 22–26; representatives to, as "we" in Declaration of Independence, 16; and slaves as proxies of George III, 16–17, 22; unity of population as crucial for success, 15
Continental System, 155
Cook, Orchard, 133
Cooper, Thomas, 102n76, 185
Coxe, Tench, 57n51
Crawford, William H., 133, 188, 190
Creek, 23–26, 27, 182, 186, 190–91
culture, government institutions as shapers of, 3
Cunningham, Noble E., 2

Dallas, Alexander, 167
Danbury Baptists, letter to (Jefferson, 1801), 59, 69, 73
Darlington, William, 293–94
Dartmouth Gazette, 72
Daveiss, Joseph Hamilton, 227
Davids, James A., 67
Dearborn, Henry, 66, 153–54, 224–26, 228
Decatur, Stephen, 226
Declaration of Independence: accusations against George III, 16, 33, 293; committee to draft, 18, 25–26; compared to *Summary View of the Rights of British America,* 108; events during drafting of, 26–27, 36n38; exclusion used to create unity, 15, 31–32; immigration in, 93; individuals and groups of people named in, 16–17, 32n2; Jefferson's duties while drafting, 26–28; as justification for actions against slaves and Native Americans, 33; and proxies for George III, 16–21, 22–26, 34n10, 34n12; purpose of, 15; rhetoric used in, 31, 33, 285; similarities to Virginia constitution,

28; similarities to Wythe's appeal to German mercenaries, 20
Delesdernier, Lewis, 137
"Democrat, A" (pseudonym), 89–90
Democratic-Republicans, as proslavery, 254
Democratic Society of Kentucky, 45–46
Detached Memorandum (Madison), 72–73
Dew, Thomas Roderick, 256
diffusion, 9, 293; antislavery, 215–16, 251–54, 255–56; as compromise to preserve union, 298n28; and Federalists, 298n26; as moral recourse, 254–55; proslavery, 243, 254, 255, 256–57; and slave trade, 255, 293
"Draft Declaration and Protest of the Commonwealth of Virginia, on the Principles of the Constitution of the United States of America, and on the Violations of Them" (Jefferson), 122–23
Drakeman, Donald L., 76n16
Duane, William, 102n76
Dunmore, Lord, 28–30
Durrell, William, 102n76

easterners and eastern states, 44, 85
economy and national finances: attempted elimination of national debt, 154, 155; Bank of the United States, 81; consumption and production, 152, 168, 171; and Embargo Act, 156, 158; at end of War of 1812, 167; financial stability and the Constitution, 150; government institutions as shapers of, 3; Hamiltonian model as based on British, 119; and internal improvements, 272; during Jefferson presidency, 154, 155–56, 157; national currency, 168, 169; and nonimportation policy of Madison, 160; proposed Jay-Gravier Treaty, 41; slavery as essential to, 257; during War of 1812, 165, 166–67. *See also* commerce; yeomen and yeoman ideal
Edling, Max M., 156–57, 166, 173n9
Edwards, Pierpont, 69–70
election of 1800, 184, 185
Elusive Republic, The (McCoy), 3
emancipation: British offer of, for military service, 28–30; with colonization in Africa, 118, 215, 244, 245; diffusion would promote gradual, 251; and the Enlightenment, 244; Hillhouse proposal failure, 253; Jeffersonian Republicans favoring, 242; in stages, 243, 244, 292
Embargo Act (1807): and American economy and finances, 156, 158; and criticism of Virginia as having lock on presidency, 291; as enabling effective limited federal government, 270–72; enforcement of, 7, 130, 131–32, 135–38, 139–40; and Enlightenment principles, 205; failure of, 158; Federalist resistance to, 132, 134, 138, 139, 291; historiography of, 129–30; and Jefferson, 129–30, 131, 134, 140–41; Jeffersonian Republican opposition to, 132, 133, 135, 140; Lower South support for, 190; and Madison, 137, 270, 280n40; mobilization of support for, 134; Non-Intercourse Act as replacement for, 141, 159; passage of, 134; and personality conflicts, 129; as preventing war and fostering peace, 270; protests against, 7, 134–35, 137–38; as return to American roots, 158–59; and sectionalism, 128, 132–33, 134, 135, 138–39, 140
Enforcement Act (1809), 131–32, 139

English Sierra Leone Company, 248
Enlightenment, the: and emancipation of slaves, 244; existence of multiple, 202; incremental progress to improved world, 292; to other founders, 201, 217n5, 218n7. *See also* Jefferson, Thomas: and the Enlightenment
Enquirer (Richmond), 138
"Ethiopian Regiment," 29–30
exclusion, using to create unity, 15, 16–21, 31–32, 34n10, 34n12
expansionism: and diffusion of slaves, 243, 251–55; feared by Atlantic states, 44; and internal improvements, 169, 193; land as empty, 257; and land speculation in Georgia, 181, 187–88; Louisiana Purchase as beginning of, 40; and national identity, 39; and Native Americans, 45, 171; and proposed commercial treaty with Spain, 42–43; as safety valve for dangerous slaves, 43–44; into Spanish Florida, 188–89; as strengthening bonds with France, 44–45; and yeoman ideal, 1, 39, 183

faith-based initiatives, 67
Farmers-General (monopoly), 41
Federal Gazette, 95
federal government: as ascendancy of nationalism, 106; basic organization and practices set by Federalists, 4; the Constitution and containment of, 129, 277; and Embargo Act, 7, 130, 131–32, 135–38, 270–72; enforcement of state laws banning free persons of color, 186; expenditure of private funds held in trust by, 66; in extended republics, 264; as fiscal-military state, 150–51, 153–57, 160, 165, 168, 170–72; and Georgia's western lands, 186; and internal improvements, 169–70, 193, 272; Jeffersonian ideal of, 1, 2; Jeffersonian Republicans as enabling Americans to unknowingly to benefit from, 4, 266; Lower South support for strong, 8, 181, 186, 190, 191–93; monarchy as result of increase in power of, 265–66; powers of, dependent on people, 276, 288; and proposed commercial treaty with Spain, 44, 55n20; and religious freedom, 68; and revenue sources, 154, 155, 156–67; southerners and southern states, 179, 186; states' dependence on, 178; strength of, 223, 266, 278n14, 283; taxation powers of, 91. *See also* strict constructionism; War of 1812
federalism: as basic to Jeffersonian creed, 87, 108–9, 123, 124n11; and containment of sectionalism, 129; as defined by Jefferson, 290; as exploitative system, 178; in Jefferson's constitution for Virginia, 111; requirement of limited central power, 264–66; and *Summary View of the Rights of British America,* 108. *See also* states
Federalists: accused of neglecting south, 179; anti-southern ideology of, 129; and backcountry "ruffians" of Lower South, 181, 182–83; basic federal government organization and practices set by, 4; and Burr Conspiracy, 229–30; championing of Atlantic/global marketplace, 151; as copyists of British system, 85; and diffusion, 298n26; and Embargo Act, 132, 134, 138, 139, 291; Hartford Convention, 262; Jeffersonian Republicans as waging "war on religion," 72; Jefferson's fear

of resurgence of, 292; and Jefferson's response to Burr Conspiracy, 223; and Lower South, 181, 182–83; monarchy as result of agenda of, 265–66; national government basic administrative organization and practices set by, 4; as party of common good, 5; policies of, as not serving American people, 80, 81; Republican opposition to policies, 1; response to Whiskey and Fries's Rebellions, 228; revenue sources under, 156–57; rhetoric used by Jefferson to describe, 1, 212, 287, 288; and spread of slavery, 254; strict constructionism and opposition to policies of, 81; westerners' increase in rift with, 45–46. *See also* Alien and Sedition Acts; Bank of the United States

Ferguson, E. James, 150

financial elite: as beneficiaries of Bank of the United States, 85, 86; as dishonest, 112; in rhetoric of Jeffersonian Republicans, 161, 162

Findley, William, 47

Fischer, David Hackett, 139

Fisk, Jonathan, 148

Fletcher v. Peck (1810), 187

Fliegelman, Jay, 295

Foster, Augustus, 189

Foster, George, 23, 24

France: commerce with, 41, 44–45, 46, 48, 51, 56n39, 154; and expansionism, 44–45; French Revolution, 46, 81, 87–91, 206–11, 290; issue of, in control of Louisiana, 50–51; Jeffersonian Republicans hope for close relations with, 51; Napoleonic Wars, 154, 155–56, 157–58; obligations to, 88, 89; Quasi-War with (1797–99), 1, 95–96; suspension of commerce with, 48, 56n39; and Treaty of Mortefontaine, 154; war debt owed to, 41; XYZ Affair, 91

franchise, 110–11, 112–13

Franklin, Benjamin, 26, 217n3, 217n5

Freneau, Philip, 83, 86, 88

Fries's Rebellion, 228

Frothingham, David, 102n76

Gabriel Prosser rebellion, 246–48

Gallatin, Albert: background of, 148–49; and Burr Conspiracy, 224–26, 239n25; cost of nonimportation policy, 160; diplomatic mission to end War of 1812, 166; and Embargo Act, 131, 136, 138, 291; and fiscal military state, 153–57, 160; on Florida, 189; Gallatinian-Hamiltonian system during War of 1812, 165; and Georgia land grants, 187; objections to Alien and Sedition Acts, 93–94, 95; on official duties of and private actions by officials, 63; and renewal of charter of Bank of the United States, 161–62, 165; and spread of slavery, 252; and taxation powers, 91

Garrard, James, 30

gender equality: in "A Bill Concerning the Course of Descents" in Virginia, 114; in education, 115–16; in Jefferson's constitution for Virginia, 110

General Advertiser (Bache), 84

Genet, Edmond-Charles, 87, 89, 133

George III (King): accusations against in Declaration of Independence, 16, 33, 293; proxies for in Declaration of Independence, 16–21, 22–26, 34n10, 34n12; proxies for in Virginia constitution, 28–29

Georgia. *See* Lower South

German mercenaries: as characterized by patriot leaders, 31; colonists' appeal to, 19–20; evidence of British hiring of, 17–18; intelligence about, 17–18; as proxies of George III in Declaration of Independence, 16–21, 34n10, 34n12; as proxies of George III in Virginia constitution, 28
Gerry, Elbridge, 30, 36n38, 84
Giles, William Branch, 82, 118–19, 252
Gore, Christopher, 249
government: institutions shape society, 3; limited, has limited sovereignty, 277; powers of, derive from the people, 8, 87, 90, 92, 108, 124n11, 273; purpose of, is protection of property and beliefs and thus liberty, 267; removing, as source of war, 269–70; types of republican, 279–80n33
Government Out of Sight, A (Balogh), 4, 266
gradualism policy of emancipation, 243, 244, 292. *See also* diffusion; repatriation
Graham, John, 225, 233
Granger, Gideon, 68, 228
Gravier, Charles, 41
Grayson, William, 42–43
Great Britain: accusations against people of and proxies of, in Declaration of Independence, 16–21, 22–26, 34n10, 34n12; Admiralty Court decision in *Polly* case, 154; as benefactor of U.S.-Spain rupture, 45; commerce with U.S., 40–41, 268–69; deportation of rebellious maroons, 249; as fiscal-military state, 150; and Jay Treaty, 46–47, 48, 51–52, 55n32, 183; Jefferson on Virginia's relationship with, 107–8; Jefferson's hostility toward, 219n22; and Napoleonic Wars, 154, 155–56, 157–58; and *Polly* case, 156; reconciliation with, 107; seizure of ships carrying goods to France, 46. *See also* Revolutionary War
Green, Steven K., 73
Greenleaf, Ann, 102n76
Greenleaf, Thomas, 92, 102n76
Griffin, Patrick, 182
Griswold, Stanley, 73–74
Grotius, Hugo, 89
Gunn, James, 181, 183
Gutzman, Kevin R. C., 280n40
Gwynn's Island, 30–31, 37n52

Haiti, 118, 184
Hamilton, Alexander: assumption of interdependence between nation's domestic system and place in world requiring commerce, 279n32; characteristics of, 149; as desiring to follow political and economic British model, 119; as "monocrat," 266; passage of fiscal policies, 181; on police power, 278n14; Republican opposition to policies of, 1; and Washington's Neutrality Proclamation, 88, 91. *See also* Bank of the United States
"Hancock" (pseudonym), 135
Hancock, John, 16
Harper, Robert, 185
Harrison, William, 186
Hartford Convention, 262
Haswell, Anthony, 102n76
Hatter, Lawrence B. A., 46–47
Hawkins, Benjamin, 186, 189
Hayne, Robert, 178, 182, 192, 193
"Helvidius" (Madison pseudonym), 88
Hemings, Sally, 221n41
Hendrickson, David C., 138
Henry, Patrick, 109, 242, 244, 285
Hillhouse, James, 134, 253
HMS *Leopard,* 130, 156, 158

Hook, Josiah, 137
House Committee of Commerce and Manufactures report (1803), 51–52
Hume, David, 84, 266
Hutcheson, Frances, 219n17

immigrants and immigration, 93, 115
independence: actions of Continental Congress while considering, 25–26; hiring of mercenaries as deciding factor to fight for and declare, 21; and international commerce, 40–41; motion to declare, in Continental Congress, 26
Independent Chronicle, 86, 102n76
internal improvements: constitutionality of, 272; and economy, 272; and expansionism, 169, 193; federal government, 169–70, 193; and Jeffersonian Republicans, 169–70; in Lower South, 193; and Madison, 272, 273
international law and abrogation of treaties, 89
"Ionotus" (pseudonym), 90
Iroquois, 22, 23

Jackson, Andrew, 190–91, 287
Jackson, James: and Bank of the United States, 82, 84; and commerce in southern states, 181; constituency of, 181; and fear of West Indian slaves, 184; and land grants, 187; and patronage, 185
Jackson, Robert, 63
Jay, John, 42–44, 46
Jay-Gardoqui agreement, 42–46, 55n20
Jay-Gravier Treaty, 41
Jay Treaty, 5–6, 46–47, 48, 51–52, 55n32, 181, 183, 268
Jefferson, Peter, 107
Jefferson, Thomas: ability to ignore contentious divisions, 290; belief in self-government, 204–5, 206, 214; belief in similarity of opinion among Americans, 1, 110–11, 112–13, 119, 120; and Cedars, 26–27; and College of William and Mary, 106, 115–16; commerce and finances while president, 154, 155–56, 157–58; commercial realignment as necessary for genuine independence, 40–41; confidence in American people, 8, 92, 129, 209, 223–24; and election of 1800, 1, 59–60; and Embargo Act, 129–30, 131, 134, 139, 140–41; on equal representation, 113; exhortation to colonists to fight, 19, 34n12; family background of, 107; fear of resurgence of Federalists, 292; and federalism, 68, 87, 108–9, 123, 124n11, 288, 290; and fiscal-military state, 170–72; and French Revolution, 209–11, 290; friendship as extending to national community, 284, 294, 295, 296; and gender equality, 110, 114; grave marker of, 105; as having prophetic pretensions, 294, 299n29; hostility toward Great Britain, 107, 219n22; as impenetrable mystery, 202, 218n10; and intelligence about German mercenaries, 18, 19; limitation of political activity due to age, 118; and Louisiana Purchase, 38, 49–50, 52–53, 57n47; as minister plenipotentiary to France, 41; on Monroe as minister plenipotentiary to France and Spain, 49; and Monticello, 201; and Native Americans, 31, 186, 284; on need for manufacturing, 121; and numeracy, 149; objections to Alien and Sedition Acts, 92; objections to Bank of the United States, 83, 86–87; perception of northerners, 283; promotion of

Jefferson, Thomas (*continued*)
international trade, 153; reaction to political disagreements, 211, 287; replacement of laws and constitutions, 111–12; Revisal of the Laws, 113–16; rhetoric used to describe Federalists, 1, 211–12, 287, 288; rhetoric used to describe Republicans, 287; sketch of Gwynn's Island, 30–31, 37n52; source of strength of federal government, 223, 288; state of mind at end of life, 122–23; on suspension of commerce with France, 56n39; and University of Virginia, 116, 121; on use of presidential veto, 87; use of word "sacred," 288–89; and Virginia constitution, 28–29, 30–31, 109–12, 111, 114, 121–22, 127n66; as Virginia governor, 117; on Virginia's relationship with Great Britain, 107–8; and War of 1812, 121; and Washington's Neutrality Proclamation, 88, 89; wish for egalitarian Virginia, 105–6. *See also* Burr Conspiracy; Declaration of Independence

—, and the Enlightenment: basic Enlightenment principles, 202; belief in self-government, 204–5, 206, 214; as compared to other founders, 201, 217n5, 218n7, 218n13; at core of self-image, 201, 203, 205, 257–59; and Embargo Act, 205; French Revolution, 206–8; and Louisiana Purchase, 213; Missouri crisis as abnegation and annihilation of, 214–15; moose request, 199–200, 216–17n3; necessity of always representing will of people, 211–12; principles of, and governing, 203–4, 213; rhetoric used to describe Federalists, 1, 212; and Shays's Rebellion, 205–6, 210; and slavery, 215–16, 220n41, 242–43, 250, 257; support of "the people," 209–10

—, and religion: attacked for lack of, during 1800 election, 59–60; and Christianity, 73, 75n3, 114, 125n28; convergence of revivalists and rational religious individuals, 287; and dismissal of Federalist appointees, 70–71; enforcement of Sabbath and service decorum, 114; freedom of, as "most inalienable and sacred of human rights," 65–66; government recommendations concerning, 61, 75n6; incorporation of churches, 65; as matter regulated by state, 61, 68; as out of government but in lives of government officials, 63; prayer at inaugurals and annual addresses to Congress, 62; prayer proclamations as violations of Constitution, 61–62; references to God, 287; Revisal of the Laws, 114; treaty with Kaskaskia, 66–67; use of House of Representatives for religious services, 64, 65, 76n14; use of presidential "bully pulpit," 69–72; in Virginia constitution, 111; Virginia Statute for Religious Freedom, 59, 60, 74, 106; on "wall of separation between Church & State," 59

—, and slaves/slavery: African Americans' sense of selves as Africans, 250; as countryless, 284; deportation of, 117–18, 246, 247–48; diffusion of, 9, 215–16, 243, 251–57, 293; and emancipation, 115; emancipation in stages, 243, 244, 292; and the Enlightenment, 215–16, 220n41, 242–43, 250, 257; on harm of slavery to America in international affairs, 245; on northern restrictionists, 254; preparation for freedom

on plantations, 245; as threat to union, 256; trade in, 115; on treatment of, 245; views of African Americans' abilities, 117, 250; in Virginia constitution, 111; as at war with United States, 284
Jeffersonian Republicans: belief in marketplace of ideas, 81, 88; challenge of balancing ideals and realities, 4, 68; as coalition based on convergence of interests, 6, 39, 45–46, 53; and compensation for NEML investors, 187–88; consumers and policies of, 152, 168, 171; as demystifying polity, 287; development of philosophy of, 96–97; as enabling Americans to unknowingly to benefit from government, 4, 266; as establishment party in Virginia, 7; federalism as creed of, 108–9, 123, 124n11; and internal improvements, 169–70; and Louisiana Purchase, 49–51, 57n51; in New England, 69–74; opposition to Alien and Sedition Acts, 91–96; opposition to Bank of the United States, 1, 82–87, 161, 162–64, 176n28; opposition to Embargo Act, 132, 133, 135, 140; opposition to Federalist policies, 1; opposition to Washington's Neutrality Proclamation, 87–91; as party finding identity, 96–97; as party of the American people, 5, 211–12; producer ethos, 151–52; relations with France, 51; and religious freedom, 3, 6, 59, 60, 62, 65–66, 72–74, 76n8, 78n39; response to capture of *Chesapeake,* 130–31; rhetoric used by Jefferson to describe, 287; sectionalism within, 292; as southern party, 133; as strict constructionists of Constitution, 80, 82; and wartime expansion of federal government powers, 167–68; will of people as supreme, 8, 87, 90, 92
—, rhetoric of: about financial elite, 161, 162; about holding office, 218n8; about "the people," 286; actions as mismatching, 7, 153, 170–71; extolling yeomen, 183; as making accomplishment of goals impossible, 296, 299n29
Jefferson's Empire: The Language of American Nationhood (Onuf), 283
Jennings, Walter W., 129
Jeremiah, Thomas, 28–29
John, Richard R., 3
Johnson, Andrew, 76n16
Johnson, Guy, 22, 23
Johnson, William, 187
Jones, William, 166

Kaskaskia, treaty with, 66–67
Kentucky Gazette, 48
Kentucky Resolutions, 92, 95
Kerber, Linda K., 129
Kernell, Samuel, 278n7
King, Rufus, 248
Knox, Henry, 153

Lafayette, Marquis de, 251
Lambert, John, 128
Lampi, Philip J., 132
land: acquisition of Native American, 66–67, 153–54, 186; ceded by Spain, 183; and Enlightenment yeoman ideal, 213; proposal to give state, to yeomen, 110–11, 112–13, 119; public sale of, 179; speculation in Georgia, 181, 187–88; and War of 1812, 189, 191; western, seen as empty, 257. *See also* expansionism
Langdon, John, 17
Lawrence, John, 84

Leclerc, George Louis. *See* Buffon, Comte de (George Louis Leclerc)
Lee, Henry, 55n20
Lee, John, 18
Lee, Richard Henry, 18, 21, 26, 108
Legion of the United States, 182
Letters from England (Voltaire), 267
Levy, Leonard W., 13
Lewis, James E., Jr., 129, 130
Liberia, 118
Lincoln, Benjamin, 137
Lincoln, Levi, 140, 187
Livingston, Edward, 91, 93, 95
Livingston, Robert, 38, 52
Livingston, William, 18, 26
Lloyd, James, 92
Locke, John, 88, 201, 219n17
Louisiana Purchase: benefits of, 50, 52, 57n51; concerns about, 39; details of, 38; development of support for, 49–51, 57n51; and Enlightenment beliefs of Jefferson, 213; financing of, 154–55, 174n12; importance of Mississippi River and New Orleans, 38, 39, 43, 48, 49, 50–51, 56n41, 154; necessity of constructing political economy in support of, 50; and Spain, 188; as surprise to Jefferson administration, 38, 49–50, 57n47; and westerners, 52–53
Louisiana Territory, 253
Love, John, 162
Lower South: Anglophobia of, 189, 192; coastal versus backcountry residents, 184–85; conditions during Confederation era, 180; and election of 1800, 184, 185; and Embargo Act, 190; and free persons of color, 186, 192–93; and internal improvements, 193; and Jay Treaty, 181, 183; land speculation in Georgia, 181, 187–88; Native American lands in, 182, 183; perception of national government of westerners in, 182–83; and Spanish Florida, 8, 188–89; support of Federalists, 181; support for strong central government, 8, 181, 186, 190, 191–93; and War of 1812, 190–91; western lands and federal government, 186
Lyon, James, 96

Macaulay, Zachary, 248
Macon, Nathaniel, 93
Macon's Bill no. 2 (1810), 159–60
Madison, James: on America as compound republic, 263–64; and Bank of the United States, 82, 84, 85, 162; and Bank of the United States charter renewal, 163, 164, 176n28; and Bonus Bill, 170, 271–73; and Burr Conspiracy, 224–26, 229, 230, 238n10, 239n31; and commercial coercion, 268–69, 279n32; commercial realignment as necessary for independence, 40–41; on constancy of meaning of Constitution over time, 274; on Constitution as source of party distinctions, 281n54; Constitution's amendment process, 272–73, 274, 277; discriminatory duties proposal, 46; and emancipation, 118, 242; and Embargo Act, 137, 270, 280n40; endorsement of "American System" in second term, 262–63; and the Enlightenment, 217n5; and fiscal-military state, 150–51, 153–57, 160, 165, 168; and Florida, 189; and Georgia land grants, 187; on guillotining of Louis XVI, 290; and internal improvements, 272, 273; on limited sovereignty of limited government, 277; and Louisiana Purchase, 39, 49, 52; nonintercourse policy of, 158–59, 159–60; objec-

tions to Washington's Neutrality Proclamation, 88; promotion of international trade as secretary of state, 153; on proposed commercial treaty with Spain, 43, 44–45; on Republican newspapers, 94; on republics as only hope for peace, 269; on sacrifices by American people, 271; and Second Bank of the United States, 168–69; on supremacy of will of the people, 275; and treaty with Kaskaskia, 66–67; types of republics, 279–80n33; U.S. as compound commercial republic, 266, 267; on war and peace, 268, 269–70, 280n36, 280n43
—, and religion: on advisory prayer proclamations, 62; enforcement of Sabbath and service decorum, 114; government gifts to religious organizations, 67; incorporation of churches, 64–65; multiplicity of sects important for freedom of religion, 266–67, 279n20; prayer at first inaugural, 75n7; prayer proclamations, 62–63; on religious actions by government officials, 61; on "sacred principle of religious liberty," 72–73; and Statute for Establishing Religious Freedom, 106
Magruder, Allan Bowie, 30
"Making Sense of Jefferson" (Onuf), 296
Malone, Dumas, 115
Malthus, Thomas, 120
manufacturing, 121, 129, 262–63
marketplace of ideas, 81, 88, 90, 93–94. *See also* religion, freedom of
Marshall, John, 187, 276, 277
Martin, Josiah, 28
Martínez de Yrujo, Carlos Fernandez, 49
Mashaw, Jerry L., 130
Mason, George, 109
Massachusetts, 72
Mathews, George, 188–89
Mattes, Armin, 279n32
Mayo-Bobee, Dinah, 130
McCoy, Drew R., 3, 6, 39, 173n9, 268
McCullough v. Maryland (1819), 276–77
McDonald, Forrest, 129–30, 140
McDowell, Joseph, 93, 94–95
McGillvary, Alexander, 182
Merchant, George, 17–18
merchant class: as beneficiaries of Bank of the United States, 84, 85, 86; and Embargo Act, 130, 136–37
Milan Decree (Napoleon), 155–56
Mind of James Madison, The (Sheehan), 264
"Mississippi Question, the": commerce and control of Mississippi River and New Orleans, 38, 39, 43, 48, 49, 50–51, 56n41, 154; and convergence of interests of southerners and westerners, 39–40, 42, 43, 44–46; France in control of Louisiana, 50–51; New Englanders and proposed commercial treaty with Spain, 42; southerners and proposed commercial treaty with Spain, 42–44; Treaty of San Lorenzo, 47–48; westerners and proposed commercial treaty with Spain, 42, 44–46. *See also* Louisiana Purchase
Mississippi Territory, 252
Missouri crisis and Compromise, 122, 214–15, 254, 255
Mitchell, David, 189
moneyed class: as beneficiaries of Bank of the United States, 85, 86; as dishonest, 112; in rhetoric of Jeffersonian Republicans, 161, 162
Monroe, James: and deportation of emancipated slaves, 118; and Louisiana Purchase, 38, 52; as

Monroe, James (*continued*)
minister plenipotentiary to France and Spain, 49; and Missouri Compromise, 122; on Prosser rebellion, 247; and Spanish Florida, 191
Montesquieu, 264
moose request, 199–200, 216–17n3
Morales, Juan, 48

Napoleonic Wars, 154, 155–56, 157–58
National Gazette (Freneau), 83
national identity: government institutions as shapers of, 3; Jeffersonian, 1; and westward expansion, 39. *See also* "American people, the"
National Intelligencer, 291
nationalism, ascendancy of, in federal politics, 106
National Magazine proposal, 96
National Republican Party, 7
Native Americans: acquisition of land from, 66–67, 153–54, 186; as characterized by patriot leaders, 31; Declaration of Independence justifications for actions against, 33; as depicted in Virginia constitution, 28; education of, 116; expansionism and, 45, 171; federal protection against, 45; Jay Treaty provisions, 47; Jefferson's call for physical removal of, to west of Mississippi, 31; Jefferson's civilization project, 186; Jefferson's views on, 284; lands in Lower South, 182, 183; language used to described, 17, 24; Louisiana Purchase as removing threats from, 50; as proxies of George III, 16–17, 22–26; during Revolutionary War, 23–26, 27, 28–30, 36n38; and Spanish Florida, 189, 191; Treaty of Fort Jackson land cession, 191; written out of Declaration of Independence, 32. *See also specific groups by name*
natural rights: immigration, 115; individual freedom, 207–8; self-government, 74, 89, 107, 108, 202, 204–5, 206, 214
Neem, Johann N., 73
Newburyport Herald, 134
New Englanders and New England states: anti-southern ideology of, 129; and Embargo Act, 130, 131, 135–37; and Georgia land speculators, 187; Jefferson's attitude toward, 141; Jefferson's yeoman ideal, 130; mixing of church and state, 69–71; proposed commercial treaty with Spain, 42; slave trade, 180
New England Mississippi Land Company (NEML), 187–88
New Hampshire, 60
New Hampshire Gazette, 86
New London Gazette, 134
Newton, Sir Isaac, 201
New York, 60
New York Daily Gazette, 85
New York Journal (Holt), 25
Nicholas, George, 47
Nicholas, John, 93
Non-Intercourse Act (1809), 141, 159
North African Maghreb, 154
North Carolina, 72
northerners and northern states: and Embargo Act, 129, 135; and Embargo Act violations, 136, 137–38, 139; Jefferson's attitude toward, 140–41, 283; redistribution of capital into, 178; and slave trade, 294; and spread of slavery, 254
Northumberland Gazette, 102n76
Notes on the State of Virginia (Jefferson), 60, 117, 119, 151–52, 200, 201, 218n7, 246

Öhman, Martin, 5–6
Olney, Jeremiah, 13, 139
Onuf, Peter S.: approach to historical analysis, 283, 284; on Embargo Act and disunion, 138; focus on politicians in real time, 3; on Jeffersonian Republicans' challenge of perfect republican government, 68; on Jeffersonian Republicans' reaction to opposition to Embargo Act, 132; on Jefferson's ability to ignore contentious divisions, 290; on Jefferson's application of friendship to executive functions, 296; on Jefferson's belief in convergence of revivalists and rational religious individuals, 287; on Jefferson's perception of northerners, 283; on Jefferson's sense of national community, 284; on Jefferson's state of mind at end of life, 122; on nation imagined by Jefferson, 128; on political and religious toleration called for by Jefferson, 74; on sectional interests in union, 128–29
Origins of the Federal Republic, The (Onuf), 283
Otis, Harrison Gray, 132

"Pacificus" (Hamilton pseudonym), 88
Page, John, 31
Paine, Thomas, 84
Parkinson, Robert G., 5, 285, 286
Pasley, Jeffrey L., 134
Patriot (newspaper), 291
patronage, 185–86
Pendleton, Edmund, 34n10, 109, 113
Pennsylvania Evening Post (Towne), 22–23, 29
Pennsylvania Gazette (Hall and Sellers), 18
Pennsylvania Journal (Bradford), 18
Pennsylvania Packet (Dunlap), 18–19
"people, the." *See* "American people, the"
Perceval, Spencer, 160
Peskin, Lawrence A., 189
Peterson, Merrill D., 115, 218n10, 298–99n28
Pharoah (slave), 247
"Philadelphius" (pseudonym), 89
"Philoveritas" (pseudonym), 88
Pickering, Timothy, 132–33, 134, 253
Pinckney, Charles, 181, 183, 184, 186, 192–93
Pinckney, Charles Cotesworth, 184
Pinckney, Thomas, 47, 181, 183, 184
police power, 278n14
Polly case, 154, 156
Preble, Edward, 226
prejudices, as unifying force, 15, 31–32
press: and Alien and Sedition Acts, 92, 93, 94, 95, 102n76; and the Bank of the United States, 82–83, 84, 85, 86; on British offers to Native Americans, 22–23; Burr Conspiracy in, 223, 224, 229–30, 231; and Cedars stockade incident, 24–25; diffusion in, 298n26; on Dunmore's germ warfare, 30; and Embargo Act, 134, 135, 270; on German mercenaries, 18–19; government printing contracts, 34n8; Jeffersonian Republicans as party of south, 133; Jefferson letter to Danbury Baptists, 69; in Jefferson's draft for Virginia constitution, 111; in Lower South, 185; *National Magazine* proposal, 96; on religious freedom laws, 72, 73; and risk of massacre by Native Americans, 27; and threat from Dunmore emancipation, 27; as vigilant guardians for republic, 88; and Washington's Neutrality Proclamation, 88, 100n36; western, on Jay Treaty, 48

"Principles of '98," 153, 170, 171, 178, 185
producer ethos, 151–52, 168, 171. *See also* yeomen and yeoman ideal
"Property" (Madison), 267
Puffendorf, Samuel von, 89
Purdie, Alexander, 27

Quasi-War with France (1797–99), 1, 48, 49, 56n39, 95–96, 154
Quincy, Josiah, 131, 133
Quincy, Josiah, III, 64

Ragosta, John A., 6
Rakove, Jack, 280n48
Randolph, Edmund, 109
Randolph, John, 107, 231, 240n34
Randolph, Peyton, 107
Randolph, Thomas Jefferson, 118
Read, James, 181, 183
realities, challenge of balancing ideals with, 4
"receptacle" proposal, 246, 247–50
Red Stick Creeks, 190–91
Rehnquist, William, 76n14
religion, freedom of: and church incorporation, 64–65, 76n16; and church land, 67, 114; and enforcement of Sabbath and service decorum in Virginia, 114; mixing of church and state in New England, 69–71; multiplicity of sects important for, 266–67, 279n20; as natural right, 74; as necessary for functioning of republics, 59, 73, 74; and neutrality in use of government buildings, 65–66; nonsectarian monotheism, 287–88; official prayer proclamations, 61–62; postindependence reforms by Jeffersonian Republicans, 72–73, 78n39; and prayers at public events, 62–63, 76n9; and recognition of religiosity of government officials, 61, 62, 63, 76n8; in Revisal of the Laws, 113–14; states as regulators of, 60, 61, 68, 114; and use of government buildings for religious services, 64, 65, 76n14, 76n17, 77n18. *See also* Jefferson, Thomas: and religion; Madison, James: and religion
repatriation: deportation as, 118, 246, 247–48, 250–51; by Great Britain, 249
Repertory (newspaper), 135
"Report of 1800" (Madison), 265
"Republican, A" (pseudonym), 89
Republican Notes on Religion (pamphlet), 60
republics: bloodshed as necessary for achieving, 209, 210; classic, small, 264, 267; elements needed for, 68; extended, as best check on tyranny, 263, 264; and French Revolution, 208, 210–11; inevitable decay of, 3; Madison's types of, 279–80n33; necessity of popular responses to threats, 236; newspapers as vigilant guardians of, 88; as only hope for peace, 269; religious freedom as necessary for functioning, 59, 73, 74; rhetoric of Revolutionary American, 285–86; U.S. as a compound, 263, 265, 266; U.S. as a compound commercial, 266, 267; and yeoman ideal, 1, 110–11, 112–13, 119, 120
Revisal of the Laws, 113–16
Revolutionary War: Cedars stockade incident, 23–27; financing of, 41, 149–50; invasion of and retreat from Canada, 23; Native Americans during, 23–26, 27, 28–30; rhetoric of, 285–86; unified population necessary for success of, 15
Rhode Island, 72
rice, 41

Richmond Enquirer, 118
Richmond Examiner, 102n76
Robinson, W. A., 72
Rothman, Adam, 294
Rutledge, Edward, 19, 26

St. George's Bay Company, 248
Salem Gazette, 139
Saler, Bethel, 186
Scalia, Antonin, 75n6
Schoen, Brian, 130, 133
Schuyler, George, 22
Schuyler, Philip, 25
scientific racism, 220n41
Sears, Louis Martin, 129
Second Bank of the United States, 9, 167, 168–70, 275–76, 287
Second Maroon War, 249
"Secretarius" (pseudonym), 89
sectionalism: and drafting of U.S. Constitution, 128–29; and Embargo Act, 128, 132–33, 134, 135, 138–39, 140; in historiography of Embargo Act, 129–30; within Jeffersonian Republicans, 292; and Jefferson's belief in friendship as extending to national community, 284, 294, 295; and Missouri Compromise, 122; and War of 1812, 141
Sedgwick, Theodore, 84
self-government: and the Constitution, 74, 204–5, 213; as natural right, 74, 89, 107, 108, 202, 204–5, 206, 214
Seminole, 191
Sharp, Granville, 248
Shays's Rebellion, 205–6, 210, 219n16
Sheehan, Colleen, 264, 266
Sheppard, Mosby, 247
Sherburne, Henry, 24, 27
Sherman, Roger, 18, 26
Short, William, 207, 209, 210, 292
Sierra Leone Company, 248–49
slaves and slavery: and African Americans' collective sense of themselves as Africans, 250; as characterized by patriot leaders, 31; escape to Spanish Florida, 189, 191; as essential to economy, 257; as eventually disappearing, 215–16; and expansion into west, 43–44; and expansion of transatlantic trade, 175n13; as foreign nation on American soil, 246; and free persons of color, 186, 192–93; and Haitian revolution, 184, 185; as jeopardizing American experiment, 244–45; as justification for actions against George III, 33, 293; language used to described, 17; and Louisiana Purchase, 50; in Louisiana Territory, 253; in Lower South during Confederation era, 180; and New Englanders, 180; population, 256; procreation and purchase of females, 292; as proxies of George III, 16–17, 22; relationship to masters, 256; in Revisal of the Laws, 115; as threat to union, 255–56; trade in, 115, 180, 242, 251–52, 253, 255, 293, 294; transformation from state to national issue, 254; in Virginia constitution, 28. *See also* African Americans; diffusion; emancipation; Jefferson, Thomas: and slavery
Sloan, James, 133
smallpox, in Dunmore's African American regiment, 30
Smith, John, 253
Smith, Joshua M., 137
Smith, Margaret Bayard, 65, 76n17
Smith, Robert, 224–26, 229, 234, 240n47
Smith, Samuel, 93
Smith, William Loughton, 181
South Carolina. *See* Lower South

southerners and southern states: and Atlantic system after Revolutionary War, 40; claim of neglect by federal government, 179; commerce concerns of, 39, 40; and Democratic-Republicans, 254; and Embargo Act, 129, 132, 133, 136–37; expansionism as safety valve for dangerous slaves, 43–44; free persons of color in, 186, 192–93; and Jay Treaty, 5–6; Jeffersonian Republicans as coalition based on convergence of interests of west with, 39, 53; Jeffersonian Republicans as party of, 133; and Louisiana Purchase, 39–40; and Native Americans during Revolutionary War, 27, 28–30, 36n38; proposed commercial treaty with Spain, 42–44; and suspension of commerce with France, 48, 56n39. *See also* Lower South

Spain: and Burr Conspiracy, 222, 226–27, 230, 233; Florida territory, 8, 183, 188–89, 191; Great Britain as benefactor of rupture with, 45; and Louisiana Purchase, 188; proposed commercial treaty with, 42–46, 55n20; Treaty of San Lorenzo, 47–48

speech, freedom of, as First Amendment right, 91

Spirit of the Laws (Montesquieu), 264

Spivak, Burton, 130

Stagg, J. C. A., 268–69

statecraft: Americans' own self-interest as tool of, 4; assertive use of, 3; under Federalist administrations, 1; and financial resources, 150; and objections to Alien and Sedition Acts, 91, 92–96; and objections to Bank of the United States, 83–87; and objections to Washington's Neutrality Proclamation, 89–91; under Republican administrations, 2

states: and Bank of the United States, 83, 84–85; and the Constitution's contract clause, 187; defense of territorial claims, 283; dependence on federal government, 178; land sales, 179, 181, 187–88; militias and Burr Conspiracy, 223, 233; militias in War of 1812, 190, 191; mixing of church and state in New England, 69–74; postindependence reforms, 72; protection of coastal areas by, 183–84; refusal to enforce Embargo Act, 139–40; regulation of religion by, 60, 61, 68, 72; rights of, 8, 192–93, 214–15, 288; Sedition Act and transfer of nondelegated powers to, 92; violations of federalism by, 122–23. *See also specific states by name*

Statute for Establishing Religious Freedom (Jefferson), 59, 60, 72, 74, 106, 203

Stone, Michael, 82, 84

Story, Joseph, 140

Stow, Joshua, 78n39

strict constructionism: and containment of federal government, 129, 277; label of, 80; legislative supremacy as superseding, 87, 88; and objections to Alien and Sedition Acts, 91–92; and objections to Bank of the United States, 82–83, 85; and objections to Bonus Bill, 169–70, 271–72; and opposition to Federalist policies, 81; as policy mindset, 81–82; and Washington's Neutrality Proclamation, 90–91

Stuart, Henry, 27, 28–30, 36n38

Stuart, John, 27

Stuart, Reginald C., 134

Sullivan, James, 136, 139

Summary View of the Rights of British America, A (Jefferson), 107–8, 273

"Tammany" (pseudonym), 164
Taylor, Alan, 190
Taylor, Hubbard, 45
Taylor, John, 245
Thacher, George, 252
Thomas, Clarence, 75n6, 76n14
Thompson, Daniel Pierce, 242
Thomson, Charles, 16
Thornton, Henry, 248, 249
Time Piece (newspaper), 102n76
tobacco, 41, 43, 46, 48, 49
Tom (slave), 247
Towne, Benjamin, 22–23
trade. *See* commerce
treaties, abrogating, 87, 89
Treaty of Fort Jackson, 191
Treaty of Ghent, 167, 292
Treaty of Mortefontaine, 154, 184
Treaty of Mount Dexter, 186
Treaty of San Lorenzo, 47–48, 181
Trees, Andrew, 250, 257
Troup, George, 188
Trumbull, Jonathan, 140
"Truth" (pseudonym), 89
Tucker, Robert W., 138
Tyler, John, 118
tyranny: and Alien and Sedition Acts, 92; and concentration of wealth, 85; intermingling of church and state as foundation of, 59; and republic size, 263, 264; sovereignty as, 281n62

"Uniform Federalist, A" (pseudonym), 88
unity: necessary for success of Revolution, 15; using exclusion to create, 15, 16–21, 31–32, 34n10, 34n12
"Universal Peace" (Madison), 269
University of Virginia: establishment of, 116, 121; and failure of reform of College of William and Mary, 116; importance to Jefferson, 105; as nonegalitarian, 106
USS *Chesapeake,* 130, 156, 158

Valsania, Maurizio, 299n29
Varnum, Joseph, 252
Vattel, Emmerich de, 89
Vergennes, comte de (Charles Gravier), 41
"Veritas" (pseudonym), 90, 101n52
Vermont, 72
Vermont Gazette, 102n76
Virginia Gazette (Dixon and Hunter), 18, 30, 34n8
Virginia Gazette (Purdie), 27
Virginia Quid, 231, 240n34
Voltaire, 266, 267

war: causes of, 268, 269–70; incurrence of debt for, 270; preparations for, 280n43; and standing army, 1, 169, 262, 280n36
War of 1812: and absence of national bank, 165; American diplomatic mission to end, 166; causes of, 160, 189, 192; cost of, 160; funding of, 7, 165, 166–67; and Jefferson, 121; and Lower South, 190–91; and sectionalism, 141; state militias, 190, 191; Treaty of Ghent, 167; wartime expansion of powers of federal government, 167–68
Washington, George: and Bank of the United States, 82, 83, 85, 86–87, 276; characteristics of, 149; and French Revolution, 210; Neutrality Proclamation, 87–91, 100n36
Wayne, Anthony, 182
Webster, Daniel, 178, 182
westerners and the west: and Burr Conspiracy, 224, 225; commerce with France, 51; increase in rift with Federalists, 45–46; and Jay Treaty, 5–6,

westerners and the west (*continued*) 47, 48, 55n32; land seen as empty, 257; and Louisiana Purchase, 52–53; and "Mississippi Question," 39–40, 42, 43, 44–46, 49, 56n41; and Monroe as minister plenipotentiary to France and Spain, 49; Native American raids against, 45; in northwest as beneficiaries of Federalist administrations, 182; perception of national government of, in Lower South, 182–83; as trade competitors of southerners, 39–40, 43. *See also* expansionism
Whig (newspaper), 164
Whipple, William, 25
Whiskey Rebellion, 228
Whitaker, Arthur Preston, 39–40
Wilberforce, William, 248
Wilkinson, James, 226, 228, 233, 239n23
"William Tell" (pseudonym), 94
Wirt, William, 262, 285
Wolf, Christian, 89
Wood, Gordon, 218n13
Wythe, George, 19–20, 26, 109, 286

XYZ Affair, 91

yeomen and yeoman ideal: desire for goods and access to markets, 152, 268; and Embargo Act, 130; and the Enlightenment, 213; and expansionism, 1, 39, 183; in Jefferson's vision for Virginia, 110–11, 119; loss of markets after Revolutionary War, 39–40; as model for American people, 119, 183; and objections to Bank of the United States, 84, 85, 86, 97; proposal to give state land to, 110–11, 112–13, 119; rhetoric of Jeffersonian Republicans extolling, 151; role of, in republics, 1, 110–11, 112–13, 119, 120

Recent Books in the Jeffersonian America Series

Nature's Man: Thomas Jefferson's Philosophical Anthropology, Maurizio Valsania

Religious Freedom: Jefferson's Legacy, America's Creed, John Ragosta

Sons of the Father: George Washington and His Protégés, Robert M. S. McDonald, editor

Paine and Jefferson in the Age of Revolutions, Simon P. Newman and Peter S. Onuf, editors

Era of Experimentation: American Political Practices in the Early Republic, Daniel Peart

Collegiate Republic: Cultivating an Ideal Society in Early America, Margaret Sumner

Amelioration and Empire: Progress and Slavery in the Plantation Americas, Christa Dierksheide

Becoming Men of Some Consequence: Youth and Military Service in the Revolutionary War, John A. Ruddiman

Patriotism and Piety: Federalist Politics and Religious Struggle in the New American Nation, Jonathan J. Den Hartog

Between Sovereignty and Anarchy: The Politics of Violence in the American Revolutionary Era, Patrick Griffin, Robert G. Ingram, Peter S. Onuf, and Brian Schoen, editors

Citizens of a Common Intellectual Homeland: The Transatlantic Origins of American Democracy and Nationhood, Armin Mattes

The Haitian Declaration of Independence: Creation, Context, and Legacy, Julia Gaffield, editor

Confounding Father: Thomas Jefferson's Image in His Own Time, Robert M. S. McDonald

Blood from the Sky: Miracles and Politics in the Early American Republic, Adam Jortner

Pulpit and Nation: Clergymen and the Politics of Revolutionary America, Spencer W. McBride

Jefferson's Body: A Corporeal Biography, Maurizio Valsania

Jefferson on Display: Attire, Etiquette, and the Art of Presentation, G. S. Wilson

Jeffersonians in Power: The Rhetoric of Opposition Meets the Realities of Governing, Joanne B. Freeman and Johann N. Neem, editors